WOMEN AND THE CRUSADES

WOMEN AND THE CRUSADES

HELEN J. NICHOLSON

OXFORD
UNIVERSITY PRESS

OXFORD
UNIVERSITY PRESS

Great Clarendon Street, Oxford, OX2 6DP,
United Kingdom

Oxford University Press is a department of the University of Oxford.
It furthers the University's objective of excellence in research, scholarship,
and education by publishing worldwide. Oxford is a registered trade mark of
Oxford University Press in the UK and in certain other countries

First Edition published in 2023

Impression: 1

Published in the United States of America by Oxford University Press
198 Madison Avenue, New York, NY 10016, United States of America

British Library Cataloguing in Publication Data
Data available

Library of Congress Control Number: 2022942544

ISBN 978-0-19-880672-1

DOI: 10.1093/oso/9780198806721.001.0001

Printed and bound in the UK by
Clays Ltd, Elcograf S.p.A.

Preface

How could women play any role in crusading? If the crusades were a military undertaking and only men could fight, then obviously women could play no practical part in them. Furthermore, clergy and canon lawyers condemned their involvement and commentators blamed women for leading crusaders into sin and bringing God's wrath down on them.

Yet evidence from medieval Europe and the Middle East during the period of the crusades (broadly the second half of the eleventh century to 1570 when Cyprus, the last crusader state, was lost to the Ottoman Turks) reveals that women played a large part in these wars, from propaganda for crusades through supplying resources and personnel, taking on some combat roles (although their menfolk generally tried to keep them out of the front line), giving support on the battlefield, raising money, and commemorating crusaders. They suffered or enjoyed the results of crusading. It can be difficult to establish *exactly* what they did, however, because their contemporaries and writers since tend to fit them into certain categories: women could be perfect wives, pious martyrs, and evil jezebels, but it was difficult for them to be simply people. In the period of the crusades, as now, those writing about the crusades always wanted to make a good story from events, with an appropriate happy or moral ending. Women's involvement was usually depicted as exceptional rather than routine, romantic rather than mundane.[1]

While it is true that women did have to face considerable barriers, not least from cultural expectation and misogyny, this book argues against the assumption that women's participation was exceptional, seeking to show that women's involvement in the crusades was wide-reaching and normal.[2] That said, like the contribution of most men, their contribution was often passive rather than active.

The crusades were holy wars in which Latin Christians (those following the Roman tradition and acknowledging the pope as their spiritual leader) fought those of other faiths—heretical and schismatic Christians, and Muslims, and pagans—in defence of people and territory, with spiritual rewards promised to participants. They began in the late eleventh century, as economic and commercial growth spread throughout Christian Europe. The rulers of what were later Spain and Portugal started to expand their territories south into Muslim al-Andalus while growing Italian mercantile cities such as Genoa and Pisa harassed the North African coastal cities. In the Middle East in 1098–1099 the crusaders took advantage of political divisions to capture the cities of Antioch—conquered by the Seljuk Turks in 1084–85—and Jerusalem, which had been conquered by Caliph Umar in around 637. Less than a century later Jerusalem was lost to Saladin (d. 1193), but the concept of crusading continued into the sixteenth century and beyond as a structure for organizing and recruiting for wars with an underlying religious justification.

This book does not set out to re-narrate the crusades. Its purpose is to examine the contribution that women made to the crusading movement from the eleventh century to the sixteenth, in all the theatres of war where the concept of crusading was applied. Many of the women considered in this book did not take the cross in the sense of taking a formal vow to go on crusade and sewing the symbol of the cross on to their clothing, but were involved in the crusade indirectly by urging family members to take part in a crusade, looking after the family estates during a crusader's absence, purchasing a crusade indulgence which would give them the spiritual benefits of crusading without taking part in person, or taking part in a religious ritual that supported crusading. As it was not necessary to have taken a formal crusade vow to play a significant role in crusading I have not set out to identify every female crusader or to produce a list of female crusaders, which would give too narrow an impression of women's involvement.[3]

Considering the roles of women in crusading shows us that although the crusades were indeed a military undertaking involving fighting men, they were very much more than that: the whole of Latin Christian society throughout Europe was deeply involved in crusading in some way or another. By studying women in the crusades we gain a greater insight not only into the campaigns of the crusades but also into European society itself over half a millennium ago.

Acknowledgements

I am very grateful to my colleagues in the History Department at Cardiff University for granting me research leave in 2020–2021 so that I could complete this book, and to the School of History, Archaeology and Religion for confirming their decision. I am also extremely grateful for the help of staff in Cardiff University Arts and Social Studies Library, especially the staff in Scolar (Special Collections and Archives) and in Inter-library Loan for their assistance in obtaining copies of research materials during the COVID-19 restrictions. Regrettably these restrictions have meant that despite their efforts some items have not been accessible to me. I also thank Luciana O'Flaherty of Oxford University Press for commissioning this book and for her support throughout its production, and the publisher's anonymous expert reviewer for their constructive comments. As I have been working on this research project for many years my debts to other researchers are too numerous to set out individually here, but I have referred to as many as possible in the notes. My husband Nigel Nicholson drew the maps and has patiently and generously provided assistance as required. I drew up the family trees and made all the translations which are not otherwise attributed. All errors are, of course, my own.

Contents

A Note on Names   xi

Maps   xiii

1. Locating Women in the Crusades: Definitions
   and Evidence   I

   Women's roles in crusading   2

   Definitions of crusading   5
      What was a crusade?   5
      Crusade or pilgrimage?   7

   Some problems with evidence   9

   Motivation   19

2. Initializing Crusades   21

   Beginnings   23

   The Reconquest of the Iberian Peninsula and beyond   25

   The Crusader States and the eastern Mediterranean   35

   Family connections   37

   Recruiting for crusades   42

3. Crusade Campaigns   53

   Women's roles in crusades: plans and practice   53
      Accompanying husbands   56
      Caring for the sick   63
      Diplomacy and intelligence   65
      Women acting alone   70
      Making a living   77
      Military action   79

   Victims and prisoners of crusades   87

4. **The Home Front: Supporting the Crusade**   97

   The costs of crusading for those left behind   98

   Administering estates   103

   After the crusade   109

   Financing crusaders   114

   Spiritual support: prayer, holy women, and saints   121

5. **After the Crusade: Memory and Imagination**   129

   Memorials and foundations   130

   Liturgy and ritual   141

   Written record   142

   Cultural patronage   147

Summing Up   157

Chronology of the Crusades   163

List of Popes   171

Family Trees   175

Endnotes   185

Bibliography   241

   Primary sources   241

   Secondary works   251

Index   277

A Note on Names

It is always difficult to know how best to render personal names for a work of this geographical breadth and chronological length, especially as there may have been no single contemporary spelling. Where there is a general modern consensus on the rendering of a name into English, I have used it: so I have rendered the name of Queen Giovanna of Naples as Johanna, but Jeanne daughter of King Henry II of England and Eleanor of Aquitaine as Joanna. For individuals who are less familiar I have tried to use the spelling of their name in their original language. I have given alternative versions of names in brackets the first time each individual is mentioned.

Maps

Map 1. Europe, North Africa and the Middle East

Map 2. Spain, France, and Italy

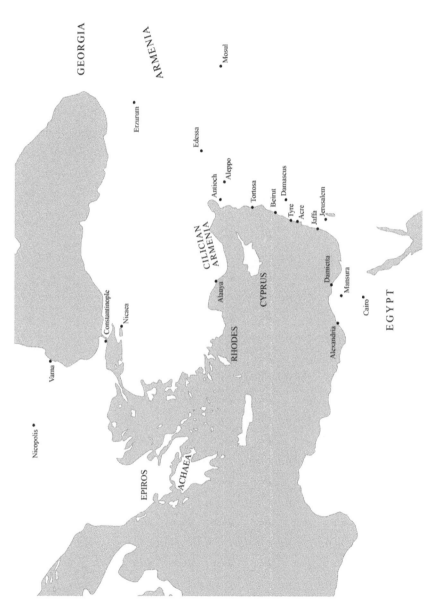

Map 3. The Middle East

I

Locating Women in the Crusades

Definitions and Evidence

Could women even take part in crusades, let alone fight? Contemporary narrative accounts of the First Crusade (1096–1099) and the strictures of medieval canon lawyers certainly suggest that women contributed little to crusades and cast doubt on their status as crusaders, *crucesignatae* (literally 'cross-signed'), the status accorded to those who took a formal religious vow to participate and wore a cross on to their clothing as a symbol of their vow. Women's involvement in crusades was depicted as undesirable, consuming resources that were needed by the fighters and undermining the moral fibre of the army.[1] Albert of Aachen, writing his history of the First Crusade shortly after its conclusion, described how the clergy in the crusading army blamed famine in the siege camp on sin, including adultery and fornication. Fulcher of Chartres, who took part in the crusade, reported that women were expelled from the crusader camp 'lest perhaps [the men] should displease the Lord [God] through being contaminated with the filth of dissipation'.[2] Some crusaders took clerical admonitions to avoid all sexual activity seriously, even though contemporary medical opinion held that sex is essential for good health. Ambroise and Richard de Templo, recording the events of the Third Crusade, even claimed that many participants on the Third

Crusade had died because they abstained from sexual intercourse with women.[3]

Yet women did play a constructive role in medieval European warfare and some sources show that women were expected to take part in conflict in certain circumstances.[4] Indeed, scholars have identified so many women engaged in military activity in medieval Europe that women's involvement in war now appears commonplace.[5] Likewise, when researchers have actively looked for women's involvement in crusading they have found that women were involved in and affected by crusades in many different ways.[6] Nevertheless, women's roles in crusades are still much less well known than men's contributions, and outside specialized academic research there is very little awareness that women played any role in crusading, beyond a few high-profile queens of England such as Eleanor of Aquitaine (d. 1204) and Eleanor of Castile (d. 1290).

Women's roles in crusading

Historian Sabine Geldsetzer's 2003 study of women on crusades to the Holy Land between 1096 and 1291 established that women certainly took part in crusades. She identified fourteen women who had definitely taken a formal crusade vow, ninety-one who took part in a crusade with or without a formal vow, and fifty-nine more who may have taken part in a crusade expedition (although some of these may have been on peaceful pilgrimages rather than a crusade).[7] This may not seem very many, but just as most women who were involved in crusade campaigns were not formally called *crucesignatae*, most men in crusade armies were not *crucesignati*, the male equivalent.[8] Women present in the armies of the First Crusade, for instance, were full participants in the expedition even if they had not formally taken the cross.[9] Just as men did, women accompanied crusaders as servants and companions. Just as men did, women also suffered at the hands of crusaders: they were abused, taken prisoner, enslaved, and killed.[10]

Women involved in the crusades usually did not play an active military combat role except in emergencies and few took on command roles. Some men, notably priests, were also not expected to fight in the field, and instead performed essential support roles in time of war. Like their male counterparts women were allocated specific support roles in wartime, such as herding livestock to safety, loading crossbows, boiling water, collecting or preparing munitions for use against the enemy and sometimes also delivering them, and performing labouring tasks. These were essential roles and the fact that they were performed by women did not make them any less militarily valuable.[11] Royal and noble women initiated and organized campaigns, mustered and led armies to the front, but were not recorded fighting in the field. They also provided diplomatic support. The roles played by women were as essential and often the same as the roles played by men, and the fact that they were not regarded as newsworthy and so were not usually noted does not mean that their fellow-crusaders thought they were unimportant.

That said, most women of child-bearing age would face certain limitations on crusade which men did not experience. Women's monthly bleeding rendered them spiritually impure in the eyes of the clergy so that they were barred from entering some holy sites, and could leave them unable to operate for a few days each month due to 'period pains'.[12] As a married couple travelling together would probably continue sexual relations throughout the crusade for their health and to avoid the temptation to adultery, and as there were no safe and effective means of birth control, a woman travelling with her husband was likely to become pregnant during the crusade, and then might suffer from the various conditions which commonly arise in pregnancy, from morning sickness through to life-threatening conditions such as eclampsia. She might die in childbirth. If she survived, after the child's birth she would be occupied in feeding and caring for it. Noble and wealthy women would be able to employ assistance to help them with this work, but poor women would be expected to carry the extra burden regardless and some could not do so: Albert of

Aachen describes women giving birth prematurely because of the harsh conditions and abandoning their dead or dying infants.[13] As a result, women of child-bearing age were not always as mobile as men of a similar age and not always able to take on heavy physical work, although they might also be able to call on the assistance of their children to help with simple labouring tasks: when the crusaders captured Damietta in 1219, women and children were paid for the help they had given the warriors during the siege.[14]

Women's involvement in the crusades was also limited by social status. In Europe and the Middle East during the time of the crusades opportunities available to noble women for travel and individual choice would have been very different from those available to merchant women, and even further removed from those of poor women. Noble women might raise troops, finance the construction of fortifications, act as patrons for literature connected with the crusade, commission a tomb for a dead crusader, and so on. Such contributions would probably have been beyond the financial resources of other women; yet non-noble holy women could act as effective advocates of crusading, as their spiritual authority gave them a public voice. We shall encounter several such women later in this book.

All non-combatants, male and female, could be a drain on a crusade army's resources. Popes encouraged those who could not fight to make a financial contribution to the crusade in return for a part of the spiritual reward promised to those who took part in person. The promised spiritual reward changed as the concept of crusading developed, but in general participants in the crusades believed that God would cancel some or all of the punishment due for their sins in return for their taking part; this was called an 'indulgence', as God indulged or remitted their punishment.[15] At the end of the twelfth century Pope Innocent III formalized this arrangement of payment for the crusade indulgence, offering those who donated towards the cost of going on crusade or who sent someone else in their place the same spiritual reward as those who went in person. Experts in canon law, the law of the Church, assumed that women would always redeem their crusade vows by payment rather than going in person, unless they could afford to raise and lead a military force themselves.[16]

As most of the fighting on a crusade would be carried out not by vowed crusaders but by warriors hired to fight, most members of society—women, clergy, non-military classes, those too old or too young to fight—supported crusading not by fighting but by donating money and taking part in special liturgies (religious rituals and prayers) to win God's help for the warriors.[17] So to assess women's full contribution to the crusades we need to look not only at the campaigns themselves but to the physical and spiritual support network for crusaders in Europe, the culture which supported the crusades and the memorialization of crusaders—activities which involved women from all levels of society.[18]

Definitions of crusading

What was a crusade?

In addition to considering a broad range of activities which supported crusading, we should consider a broad range of campaigns. Perhaps the most commonly held view of a crusade is that it was a military expedition to the eastern Mediterranean to assist Christians or to liberate or defend Jerusalem and the Church of the Holy Sepulchre (built on the site in Jerusalem where Christ's body is reputed to have lain between burial and resurrection). On this basis, crusades began in the late eleventh century and ended at the end of the thirteenth century when the final strongholds of the so-called 'crusader states' (polities created after the First Crusade and based around the cities of Antioch, Edessa, Jerusalem, and Tripoli) were captured by the Mamluk sultans of Egypt (a military oligarchy made up of former slaves of Central Asian origin and their descendants).[19] However, contemporaries used the same terminology in referring to a much wider range of campaigns, which took place over a longer period of time and a greater geographical area. Hence the word 'crusade' is now used to designate variously any military expedition originated, authorized, and organized by the papacy (including campaigns in the Iberian Peninsula, the Baltic region, or against heretics), any expedition which its participants depicted as a crusade (including popular movements such as the Children's Crusade of 1212 which were not authorized by the papacy), or any instance of penitential warfare, holy war which justified fighting in defence of the Christian faith with the expectation of spiritual reward.[20]

According to these wider definitions, crusading began in the second half of the eleventh century, when Pope Gregory VII first proposed a penitential military expedition to help the Christians of the East, and continued into at least the sixteenth century. In the sixteenth century Latin Christians still talked of recovering Jerusalem although their main focus was to halt the advance of the Ottoman Empire.[21] The language of crusading was used in a range of conflicts in defence of Christians: for example, by the military-religious Hospital of St John (the Hospitallers) defending themselves against the Ottoman Turks on Rhodes (1522) and Malta (1565), and by the Portuguese in Ethiopia (1541–1543), where a Portuguese force under Cristóvão da Gama assisted Queen Säblä Wängel (Seble Wongel) and her son King Gälawdewos to defeat the jihadi forces of Imam Ahmad ibn Ibrahim al-Ghazi of the Muslim kingdom of 'Adal.[22] The campaign was described by the eye-witness and soldier Miguel de Castanhoso in crusading terms: the Portuguese came in 'the service of God' to 'die for the faith of Christ'; it was a 'holy enterprise', fighting 'the enemies of our holy faith', and Cristóvão da Gama was 'the apostle of God come to deliver [the Ethiopians] from captivity and subjection'. Castanhoso called da Gama's death at the hands of Imam Ahmad a martyrdom and described miracles occurring at the site and on the day of his death, as if this war was a crusade, even though it had not been formally launched by the pope.[23]

The Spanish conquerors of Mexico led by Hernán Cortés (1519–1521) also referenced some aspects of crusading as they set up altars with the symbol of the Holy Cross and images of the Blessed Virgin Mary and the Infant Christ, called on St James of Santiago for aid (traditionally the helper of the crusaders in Spain against the Moors), gave Christ credit for their victories, and maintained that they were carrying out holy work (but their holy work was the conversion of non-Christians rather than the protection of Christians and Christian territory which had been the role of the crusades).[24] Unlike crusaders they did not claim to be giving their lives for Christ, and they did not have papal endorsement for their campaigns.

These crusades and holy and/or penitential wars were not simply between Christians and Muslims or Christians and pagans: Christians allied with Muslims and Muslims with Christians, Christians with pagans and so forth. The difference between these wars and traditional raiding for plunder and captives or a war over territory was that the pope was involved in initiating and/or organizing many of the campaigns, and they were fought in the name of Christ for a spiritual reward. Many of the women discussed in this book supported or were involved with these wider expeditions rather than expeditions to Jerusalem, but all these expeditions used the same terms to describe their purpose: referring to taking up the Holy Cross, carrying out Christ's business, dying for Christ, and fighting an enemy who threatened Christians and Christendom.

Crusade or pilgrimage?

Not every woman who set out for Jerusalem was going on crusade; many were going on pilgrimage.[25] It can be difficult to separate pilgrimage from crusade, because by the time of the Second Crusade (1147–1148) the armed expeditions to assist Christians and protect Christian holy places were known as 'pilgrimages' (in Latin, *peregrinationes*). Those taking part in a crusade took a vow in a liturgical rite similar to a vow of pilgrimage, both crusades and pilgrimages were deeply pious acts undertaken in expectation of a spiritual reward, and crusaders called themselves 'pilgrims', *peregrini*.[26] Crusaders' property was under Church protection during their absence as was pilgrims' property (although the protection for crusaders' property was extended to cover their wives and children too).[27] Pilgrimages are penitential journeys to a sacred place; crusades were penitential undertakings with a holy aim. Contemporary descriptions did not always make clear the difference between the two, even if they were aware that there was a legal difference.[28] The liturgical connection between pilgrimage and crusade continued even after the loss of Jerusalem and the crusader states of the Holy Land, and only gradually faded in the fifteenth century as the Ottoman Turks came to be seen as the greater threat to Christendom.[29]

This use of the single term 'pilgrimage' both for peaceful journeys to holy sites and for penitential military expeditions can, of course, make it difficult to tell whether a particular woman 'pilgrim' was on a peaceful pilgrimage or taking part in a crusade. To compound the confusion, a woman might commute or change a pilgrimage to a holy place into a financial contribution towards the military defence of the Holy Land, as when in 1275 Helewyse Palmer and her daughter Isabel from Preston in Lancashire, England, commuted a vow of pilgrimage to the shrine of St James of Compostela into a donation to aid the Holy Land, meaning that the money would pay for warriors to defend the crusader states, and suggesting that a peaceful pilgrimage was the equivalent of military action in God's cause.[30]

Women travelled in significant numbers to the Holy Land even after the destruction of the crusader states in Palestine and Syria in 1291, demonstrating that the Holy Land and Jerusalem remained important to Latin Christians.[31] Some went on pilgrimages with husbands and parents, but many travelled alone.[32] Margery Kempe (fl. 1438), a wealthy merchant woman from King's Lynn in Norfolk, England, now famous for her mystical visions, was one such who made the journey to the Holy Land without husband or family, visiting Jerusalem, the Jordan, and the Mount of Temptation, and returned bearing holy relics to recount her spiritual experiences.[33] However, although her pilgrimage was a physical and spiritual struggle, it was not a military expedition and she did not get caught up in military activity—unlike Isolda Parewastell from Somerset in England who in 1365, having travelled to Jerusalem, was caught up in Mamluk reprisals against Christians for the Latin Christians' conquest of Alexandria in that year.[34]

Those who went on pilgrimage to Jerusalem or dreamt of doing so would have wanted to retain access to the holy city for pilgrims, which meant at least maintaining the possibility of military action if necessary. Interest in the Holy Land—as evinced by women such as Elizabeth of Asheton, about to set out from Dover in March 1348 for the Holy Land on pilgrimage accompanied by a chaplain and two yeoman, or Elizabeth of Combe Keynes in Dorset, who set out with some of her neighbours for the Holy Land in Christmas week of 1373 but died during the journey, and which led three named men and five unnamed women to make arrangements for a journey to the Holy Land in 1386—could translate into support for holy war against non-Christians to recover or protect the Holy Places.[35] The six wealthy and devout old women who joined the same pilgrimage ship as Felix Fabri on his first pilgrimage to the Holy Land in 1480, the year of the first Ottoman siege of the Hospital of St John on Rhodes, testify to women's continuing willingness to brave the perils of the eastern Mediterranean at a time of increasing danger to travellers.[36] Although some of the women who are discussed in this book were in fact on pilgrimage when they became mixed up in a crusade, they were involved in crusade activity even if unintentionally. Other women discussed here may have been connected with a crusade expedition, or may have been independent pilgrims. All of them were involved in some way with penitential warfare, whether supporting the use of force or taking part in it themselves, rather than peaceful pilgrims.

Some problems with evidence

Establishing exactly what women did on crusade is not as straightforward as might first appear. The narrative accounts of the crusades are perhaps the most attractive sources for studying these campaigns, with their gripping accounts of battles and the difficulties faced by the crusaders, but they do not necessarily give an accurate account of what took place.

Crusade chronicles were a distinctive type of historical writing that told the story of a crusade campaign from beginning to end.[37] Typically they were composed either while the crusade was in progress (to encourage recruitment), in the immediate aftermath (to explain success or defeat), or in preparation for the next one (to encourage recruitment and remind the leaders of what went wrong last time). Many were written by clerics such as Albert of Aachen and Fulcher of Chartres, whose accounts of the First Crusade have already been mentioned. Clerics often wrote in the scholarly language of Latin, which gave their work more authority, but some wrote in their own language—French, Occitan, and so on—and might use verse to make their work accessible to a wider audience. For instance, two writers recorded the events of the Third Crusade (1189–1192) with similar content but very different presentation: the *Estoire de la Guerre Sainte* ('the history of the holy war') was written in French verse, probably by a Norman priest named Ambroise, while the *Itinerarium peregrinorum et gesta regis Ricardi* ('the pilgrims' journey and the deeds of King Richard') was written in Latin prose: the author was probably an English Augustinian canon, Richard de Templo.[38] But not all historians were clerics: some crusade chronicles were written by secular warriors, such as Geoffrey of Villehardouin, one of the leaders of the Fourth Crusade, or John, lord of Joinville and seneschal of Champagne in north-eastern France, who took part in King Louis IX of France's first crusade, to Egypt (1248–1254). Geoffrey wrote soon after the Fourth Crusade to explain and justify the course of events. John wrote some fifty years after events as an old friend of the king, incorporating his account of King Louis's crusade into his account of Louis's holy life.[39]

Some writers incorporated descriptions of crusades within wider commentaries on current and recent events, as did Archbishop William II of Tyre (d. *c.* 1185), historian of the kingdom of Jerusalem, and the

English monastic chronicler Matthew Paris of St Albans Abbey
(d. 1259), both writing in Latin. Matthew's work—well-informed,
readable, and enlivened by his own strong prejudices—was continued
by other monastic writers, although his histories probably did not
circulate outside monastic circles.[40] William's history was translated
into French and continued in both Latin and French by writers working in Europe and in the kingdom of Jerusalem. In its French form
(known as 'the History of Eracles' from its opening chapter, which
tells how the Byzantine Emperor Heraclius recovered the relic of the
True Cross on which Christ was crucified from the Persian king
Chosroes II), this history circulated very widely among the secular
nobility of Europe as well as clerical scholars. Both William and his
French continuator were so prejudiced in favour of certain members
of the nobility of the crusader states that at times their accounts border on fiction.[41] The anonymous northern French writer known as
the 'minstrel of Reims', writing in 1260, composed an entertaining
and semi-fictionalized account in French prose of events in the Holy
Land, France, Flanders, and England over the previous eighty years.[42]

It was not only western Europeans who wrote about the crusades.
Anna Komnene or Comnena (d. c. 1153), eldest child of the Byzantine
emperor Alexios I Komnenos whose appeal to the West had initiated
the First Crusade, incorporated extensive commentary on that campaign in her biography of her father, the *Alexiad*. Written in 'high style
Greek', this was a learned and deliberately antiquarian work aimed at
an elite readership and intended to exalt her father's memory.[43] The
conflict between Saladin and the Third Crusade was recorded by
Saladin's secretary 'Imād al-Dqīn al-Iṣfahānī and the *qadi* Bahā' al-Dīn
Ibn Shaddād, who wrote to praise Saladin.[44] Their contemporary, the
scholar and historian Ibn al-Athīr, used their work and developed it
in his history of the period.[45] In contrast, the Arab-Syrian nobleman,
warrior, and poet Usama ibn Munqidh included stories of crusaders
and women's involvement in conflict as part of his collection of
improving anecdotes, which he may have intended to present to his
patron Saladin.[46]

Just as no modern reader would accept a news report without questioning whose political interests it serves, we should not accept a contemporary commentary on a crusade expedition without pausing to ask whose interests or what agenda the writer was promoting. No writer set pen to parchment without an objective in mind, be it to present a moral lesson to edify the reader, praise the deeds of a noble person in hopes of receiving their patronage, vindicate the actions of themselves or their friends or patrons, offer a moral lesson, or give a warning to future generations. Each character presented in these crusade narratives had their role to play in the author's overall plan. Writers on all sides of the conflict depicted women in traditional gendered roles: they could be pious virgins, faithful wives and carers, pure-hearted devotees of chivalry; or they could be impious whores, weak-willed frail creatures easily led astray by their lusts, or powerful temptresses; or they could be innocent victims and suffering martyrs, or depicted as spoils of war, the just reward of the victor. Writers anxious that the presence of women in crusading armies could destroy the crusaders' spiritual purity and lead them into sin would tend to stress the destructive influence of women in the army rather than giving them credit for their courage in undertaking the journey.[47]

The mother of the Muslim general Kerbogha in the account of the First Crusade known as the *Gesta Francorum* ('the deeds of the Franks') is a good example of a fictionalized character which reflects the narrator's aims and audience expectations rather than actual events. The *Gesta Francorum* describes Kerbogha's mother hurrying to reprimand her son when she hears that he is besieging the crusaders, who have just captured Antioch. She beseeches him not to fight 'the Franks' (the Latin Christians, who called themselves 'Franks'):

> The Christians alone cannot fight with you—indeed I know that they are unworthy to meet you in battle—but their god fights for them every day, and keeps them day and night under his protection, and watches over them as a shepherd watches over his flock.[48]

She predicts that if her son ignores her advice he will suffer the greatest loss and dishonour, and die later in the year. This does not mean that Kerbogha's mother did in fact arrive at the siege of Antioch and make such a speech; the character has an important narrative role in presenting the author's propaganda for the crusade. It also reflects contemporary European Christian views of a mother's social role and responsibilities, and what European Christians imagined about Muslim women and believed about crusades.[49]

Eleanor, duchess of Aquitaine, queen first of France and then of England, is a slightly different case: she did take part in a crusade but her role was elaborated by her contemporaries and later generations. Eleanor accompanied the Second Crusade with her first husband, King Louis VII of France, but the eye-witness account by the monk Odo of Deuil and the course of events indicate that her active role during the crusade was in diplomacy, not on the battlefield. The crusade was a failure: it made no territorial gains, and arguably its abortive siege of Damascus drove that influential city into the hands of Nūr al-Dīn, ruler of Aleppo and Mosul, and formidable champion of Islam. Eleanor was among those whose actions were blamed for undermining the crusade: she was accused of having an affair with her uncle, Prince Raymond of Antioch. Raymond had hoped to persuade Louis to help him attack Aleppo, but Louis preferred to take his army on to Jerusalem. It is possible that Eleanor's attempts to negotiate between her uncle and her husband were misinterpreted by her husband and his northern French advisors; but whatever the origin of the accusations against her, later writers developed and embellished the story, adding additional romantic liaisons. By 1260 the 'Minstrel of Reims' was telling a story of Eleanor having an affair with the Muslim sultan Saladin—who in 1147 would have been only ten years old. In the seventeenth century the English clergyman and historian Thomas Fuller recorded Eleanor falling in love with 'a base Saracen jester'. Some writers imagined a military role for Eleanor. The Byzantine historian Niketas Choniates (d. 1217) wrote that there was a group of women among the crusaders who rode astride like men, 'bearing lances and weapons as men do; dressed in masculine garb, they conveyed a wholly martial appearance more mannish than the Amazons' led by 'another Penthesilea', the queen of the Amazons at the ancient siege of Troy. He was probably referring to Eleanor and her ladies, but as he was not even born at the time of the Second Crusade, his account must have been based on a previous generation's hostile memories of the crusaders, as seen through the distorting lens of the Fourth Crusade's sack of Constantinople, which Niketas himself witnessed. For Niketas, the fact that noble women accompanied the crusade was an indication of the crusaders' barbarity.[50]

Another stereotypical role for women was as victim. Preachers recruiting for crusades dwelt on the sufferings Islam had inflicted on Christian women in the Holy Land.[51] Latin Christian writers also warned that Christian attacks on Muslim women would cause lethal Muslim reprisals: the continuations of Archbishop William of Tyre's History stated that the immediate cause of the loss of kingdom of Jerusalem to Saladin in 1187–1188 was that Renaud de Châtillon, lord of Transjordan, captured a caravan in which Saladin's mother or sister was travelling and refused to obey King Guy of Jerusalem's order to release her. The mother or sister appears to be a later invention, as contemporary Muslim and Christian writers recorded the attack on the caravan but not Saladin's relative.[52] Similarly, Francesco Balbi di Correggio, an eyewitness of the Ottoman invasion of Malta in 1565, blamed the Ottoman attack on the Hospitallers' capture of an elderly and influential Turkish noblewoman on her way to Mecca.[53]

The stereotype of the foolish and greedy woman who manipulated her loving husband into rash actions was cited as a cause of unjust campaigns. The Catalan author Ramon Muntaner blamed Beatrice of Provence for Charles of Anjou's invasion of Sicily in 1266, a campaign that was devised and organized as a crusade against the pope's enemies. According to Ramon, Charles had found his wife Beatrice weeping because her elder sister Margaret was queen of France while she was a mere countess, and promised her a crown. To fulfil his promise, he then informed the pope that he was prepared to undertake the conquest of Sicily.[54] By claiming that Charles's original motivation in invading Sicily was merely to please his wife rather than for pious reasons, Ramon strengthened the justification for the revolt of the Sicilian Vespers in 1282 against Charles.

For critics of crusade campaigns, women's involvement was evidence of the futility of the exercise and the foolishness of the participants. Commentators told humorous stories of ordinary women's involvement in recruiting crusaders to highlight the gullibility of the common people, such as the famous story of the woman who set out with her goose to join the First Crusade—or, according to some reports, the goose led her and she followed it, accompanied by a credulous crowd.[55]

Some crusade chroniclers apparently invented women crusaders to improve their narrative. Historian Hilary Rhodes has discussed the case of Florina, supposedly daughter of Duke Odo I of Burgundy. Albert of Aachen described Florina's death in battle during the First Crusade, probably in late autumn 1097. According to Albert, she was the widow of a prince of Philippi and was accompanying the army of Svend, son of the king of Denmark, hoping to marry him after the expedition was successful. After passing through Constantinople and crossing the kingdom of Rum (in what is now Turkey), the army was attacked by Turks, and both Svend and Florina were killed. However, Rhodes points out that Albert's dates do not add up: if Florina existed, she could have been aged only fourteen at the time of this alleged incident. What is more, Duke Odo I did not mention his supposed daughter in any of his charters before setting out on his own crusade in 1101, whereas it would have been appropriate for him to have at least made a donation for her soul to a local monastery before setting out to the east himself. Rhodes concludes that Florina was an invention and that her name was possibly taken from the city of Florina in Macedonia, where there is also a city named Philippi.[56]

It is likely that Albert included the story for its moral value, to join his other stories warning women of the dangers of going on crusade. Just one of Albert of Aachen's stories of a noblewoman dying on crusade can be confirmed, at least insofar as the woman in question actually existed: Ida, widow of Leopold II of Austria, did take part in the crusade of 1101.[57] Women did come to unhappy ends during the crusades just as their male comrades did, but Albert's depiction of their experiences was not objective; it was deliberately framed to make his moral point.[58] Reluctant to 'lose' a named female crusader, modern scholars have continued to list Florina as a woman crusader despite the lack of evidence for her existence. In the same way, an entirely fictional woman crusader named Valette has appeared in modern histories of the Fifth Crusade, apparently created by a misprint: in reality this was a male crusader named Jordan Valette.[59]

When a writer gave no name or provenance to a character we have no means of checking whether they existed. For example, both Ambroise and Richard de Templo describe the death of a woman during the siege of Acre of 1189–1191. According to their story, she was labouring with other crusaders, helping to fill in the ditch around the city with earth, when she was hit by a missile and killed. Her pious dying wish was for her body to be laid in the ditch so that even after her death she would continue the good work. Both authors mention her husband but Richard de Templo particularly emphasized that she was respectably married, depicting her making a dying request to her husband, addressing him as '*Dilectionem tuam, Domine carissime*' (you darling, dearest lord) and imploring him in the name of 'the sacrament of marriage, by our long-ago marital vows' to fulfil her wish to be buried in the ditch.[60] This is a heart-warming tale that could have inspired listeners to greater acts of piety, but the incident may have been invented to make a moral point. Because these writers represent her as one among many women working to fill in the ditch we may suppose that this woman represents the non-noble women who joined the Third Crusade, but the story itself cannot be validated.

Stereotypes aside, it is easy to miss references to women in crusade armies. Although contemporary crusade accounts sometimes mentioned noble women by title and, less often, by name, they usually mentioned non-noble women as a group rather than as individuals (and hardly ever named them). Anna Komnene, for example, simply mentioned that the civilians accompanying the armies of the First Crusade included women and children, but gave no details.[61] Often writers simply described the whole army as a group and did not specify men and women separately, as the language they used included both. A commentator writing in Latin, wishing to inform readers that a leader was accompanied by their followers, would refer to the followers as '*suis*' (literally, his or hers—the Latin does not specify gender); or they might refer to '*gens*', a feminine noun meaning 'people' as a group of men and women. These words have often been translated into modern English as 'men'; so although the original text allowed for the possibility that women were involved, the modern translation does not.[62]

It is possible, of course, that some women went unnoticed by their contemporaries because they did not appear to be women—because they were dressed as men. There are a few references in both Christian and Muslim writings about the crusades and pilgrimage to women dressing as men, either to take part in the fighting or for safety when travelling.[63] Muslim descriptions of Christian women disguised as male warriors in the crusader armies may be inventions because they are so obviously moral stories emphasizing the barbarity of the Latin Christians, their perverted religious fanaticism and their godlessness, demonstrating that their cause was doomed to failure.[64] Given that one of these women pilgrims in male disguise, Hildegund von Schönau (d. 1188), was depicted as constantly anxious that others would realize she was really a woman, there were obviously problems in trying to maintain such a disguise for a long period.[65] We can only speculate how many women might have taken part in crusading in disguise, because if their disguises were successful then they would not have been recorded.

As the narratives sources present so many challenges of interpretation we might question how we may ever know that any women were involved in the crusades. However, the narrative accounts of crusades are not the only source of evidence. There are also personal letters, records in bishops' registers commuting women's vows (changing their crusade vow to a pilgrimage to a nearer destination, or to a money payment, as Helewyse Palmer and her daughter Isabel did), records in the papal registers recording various aspects of women's involvement, charter evidence (documents recording legal transactions, such as loans taken out to finance a crusade), evidence from legal cases (such as disputes between the heirs when a crusader died overseas), references to crusades and crusade-related matters in the lives of saints (such as Hildegund von Schönau), and so on. Again, more evidence survives for nobles than for non-nobles. In contrast to the narrative records these documentary records give us the names of non-noble women involved in the crusades: for example, making a will when they were about to set out. Some of them offer us glimpses of the motivations behind women's interest in the crusades. All of these sources require interpretation, and (as we will see) some personal letters may be later forgeries; but they generally take a positive view of women's involvement. Unfortunately, as they are scattered throughout the archives of Europe and only a small proportion of them have been published, it is impossible to judge whether the sample that we have is representative of the whole.

For example, a passenger list from a ship named 'St Victor' which was at Messina in Sicily in July 1250 lists many women among wouldbe 'pilgrims' going to join a crusade. To judge from the passengers' names the ship had set out from France, and it was sailing to Damietta to join Louis IX's first crusade. Of 453 passengers, forty-two (almost ten per cent) were women. As none of these were noble crusaders, the chance survival of this record gives us a rare insight into how non-noble women could travel to join a crusade. Half of these women were travelling with male companions—fourteen with a husband, one with husband and son, one with father, one with her brother, two with brother and sister-in-law and two with a 'socius' (a male companion, undefined)—and half without male company. Nine of the remaining women travelled alone, ten may have have been travelling with another woman or women, and two were identified as travel companions: one may have been the other's servant.[66] It is tempting to assume that this list is typical of crusader ships and that all crusades would have included a similar proportion of women, but regrettably it is the only such list which has so far been identified. There is no information about why they had joined the crusade, but the fact that they were collectively called 'pilgrims' indicates that they had joined for spiritual reward.

Motivation

Like our own age, the people of Europe in the period of the crusades were extremely concerned about health and purity, going to enormous lengths to ensure that they and their society were safe from infection. Nowadays this concern is primarily focussed on physical health and what damages the physical body, but their focus was on spiritual health and those things which destroy the soul. The infection that they sought to avoid was the infection of sin rather than physical disease.

To ensure their spiritual health, Latin Christians fasted at certain times, endowed religious houses and hospitals, undertook other charitable giving, and travelled on pilgrimage to holy sites to gain a spiritual reward. Support for the crusade, with its call to recover Christ's patrimony from unbelievers and protect other Christians from persecution, was a means of cleansing the soul from the taint of sin through fighting against the infection of false belief. The enormous challenges and personal costs of crusading made it a penitential exercise that would bring spiritual health to both the individual and wider society, but the costs and the need to protect family interests limited how far any woman or man could participate.[67]

Women's ability to join a crusade was primarily dependent on their social class.[68] Crusading was very expensive: it has been estimated that 'a poor knight would have to find at least four times his average annual income' in order to join the First Crusade. As most crusaders would have made a considerable financial loss in crusading, the obvious conclusion to draw is that they and the families who supported them were inspired by religious idealism.[69] The fact that men and women vowed to go on crusade and then commuted their vow to a cash payment also suggests that piety was an important factor in crusading; the spiritual reward was worth the payment. The enormous personal cost which some women paid to support a crusade again strongly suggests that piety was a major stimulus. Yet we have to deduce this from events and actions; few of the sources state this explicitly.

Motives are seldom straightforward, and everyone involved will have had many reasons for venturing on a crusade over and beyond simple piety. Dynastic interests and the need to escape difficult situations at home could be motivations for crusading in addition to the desire to serve God and win a spiritual reward.[70] Many women took part in crusades because they were accompanying their husband, father, brother, or son, and they may have had no choice over whether they participated.[71] Others were in employment and accompanied their employer (for example as ladies' maids), or conducted their business (for instance, as merchants selling food to the army). Family tradition was perhaps the most important motivation for crusading, after piety, and women played a significant role in upholding this tradition and introducing it to each new generation.

2

Initializing Crusades

Jherusalem, grant damage me fais,
Qui m'as tolu ce que je pluz amoie.[1]

> (Jerusalem, you do me great harm; you've taken
> from me what I loved most).

This 'crusade song' presents a common image of women's involvement in the crusades: the young woman weeping because her
brave knightly lover is far away crusading. Vividly expressed in poign-
ant verse, the emotions are raw, honest, and shocking: the speaker
declares that she is on the point of turning against God because he has
taken her from her great joy. Medieval French 'crusade songs' also
depict male crusaders expressing similar views, each declaring that
although he is fighting for Christ he longs for his sweetheart. But do
these songs reflect actual opposition towards crusading, or are they
simply a version of the courtly love lyric, adapted to reflect the interests of the moment? As the love aspect of these songs overshadowed
the crusading aspect, it seems that audiences were more interested in
love's pangs than in fighting.[2]

Still, the song raises the question: did women oppose crusading?
Canon law laid down that neither party to a marriage could make a
vow without the other's consent, which allowed women to veto their
husband taking a crusade vow, and vice versa. As women's veto on
crusaders was abolished in the early thirteenth century it appears that

wives had been preventing their husbands from taking part.[3] The Cymro-Norman cleric Gerald of Wales recounted how a married woman of Cardigan who had held her husband back from taking the cross during Archbishop Baldwin of Canterbury's crusade preaching tour of Wales in 1188 then went on to suffocate her baby by accident. Convinced that this was a punishment from God, her husband then took the cross, and she sewed it to his clothes herself. Told out of context, this suggests that Gerald saw women as an impediment to the crusade cause, but just before recounting this anecdote he had described an old woman ardently supporting her son in taking the cross, thanking Christ for judging her worthy to bear a son who would now serve Him. By juxtaposing the two extremes—heartfelt praise and absolute opposition—Gerald strengthened the emotional impact of his work.[4] Such stories warned men not to use their wives and mothers as an excuse to avoid the crusade.

Other writers suggested that women were as enthusiastic about crusading as their menfolk and could play informed, direct, and active roles in recruiting for crusades. One of Archbishop Baldwin of Canterbury's companions on the Third Crusade depicted women encouraging their menfolk to go. His view of women's contribution to recruitment was wholly positive: 'brides urged their husbands and mothers incited their sons to join such a notable contest, their only sorrow being that they were not able to set out with them because of the weakness of their sex'.[5] The Muslim historian Ibn al-Athīr recorded a conversation he had had with a Christian prisoner who told him that although he was his mother's only son, she had sold the family home in order to equip him for the Third Crusade, and had sent him to recover Jerusalem.[6] In the mid-fifteenth century, writing his novel 'Jehan de Saintré', Antoine de la Sale depicted his young hero's lady love instructing him to join a campaign against the 'Saracens' (Lithuanians) on the Prussian frontier to help him on the path to becoming the most valiant man in the world and to emulate his ancestors: 'it seems to me that you cannot do it in a holier or more honourable way than on this very holy journey to Prussia, at this very holy battle which must take place at the encounter with the Saracens'.[7] All these writers regarded women as crucial in encouraging men to join crusades.

Beginnings

From the very beginning of the crusade movement high-status women were involved in initializing crusades. A noblewoman played a central role in the first papal attempt to organize a military expedition to help the Christians of the eastern Mediterranean. At the end of 1074 Pope Gregory VII enlisted the aid of Countess Matilda of Canossa (also known to modern scholars as Matilda of Tuscany) and her mother Countess Beatrice for his proposed campaign to aid the Byzantine Greeks against the Seljuk Turks. Matilda, who had inherited her lordship as her father's only surviving heir, was an effective military leader in her wars in support of papal reform and against the western emperors from the 1070s until 1114.[8] Gregory's plan in 1074 was that Beatrice should remain in Italy to safeguard their common interests, while Matilda would lead her own troops to the East. Gregory also hoped that the dowager empress, Agnes of Poitou, would assist them with her prayers, and that she and Matilda would encourage wide recruitment. He informed Agnes's son King Henry IV that more than 50,000 were preparing to set out under papal command. In a letter addressed to all his loyal followers, Gregory appealed to warriors to cease fighting for earthly gain, and to come with him to help the Christians in the East and to give up their lives for their brothers. In return for defending the Christian faith they would win an eternal reward. In the event this expedition did not set out: perhaps the pope had decided that—with the exception of Countesses Beatrice and Matilda—his secular allies could not be relied upon.[9] Nonetheless the pope's proposals show that the ideas that would underlie crusading were already circulating at the papal court more than twenty years before the First Crusade set out for the eastern Mediterranean, and

that from the start noblewomen were at the forefront of putting penitential warfare into practice.

This abortive expedition was not the end of Matilda's involvement
in war against the enemies of Christians. In 1087 Matilda contributed
troops to a Pisan-Genoese expedition against the Muslim port city of
al-Mahdiya (or Mahdia) and its suburb Zawīla on the coast of what is
now Tunisia in North Africa. They captured the city, plundered it,
released Christian captives, and took Muslim prisoners. There was a
compelling commercial and strategic reason for their attack: the city's
ruler, Tamīn, had been encouraging raids on Christian shipping and
lands. The Latin song written to celebrate the expedition's success
(the *Carmen in victoriam Pisanorum*: the 'Song about the Pisans' victory')
compared the campaign to classical wars but also described it as a holy
war, similar to Gideon's miraculous triumph brought about by God
(Judges 6–8). Although Matilda did not personally take part in the
campaign, by contributing troops she demonstrated her support for
its aims and assisted its success.[10]

Despite the religious propaganda which accompanied it, this expedition was merely a raid to weaken a commercial rival and take captives
for ransom or sale: elsewhere in the Mediterranean more permanent
conquests were in train. The eleventh-century Mediterranean was the
scene of increasing commercial conflict between the expanding
Christian ports of Italy (including Amalfi, Genoa, Pisa, Venice), the
south of France (especially Marseille), and the northern Iberian peninsula (particularly Barcelona), and the more established Muslim city
ports of North Africa, the southern Iberian peninsula, and the islands
of the central and eastern Mediterranean. This conflict was stimulated
by climate change, population growth and migration, and the economic and commercial revival of much of Europe in the eleventh
century. During the tenth and eleventh centuries the nomadic peoples
of central Asia, driven by famine caused by environmental change,
migrated west in search of food, and moved into the sedentary and
settled Byzantine and Fatimid empires of the Middle East. In response,
the Byzantine emperor appealed to European Christians for military

assistance. In contrast, in Europe the same climate change assisted agricultural growth and a population surplus looking for new lands for expansion, while economic development produced surplus wealth which could finance military expeditions to capture and hold new lands.[11] At the end of the eleventh century these developments stimulated and enabled the First Crusade.

At the other end of the Mediterranean, Latin Christian rulers had been expanding their authority into territory that before being conquered by Islam in the eighth century had formed part of the Roman Empire and then the Visigothic Empire. They depicted this expansion as a reconquest of lands which were rightfully Christian.

The Reconquest of the Iberian Peninsula and beyond

The Christian kingdoms of the northern Iberian Peninsula, which had not been conquered by the Muslim invasions of the early eighth century, took advantage of the weakening power of the Cordoban caliphate after 1008 to expand southwards along the rivers Duero and Ebro into Muslim-controlled territory. Small states known as 'taifas' emerged across al-Andalus (Muslim Spain), based around the major cities and effectively independent of Cordoba. They alternately formed alliances or fought among themselves, allied with and waged war on the Christian rulers of the north, and paid tribute to Christian rulers in return for military aid and protection. In 1085 King Alfonso VI of León and Castile captured the taifa of Toledo, the ancient Visigothic capital of Spain, a military and a propaganda victory which allowed him to depict himself as restoring the Christian empire of the Visigoths. The power of Cordoba, Granada, and the other taifas was far from broken, however, and the Muslim rulers of the peninsula called on North African Muslim rulers for assistance against the Christians. Assistance came from the Murabitun, also known as the Almoravids, radical Islamic warriors who dominated north-west

Africa as far south as the Ghana Empire. The struggle for domination of the Iberian Peninsula would continue for another five centuries until Ferdinand and Isabel of Aragon-Castile conquered Granada in 1492.[12] The Christian rulers of the Iberian Peninsula used crusading language to assist recruitment and justify their campaigns, but the conflict between Christian and Muslim was as much a conflict over territory as a holy war.[13]

King Alfonso VI, conqueror of Toledo, died in 1109. His one surviving legitimate heir was his daughter Urraca, daughter of his second wife Constance of Burgundy (see family tree 2, showing King Alfonso's descendants).[14] Urraca faced considerable threats to her authority. There was the constant danger from the Almoravids to the south, who raided the area around recently conquered Toledo and its fortresses, and conquered the taifa of Zaragoza. Within Christian Spain, she fought to retain her kingdom against her estranged second husband, King Alfonso I 'El Batallador' (the Battler) of Aragon; she also combatted her illegitimate sister Teresa, married to Count Henry of Portugal and with ambitions to rule Galicia-León.[15]

The contemporary commentators, charters of donation, and the later Muslim historian Ibn al-Kardabus described Urraca as a leader of armies in her wars against both Alfonso I and against her rebellious magnates.[16] But although much of her reign was spent fighting Christians, Urraca's reign also saw some advances against the Almoravids. Among her extensive patronage to churches and religious houses she gave property on the border with Portugal to the new Jerusalem-based Hospital of St John of Jerusalem, which at this time was not yet formally a military order (its members would later become the Knights Hospitaller), but did represent God's holy city and was symbolic of Christ's cause.[17] She did not lead her army to defend Toledo when it was under attack from the Muslim Almoravids between 1113 and 1118, but as Toledo was still effectively a separate realm during her reign it is not surprising that its defence was in the hands of its local lords.[18] At that point there was no urgent need for Urraca to divert her resources from fighting her Christian rivals.

When she had sufficiently established her authority in León and Castile, she was able to go on to the offensive against the Almoravids.

The queen was probably involved in the campaign of winter 1123–1124 which captured the city of Sigüenza (about halfway between Toledo and Zaragoza). This was not a formal crusade, but at the end of November 1123, as the queen, bishops, and magnates would have been assembling at Toledo for the campaign, Pope Calixtus II's chaplain was present in Toledo confirming a generous donation Urraca made to the archbishop of Toledo; so presumably the pope was taking an interest. The campaign secured Toledo from the east and cut Almoravid communications between Zaragoza and Seville. Urraca's gains from the Almoravids laid the groundwork for further gains by her son and heir Alfonso VII.[19]

Urraca's half-sister Teresa of Portugal also ruled a country that had a frontier with the Muslims, and therefore was also responsible for defending her territories against them. Unlike Urraca, she ruled not in her own right but as widow of the count of Portugal and mother of his son and heir. Like Urraca, she endowed a Jerusalem-based religious order: in March 1128 she gave the fortress of Soure near Coimbra to the 'knights of the Temple of Solomon', later known as the Templars, 'for the remedy of my soul and the remission of my sins', indicating both her concern to ensure that this strategic fortress was effectively defended and a wish to associate herself with the holy city of Jerusalem, which the Templars had been set up to defend.[20]

Muslim attacks on León were clearly a problem in November–December 1110 when Urraca and Teresa made a pact of friendship: Urraca passed direct responsibility for some territories in León to her step-sister and Teresa promised to defend these lands and their people against both Moors and Christians, as a good sister to a good sister. In the immediate aftermath of Count Henry's death in 1112 the Almoravid threat subsided. Then in 1116 the Almoravids advanced on Coimbra, which had been captured from the Muslims only in 1064, and captured the fortresses which formed its outer defences. In 1117 the Almoravid emir 'Ali ibn Yusuf led Islamic troops from North

Africa and Andalusia to besiege Coimbra itself, apparently in a sur-
prise attack as Pope Paschal II was informed that Teresa had barely had
time to get safely into the city and defend herself. Nevertheless, the
city was strongly defended, and despite suffering considerable destruction and death the defence held fast. After a twenty-day siege the
Almoravids withdrew.[21]

Both at Toledo in 1123 and at Coimbra in 1117 the queens were
present during hostilities against Muslims but Christian commentators did not depict them as leading the army themselves. Queens were
generally shown supporting their husbands and especially their sons
in fighting the Muslims, rather than fighting on their own behalf. For
example, the anonymous *Latin Chronicle of the Kings of Castile*, composed probably in the 1220s and 1230s, showed Queen Sancha of
Aragon (d. 1208) encouraging her son Pere to assist her nephew King
Alfonso VIII of Castile in fighting the king of Morocco in 1196. It also
depicted Alfonso VIII's daughter Queen Berenguela of Castile (d. 1246)
supporting her son Fernando III when in 1224 he expressed a wish 'to
serve the Lord Jesus Christ, by whom kings reign, against the enemies
of the Christian faith, to the honour and glory of His name'—a dec-
laration that this was holy war, even though this was not a crusade
specifically authorized by the pope.[22] The *Chronicle* recorded that in
the long war of conquest that followed, Fernando kept his mother
informed on his undertakings and achievements, took her advice on
strategy, and returned to her and the seat of government after each
campaign. Berenguela's authority as queen enabled and supported
Fernando's holy war; but she did not take an active role herself.[23]

On the other hand, the *Chronica Adefonsi Imperatoris* ('Chronicle of
the Emperor Alfonso') had depicted the Empress Berenguela of
Castile (or Berengaria), wife of Queen Urraca's son and heir Alfonso
VII, defending the city of Toledo against Almoravid attack, but through
diplomacy rather than arms. According to this account, when the
Almoravid army reached the outskirts of Toledo and began to destroy
the vineyards and orchards:

The Empress Berengaria was in Toledo with many knights, archers and infantrymen who were guarding at the gates and walls of the city. When she realized what the Moors were doing, she sent messengers to their kings bearing the following communication: 'Do you not realize that you are fighting against a woman, and that this is in no way advantageous to your own honour? If you wish to fight, go to Oreja and fight with the Emperor who is awaiting you there with his forces in battle array.' When the enemy rulers heard this message, they looked up, and saw the Empress seated on a royal throne in the high tower of the Alcazar. She was adorned and attended as befits an Empress. Around her there was a large group of distinguished women singing to the accompaniment of tambourines, lutes, cymbals and psalteries. Upon seeing her, the Moors were not only totally astonished, but they were also very ashamed. They bowed their heads before the Empress, turned back and did not cause further destruction in the area. They gathered their forces that had lain in ambush, and they returned to their own lands without victory and without honour.[24]

This story was probably intended to be humorous, showing the enemy trapped by his own sense of honour and dignity.[25] It enabled the chronicler to depict Alfonso VII's wife as supporting her husband by defending his chief city from attack without suggesting that the Emperor had failed her or the kingdom. This, the chronicler believed, was how queens should act in warfare, not having to demean themselves by being physically involved in fighting. Notice, however, that Berenguela had 'many knights, archers and infantrymen'. It is more likely that she informed the Almoravid general that she could easily defend the city until it was relieved by the Emperor, who was nearby with his army at the fortress of Oreja. The general would have withdrawn because he realized he could not capture Toledo before the Emperor arrived.

Later queens were also depicted offering diplomatic support for war against the Muslims. According to the contemporary Álvar García de Santa María in his history of the reign of King Juan II of Castile-León, in 1407 Fernando, brother of the late King Enrique III of Castile and co-regent for the infant King Juan II, announced that he would go to war against Muslim Granada in retaliation for the capture of the castle of Ayamonte from Castile in 1405, and subjugate Granada 'to the sovereignty of our Lord Jesus Christ and the king.' The war would lead to 'the exaltation of the Catholic faith' and was 'a holy work' which would 'save our souls' as well as recovering the young king's property. Fernando's co-regent Catalina (or Catherine) of Lancaster, Juan II's mother, approved of Fernando's intention to conquer the 'infidels' and return her son's land to him. Conceived as a holy war, the campaign was supported by the Avignonese Pope Benedict XIII, who authorized the Castilian crown to take Church funds, the *tercias* or one-third of the tithe, to finance it. As in the case of King Fernando III's campaigns of almost two centuries earlier, the queen provided the authority for the campaign without herself being involved in the war. (The expedition set out but failed to make any territorial gains.)[26]

In 1411, Catalina negotiated with her brother-in-law King João I of Portugal to assist Castile in a joint campaign against Granada, and in 1415 she may have discussed plans for the conquest of Granada with João's wife, her own half-sister Philippa of Lancaster. In the following year Queen Catalina was again discussing plans for the conquest of Granada with Fernando, now king of Aragon; but Fernando's death that year brought this to an end. Instead Catalina turned her diplomacy to her Muslim opponents and in 1417 she made a truce with Yūsuf III of Granada for two years.

Meanwhile, although Philippa of Lancaster had died in 1415, João I and their sons pressed ahead with an expedition she had supported, the conquest of Ceuta in Morocco. The expressed aim was to spread Christianity and crush Islam, but the conquest also gave Portugal a strategic foothold and challenged Castilian dominance of the holy war in the Iberian Peninsula.[27]

Philippa and Catalina came from a family imbued with the crusading ethic (see family tree 4 showing the daughters of John of Gaunt). Philippa's maternal grandfather, Henry of Grosmont, duke of Lancaster, had crusaded in Prussia and in Spain.[28] As a young man their father, John of Gaunt, took an interest in crusading, stipulating that his knights should provide military service against the 'enemies of God'. In 1386–1387 he led a military expedition to claim the throne of Castile in the name of his second wife, Constanza of Castile, daughter of Pedro I: this was promoted as a crusade by the Roman pope Urban VI, as the campaign was against Henry of Trastamara, supporter of the Avignonese pope, Clement VII. Gaunt also patronized the Castilian military religious orders and was involved in plans for crusade expeditions in eastern Europe, while his sons Henry Bolingbroke—later King Henry IV of England—and John Beaufort took part in crusades against the Lithuanians and elsewhere.[29]

The fifteenth-century Portuguese historian Gomes Eanes de Zurara (c. 1410–c. 1474) indicated that Philippa of Lancaster's English chivalric values had an ongoing influence on her husband João I and on their three sons. Zurara depicts Philippa giving her wholehearted support to the plans of her husband and sons to capture Ceuta, because this would enable her sons to accomplish great chivalric deeds as their ancestors did. Unlike the reported comments of Berenguela of Castile to her son Fernando III in 1224, or Catalina of Lancaster to her brother-in-law Fernando in 1407, Zurara depicts Philippa highlighting the chivalric rather than the spiritual aspects of the campaign. On the eve of the crusade's departure Philippa falls ill with plague, and on her deathbed she gives each of her three sons a sword and asks her husband the king to use these swords when he knights them. She tells each of her sons: 'I require you to accept this sword from my hand with my blessing and that of your forefathers from whom I am descended', making explicit the link between them and her father's chivalric past.[30]

In this scene crusading has become inextricably entwined with chivalry. Philippa appears as a new Niniane, the Lady of the Lake, teaching the young Lancelot about knighthood and giving him his arms, or presenting Arthur with his sword from the lake.[31] However, although Philippa's son Henry 'the Navigator' did appear to take her chivalric and crusading ideals seriously, his campaigns in North Africa and attacks on the Canary Islands may have been more focussed on acquiring gold and slaves than winning land and people for Christ.[32]

By the early fifteenth century, war against the Muslims on the southern frontier of the Iberian Christian kingdoms was no longer an absolute necessity to ensure the security of the realm. Although border raiding continued, captives and property were taken, and crops burned, there was no realistic possibility of the Muslim kings of Granada or Morocco recapturing Toledo or Seville, for example. Nevertheless, when Isabel of Castile and her husband Ferdinand of Aragon secured control of the throne of Castile in 1479 they stated that they had always intended to conquer Muslim Granada and that 'they ought not to undertake any war except for the faith and for security'. In her marriage agreement with Ferdinand in 1469, Isabel had insisted that the conquest of Granada was a priority: Ferdinand undertook 'to wage war against the Moors, enemies of the holy Catholic faith'.[33]

After initially confirming her late brother Enrique IV's truce with Granada while she dealt with the rival claim to the throne of Castile from her niece Juana, Isabel with her husband Ferdinand petitioned Pope Sixtus IV to proclaim a crusade against Granada and allow them to finance it with ecclesiastical tithes. Isabel and Ferdinand told the pope that they were not undertaking this campaign to enlarge their realms or win wealth, but to serve God, multiply the holy Catholic faith, and remove the constant danger of the infidels from Spain.[34] Three years later, they declared that the war was 'holy and just and for the exaltation of our holy Catholic faith'. It was just because they were recovering territories invaded by the Muslims more than seven centuries earlier; Ferdinand declared that the war was no less just and necessary than the war in the eastern Mediterranean.

As in the previous conflicts, the king led the military forces while the queen provided her authority and support. In November 1489 she even attended the siege of Baza in person, accompanied by her daughter, ladies, and members of her council. The royal secretary and chronicler Fernando de Pulgar, who was present, described the king going with all his military commanders and knights to meet the queen and her entourage, and the delight of everyone in the besieging army because they thought her arrival foreboded the successful conclusion of the siege. Pulgar speculated on the reaction of the besieged Muslims to the queen's arrival but commented that he himself observed that after the queen arrived the enemy appeared less ferocious, as if they became tame.[35]

The monarchs were depicted acting together in everything; if Ferdinand was distracted by other affairs, Isabel would recall him to the religious necessity of conquering Granada. Isabel's role in promoting the war was acknowledged in March 1490, before the fall of Granada, when Pope Innocent VIII awarded her the papal honour of the Golden Rose for her work in extending the Christian faith. Isabel died in 1504; in her testament she urged her successors to continue the conquest of Africa (claimed by the rulers of Castile through their Visigothic predecessors) and 'fight for the faith against the infidels'. By 1526 the Spanish generally credited Isabel with having initiated the conquest of Granada.[36] All this said, it was a historiographic tradition among Christian commentators in the Iberian Peninsula to assign the spiritual initiative in the holy war to the queen and the actual implementation of military operations to her husband or son. The fact that Ferdinand continued the same policies after Isabel's death indicates that he was as devoted to them as she was, and that both were equally interested in the territorial as well as the spiritual gains from the war.

The Catholic monarchs' commitment to conquering Muslims and expanding the Christian faith was taken up by Christopher Columbus when he sought support for his proposed voyage to China via the western ocean, arguing that if successful this could provide a new route to Jerusalem. In a letter of 1501, following his recent discovery of 'the Indies', he wrote to Isabel and Ferdinand stating that his discovery was a miracle from God in compensation for the loss of the 'Holy House' in Jerusalem, that it was foretold by the Old Testament prophet Isaiah, and that it was prophesized that the person who would rebuild God's House upon Mount Zion (Jerusalem) would come from Spain—indicating that the Catholic monarchs should expect to recover Jerusalem from Islam. In fact the Spanish and Portuguese expansion into the New World never received papal approval as a crusade, although the *conquistadores* took with them the attitudes and language of the crusade, carrying banners showing the Holy Cross and appealing to Christ, the Blessed Virgin Mary, and St James of Compostela just as they had in Spain when fighting the Moors. Bernal Díaz del Castillo, one of Hernán Cortés's companions in his conquest of Mexico (1519–1521), also emphasized the assistance they had received from a local high-status woman whom they knew as Doña Marina, 'a person of the greatest importance [who] was obeyed without question by the Indians throughout New Spain' and who converted to Christianity, similarly to the fictional assistance given to the crusaders by Muslim noblewomen who converted to Christianity in European epic-romance literature about the crusades.[37]

Even as the Spanish and Portuguese explored the New World and the Portuguese found the maritime route to India, the Muslim Ottoman Turks of the eastern Mediterranean were becoming a threat to their interests in North Africa. In 1509 Queen Eleni of Ethiopia, regent for her step-great-grandson Lebnä Dengel, replied to an appeal for military aid from King Manuel I of Portugal with envoys bringing the gift of a cross made from the wood of the True Cross and a letter offering an alliance against the Muslims, support in fighting men, and supplies for a campaign by land and sea to 'wipe the Moors from the face of the earth'. However, Manuel's return embassy did not reach Ethiopia until 1520, by which time Lebnä Dengel had come of age, the old queen had stepped down as regent, and the young emperor was not interested in pursuing an alliance. Two decades later a Portuguese force would go to assist the king's widow and son against Muslim invasion in a campaign described in crusading terms as a 'holy enterprise'.[38]

The Crusader States and the
eastern Mediterranean

At the eastern end of the Mediterranean, queens regnant were also responsible for the defence of their territory against Muslim enemies and for this purpose recruited troops and organized campaigns, although for the most part these were not formal crusades. In the generation following Queens Urraca of León-Castile and Teresa of Portugal, Queen Melisende of Jerusalem (ruled 1131–1153), daughter of King Baldwin II and queen in her own right, ruled with her son Baldwin III. Archbishop William of Tyre recorded in his history of the kingdom of Jerusalem that when the news of Zengī's siege of Edessa (1144) reached the queen and her son in Jerusalem, after consulting her nobles she sent a military force with all speed to help. William drew a sharp contrast between Melisende's quick action and the reaction of Prince Raymond of Antioch, who (he wrote) rejoiced at the adversities of Count Joscelin II of Edessa because of his personal enmity against the count rather than remembering that personal quarrels should not affect public policy. Melisende's action, however, was not enough to save the city, which fell to Zengī with great slaughter.[39] William also recorded that Baldwin III and his mother, 'a wise and cautious woman, having a manly heart and wise in nothing inferior to any learned prince', were present at the council of the leaders of the Second Crusade which assembled at Acre in June 1148 to decide what strategy the crusade should adopt.[40] The council eventually decided to attack the major city of Damascus, which turned out to be a disastrous mistake—but William and the other contemporary commentators do not make clear whose decision this was. William blamed Count Thierry of Flanders for the failure of the siege, while commentators from Europe blamed the people of Jerusalem, but no one specifically blamed Melisende.[41]

Melisende's granddaughter Sybil, likewise heiress to the kingdom
of Jerusalem, took some military initiative after Saladin captured her
husband Guy de Lusignan at the battle of Hattin in 1187, and after
Guy's release she supported her husband gathering a military force of
crusaders from Europe to recover their kingdom, but unlike her
grandmother she did not take a prominent role in arrangements for
the crusade.[42] Almost three centuries later Sybil's titular successor,
Charlotte de Lusignan, queen of Cyprus and Jerusalem, appealed to
the West for aid against Muslim-sponsored attack but to no avail. In
1463 she and her second husband Louis of Savoy were driven out of
Cyprus by her illegitimate half-brother James in alliance with the
Mamluk sultan of Egypt.

Since 1426 when King Janus had been defeated by the Mamluk
sultan Barsbay, Cyprus had been a tributary of the Mamluks and
under constant threat of Mamluk invasion. In response, popes had
issued regular crusade indulgences to encourage Latin Christians
to give aid to the island: by purchasing one of these indulgences,
the donor received the spiritual benefit of going on crusade, while
the money raised would go to assist the defence of Cyprus. However, the
crusading status of the island did not help Charlotte to raise effective
military aid. She went to Rome to appeal to the pope, and also sought
help from the Hospitallers on Rhodes. The Hospitallers allowed her to
set up court on Rhodes and supported her case, showing that they saw
her cause as just and appropriate for their involvement as a military
religious order of the Christian Church fighting against the enemies
of Christendom. But Charlotte could get no assistance from the
powerful maritime power of Venice, because James's wife Catherine
Cornaro was a Venetian. After James's death in 1473 rumours reached
Venice that the sultan would now back Charlotte's claim, whereupon
Venice sent a fleet to Cyprus to support Catherine. At last Charlotte
was forced to give up, ceding her claims to Cyprus and the kingdom
of Jerusalem to the House of Savoy, her husband's family.[43]

Charlotte's sad experience demonstrated that even when a Christian
queen had a just cause against a Muslim-backed adversary, and the

support of the papacy, she could not necessarily inspire a full crusade to come to her assistance. Catherine remained queen of Cyprus, paying tribute to the sultan of Egypt but in reality only an agent for the Republic of Venice.[44]

Family connections

Although these women recruited and organized armies which fought Muslims, with the possible exception of Isabel the Catholic they were not themselves crusaders. But it was not necessary to be a crusader in order to promote crusades. In the late eleventh century and first half of the twelfth the women of the families of the counts of Burgundy, the counts of Nevers, the Montlhérys, and the Le Puiset family, among others, played a central role in encouraging their menfolk to become involved in crusading, bringing the crusade tradition to the families into which they married.[45] In 1216 James of Vitry, newly consecrated bishop of Acre and preacher of the Fifth Crusade, wrote that the women of Genoa had led their husbands to take the cross.[46] We have already seen that in the Iberian Peninsula in the early fifteenth century the sister-queens Catalina of Castile and Philippa of Portugal encouraged their male relatives to take up holy war against the Muslims. Philippa's ideals would also have influenced her daughter Isabel, who in 1430 married the twice-widowed Duke Philip the Good of Burgundy, an enthusiastic promoter of crusading. As duchess, Isabel may have planned a naval crusade against Tangier. She may also have initiated the ill-fated 1456 marriage between her nephew John of Coimbra and Charlotte de Lusignan, heiress to the kingdom of Cyprus, to provide Burgundy with a naval base in the eastern Mediterranean. Again, it is possible she contributed towards her son Charles the Bold's interest in crusading—although he did not go so far as his father in organizing crusades.[47]

Marriage alliances linked crusading families and reinforced their capability for crusading. In 1224 when the widowed John de Brienne (king of Jerusalem 1210–1225) came to Castile on his way to the pilgrim centre of Santiago de Compostela, Queen Berenguela of Castile negotiated a marriage between him and her daughter Berenguela, younger sister of her son King Fernando III of Castile. This marriage linked the ruling house of Castile to Jerusalem, connecting King John not only to the rulers of Castile, victorious propagators of holy war against Islam, but also—through his wife's aunt Blanche of Castile—to the Capetian royal house of France (see family tree 3, showing Blanche of Castile's family). These connections would later prove valuable to John de Brienne's sons and his daughter Marie de Brienne.[48]

Queen Berenguela of Castile's younger sister Blanche had married Louis of France in 1200 (later King Louis VIII, 1223–1226). Blanche appears to have maintained an interest in events in Castile and may have corresponded with her sister and one of their cousins on the victory of their father King Alfonso VIII of Castile over the Almohad caliph Muhammad al-Nāṣir at Las Navas de Tolosa on 16 July 1212.[49] In addition to their father being the hero of La Navas, Berenguela and Blanche were daughters of Leonor or Eleanor Plantagenet (d. 1214) (see family tree 1, showing the descendants of Eleanor of Aquitaine), who was second sister of King Richard I of England, hero of the Third Crusade, daughter of Eleanor of Aquitaine and of King Henry II of England (reigned 1154–1189), who supported the kingdom of Jerusalem with donations and vowed to go on crusade—although he never went, and great-granddaughter of Fulk V of Anjou, husband of Melisende of Jerusalem and king of Jerusalem from 1131 to 1143. Blanche was further linked to crusading through her in-laws: she was the daughter-in-law of King Philip II of France, who took part in the Third Crusade, and her husband Louis took part in the crusade against the Albigensian heretics in 1215, 1219, and 1226.

Louis died during his final campaign in the south, leaving Blanche a widow in a foreign land at the age of 38 with seven living children (three of whom were under the age of five) while her eldest son Louis, heir to the French throne, was only twelve years old. As regent for Louis she faced considerable opposition from the French nobility in establishing her son's authority securely, but she was eventually successful in winning the respect of the people and enforcing royal authority, both through peaceful means (charitable giving, religious endowments, and building projects) and force, leading her army to crush the opposition. She brought the Albigensian Crusade to a successful conclusion in April 1229 with the Treaty of Paris (or of Meaux).[50]

Blanche was a severely pious woman, devoted to the protection of the Christian faith and the eradication of heresy.[51] But given her husband's death during the Albigensian Crusade and the challenges that this had brought for her, her children, and the kingdom of France, it is not surprising that (according to John, lord of Joinville—writing over 60 years later) when Blanche heard that her son Louis had taken the cross she mourned as deeply as if she had seen him dead, and— according to Matthew Paris—she tried to have the vow nullified on the basis Louis made it when he was unwell. The fact that his three surviving brothers followed Louis's example would only have increased her anxiety. Writing around twenty years after events, the Minstrel of Reims described Blanche refusing to leave Louis's side as he set off on his journey, and when he told her that he must leave her, she wept and fainted with grief. Nevertheless, Blanche did assist her son in his preparations for the crusade, lending the count of Toulouse 20,000 *livres parisis* to encourage him to join the crusade. She acted as an effective regent during Louis's absence and raised money to pay his ransom after his capture in Egypt, but she died in November 1252 while he was still in the Holy Land.[52]

Blanche also offered support to a non-papal crusade. During her second regency a popular movement arose in north-eastern France whose members were known as the *pastoureaux* (shepherds). Their leader, known as the 'Master of Hungary' ('master' in the sense of 'learned man' or 'scholar') claimed to have had a vision of the Blessed Virgin Mary telling him to lead all the shepherds to the East to rescue Louis, who had been captured by the Muslims in Egypt in April 1250. Matthew Paris described Blanche's handling of the situation favourably, depicting her giving the movement the benefit of the doubt and remaining calm in the face of great provocation. He explained that she initially welcomed them: 'Blanche the governor and queen of the French, hoping that they would reach the Holy Land and avenge her sons, bestowed grace and favour on them.' But then they rioted at Orleans and killed a scholar, attacked the clergy and looted and destroyed their property. Outcry and complaints reached the ears of Blanche and the magnates. Blanche modestly (according to Matthew) responded: 'God knows, I believed that they would gain the whole world in simplicity and sanctity. But as they are deceivers, let them be excommunicated, captured, destroyed.' Before this could be done the group moved on to other cities, doing more damage, until at last they were suppressed.[53]

Other women of the family also supported the crusades. Agnes of Harcourt, biographer of Blanche's pious daughter Isabelle, wrote that after the death of her father, King Louis VIII, on the Albigensian Crusade Isabelle used some of the money he left her to send ten knights overseas: that is, to help protect the kingdom of Jerusalem. By noting this action by her subject, Agnes linked Isabelle's piety to the holy undertaking of the crusade.[54]

Blanche's great-great-granddaughter Queen Johanna (or Giovanna) of Naples (d. 1382) maintained the family interest in organizing a crusade to Jerusalem, especially because as the descendant of Blanche's youngest son Charles of Anjou she had inherited his claim to the throne of Jerusalem, purchased from Maria of Antioch in 1277. Like her ancestress Blanche she cultivated a reputation for piety, religious patronage, and support for holy women (such as Birgitta of Sweden, Birgitta's daughter Katherine of Vadstena, and Catherine of Siena), and she was loyally obedient to the papacy—which eventually led to her being caught up in the controversy over the election of Pope Urban VI at Rome in 1378 which resulted in the Great Schism with rival popes in Rome, Avignon, and later in Pisa too.[55] As early as 1343, when she was still in her teens, Pope Clement VI solicited her support for a naval expedition against the Turks in Greece.[56]

In 1372 Pope Gregory XI wrote to Johanna asking for aid for the Christian kingdom of Cilician Armenia: Margaret of Soissons, wife of King Leon VI of Cilician Armenia, had informed him that much of the kingdom had fallen to the Turks. The pope also wrote to the leaders of Venice, Genoa, Philip II, titular Latin Emperor of Constantinople, John de Lusignan, titular Prince of Antioch and regent of Cyprus, and Brother Raymond Bérenger, Grand Master of the Hospitallers, asking them to send aid. But as the Genoese were on the point of invading Cyprus at that point with the support of Johanna and the Hospitallers, none of the addressees took action.[57]

As titular queen of Jerusalem Johanna had an obvious interest in the political crisis on Cyprus which followed the assassination of King Peter I in 1369, particularly as the Lusignan rulers of Cyprus also claimed the title of kings of Jerusalem. Peter's widow Queen Eleanor may have asked for her support for a Genoese invasion to avenge Peter's death, for which Eleanor held the regent John de Lusignan responsible; she may also have approached Pope Gregory XI and her cousin King Pere IV of Aragon. Johanna worked with the Hospitallers, sending provisions to support Genoese intervention in Cyprus. Although in June 1373 Pope Gregory XI instructed them not to help the Genoese and tried to reach a peaceful solution, peace talks failed, and the Genoese invasion of Cyprus proceeded.[58] Meanwhile Johanna and her allies left Cilician Armenia to fall into the hands of the Mamluks. In April 1375 the Mamluks of Egypt captured the Armenian capital of Sis and took Leon, his wife, and his daughter as captives to Cairo. Leon was ransomed in 1382, but his wife and daughter had died in prison the previous year.

In October 1375 Gregory XI wrote to Johanna, acknowledging that he knew that she had very much desired to make a 'general passage' (a major expedition) to the Holy Land but asking her to redirect her plans. Setting out a pessimistic summary of the increasing threat posed by the Ottoman Turks to Constantinople, the Balkans, Achaea, and her own kingdom, Gregory explained that he intended to oppose the Turks' crossing into the Balkans by sending men-at-arms from the

Hospitallers and other Christian faithful, and he hoped that she and other Christian faithful would provide many galleys for them. This naval expedition, he wrote, would be a work of faith, *opus fidei*, and a better contribution to the Christian cause than trying to recover the Holy Land at this point, because if the Turks were not stopped now there would be no hope of recovering the Holy Land in future.[59] The influential letter-writing holy woman Catherine of Siena also wrote to Johanna about her planned crusade against the Turks. She was already urging the English mercenary captain John Hawkwood to lead his company against the 'infidels' who held 'our Holy Place', and in July 1376 she wrote to Johanna, asking for her support to take back 'the Holy Place of Our Lord'; she also wrote to Pope Gregory.[60] In the event there was no general passage, but we will return to Catherine of Siena's crusade plans below.

Johanna, then, continued her paternal family's crusade traditions but in name rather than in practice. Even when women themselves took no action to promote crusading, family links through women could provide connections which contributed towards the organization of a crusade. According to the hostile Byzantine historian Niketas Choniates, Irene Angela (also known as Eirene Angelina, d. 1208) provided the link between her husband Duke Philip of Swabia, and her brother Alexios Angelos, who in 1201 appealed to Philip for aid in winning the Byzantine throne, to which he claimed to be the rightful heir. The result was the diversion of the Fourth Crusade to Constantinople, which won Alexios the throne but was followed shortly afterwards by his deposition and murder. However, although according to Niketas she enabled her brother's escape to the West and besought her husband to help him and her father, Irene was not involved in organizing the expedition that ensued.[61]

Recruiting for crusades

Women also recruited in person for crusades on behalf of their husbands and sons. Alice de Montmorency, countess of Montfort (d. *c.* 1221), tirelessly recruited warriors for the Albigensian Crusade on behalf of first her husband Simon de Montfort and then her eldest son Amaury. Peter of les Vaux-de-Cernay, an eye-witness of the crusade, described her as the ideal Christian wife: she was 'a helpmate like' her husband, 'pious, wise, and caring. Her piety adorned her wisdom and her concern for others, her wisdom shaped her piety and concern, her concern stimulated her piety and wisdom.' Alice did not initially accompany her husband on the crusade, but he summoned her after the crusade had begun and she arrived in the Languedoc at the start of March 1210 with a force of knights. Throughout the crusade she supported the crusade by raising troops and leading them to join her husband. She was also one of the military council advising her husband, and she worked with her husband negotiating with the crusaders to encourage them to remain with the campaign rather than departing after one season. However, she did not take an active part in combat, so (for example) when in March 1210, just after her arrival in the south, de Montfort heard that the citizens of the fortified town of Montlaur had attacked his garrison in the castle he ensured that Alice was safely in a nearby castle before setting off to deal with them.

Alice was based at Carcassonne for much of the war, but she was with de Montfort at the siege of Termes in October 1210, and at Lavaur during the siege of Castelnaudry in September 1211—while her children were safely elsewhere. In the summer of 1212 Alice travelled with Peter of les Vaux-de-Cernay and his uncle Guy from Carcassonne, leading a troop of crusaders to join her husband at the siege of Biron in the Agenais. In 1216 she moved to the Château Narbonnais at Toulouse and was there at the start of the rebellion of Toulouse in September 1217, with her daughters-in-law and nieces and nephews, Guy de Montfort's wife, and the papal legate Bertrand. Alice sent the news of the rebellion to her husband and organized the castle's defences. As the siege dragged on she went north to recruit additional troops, especially asking her brother the Constable of France for his help. She returned in May with a large party of crusaders.

Like Blanche of Castile in the following decade, Alice lost her husband during this crusade: Simon de Montfort was killed in June 1218

while he commanded the siege of Toulouse. Alice then travelled north
again to raise support for her son Amaury, returning around Christmas
1218. But without Simon's leadership, Amaury was unable to withstand the southern nobility whose lands his father had conquered
during the crusade. In 1224, rather than continue the war himself,
Amaury gave up his claim to the county of Toulouse and his father's
other lands in the Languedoc to King Louis VIII of France, who
launched a new expedition against the Albigeois but (as mentioned
already) died of illness on his way back north, in November 1226.[62]

Both Alice de Montmorency and Blanche of Castile, Louis's widow,
were deeply pious, even fanatical, noblewomen married to equally
pious noblemen, personally devoted to the holy cause of the crusade,
who supported their husbands' crusading enterprises wholeheartedly—
and both paid a great price for their involvement, with the deaths of
their husbands. Less personally costly were the efforts to raise money
and men by Marie de Brienne, daughter of John de Brienne and the
younger Berenguela of Castile, and married in the mid-1230s to her
father's ward Baldwin, heir to the Latin Empire of Constantinople. In
1249 Marie travelled to Cyprus to meet King Louis IX of France and
his crusaders, who were over-wintering on the island before beginning the campaign. Her aim was to gain military aid for the Latin
Empire, which was under severe pressure from the Greek rulers of
Epirus and Nicaea and the king of the Vlachs and Bulgars. Calling first
on her own kinsmen and then appealing more widely to the crusading knights of Louis's host, she obtained written undertakings from
over 200 knights in the crusade army (according to John of Joinville,
who was one of those promised her aid) that if King Louis decided to
lead an army to assist Constantinople after completing his crusade,
they would join it. She then went on to France with her brother John
of Acre, with the aim of raising funds to support the Latin Empire.[63]

In the event, Louis IX did not go to Constantinople after completing his crusade to the Holy Land. Instead, Marie extracted what funds
she could from her family estates in the West, through taxation and
sale, and then went on to the Iberian Peninsula, where she persuaded

another of her relations to give financial aid, King Alfonso X of Castile (the son of her mother's eldest brother). As Alfonso was a candidate for the throne of the western Empire, one prospective emperor was helping another to hold his throne, but this was not enough to prevent Michael VIII Palaiologos, ruler of the Greek Empire of Nicaea, from reconquering Constantinople in 1261. Marie and Baldwin did not give up, and in 1267 they made an agreement with Louis IX's youngest brother, Charles of Anjou, king of Sicily, that his daughter Beatrice would marry their son and heir Philip of Courtenay, and that Charles would provide 2,000 cavalrymen for a year to recover Constantinople. The marriage took place in 1273, but Charles's expedition to Constantinople never took place.[64]

Another expedition which never took place was the project proposed by a group of Genoese noblewomen in 1301, endorsed in several letters from Pope Boniface VIII. The pope's list of those involved included some of the leading families of Genoa: S. Spinola, M. de Grimaldi, A. Doria, J. de Ghisolfi, S. and P. de Cibo, and also 'A. de Carmendino', 'C. Francie', 'P. de Caris, and many other women, female comrades and followers'. Their plan was to take advantage of the weakness of the Mamluks in the Holy Land (resulting from their defeat at the hands of the Mongol il-Khan Ghazan in the previous year) and recapture Jerusalem. The women had selected a leader, the famous Genoese admiral Benedetto Zaccaria, and planned to join the expedition themselves, 'choosing to be afflicted with God's people rather than to have the pleasure of worldly life, aspiring to the remuneration which the eye does not see, nor the ear hear, and which does not enter into a person's heart' (a quotation to 1 Corinthians 2:9, meaning that the women were seeking a heavenly reward). The pope noted that 'kings and princes of the world are running away from aiding [the Holy Land], even when they have been asked, whereas feeble women are offering themselves [to bring aid]'. The scheme came to nothing when the Genoese discovered that the pope would not allow them to conquer and fortify the towns of Syria for their own benefit. Benedetto Zaccaria conquered the island of Chios instead.[65]

As women were not licensed to teach or preach religious matters in public, women could not act as official preachers of crusades. However, there could be exceptional circumstances. In La Palma in the Canary Islands in the latter part of the fifteenth century an indigenous convert, baptized as Francisca de Gazmira, was licensed to preach Christianity and may have encouraged her compatriots to accept the invasion of Alonso de Lugo in 1492, which was presented as a crusade.[66] The Cistercian preacher and author Caesarius of Heisterbach recorded a rather different case in Germany early in the thirteenth century. One Master Theobald, cantor of St Stephen's church in Mainz, was trying to preach the crusade at Kaisersleuten, but on the first day the wind blew so loudly that he could not be heard and the following day he was repeatedly interrupted by a woman making mooing noises. Believing both these problems to be caused by a demon, he had the woman led to the magistrate and interrogated her—or rather, him, because he identified the demon as male. The demon stated that his name was Abrianus and he had been sent to sow doubt about what Theobald was promising in his preaching. Theobald threw part of his stole around the other's neck and told the demon (within the woman) that because he had impeded the preaching, he now commanded him, through the virtue of the Holy Cross, to preach with him. Forced by the Cross, the unwilling demon began to preach (still in the woman's body). When a man came and took the cross for himself and his father's soul, the demon rushed on him telling him that the cross would not help him, but when pressed had to admit that his father's soul was now freed. People then came flocking to take the cross. Caesarius stated that he had heard this directly from Theobald: 'who is a literate and religious man'. We may not accept that a demon inspired the woman, but through her disruptive behaviour and impersonation of a male demon she gained authorization to preach.[67]

While noblewomen held authority through their social status and had the financial means to recruit crusaders, holy women promoting the crusades drew their authority from visions, sometimes linked to extreme ascetical exercises, and the support of their male priest-confessors who recorded and presented their work. A holy woman's approval of crusading would be recorded as evidence of her piety, and also underlined the piety of the enterprise, thus encouraging others to take part. So, for example, in his hagiographical life of Mary of Oignies (d. 1213), James of Vitry depicted this holy woman burning with ardour to 'honour the Lord by confessing his name' on crusade against heretics. According to James, Mary had experienced a vision of the crusaders taking the cross to fight heretics in the Languedoc three years before the Albigensian crusade actually started, and then after the battle of Montgey in spring 1211, when the crusaders were defeated by Languedocian forces led by the count of Foix, she saw in a vision the souls of the dead crusaders being carried by angels directly to heaven without any purgatory. Dedicated to Bishop Fulk of Toulouse, who like James of Vitry was one of the preachers of that crusade, this account was clearly intended as crusade propaganda.[68]

In the fourteenth century a succession of women visionaries and recluses promoted the crusades. The first and perhaps most famous of these was St Birgitta of Sweden, an extremely influential figure on the European stage during her lifetime and after her death in 1373: she founded a monastic order, she travelled to Rome and became an advisor to the pope, and she was the only woman in the fourteenth century who was canonized as a saint—out of just eight canonizations in that century. Her visions or revelations—around seven hundred—were read across Latin Christian Europe and widely quoted.[69] Birgitta came from a noble family and was briefly an advisor to Blanche of Namur, queen of Sweden; she married a nobleman, Ulf Gudmarsson, and had eight children. Although the traditional Latin Christian view was that only a virgin could achieve full spiritual development, Birgitta maintained a life of piety during marriage and after her husband's death she took up a religious life as a visionary, advising others on God's will for them as she had seen it in her visions.

Among her visions were around twenty justifying crusades, but she also criticized the motivation of the crusaders. The crusades which concerned her were two expeditions by King Magnus Eriksson (Magnus IV, d. 1374) to Finland and Russia in 1348–1351. Sweden already controlled part of the east Baltic area and Magnus's invasion was prompted by a dispute with the city of Novgorod over borders, but he also proposed to debate doctrinal differences between the Latin and the Russian Orthodox Churches, and his campaign included conversions of the peoples he conquered. However, he made no gains in territory. Birgitta's revelations depict these crusades as justified by the need to convert pagans and impose justice on them, providing the minimum of force was used and the aim was to establish peace. Crusaders should desire 'nothing but to die for God's sake and to live for God', their only aim being to win the pagans' souls. Later Birgitta criticized the king's actions on crusade, accusing him of not following the advice given and failing to convert the infidel.[70]

Prompted by a vision, Birgitta travelled to Rome for the Holy Year of Jubilee in 1350, from where in 1365–1367 she travelled to Naples and met Queen Johanna, who became her friend and later gave evidence at her canonization process. Despite their friendship, Birgitta criticized the queen's worldly lifestyle: 'she should be content with the colouring and beauty with which God has adorned her face, because artificial colouring is very displeasing to God...she should distance herself from worldly customs and fawning women'.[71] Similarly she criticized Blanche of Namur, queen of Sweden, and King Magnus for their worldliness. Blanche was reminded that 'she will render an account to God for all her temporal goods down to how the least obol was earned and spent;...her time is very short and she will die before she knows it', and she should repent of her sins and go on pilgrimage. Magnus was criticized as 'a robber in God's sight and a traitor of souls and a prodigal squanderer of riches' who had spiritually betrayed many people.[72]

Birgitta returned to Naples in 1371 on pilgrimage to Jerusalem, and then travelled on to Cyprus bearing letters of recommendation from Queen Johanna and from the Empress of Constantinople. Cyprus was in a state of political upheaval following the murder of King Peter I in

1369, but Peter's widow Queen Eleanor of Aragon welcomed Birgitta and asked for her advice. Birgitta then travelled on to Jerusalem, where she received further visions advising the leaders of Cyprus. She and her party returned to Rome via Queen Johanna's court at Naples, and Birgitta died in Rome, aged around seventy.[73]

Although she was friends with one would-be crusading queen and another who may have promoted a crusade, and travelled to Jerusalem on pilgrimage, and despite her family interest (her brother Israel Birgersson took part in Magnus's 1350 expedition), crusading was hardly the focus of Birgitta's spiritual life.[74] Her immediate successor as papal spiritual advisor took a very different view.

Birgitta may have had an indirect influence on the holy woman Catherine of Siena (d. 1380), as Catherine met Birgitta's confessor Alfonso da Vadaterra in 1373/4, after Birgitta's death.[75] Birgitta had been advising the pope about the state of the Church and the need for the pope to return to Rome from Avignon, providing the pope with spiritual authority for his actions. Whether or not Birgitta's example or writing directly influenced Catherine, she may be characterized as Birgitta's successor in that she took over the role of political visionary for the papal court.[76] Unlike Birgitta, Catherine was not a noblewoman by birth, but she came from an influential family of Siena that was part of the dominant political class of that city, the family's successful business had expanded to Florence, and her siblings married into socially prominent families. From at least her mid-teens, Catherine chose to follow the contemplative life of a recluse within the family home, and became associated with the Dominican order, wearing their mantle as a symbol of her religious way of life. In 1374 she attended the Dominican General Chapter in Florence, after which the Dominican friar Raymond of Capua was assigned to her as confessor and biographer. The pope later wrote that Raymond had been appointed to guide Catherine 'for the saving of souls, the crusade, and other business of the Holy Roman Church'.[77]

Catherine pursued a letter-writing campaign to public authority figures promoting a reform programme which included unifying

Christendom, bringing the papacy back to Rome, and converting Muslims. A crusade against the Turks would be a vital part of this programme; she intended to join it herself and find martyrdom in the East. Even to the most powerful and potentially dangerous figures Catherine wrote as a friend, implying that her spiritual authority made her their equal or superior. In the first half of 1375 she wrote to the famous military leader Sir John Hawkwood and his mercenary company calling them 'my brothers in Christ' and advising them that as a crusade had been called they should no longer wage war against Christians but go to fight the infidels.[78] She also wrote to Barnabò Visconti, despot of Milan, calling him 'dearest father and brother in Christ gentle Jesus', and solicited the support of his wife Regina della Scala, urging him to be loyal to the pope and to fight the infidel rather than Christians.[79] Queen Johanna of Naples was her 'mother and sister in Christ'; Catherine praised her for her readiness to be involved in a crusade and urged her to be a leader and patron of the enterprise.[80]

Catherine repeatedly urged Pope Gregory XI to press on with his return to Rome and his plans for crusade: he should 'raise the standard of the most holy Cross' (her metaphor for calling a crusade), which would enable him to win peace in Christendom and turn all war against the infidels. She believed the crusade would lead all his enemies to unite eagerly with him because 'they are ready to give their life for Christ...you will see the wolves become lambs'. She urged the pope to 'minister the Blood of the Lamb to those wretched infidels'—first he should fight them and then convert them to Christ.[81] Everywhere she tried to make peace so that a crusade could be launched. She pressed King Charles V of France to stop fighting Christians, because his wars had harmed both Christians and infidels by preventing the start of a crusade and the conversion of the infidel. Instead, he should follow in Christ's footsteps by undertaking the crusade. She urged the Florentines to make peace with the pope, because Christians should only fight infidels, not their fellow Christians.[82]

Catherine's campaigning certainly had some effect, as around this time the Tuscan hermit Giovanni dale Celle of Vallombrosa wrote to

one Domatilla, a woman under his spiritual care who had taken religious vows, to advise her not to follow Catherine's advice. He had
heard that with Catherine's encouragement she wished to go 'beyond
the sea' (a metaphor for joining a crusade to the Holy Land) with
many virgins, honest women, and other youths. But Giovanni was
concerned that this was not the right step for Domatilla. Christ is to
be found by prayer, not pilgrimage, Domatilla could obtain an indulgence for sin through a pilgrimage to Rome, and travelling to
Jerusalem was perilous: the sea voyage was dangerous, she might suffer
from seasickness, and she could be captured and sold as a slave; her
virtue would be at risk, and her presence and that of the other young
women on the expedition might distract the warriors. Nevertheless,
Giovanni was willing to allow Domatilla to take part in a crusade
when she was spiritually fit to go.[83]

In 1378 the election of two rival popes and the beginning of the
Great Schism put an end to Catherine's hopes of a crusade. Her final
years were spent campaigning for Urban VI, the pope in Rome, and
criticizing those like Queen Johanna of Naples who supported the
rival pope in Avignon. She died in 1380 after a long illness, aged
around 33.

Catherine was not the last Christian mystic to declare her wish to
organize a crusade. Joan of Arc (d. 1431) also stated her intentions to
start a crusade. In March 1429, after undergoing questioning at Poitiers
by a group of ecclesiastics appointed by the Dauphin to establish
whether or not she really had been called by God to restore the kingdom of France, Joan announced that she would lead a crusade as soon
as her war with England was over. Writing a challenge to the king of
England and the duke of Bedford to warn them to withdraw before
she led her army to relieve Orleans, she declared that if they would
make peace they would be able to join her crusade, in which 'the
French will do the fairest deed which was ever done for Christianity'.
Her contemporary and admirer Christine de Pizan (or de Pisan: d. 1430)
wrote that Joan would destroy unbelievers and heretics, and lead
King Charles VII of France to the Holy Land to conquer the Saracens;

and that both Joan and Charles would die in the Holy Land, in fulfil-
ment of prophecy. To underline Joan's potential as a crusade leader, in
describing her achievements to date Christine added: 'Greater things
were not done before Acre', an allusion to the Third Crusade. Such
plans demonstrated and reinforced Joan's self-presentation as a devout
Christian military commander.[84]

But holy women did not recommend all warriors to join the crusades. When in spring 1176 Count Philip of Flanders approached the
visionary Abbess Hildegard of Bingen (d. 1179) for advice on his
forthcoming expedition to the kingdom of Jerusalem, she replied that
he should purge his own sinfulness before waging war on the infidel.[85]
Crusaders needed to have the correct frame of mind, and focus on
God rather than worldly advantage.

It was one thing to promote a crusade, either as Christ's work or as
an honourable deed of chivalry, but it was quite another to take part.
Let us now consider those women who were physically involved in
crusading and holy war, either as aggressors or as sufferers.

3

Crusade Campaigns

Not all women would have shared the view of the five officials of the military-religious Teutonic Order who argued in 1395 that women's spiritual warfare in prayer was as valuable a front-line role as male warriors' physical warfare against the enemies of Christ.[1] For those women whose enthusiasm for the crusade led them not only to take the cross but also to set out on an expedition, there were many roles other than prayer which they could perform.[2] Some of these—such as caring for the sick—were prescribed by social and cultural tradition as acceptable roles for women; others, such as wielding weapons in emergency situations, were equally essential to military success but presented by contemporary commentators as exceptional. In every case, there was the constant danger of death or capture.

Women's roles in crusades: plans and practice

Pope Urban II did not intend women or other non-combatants to join the First Crusade. By requiring everyone who intended to take the cross to obtain their parish priest's agreement, he hoped that non-combatants could be excluded. One noblewoman who took the cross, Emerias of Alteias, was persuaded by her bishop to establish a hospice to care for the poor instead of joining the crusade as a pilgrim; but even if some were persuaded to redirect their vows in similar ways, many women joined the expedition.[3]

By the late thirteenth and the fourteenth century, theorists drawing up more or less fanciful plans for reconquering the Holy Land from the Mamluks assumed that women would take part in one way or another. The anonymous author of the tract entitled 'Via ad Terram Sanctam' (the way to the Holy Land), writing between 1289 and 1293, set out overwintering arrangements for the ships carrying the army's equipment and food, and the ladies, women and children of the army, indicating that women of all social ranks would be present.[4] Marino Sanudo, a Venetian layman who composed a well-informed crusade plan sometime between 1300 and 1321, noted the presence of women in past crusade armies and included provision for women who would join his proposed crusade to reconquer the Holy Land, assuming that women would accompany their husbands, with their children. Women married to soldiers in the crusade army should receive the same ration as the men, and widows of soldiers who died on the campaign should continue to receive their ration. A dead man's children and other dependants should also be provided for until adulthood.[5] Writing in 1389, the soldier and veteran crusader Philippe de Mézières, former chancellor of Cyprus and counsellor of the late King Charles V of France, drew up a long treatise proposing Europe-wide religious, social, and political reform which would culminate in the Christian kings of Europe leading a great crusade to drive the Turks out of Europe and recover the Holy Land. He recommended that women should accompany their husbands. Kings, princes, barons, and knights should take their wives 'to remove the grounds and matter of all fleshly sin', which had offended Christ in the past and caused Him to withhold many victories from the Christians. The men at arms and other troops should have a regulated number of women, 'who are necessary for their service', and who should be decently dressed because they were going to serve men on the holy expedition for love of Jesus, 'as was seen at other times with worthy ladies who formerly on expeditions served the Christian army and all manner of people humbly and devotedly'. The army should arrive in Egypt or Syria in September or October rather than at the beginning of summer to allow the army time to acclimatize, otherwise many of the soldiers, 'and especially the women', would perish in the heat. Reinforcements of troops and women to serve the men should be sent overseas as required.[6]

Insofar as they accepted that women would accompany the crusade army, these were realistic plans; they also acknowledged contemporary medical opinion that a lack of sexual intercourse was unhealthy because retaining semen caused an imbalance in the body and so could cause illness. Even virginity was harmful. On this basis married couples should travel together on crusade, to ensure their mutual health and avoid the temptation to commit the sin of adultery.[7]

Writing in around 1306 and addressing himself to the former crusader King Edward I of England, Pierre Dubois advised that women—married and widowed—as well as men should contribute troops to the crusade, but he also had a different plan for how women could aid the crusade effort: through education. He wished to convert the European properties of the Templars and Hospitallers into schools for boys and girls from the age of four or five years, to learn Latin, Greek, and Arabic. Boys would then train for the priesthood, but would also be taught medicine, including human and veterinary surgery, so that they could assist the crusade army. The girls would learn medicine and surgery, then be adopted by Latin Christian princes in Europe and the Holy Land to give them noble status, and eventually marry the clergy and nobility of the Eastern Church. They would teach their Greek and Syrian husbands and children Latin Christianity, and spread the teachings of the Latin Church through ministering their medical skills to women. Spreading Latin Christianity in this way would assist trade. Some of these women could marry 'Saracens' (meaning Muslims) and convert them to Christianity. Dubois also believed that Muslim women would readily embrace Christianity because then their menfolk could have only one wife each rather than 'seven or more'. The children thus educated in Dubois's schools would have to repay the costs to the educational foundation which had educated them, so ensuring a continual income for the schools.[8] Unlike Sanudo and de Mézières, Dubois did not expect women to travel with the military; their role would be diplomatic and caring.

These, then, were acceptable roles for women in crusade campaigns: accompanying their husbands, caring for the sick, and diplomacy. How far did women take on these roles in reality?

Accompanying husbands

The surviving evidence indicates that women who took part in crusade expeditions were indeed usually accompanying their menfolk. Many lower status women on crusade would have had no choice in this, as they would have been destitute if they had stayed behind. Although some leaders of the First Crusade left their wives at home to act as their regents during their absence overseas (Count Robert II of Flanders appointed his wife Clemence of Burgundy as his regent, while Count Stephen of Blois appointed his wife Adela of Normandy), others travelled to the Holy Land with their wives: Baldwin of Boulogne, later King Baldwin I of Jerusalem, was accompanied by his wife Godvere of Tosni, who died on the journey, and Raymond of Saint-Gilles travelled with his wife Elvira of Castile.[9] Later crusades saw queens accompanying their menfolk: we have already seen that Eleanor of Aquitaine accompanied her husband King Louis VII of France on the Second Crusade (in contrast, Count Thierry of Flanders left his wife Sybil at home to rule as his regent), and Eleanor's son Richard I of England was accompanied from Sicily on his way to the Third Crusade in spring 1191 by his sister Joanna, widow of King William II of Sicily, and his wife-to-be Berengaria of Navarre.[10] The viscount of Châteaudun and his mother also joined the Third Crusade and died during the siege of Acre (1189–1191).[11] Adolf IV, count of Holstein, was accompanied by his wife Heilwig of Lippe on crusade to Livonia in 1238.[12] On King Louis IX's first crusade he was accompanied by his wife Margaret of Provence (his mother Blanche of Castile remained in France as regent), while his younger brothers

Counts Robert I of Artois, Alfonse of Poitiers, and Charles of Anjou were accompanied by their wives Matilda of Brabant, Jeanne or Joanna of Toulouse and Beatrice of Provence; and other noble women also accompanied their husbands.[13] In 1270 Louis IX set out on a second crusade, this time to Tunis: this time his wife did not accompany him, but their daughter Isabelle accompanied her husband Thibaut V (or Theobald) of Champagne, king of Navarre, while Jeanne of Toulouse again accompanied her husband Alfonse, and Louis's eldest living son Philip, soon to be King Philip III, had his wife Isabelle of Aragon with him. This crusade in particular demonstrated that crusading was not safe even for non-combatants, as many participants died from disease including Louis himself, Isabelle and Thibaut, Jeanne and Alfonse, while Isabelle of Aragon died in childbirth on the way home, following a fall from her horse.[14] In 1345–1347 Marie des Baux accompanied her husband Humbert II of Viennois on his crusading expedition to Smyrna and Rhodes; he fell ill and recovered, but she died of sickness at Rhodes.[15]

These noblewomen would have joined crusade expeditions for the same spiritual motives as their menfolk—Joanna of Sicily, for instance, had probably taken the cross with her late husband King William II— but they also acted to benefit their family. Richard I of England would have wanted his sister Joanna to accompany him on the Third Crusade because he needed her dowry to help finance the expedition, and because she would be noble company for his wife-to-be Berengaria.[16] In 1386 Constanza of Castile, wife of John of Gaunt, duke of Lancaster, and John's three daughters accompanied the duke on his crusade against Castile. Constanza's presence was essential as the crusade was to enforce her claim to the throne of Castile; perhaps she and John hoped to employ the daughters in marriage alliances, as their daughter Catherine (or Catalina) married Enrique, heir of King Juan of Castile, and John's daughter Philippa married King João I of Portugal.[17] John de Brienne apparently brought his niece Margaret on the Fifth Crusade to marry her to Balian, lord of Sidon; but the marriage did not take place.[18]

Richard I of England may have brought his sister Joanna into his negotiations with Saladin. According to contemporary Muslim accounts and the 'History of Eracles', Richard used the possibility of marriage between Saladin's brother al-ʿAdil and his sister Joanna as a bargaining tool with Saladin. The only condition proposed was that al-ʿAdil should become a Christian. According to the Muslim commentators, al-ʿAdil was in favour of the match, but the scheme fell through because Joanna refused.[19]

Although in Sicily, where Joanna had been queen from 1177 to 1189, interfaith marriages had only taken place among the backward rural population (at least, according to the tenth-century commentator Ibn Ḥawqal),[20] in the Middle East and north-east Africa marriage between Muslim and non-Latin Christian ruling families was commonplace. Such marriages did not necessarily require either of the spouses to convert. In fact, two of al-ʿAdil's sons contracted such a marriage. In 1210 the Armenian noblewoman Tʿamtʿa (daughter of Ivane Mqargrdzeli, an Armenian noble of the influential Zakʿarid family and Georgian military commander, and of Xošakʿ (Khoshak), a powerful Armenian noblewoman), was married to the Muslim commander of the city of Akhlat (Xlatʿ): al-Awhad, a son of al-ʿAdil. When al-Awhad died a few months later his brother al-Ashraf Musa married Tʿamtʿa to preserve the alliance, but Tʿamtʿa did not convert to Islam or accompany her new husband: she remained at Akhlat and exercised authority there, to the benefit of the local Christians. When the city fell to the Khwarazmian ruler Jalal al-Din in 1230 he married Tʿamtʿa, so reinforcing his authority over her city. Again, T'amt'a remained in her city and did not accompany him; when he was killed in the following year, she returned to being al-Ashraf's wife but did not live with him, continuing to govern Akhlat.[21] It would appear in this case that whoever was overlord of the city was husband of the lady, and that the marriage was only an expression of authority over territory.

To the south of Saladin's Egyptian domains, marriage alliances between Nubian Christians of Makuria and ʿAlwa and Arab Muslims were also unproblematic. According to the historian Ibn Khaldūn (d. 1406), the disintegration of the Nubian kingdoms in the four-teenth century and their conversion to Islam was partly due to the Nubian kings marrying their daughters to the sons of Juhayna Arabs. As sisters and their sons inherited land, the kingdoms were divided between the Muslim children of these marriages.[22] In Christian Ethiopia, noble families routinely used interfaith marriages as a means of making alliances; here usually the wife converted to her husband's religion. Queen Eleni of Ethiopia, who in 1509 as regent for her step-great-grandson Lebnä Dengel proposed an anti-Muslim alliance to King Manuel of Portugal, had been born a Muslim princess of Hadiyya, to the south of Ethiopia, but converted to Christianity when she married King Zär'a Ya'eqob of Ethiopia.[23] In the case of Joanna and al-'Adil there was no mention of conversion by either party and they would have shared authority over Jerusalem and the castles of the kingdom. Richard's proposal may or may not have been serious, but in any case his suggestion put his opponents at a disadvantage as they tried to guess at his motives, and so bought him valuable time.

As they would have done at home, wives who accompanied their husbands on crusade acted on their behalf in times of crisis. When King Louis IX was captured in early April 1250 during his campaign in Egypt, his wife Margaret was at the recently captured Egyptian port of Damietta about to give birth to a son. Patriarch Robert of Jerusalem wrote to the College of Cardinals of the Roman Church in May to inform them of the king's capture and the truce which Louis eventu-ally made, including the information that on 8 April, when no news had come of the king's fate, the queen had given orders for ten galleys and many other armed vessels with a great number of armed men to go up the Nile to help the king. Finding many recently massacred bodies and dead horses and no sign of the king, they returned to Damietta to report.[24] Writing his 'Life of Saint Louis' over fifty years later, John of Joinville had nothing to say about this decisive action by the queen but only recorded her fear:

> She was so terrified by this news [that the king had been captured] that
> whenever she slept in her bed it seemed to her that her chamber was
> absolutely full of Saracens, and she cried out: 'Help! Help!'

John recalled that to protect her unborn child Margaret arranged for
an old knight, aged eighty, to sleep in her room, hold her hand, and
reassure her if she had nightmares. When she was about to give birth,
she requested him to kill her if the Saracens captured the town.
However, as well as recording the queen's fear, John also remembered
that she had acted to protect Damietta. Having just given birth, she
was informed that the Pisans, the Genoese, and members of the other
of the Italian communes in the city were intending to flee the city,
leaving it undefended. She summoned their representatives to her
bedside and begged them to stay, 'for you see that my lord the king
and all those who have been captured will be lost if the city is lost'—
or, if they would not, she begged them to stay until her lying-in was
complete. They replied that they had to leave because they were dying
of starvation in the town. Margaret promised them that she would
buy all the food in the town and retain all the Italians in her service
at the king's expense. They agreed to stay on these terms, and the
queen bought the food as promised, at enormous cost.[25] Nevertheless
Margaret had to cut her lying-in short and leave the city as it was surrendered on 6 May 1250 as part of the terms for Louis's release.

The head of the Egyptian government as these negotiations were
completed was also a woman, Shajar or Shajarat al-Durr, acting for
her late husband Al-Ṣāliḥ Ayyūb, sultan of Egypt.[26] When the sultan
died from illness in his military camp in November 1249, at a crucial
point in the campaign, his wife Shajar realized that if his death became
known the Egyptian cause was lost. She and Jamāl al-Dīn Muhassan,
the cavalry commander in charge of the late sultan's mamluks, agreed
with emir Fakhr al-Dīn, commander of her late husband's armies, to
keep the sultan's death a secret. The three worked together to maintain control of the government until the heir, al-Malik al-Mu'azzam
Ghiyath al-Dīn Tūrān-Shāh, could arrive from Hisn Kaīfā (now
Hasankeyf in south-eastern Turkey), where he was governor.

Emir Fakhr al-Dīn commanded the army, controlled the mamluks, and took an oath of loyalty to Sultan Ṣāliḥ and to Tūrān-Shāh as heir. Meanwhile the crusaders had heard rumours of the sultan's death and advanced towards Cairo. Fakhr al-Dīn's forces defeated them at Mansura on 8 February 1250, but was himself killed.

Shajar al-Durr continued to conduct affairs of state in the name of her dead husband until Tūrān-Shāh arrived at Cairo and was proclaimed sultan. Louis IX's forces began to retreat, but were surrounded by Egyptian troops commanded by Tūrān-Shāh and forced to surrender. Tūrān-Shāh now wished to recover Damietta (commanded by Margaret of Provence), and demanded that Shajar hand over to him the dead sultan's treasure and her jewellery. Shajar denied having the treasure and wrote to her late husband's mamluks appealing for aid.[27] While negotiations for Louis IX's release stalled, on 2 May 1250 the mamluks murdered Tūrān-Shāh, and two days later—as mother of Sultan Ṣāliḥ's dead son Khalil, and in default of other heirs—Shajar was proclaimed sultan. Negotiations with Louis IX recommenced, with the amir Husām al-Dīn ibn Abī ʿAlī acting for the Muslims. It was agreed that Damietta would be surrendered and a ransom paid. Damietta was handed over on 6 May, and Louis was released. He and the crusaders left Egypt.[28]

Presumably many women of lesser status also accompanied their husbands on crusade, but most of these women passed unnamed by contemporary commentators.[29] Like their menfolk, most women's involvement is known only when they were mentioned in a legal document that has happened to survive, such as a will or a charitable donation. Hervé de Donzy, count of Nevers, and his wife Matilda de Courtenay made their joint will at Genoa in September 1218 just before setting out on the Fifth Crusade together, while Catherine, wife of Gilles Berthout, lord of Oudenburg in Brabant, accompanied her husband and in 1219 during the siege of Damietta they together made a donation to the Teutonic Order, one of the leading military-religious orders of the crusades after the Templars and the Hospitallers.[30] Guiletta of Bologna's presence on the Fifth Crusade and that of her husband Barzella Merxadrus and their companions was recorded only because in December 1219 her husband fell ill and drew up his will, leaving his wife and companions a share of his tent, with the provision that his companions were not to disturb his wife in regard to the tent and its furnishings and she could continue to live peacefully in it as she had done until now.[31]

The passenger list of the ship 'St Victor', sailing to Damietta in July 1250 to join Louis IX's crusade, suggests that half the women who joined a crusade were travelling with their menfolk: of the forty-two women among its 453 passengers, fourteen were travelling with their husband and one with husband and son, four with other male relatives, and two with an undefined male companion.[32] But other evidence suggests that this is an underestimate and that most women on crusade were with a male relative. In England, royal licences to travel overseas (serving a similar function to the modern passport) provide evidence of a few women who were going to the Holy Land with their husbands. For example, on 25 July 1270 Juliana and her husband John Guer or de Goer were about to set out from England for the Holy Land by the king's licence.[33] On 4 July 1310 Robert son of Walter and his wife Alice were going to Jerusalem. This is the only one of the ten licences issued for travel to Jerusalem in the years 1308–1313 that mentions a woman traveller, and no further information survives on these journeys.[34]

Some women who intended to travel on crusade with their husband eventually set out alone because their husband had died or had had to commute his vow into a money payment for some reason. In so doing, a wife could hope to benefit her husband's soul as well as her own, in a 'proxy pilgrimage' (making a pilgrimage on behalf of another person).[35] In 1225–1226 one William of Hokesoure of Hampshire, England, told the king's court that he and his wife Erneburg had taken the cross together; as the pope absolved him of his vow because he was too infirm to make the journey, Erneburg had gone to the Holy Land alone.[36] Much further up the social scale, Ida of Cham, widow of Margrave Leopold II of Austria who had died in 1095, led her own army as part of the crusade expedition of 1101, with the dukes of Bavaria and Aquitaine. This expedition was defeated in Anatolia by Kilij Arslan I, sultan of Rum; the dukes escaped but Ida's fate was unknown.[37] The English royal clerk Roger of Howden, an eyewitness of the Third Crusade, noted in his 'Chronicle' that in 1196 after King Béla III of Hungary died 'his wife Margaret, sister of King Philip II of France and former queen of England as wife of Henry the young king, took the cross for the journey to Jerusalem, and remained in the land of Jerusalem at Acre in the Lord's service until the end of her life'. Although she was a *crucesignata*, Roger says nothing about what she did when she reached the Holy Land.[38] Presumably she followed a pious lifestyle of self-denial, prayer and charitable giving, to benefit her own and her husband's souls, as was later recorded of Countess Alice of Blois.

Countess Alice took the cross in 1266 or 1267. After the death of her husband John of Châtillon (who had himself also taken the cross but died in 1279 before fulfilling his vow), she travelled to Acre in 1286 or 1287 leading a large body of troops, and died in Acre in the following year. While there she reportedly 'did many good things to all sorts of people, and had a good tower and a chapel built within Acre, and established a priest to sing mass every day at the chapel', so providing for both the military defence and the spiritual protection of the city. It has also been suggested that it was Countess Alice who commissioned a *Histoire Universelle* or 'History of the World' produced at Acre in 1287: its illuminations depict the female warriors known as the Amazons in very positive roles 'as defenders of the social order'.[39] Alice was an example of the sort of woman crusader approved by the eminent thirteenth-century canon lawyer Henry de Susa, known as Hostiensis: she had sufficient resources to pay for a military contribution to the war effort.[40]

Caring for the sick

Crusade planner Pierre Dubois highlighted medicine as an appropriate role for women in crusading, but female medical practitioners were hardly ever mentioned in narrative or documentary records.

In June 1272, when Lord Edward was the victim of an assassination attempt during his crusade, his wife Eleanor of Castile did not tend his wound. The contemporary English commentator Walter of Guisborough wrote that Eleanor had to be led away 'weeping and wailing' by her brother-in-law Edmund and John de Vescy while male surgeons operated on her husband. (As Walter was not an eyewitness of events, he may have received information from eyewitnesses, or have based this touching scene on the known close affection between Eleanor and Edward.) A century later, the writer Ptolemy of Lucca gave Eleanor a more pro-active role and imagined her sucking the assassin's poison from Edward's wound: 'they say, however, that then his Spanish wife, [who was] sister of the king of Castile, showed her husband great fidelity, because she licked his open wounds all day with her tongue', removing the poison and enabling the wound to close up and heal cleanly.[41] This story, however, was clearly romantic fiction.

In most cases where medical practitioners were mentioned by con-temporary commentators they were apparently male, but noble-women did act as carers in emergency situations. In April 1542, during the Ethiopian war against Ahmad ibn Ibrahim al-Ghazi when the Ethiopian royal court was in the field with its Portuguese allies, Miguel de Castanhoso recorded that the queen of Ethiopia, Säblä Wängel, and her ladies set up a tent by the battlefield at Jarte and had the wounded placed there, and she and her ladies set about binding up the Christian wounded with their own head-dresses. In August 1542 when the Portuguese and Ethiopians suffered a defeat, the wounded were taken to the queen's house in the camp, where the queen and her women bound up their wounds while under fire from the enemy.[42]

One female medical practitioner is known from Louis IX's first crusade. In a document issued in Acre in August 1250 King Louis gave the physician (*phisica*) Hersenda a lifetime pension out of gratitude for the services she had rendered. A Hersenda who was the wife of the king's pharmacist Jacob was mentioned in a document from the Hôtel-Dieu in Paris in 1259, and the couple were mentioned again (as deceased) in a document of 1299. Hersenda *phisica* was probably the '*bourjoise de Paris*', or citizen of Paris, on whose lap Louis IX's companions laid him during the retreat to Damietta on 6 April 1250, when they thought he was dying and would not live until the evening. The king's physician would have been the obvious person to care for him at that moment of crisis.[43] But Hersenda is the only known professional female physician connected with the crusades.[44]

It has been suggested that Hersenda could have attended Queen Margaret during her lying-in at Damietta, but there is no evidence that she did.[45] Midwives or women experienced in the delivery of babies would certainly have been required during crusades, as many crusading wives gave birth while they were in the East. Countess Elvira of Saint-Gilles gave birth to a son in the East after the First Crusade.[46] Margaret of Provence gave birth to three children during her husband Louis IX's first crusade of 1248–1254, while her sister Beatrice and her sister-in-law Matilda of Brabant each gave birth to a son. Eleanor of Castile gave birth to a daughter while she was at Acre in 1271 with her husband the Lord Edward, soon to be King Edward I of England. But the names of the women who attended on them have not survived. The name of Isabelle of Aragon's *obstetrix* or midwife, Edelina, is known only because Isabelle included her among the beneficiaries in her will.[47]

Diplomacy and intelligence

Pierre Dubois envisaged the educated Christian women produced by his new schools marrying Muslims and interceding with their husbands to make peace with Christians. This plan had some precedent. Albert of Aachen included in his history of the First Crusade a story of a knight's wife whose husband had been killed by the Turks en route to the Holy Land. Forcibly married by a Turkish knight, she persuaded her Turkish husband to urge his lord, the prince of Azaz, to make an alliance with the crusader leader Godfrey de Bouillon against Ridwan of Aleppo.[48] As Albert named neither the

woman nor the Turkish knight, this story is probably wishful thinking, the stuff of romance and epic; but it does show that Latin
Christian writers believed that such conversions after marriage were
possible.[49] In a similar way the author of the Livonian Rhymed
Chronicle, which recounted the history of the Swordbrothers and
the early years of the Teutonic Order in Livonia, recorded that
Martha, wife of King Mindaugas of Lithuania, argued against her
husband when (in 1261) he decided to renounce Christianity
(although he declined to take her advice) and persuaded her husband to allow a brother of the Teutonic Order to return safely from
Lithuania to Riga.[50]

Christian noblewomen of the Middle East who married Muslim
princes, such as T'amt'a of Akhlat, certainly used their positions to
benefit local Christians. On Europe's eastern frontier in Hungary
Latin Christians and Muslims also intermarried to form alliances. For
example, in the 1240s István (or Stephen), eldest son and heir of King
Béla IV of Hungary, married the daughter of a Cuman chieftain: she
was baptized as Elizabeth, and later her parents also became Christian.[51]
In 1435 Mara daughter of Đurađ (George) Branković, Despot of
Serbia, was married to the Ottoman sultan Murad II as part of a peace
treaty which made Branković a tributary of the Ottoman sultan. In
1444 Mara initiated peace negotiations between her husband Murad
and King Vladislav of Hungary (Władysław III of Poland) which
resulted in a treaty whereby her father recovered Serbia.[52] But such
marriage alliances were not always acceptable to both parties: we have
already seen that in 1191 the proposed marriage of Dowager Queen
Joanna of Sicily and al-'Adil came to nothing.

Women's role in mediation and diplomacy during the crusades was
largely based on family ties and the defence of their own lands and
fortresses. Eleanor of Aquitaine's possible diplomatic role negotiating
between her husband King Louis VII and her uncle Prince Raymond
of Antioch during the Second Crusade has been mentioned already.
In addition, according to the eye-witness commentator Odo of Deuil,
during the crusade Eleanor received occasional letters from the

German-born Byzantine Empress Eirene (Bertha of Sulzbach before her marriage to Emperor Manuel Komnenos), sister of Gertrude of Sulzbach, the wife of King Conrad III of Germany who led the German contingent to the East in 1147. The contemporary author of the Würzburg Annals noted that Empress Eirene/Bertha intervened to ensure that the Conrad's German crusade army was well-supplied while it was camped outside Constantinople.[53]

The Fourth Crusade benefitted from the diplomacy of Byzantine imperial women. According to the French crusader Robert of Clari, when the crusaders had placed Isaac II Angelos and his son Alexios IV Angelos on the throne of Constantinople in July 1203 they sought out the 'French empress' to pay their respects. This was Anna, originally Agnes, youngest daughter of King Louis VII of France and his third wife Adela of Champagne, and thus full sister to King Philip II of France. In 1180 she had married Alexios II Komnenos, the eldest son of Emperor Manuel I Komnenos and his second wife Maria of Antioch. Alexios was overthrown and murdered in 1183, and his murderer, Andronikos, took the imperial throne and married the empress Agnes-Anna, continuing the alliance with France. Andronikos himself was murdered in 1185, but Agnes again survived. When the crusaders contacted her in 1203 they promised her their service as sister of the king of France. She was angry with them for bringing Alexios Angelos to Constantinople and said she had forgotten how to speak French, but did later speak with her nephew, Count Louis of Blois.[54] Historian Ewan Short has argued that Agnes-Anna deliberately distanced herself from the crusaders to impress on them that she was a member of the Byzantine ruling class; as she was a representative of Byzantine authority she could not allow herself to be seen as closely connected to the invaders. However, Agnes may later have used her position to assist the crusaders. When in 1206 agreement was reached between the Venetians and the cities of Adrianople and Demotika, the agreement stated that Theodore Branas, Agnes's husband, would govern the cities on behalf of the Venetians. Agnes shared the governorship with her husband. Her position as a former empress, acknowledged by the

Byzantines to represent Byzantine authority, enabled her to persuade the Byzantine population to accept this settlement.[55]

Margaret of Hungary, daughter of King Béla III of Hungary and his first wife Agnes of Antioch and empress (renamed Maria) of Isaac II Angelos, worked more openly with the crusaders than her cousin-in-law Agnes-Anna. Geoffrey of Villehardouin recorded that Margaret was present at a meeting between Isaac II Angelos, his chancellor, his translator, and four crusaders including Geoffrey. She sat next to her husband, but apart from noting her presence and her rank Geoffrey only commented that she was 'a very beautiful woman'. As the meeting involved reading and signing Latin documents, Margaret's role may have been as a translator and advisor. Following Isaac's death in 1204 she married one of the leading crusaders, Boniface of Montferrat. She negotiated with the Byzantine defenders of Adrianople and she persuaded the Byzantine people of Demotika to support Boniface. As with Agnes, Margaret was able to do this only because the people acknowledged her position as a member of the former Byzantine ruling class, and so accepted her new husband's lordship as a continuation of Byzantine authority.[56]

Women were also occasionally recorded passing on military intelligence. Two instances were recorded during the Third Crusade. The Muslim historian Ibn al-Athīr recorded that the wife of Prince Bohemond III of Antioch, Sybil, 'was in correspondence with Saladin and exchanged gifts with him. She used to inform him of many significant matters'. This previously established positive relationship worked in her favour in 1188 when Saladin captured Barziyya (or Bourzey) castle, whose lord was married to Sybil's sister; Saladin bought back and freed the lord of Barziyya and his wife, children, and wider family in recognition of the debt he owed her. The second instance appears to be a myth explaining King Richard's failure to attack Jerusalem in 1192. An insert to the oldest surviving manuscript of Ralph of Coggeshall's near-contemporary account of the Third Crusade tells how 'a certain religious woman of Syrian race' in the city of Jerusalem sent King Richard intelligence about how he could capture Jerusalem and the keys to St Stephen's gate. Everyone then decided unanimously to besiege Jerusalem, except for the duke of Burgundy, the Templars and the French, who would not support the plan because if King Richard conquered such a famous city it would offend their lord King Philip. Perhaps a veteran of the crusade (such as his informant on the Battle of Jaffa, Hugh de Neville) told Ralph of Coggeshall that even if a maiden had presented Richard with the keys to the city of Jerusalem, the French would not have supported the attack.[57]

Another example comes from the Teutonic Order's crusader state in Prussia. Writing between 1326 and 1331, Peter von Dusburg, priest-brother of the Teutonic Order, recorded in his history of the Order in Prussia how the Order's fort of Brandenburg was destroyed while the garrison was out on a raid. A Prussian woman 'of servile condition' left the castle and told Glappo, captain of the people of Warmia, that the Brothers had gone; he immediately captured the castle and destroyed it. The margrave of Brandenburg, who had originally built the castle, immediately came and rebuilt it, but the event was embarrassing for the Order.[58]

The 'History of Eracles' and the 'Chronicle of Ernoul', both describing how the kingdom of Jerusalem fell to Saladin, blamed Frankish defeat on female machinations of another sort. They told a story of how shortly before the decisive Battle of Hattin, a group of Frankish sergeants captured an old Muslim woman. She claimed to be a Syrian slave, and said she had put a spell on the Frankish army so that Saladin would capture them all. Perhaps the story arose from remarks that the Franks must have been bewitched to allow themselves to be trapped at Hattin.[59]

Women's interventions could act as a 'soft power' approach to war, although not always successfully. According to the fifteenth-century Portuguese historian Gomes Eanes de Zurara, when in 1414 or 1415 Yūsuf III of Granada became aware that King João I of Portugal was planning an attack, he got his leading wife to send Queen Philippa of Portugal a wedding trousseau for her daughter, who was about to be married. But Philippa rejected this diplomatic overture, replying that a Christian queen and princess did not interfere in her husband's business and her daughter was already well provided for.[60] Given Philippa's own family interests in crusading she had probably advised her husband to move against Granada.

Arguably Francisca de Gazmira, a native of La Palma in the Canary Islands who preached Christianity to her people, acted as a cultural diplomat for Latin Christendom and may have encouraged her people to accept Castilian conquest in 1492.[61] One of the twenty local women who were presented to Hernán Cortés and his companions in March 1519 by the leading men of the town of Tabasco (Potonchán, now in Mexico) became a key figure in Cortés's victory, as she acted as an interpreter between the Spanish and the local people. According to the eyewitness account of Bernal Díaz del Castillo, 'without the help of Doña Marina we could not have understood the language of New Spain and Mexico', and through her local knowledge and influence she saved the Spanish from many potentially fatal situations.[62]

Women acting alone

Moving on from these stereotypical roles of accompanying husbands (or in place of absent or dead husbands), giving medical aid, or acting as diplomats, there were also noblewomen who took part in holy war by virtue of their own authority. It is not always easy to establish what these women actually did. For instance, in 1148, during the siege of Tortosa in the north-east of the Iberian Peninsula, Count Ramon-Berenguer IV of Barcelona, ruler of Aragon, issued a charter in which he granted commercial privileges to the inhabitants of Narbonne in thanks for their having risked their property and lives to defend the Christian faith against the infidel. The charter indicates that his cousin the young Vicecountess Ermengarde of Narbonne had led troops from Narbonne with her uncle Berenger, abbot of Lagrasse, at Ramon-Berenguer's request, and both were present when he issued the charter.

However, the charter gives no information about Ermengarde's role during the siege itself.[63]

As the ship list from the 'St Victor' shows, women also travelled to join crusades to the East alone or with female companions. Clerical commentators criticized single women on crusades for being a temptation to sin, but most of the non-noble single women in crusade campaigns were not prostitutes but women whose male protectors, whether husbands, fathers, or employers, had died during the campaign. Many would have been domestic servants, members of crusaders' households. The non-noble crusaders were concerned to support these women when they were left without protection or employment.[64]

Single old women, in contrast, were not generally seen to be a temptation to sin, and had their own particular roles in the crusader army. One such role was entirely practical: Ambroise recorded that Richard I of England allowed no women except elderly female pilgrims working as laundresses to travel with his army when it marched south from Acre in September 1191 (Richard de Templo also mentioned the laundresses but omitted any reference to their age).[65] Another such role was religious: Saladin's secretary 'Imād al-Dīn al-Iṣfahānī wrote that the crusaders' camps were full of old women who alternately aroused and dampened the soldiers' enthusiasm to fight, telling them that the Cross would accept only renunciation and only lived by sacrifice, and that the Holy Sepulchre was in their enemy's power. He concluded: 'Marvel at how these men and women are unanimous in error!'[66]

An old woman was depicted in a similar role, encouraging warriors to self-sacrifice, in an incident in 1336 recounted by Wigand of Marburg, historian of the Teutonic Order in Prussia. Wigand reported that rather than surrender to the Teutonic Knights, the Lithuanian defenders of the fort of Pilenai killed their wives and children, and then an old woman beheaded them with an axe, finally killing herself. Reporting this story as hearsay, Wigand appears to have doubted the truth of this story, as warriors would usually regard death at a woman's hand as dishonourable. But as Lithuanian culture venerated old wise women it is possible that this old woman was one of their holy women, and the killing was a mutual act of self-sacrifice in preference to suffering religious pollution at the hands of their religious enemies. In a variation on the theme, Brother Peter von Dusburg, Wigand's predecessor as historian of the Order, told a story of a Galindian Prussian holy woman and prophetess (his translator Brother Nicolaus von Jeroschin calls her an old woman who was venerated as a seer) who, to avenge the wrongs done to Galindian womenfolk, deliberately set out to get the Galindian Prussian warriors killed by urging them to wage war on the Christians.[67]

Female rulers and noblewomen of the crusader states sometimes took an active military role. After the Second Crusade, Queen Melisende of Jerusalem continued to be involved in the defence of the kingdom as required. In 1157, while Baldwin III was campaigning in Antioch, Melisende recovered the cave-fortress of el-Hablis from the Muslims.[68] Melisende's younger sister Alice, Princess of Antioch, may have organized raiding expeditions. She may also have made diplomatic approaches to a neighbouring Muslim ruler, Zengi of Mosul, but this is uncertain because the only source, Archbishop William of Tyre's history, was implacably hostile towards her, accusing her of being inspired by an evil spirit to contact Zengi.[69]

Although Melisende's granddaughter Sybil does not appear to have been actively involved in organizing any crusade, she took some military initiative after Sultan Saladin captured her husband Guy de Lusignan with other leading nobles of the kingdom of Jerusalem at the Battle of Hattin. English commentators recorded that she took her two young daughters to the city of Ascalon—the lordship that she and Guy had held prior to gaining the throne—and defended it against Saladin, and that she and the patriarch of Jerusalem led the defence of Jerusalem. Again, after Sybil had secured her husband's release and Guy led the army to besiege the port city of Acre in August 1189, Sybil and their two daughters accompanied him.

All three died in the military camp in summer or early autumn 1190, leaving Guy without a claim to the throne.[70] This tragic end to Sybil's involvement in the conflict is a reminder of why queens usually kept out of military action.

Sybil's younger half-sister Isabel who succeeded her as queen of Jerusalem had even less involvement in war, but after the assassination of her second husband, Conrad of Montferrat, she remained in control of the city of Tyre and refused to surrender it except to King Richard I of England or his approved representative. Following Count Henry II of Champagne's election as king of Jerusalem in 1192 and King Richard's agreement, Isabel handed the keys of Tyre to Count Henry and agreed to marry him, thereby conferring her authority as heiress of King Amaury of Jerusalem to him; but she did not defend her city with weapons.[71]

Other women of the crusader states did become involved in war against the Muslims, however, even though they did not fight in the field in person. As fief holders, military service was their duty, although their feudal lord would normally expect an heiress to marry and for her husband to perform the military service due.[72] Cecilia of le Bourcq, widow of Roger of Salerno, prince of Antioch, one of the major landholders in the Principality of Antioch and styled 'Lady of Tarsus', may have helped to organize the defence of Antioch in 1119 after her husband's death in battle against the Muslim Ilghazi ibn Artuk of Mardin.[73] Eschiva de Bures, lady of Galilee, defended her castle of Tiberias against Saladin's besieging force for around a week from c. 27 June to 5 July 1187, surrendering only after the relief force led by King Guy was defeated at Hattin on 4 July.[74] Other noblewomen, such as Stephanie de Milly, lady of Transjordan, Isabel de Ibelin, lady of Beirut (d. 1282), and Countess Lucy of Tripoli (fl. 1292) negotiated with Muslim generals for their families, lands, and fortresses. 'Imād al-Dīn al-Iṣfahānī described Stephanie and her daughter-in-law Isabel weeping and humbling themselves before Saladin, imploring him to release Humfrid IV of Toron, Stephanie's son and Isabel's husband, who had been captured at Hattin. Saladin, wrote

'Imād al-Dīn, 'received both of them very well', showered them with favours, remitted the ransom due and gave them magnificent presents; but Stephanie had to surrender the castles of Kerak and Shaubak/Montréal to Saladin to gain her son's release.[75]

But although these high-status women commanded military forces and military action, the contemporary sources do not record that they bore arms on the battlefield. Similarly in 1427 Catherine of Brunswick-Lüneburg, acting as regent of Saxony during the absence of her husband Frederick or Friedrich of Wettin, margrave of Meissen and elector of Saxony, raised troops to fight the Hussite heretics but did not enter battle herself. The Hussite victory song commemorating the Battle of Ústí (in German, the Battle of Aussig) described her actions:

> The princess of Saxony was a powerful woman
> Together with barons, princes and knights
> She assembled a mighty army
> And marched into Bohemia.[76]

The poet declared that when she heard of her army's terrible defeat she fell to the ground in shock, tearing 'her golden curls from her beautiful head' and calling on God to have pity on her people, while 'other beautiful women' mourned the loss of 'brothers, uncles or fathers'. The king of Hungary (Sigismund of Luxembourg) asked what could be done 'to save the honour of the princess', but the reply was that the best solution was to leave the Czechs (that is, the Hussites) alone.[77]

Single, non-noble women on crusade were seldom mentioned in contemporary sources, and even when documents mentioned them in connection with crusades it is not always clear whether they actually took part. So, for example, when Count Henry of Rodez made his will at Acre on 18 October 1221 and left—among many other legacies—ten bezants (a coin used in the eastern Mediterranean which derived from the gold dinar) to a woman named Johannina, we have no means of knowing whether she was with him on the crusade, perhaps as a servant (as she is followed immediately in the list by the count's notary Master Bernard) or whether she was a member of his household far away in Rodez.[78] In England during the Fifth Crusade absence in the Holy Land was a frequently used excuse for non-appearance in court (for women and men), but there is no information as to whether the women in question ever reached the Holy Land. Before 1218/19 Agnes of Middleton, from Quernhow in North Yorkshire, brought a lawsuit against the blacksmith Geoffrey of Norton Conyers and his father Roger for the murder of her husband Richard, but they fled and she went to the 'land of Jerusalem' before the royal judges arrived. The accused were sentenced to be outlawed.[79] The same judicial eyre (judges' circuit) dealt with the case of Mariotta, daughter of William, who had charged Thomas le Grant with rape, but also went to the 'land of Jerusalem' before the judges arrived. In this case Thomas answered the summons but as the jurors did not suspect him he was acquitted.[80] Lecia from Walton near Wakefield in Yorkshire was summoned during the same eyre regarding the death of her son William, whom she had found drowned. When she did not appear in court the jurors said that she had gone to the land of Jerusalem and the people of the Walton agreed. The verdict on William's death was misadventure: 'no one is suspected'; perhaps Lecia's journey to Jerusalem was a proxy pilgrimage to benefit William's soul.[81] In 1221 two sisters, Cecily and Avice, were involved in a legal dispute over their mother Elena's inheritance in Warwickshire. It transpired that the pair had an elder sister, Clarice, who was in Ireland and who should also have been involved in the case; but Cecily and Avice stated that Clarice had died on her way to the Holy Land.[82]

In contrast to these piecemeal references, contemporary commentators agreed that the popular crusade movements known respectively as the 'Children's Crusade' in 1212 and the 'Crusade of the Shepherds' (pastoureaux) of 1251 and 1320 included women, presumably non-noble as none held leadership roles and none were named. The major participants in the 'Children's Crusade' were young people, both men and women—some writers specified that they were servants—but also included adults, mature women, and babes in arms. Their expressed intention, according to contemporary commentators, was to free the Holy Sepulchre from the 'Saracens'. After the movement had collapsed, according to some contemporary writers, many girls who had gone away as virgins returned pregnant. Like a modern youth movement, the participants in the 'Children's Crusade' imitated the behaviours of adults, emulating both crusaders and the chivalric elite, and seeking—like the modern 'Extinction Rebellion' movement—to right what they perceived to be the wrongs perpetuated by their parents' generation.[83]

The *pastoureaux* were older, depicted as herdsmen and farm workers rather than youths, and they set out to right the failings of their social superiors rather than their elders. Contemporaries writing about the *pastoureaux* in 1251 emphasized the men involved rather than women, but mentioned them carrying out marriages and giving the cross to 'all those who wished to take it, to women as well as children and men'. Although the stated aim of the group was to go to Egypt to rescue King Louis IX from the Muslims (the news of the king's capture in spring 1250 had reached France but not the news of his release), because of the social disruption they caused some contemporary writers accused them of being in alliance with the sultan of Egypt and even that their leaders were Muslims.[84] In 1320 again the *pastoureaux* reportedly aimed to travel to the Holy Land and defeat the Saracens, which successive kings of France had promised but failed to do. The movement again included women and recruits of all ages. As in 1250 the group became violent, but whereas previously the focus had been on the clergy, in 1320 the *pastoureaux* attacked Jewish communities, killing them and plundering their goods. The *pastoureaux* may have blamed the Jews for their recent economic hardships: the Jews had been expelled from France in 1306 by King Philip IV but were brought back in 1315 by his son Louis X, and were then encouraged to collect pre-1306 debts due to them.[85] Contemporary commentators' reference to women's involvement in these mass movements implied that they lacked organization and clear purpose, while the stories of girls returning home pregnant in 1212 underlined the dangers of being swept up in such movements. That said, there is no reason to doubt that young and older women did take part, but some may have been accompanying husbands, brothers or other male relatives rather than acting on their own initiative.

Other individual women are mentioned in the narrative sources acting for or against the crusaders. The Livonian Rhymed Chronicle included a story of an Estonian woman who with her husband's connivance secretly fed two Brothers of the Teutonic Order who had been taken captive by her fellow pagans during the Estonian rebellion against the Order. She disguised her deed by pretending that she was throwing stones at them. It also included a story of an Estonian couple who lured a German into their house and killed him with an axe. The latter were punished, according to the Rhymed Chronicle, when the pregnant wife gave birth to a deformed baby.[86]

Making a living

Some of the women with the crusade army would have been intending to make a living rather than performing a pilgrimage. Contemporary commentators—both Latin Christian and Muslim—tended to concentrate on those women who made a living as prostitutes, condemning them for polluting the spirituality of the army. Saladin's secretary 'Imād al-Dīn al-Iṣfahānī described Christian prostitutes taking the cross and coming to the siege of Acre in 1189 to provide sexual services for the crusaders, and added that Muslims also shamefully used their services. Given contemporary Latin Christian medical opinion on the necessity of sexual intercourse for good health, the women were providing an essential service.[87] But women also carried out less contentious roles. As Philippe de Mézières set out in his crusade plan, the army needed worthy ladies to look after the male soldiers humbly and devotedly, and to serve the noblewomen who should accompany their husbands.[88]

Ambroise mentioned women performing hygienic tasks for the warriors during the Third Crusade, delousing them as well as washing their hair and clothes.[89] Laundry work was almost invariably carried out by women, and was also associated with prostitution partly because washing and delousing hair was an intimate act.[90] That said, laundry work was such a stereotypical role for women that Lady Margaret Beaufort (d. 1509), Countess of Richmond and mother of King Henry VII of England, was reported to have joked that she would be willing to be a servant and laundress on crusade, if only the 'princes of Christendom' could agree to stop fighting among themselves and go to attack their common enemy the Turks.[91]

Women also sold food to the crusade army, but again this vital but mundane role was hardly ever mentioned by contemporaries except when their work impinged on military activity. So, for example, during the Fifth Crusade, in the course of the siege of Damietta, instructions were issued that everyone should be armed and organized to guard the camp, and the merchants and women with merchandise to sell should leave the army on pain of losing a hand and their property. In a more positive view of merchants' contribution, John of Joinville mentioned in his eye-witness account of Louis IX's crusade that during a Muslim attack on the king's camp on Friday 11 February 1250 the butchers, 'the other men with the army' and the women who sold provisions raised the alarm when Count Alfonse of Poitiers was captured by the enemy; the Egyptians were repulsed, and the count rescued.[92]

Presumably there were female servants among the crusaders' entourages as well as male servants. Richard de Templo mentioned three times that Berengaria of Navarre and Dowager Queen Joanna of Sicily were accompanied on their journey by servants, including girls and maids (*puellis et ancillis*); Ambroise mentioned their *meschines* or maids just once. John of Joinville mentioned the women in attendance on Margaret of Provence, queen of King Louis IX, during their voyage back from their crusade; Isabelle of Aragon, wife of Philip III of France, may have been accompanied on crusade to Tunis by the six women who received legacies in her will of January 1271.[93]

Military action

While noblemen on crusade fought the religious enemy, their wives generally kept out of harm's way. Berengaria of Navarre and Dowager Queen Joanna of Sicily remained in the royal palace in Acre while Richard I led the crusader army south at the end of August 1191, until he had occupied Jaffa, when the queens moved there; they later returned to Acre. During Louis IX's crusade to Tunis, the noblewomen were accommodated outside the camp, on ships.[94] In 1249 Louis IX had left his wife Margaret of Provence in safety at Damietta; it was unfortunate that a dramatic change in military fortune brought Damietta into the front line. In 1541–1542 Queen Säblä Wängel of Ethiopia travelled with and advised the Portuguese army which had come to assist her and her son against the Muslim invaders led by Imam Ahmad ibn Ibrahim al-Ghazi, because this 'holy enterprise' needed her presence to ensure the local people's support for the Portuguese who had come 'in the service of God' to help them. But when the king was able to join the army, the queen remained in a secure location while the king led the army to engage Imam Ahmad's forces.[95] Commanders of besieged cities generally tried to keep non-noble non-combatants, including women, in a secure place out of reach of bombardment.[96]

When noblewomen did become involved in military activity against non-Christians, contemporary commentators might try to downplay the women's danger, presenting war as a chivalrous game, as in the story in the *Chronica Adefonsi Imperatoris* of the Empress Berenguela of Castile defending Toledo from Muslim attack.[97] Again, on 25 July 1457 Juana of Portugal, recently wed queen-consort of King Enrique IV of Castile, and ten of her ladies accompanied the king on horseback on an expedition against the Muslim town of Cambil, in Andalusia to the north of Granada. Some of the ladies wore strongly woven protective material on their arms or tunics and headgear like those worn by the men-at-arms, and the queen shot several bolts from a crossbow at the walls of the city. They then returned to the city of Jaen. Afterwards the Marinid sultan of Morocco sent the queen clothing, harness for a jinette and perfume.[98] The whole event was presented like a mock conflict to amuse the ladies. That this war was in reality no game is demonstrated by the fact that the crusade campaigns that were most blatantly advertised as exercises of chivalric excellence, the Teutonic Order's *Reisen* in Prussia, do not appear to have included any women crusaders at all. Female involvement was represented only by the Order's patron, the Blessed Virgin Mary, and the female saints and prospective saints patronized by the Order.[99]

On the other hand, when enemy women were involved in holy war commentators might stress their involvement specifically to demean the enemy. We have already met in the previous chapter Alice de Montmorency, wife of Simon de Montfort the elder, who spent the years 1210–1218 recruiting troops for her husband's and then her son's campaigns against the Cathar heretics of the Languedoc and their supporters. Countess Alice was only once on the front line of military action, when in autumn 1217 Count Raymond VI of Toulouse recaptured the city of Toulouse while she was in Narbonnais castle (the castle of Toulouse). Many women and children from her and her husband's family were with her in this supposedly safe location. The anonymous continuator of the *Chanson de la croisade albigeois* (or 'Song of the Cathar Wars'), writing soon after events, described the Countess as being 'in desperate anxiety', when she realized that Toulouse had fallen to the enemy, lamenting her sudden downturn in fortune and appealing for advice. By emphasizing her panic and confusion, he impressed on his audience that the villains of his story could not withstand his hero Count Raymond. In contrast, Peter of les Vaux-de-Cernay, who supported Count Simon and Countess Alice, recorded only that Alice was one of those in Narbonnais Castle when Count Raymond captured Toulouse, and that she went to recruit additional troops in northern France.[100]

Abbot Guibert of Nogent, who was not an eye-witness of the First Crusade, imagined exotically dressed Saracen women in the Muslim camp at Antioch, carrying quivers full of arrows, who seemed to have come 'not to fight but to reproduce' and who later ran away, abandoning their children—thus clearly demonstrating their worthlessness.[101] In a similar vein Saladin's secretary 'Imād al-Dīn al-Iṣfahānī and the qadi Bahā' al-Dīn Ibn Shaddād depicted the women in the army of the Third Crusade taking an ultimately ineffective part in combat, recording that a crusader woman in a green cloak used a wooden bow against Muslim soldiers and that crusader women fought in the field against Muslims, but all were killed.[102] Their contemporary the historian Ibn al-Athīr stated that in August 1188 when Saladin was besieging the castle of Barziyya (Bourzey, near Apamea), he saw a woman operating a siege machine in the castle, which put the Muslims' siege machine out of action.[103] None of these accounts were endorsed by writers from the other side. Both Abbot Guibert and the Muslim commentators on the Third Crusade wrote to demean their religious opponents as morally corrupt barbarians who were incapable of fulfilling their social and religious duties (such as men defending their women folk) and whose society was cursed by God. 'Imād al-Dīn's and Bahā' al-Dīn Ibn Shaddād's depictions of Christian women fighting on the battlefield contributed to their wider picture of the morally corrupt enemy doomed to be destroyed by the forces of the morally upright and pious Saladin. The fact that a woman was operating a siege machine at Barziyya was a curiosity that revealed the desperate position of the defenders. Although the woman with the bow was a skilled archer, the wooden bow was a non-knightly weapon, implying that the woman using it was a low-status warrior; and she was quickly killed, restoring the proper balance to human society.[104]

Moving from propaganda to the realities of warfare, we must remember that to be effective warriors for front-line mounted combat in the field, women on crusade would have had to be trained and armed just as men had to be trained and armed. There is no evidence that they were.[105] Nevertheless non-combatants in the crusade army were expected to take an active role in combat if required, although not a role that required years of practice and expense. The dangers to non-combatants in a battle zone meant that women not connected with crusades but living in regions through which crusaders passed could also expect and be expected to take part in military activity.

The narrative accounts depict women in certain stereotypical roles in combat, in particular providing food and water for the fighting men on the battlefield. These were dangerous tasks—for example, one account of the Fifth Crusade mentions that the women bringing food and water to the footsoldiers during a battle in August 1219 were attacked by the enemy and massacred. The narratives also mention that women 'always strongly encouraged' fighters on the battlefield, perhaps yelling encouragement like modern spectators at a football match.[106] Women collected stones to be used as missiles: at Toulouse in 1217, preparing to defend their city against the crusaders, 'women and ladies' brought 'containers full of gathered stones, large ones and fist-sized pebbles'.[107]

Women carried out labouring tasks alongside other non-combatants. The *Song of the Cathar Wars* describes everyone at Toulouse—knights, citizens and their wives, men and women merchants, moneychangers, small children, both boys and girls, servants and messengers—working with a pick, a shovel or a garden fork to build defences.[108] Preparing to defend Prague against the anti-Hussite crusade in 1420, maids (in this context young unmarried women) worked alongside priests, students and Jews to dig a dry moat on the north side of Vyšehrad castle, which the radical Hussites known as Taborites (after Mount Tabor in the Old Testament) had captured in October 1419 and which protected the south side of Prague New Town; it took them five days.[109] Guillaume Caoursin, vice-chancellor of the Knights Hospitaller, described similar labouring scenes preparing to defend Rhodes against Ottoman attack in 1480: the grand master of the Order and the high officials, knights, citizens, merchants, married women, newly married, and maidens all worked to strengthen the walls and ditches, carrying stone, soil, and lime.[110] Francesco Balbi di Correggio described soldiers, women and children, and beasts of burden bringing earth into the fortified town of Birgu on Malta in May 1565 in preparation for assault by the forces of Ottoman sultan Suleiman the Magnificent.[111] Ambroise and Richard de Templo recount the death of a woman engaged in filling in the ditch defences of the city of Acre during the siege of 1189–1191, and although this example may be an invention it demonstrates the danger which women in support roles had to face.[112] Women were also depicted taking the lead in prayer and penitential actions to win God's help for the defence.[113] Performing such roles was sufficient to get them a share in the booty from a captured city, even if at the siege of Damietta in 1219 women and children were due to receive just three bezants each, while knights received twenty-four, priests and turcopoles (light cavalry) twelve, and attendants six.[114]

Contemporary accounts suggest that women fought only at times of great crisis, but they were often depicted stepping in to defend their city in emergency situations, emphasizing the desperation of the moment. Peter von Dusburg recorded that when the Teutonic Order's city of Elbing (now Elblag in Poland) came under attack from the Christian Duke Swantopolk or Swietopelk II of Pomerania during the absence of the Brothers and the men of the city on campaign, the women of the city laid aside women's adornment and put on the mind of men, buckled on swords and defended the city manfully (*viriliter*).[115] Lucy, an English sister of the Trinitarian Order, was reported to have fought in the 1480 defence of Rhodes against the Ottoman Turks.[116] The 'Song of the Cathar Wars' relates that on 25 June 1218 it was 'noblewomen, little girls, and men's wives' who were operating the mangonel that hurled the stone which killed Count Simon de Montfort.[117] The implication of this account was that Montfort's actions were so abhorrent to God that He permitted weak and feeble women to kill him—a shameful death for such a renowned warrior.

During the first crusade against the Hussite heretics in 1419, women formed part of the radical Taborite army which came to assist the people of Prague against the Catholic crusader army of King Sigismund of Hungary, heir to the throne of Bohemia. A Czech contemporary, Laurence of Březová, described the crusaders' attack on Prague New Town on 14 June 1419, and how women opposed them:

[The crusaders] strongly attacked the ...wooden bulwark....And when they tried to scale the wall erected from earth and stone, two women and one girl together with about twenty-six men who still held the bulwark defended themselves manfully, hurling stones and lances, for they had neither arrows nor guns. And one of the two women, though she was without armour, surpassed in spirit all men, as she did not want to yield one step. Before Antichrist, so she said, no faithful Christian must ever retreat! And thus, fighting with supreme courage, she was killed and gave up her spirit.[118]

A letter from the margrave of Meissen to his cousin the duke of Bavaria claimed that the king's forces had captured 156 Hussite women during this encounter who had their hair arranged like men's hair, and were wearing boots, armed with swords, and carrying stones in their hands.[119] For the Czechs, the women's involvement in military action underlined the righteousness of the Hussite cause. For the crusaders, the presence of women dressed and armed as men among the enemy's forces demonstrated their otherness and the depravity of their cause.

In such emergency situations women could use any available implement as a weapon. Ambroise and Richard de Templo depicted women of the crusader army using knives to cut off the heads of Muslims captured with their ship in a naval battle in spring 1190 during the siege of Acre; Richard de Templo explained that the women used knives rather than swords because of their physical weakness.[120] The traveller Ludolf von Sudheim noted in 1350 that on Rhodes 'it was said' that a single English woman pilgrim had stabbed and killed more than 1,000 Turkish captives *cum feru*, that is, with an iron instrument, a sword or a knife.[121] Execution of prisoners by women rather than men, and by knife rather than sword, was a means of demeaning the defeated enemy.

Women and other non-combatants were also depicted improvising helmets from metal cooking pots. Margaret of Beverley, whose life was recorded by her younger brother Thomas of Froidmont, was reportedly in Jerusalem as a pilgrim at the time of Saladin's siege of 1187, and assisted in the defence of the city. Margaret is depicted using a cauldron as a helmet so that she could carry water to the defenders on the city walls. Thomas records Margaret saying: 'like a fierce virago, I tried to play the role of a man...a woman pretending to be a man...terrified, but I pretended not to be afraid.' She was hit by a fragment of a stone hurled by one of Saladin's siege machines; the wound healed, but she carried the scar.[122]

Did Muslim women fight crusaders? The Arab-Syrian nobleman, warrior and poet Usama ibn Munqidh related a number of anecdotes of Muslim women fighting during the crusade period in the Middle East, but these were generally fighting other Muslims. Nevertheless, they show that he regarded women who fought as praiseworthy when they fought for a just cause. He recounted how when his family were fighting off an attack by a group of Nizari Isma'ilis or Batini, an heretical Islamic sect, an aunt of his cousin Shabib donned a mail hauberk and helmet, and took up sword and shield to fight the enemy. When she saw that Shabib was intending to flee from the house, she challenged him and shamed him into staying to fight. While Usama's mother protected his sister (of which more below), an old woman who had been a servant of Usama's grandfather put on her veil, took a sword, and went out to fight the Isma'ilis. Usama commented that noble women certainly had disdain for danger and courage for the sake of honour—as noble men should have. In another example of a woman's courage for the sake of honour, he recounted how the wife of a Muslim bandit who was working for a Frankish lord killed her husband because she was angry at 'what this infidel' was doing to her fellow Muslims.[123]

Another of Usama's anecdotes was about a Muslim woman from Shayzar named Nadra bint Buzurmat who went out with her fellow townspeople to attack a group of 800 or so Frankish pilgrims, men, women, and children, who had mistaken their way to Apamea. She captured three Franks, one after the other, plundered their possessions, and then called her neighbours, who came and killed them.[124] This story suggests that ordinary Muslim women could take part alongside men in raids on Frankish pilgrims. The Catalan writer Ramon Muntaner, writing in the early fourteenth century, recorded a similar incident during the French crusade against Aragon in 1285, although in this crusade both sides were Christian. Na Mercadera, a woman of Peralada in Aragon, went out of her house armed with a lance and shield so that she could defend herself if necessary against the French crusaders, who were besieging the town. She encountered a French knight, whom she captured.[125] Muntaner used this story to demonstrate God's support for the Catalans, for even their weak women could defeat the supposedly superior French knights. Similarly Peter von Dusburg recounted how a Christian woman of the Kulmerland chased into a swamp by a pagan Sudovian warrior who wanted to kill her, fought him off *viriliter* (manfully), and then succeeded in drowning him in the swamp.[126]

But valiant women who fought back did not always win. Usama repeated an anecdote about a Frankish woman who fought back under attack, told to him by a Muslim amir in Egypt, Nada al-Sulayhi. The young Nada al-Sulayhi had been one of a group of Muslim warriors who sallied out from Ascalon to attack Frankish pilgrims on the road to Jerusalem. A man hit him in the face with a spear, so he killed him; whereupon the man's wife hit him in the face with a rough-ware water jar with water in it. He also killed the woman, but was left with two scars.[127]

A Greek woman was reported to have died as a martyr fighting at Rhodes against the Turks during the siege of 1522: she was reportedly the mistress of a Hospitaller officer who had been killed during the siege. Not wishing to survive him (the report stated), she kissed and blessed their two little boys, killed them with a knife, and threw their bodies on the fire, 'so that the most vile enemy (*hostis vilissimus*) could not possess the twin nobility of their bodies alive or dead'. Then she donned the dead officer's clothes, still soaked in his blood, took his sabre, and rushed upon the Turks. She died 'fighting strongly in the manner of men'. Such accounts proclaimed the power of even weak Christian women over their Muslim enemies, but also demonstrated their dedication to Christian martyrdom.[128] Muslim and Jewish women were also reported to have preferred death for themselves and their children over capture.

Victims and prisoners of crusades

Although theorists such as Honoré Bonet (also known as Bouvet: died c. 1410) argued that women should not be compelled to go to war (although they could provide a substitute) and they should not be imprisoned,[129] in practice women were not normally spared the violence of holy war. As women and children were expected to take part in combat roles as required in time of war, they were never truly non-combatants and so were legitimate targets. Noblewomen were not exempt: Eleanor of Aquitaine's ship was captured briefly during her return from the Second Crusade, while the ship of Dowager Queen Joanna of Sicily and Berengaria of Navarre was detained at Cyprus by Isaac Doukas Komnenos during their voyage to Acre to join the Third Crusade.[130] Even baby girls were taken prisoner and sold as slaves.[131]

Contemporary writers assumed that any woman or young woman taken prisoner would be sexually abused.[132] Usama ibn Munqidh describes how the father of a young woman who had been captured by the Franks was in despair for two days until her dead body was found in the river: rather than suffer rape she had thrown herself from the horse of the Frank who had carried her away, and had been drowned. The father's anguish was then relieved by the knowledge that she had not suffered a fate worse than death. Although a victim, she had retained some agency and had chosen death rather than dishonour. While Muslim law accepted that a woman in fear of death might have to submit to enemy demands, the truly heroic woman should value honour above life.[133]

Latin Christian accounts of the First Crusade described the crusaders as routinely killing everyone in the fortified towns and cities they captured, depicting the crusaders purifying the Holy Land of unbelievers just as the Israelites of the Old Testament purified their Promised Land.[134] Given that these towns and cities were not deserted after the crusade but continued to operate, we may assume that in fact the crusaders did not kill everyone, and despite the claims that they took no prisoners there are also references to prostitutes having survived the massacres and prisoners being sold as slaves.[135] There may have been some reality behind the claims that the crusaders preferred to kill women rather than rape them, as after the crusaders' massacre of the population of Jerusalem in July 1099 the Karaite Jewish elders of Ascalon wrote lamenting the massacre but adding that they had not heard that these cursed people (the crusaders) violated or raped women as others did.[136]

The Muslim historian Ibn al-Athīr recounted how in 557 A.H. (A.D. 1162) during one of the Christian Georgians' frequent raids on their Muslim neighbours, they brought back women captives whom they had stripped and led away 'naked and bare footed', but when they arrived home the Georgian women condemned this treatment of Muslim women because the Muslims would retaliate in kind. The Georgian women then gave the Muslim women clothes.[137] But women did not necessarily spare women. When the Taborites sacked Chomútov in Bohemia in March 1421 the women in the Taborite army were reported to have taken the Catholic women and young girls out of the town with the promise of releasing them unharmed, then stripped them of their possessions, including money and jewellery, locked them in a shed and burned them all, including the pregnant women. Their action could have been retaliation for the mass burning of Hussites in February that year at Chotěboř in eastern Bohemia, where the Hussite defenders had been promised safe conduct if they surrendered the town, but were then seized and burned, or marched to Kutná Hora and burned or thrown down the mine shafts. One account recorded that a woman who saw that her husband was being burned jumped into the flames and burned with him.[138] Heretic non-combatants were treated particularly harshly by crusader armies: the massacre at Chotěboř in 1421 was matched by reports of crusader atrocities against women and young children at Louny in May 1420, Žatec in September 1421, Kutná Hora in December 1421–January 1422, and at Malín and other towns in eastern Bohemia.[139]

Likewise, during the Albigensian Crusade the crusaders dealt with the allegedly heretical women they captured just as they dealt with men, hacking them to pieces or burning them as heretics. Even captured noblewomen could expect to be killed rather than held for ransom, although a few were spared. Peter of les Vaux-de-Cernay stated that at Minerve the heretics rushed into the flames and just three women were saved from burning in the pyre with the other 'perfected' Cathars, one being a noblewoman, Matilde de Garlande, mother of one of the crusaders. The noblewoman Girauda of Lavaur, described by Peter of les Vaux-de-Cernay as 'a heretic of the worst sort', was thrown into a well and then covered in stones. William of Tudela, the author of the first part of the 'Song of the Cathar Wars' regretted her death but added that all the other noblewomen captured at Lavaur were freed by a courteous Frenchman, presumably a crusader.[140] Peter and William did not state whether the women who were spared escaped because they were noble, because they recanted their heresy, or because they had influential friends and relations among the crusader army.

Under attack from participants in the First Crusade and threatened with death or forced conversion, the Jewish communities in the Rhineland in 1096 chose mass suicide. While the crusaders were obsessed by the need to impose purity by slaying all non-Christians and heretics, the Jews were determined to protect the purity of their communities from defilement by the worshippers of a corpse, as they expressed it. Judaism has a long tradition of martyrdom in defence of Judaic law, going back to the sufferings of Daniel's friends Hananiah, Mishael, and Azariah at the hands of King Nebuchadnezzar II of Babylon (told in Daniel 1:12–32), and the gruesome deaths of a woman and her seven sons at the hands of the Hellenistic king Antiochus IV Epiphanes in the second century BC in the time of the Maccabean revolt (recounted in 2 Maccabees 6:10–41). The persecution of 1096, however, saw new forms of martyrdom, although it is difficult to discern how far the Jewish narratives of these events reflect exactly what happened, and how far they seek to justify the actions of those who died.[141]

The massacres began with the murder of eleven Jews at Speyer. The long account attributed to Solomon ben Simson of the massacres noted among the deaths 'a notable and pious woman who slaughtered herself for the sanctification of the Name. She was the first of those who slaughtered themselves in all the communities.' After killing Jews at Speyer, the crusaders came to Worms, where the short account known as the 'Anonymous of Mainz' or the 'Mainz Anonymous' recorded that they claimed that the Jews had killed one of their comrades. Then the crusaders and burghers looted and murdered the Jews, men, women, and children, and left their naked bodies in the streets. Men and women of the Jewish community refused to flee and allowed the Christian mob to kill them rather than 'deny the God on high', or used knives to kill each other and themselves to escape the mob. Their deaths were described as sacrifices, 'in the sanctification of the Name' (of God). Fathers killed their children, wives, and mothers, while mothers (most famously Rachel the daughter of Rabbi Isaac ben Rabbi Asher) killed their children. Those who died were presented as heroes; their deaths were not an indication of defeat but of victory, freely chosen in the face of evil.[142]

In contrast, at the time of the Second Crusade, according to Ephraim of Bonn's Hebrew narrative of events in *Sefer Zekhira* (probably written in the 1170s), rather than seek martyrdom Jews sought means of avoiding death in the face of Christian aggression. The martyrs Ephraim described were those who did not seek refuge in a fortress or another secure place, but travelled unprotected in dangerous situations. Among those who suffered in 1146 while travelling unwisely was the woman Mina of Speyer, who left the city of Speyer and was attacked and mutilated, although not killed. The Jews of Würzburg unwisely remained there rather than fleeing to a place of safety, and twenty-two were killed. But Rabbi Simon ben Isaac's sister managed to escape. When she was taken into a church to be forcibly baptized, she spat on a Catholic holy object (perhaps a crucifix), and feigned death under the blows of stones and fists which followed her action. She was rescued after dark by a gentile laundress who got her out of the church. By spitting on the 'abomination' she had sanctified God's name just as the Jewish martyrs of 1096 had done, but she did not have to die as a result. Arguably Ephraim wrote to advise Jewish communities on how they could survive future Christian attacks, rather than face complete destruction.[143]

But the martyrdoms of 1096 would be repeated. For instance, in England in March 1190 the Jews of York resorted to suicide and sacrificing their women and children in the face of attacks from the Christians of the city, spurred on by the imminent departure of crusaders for the Third Crusade.[144] The destruction of children in the face of the religious enemy was prompted by a similar motivation as that which led the Greek woman on Rhodes in 1522 to murder her two children before rushing out to die fighting the Turks: not to allow the vile enemy to defile them. In a similar way, during the attack mentioned above by the Nizari Isma'ilis or Batini, Usama ibn Munqidh's mother made his sister, an older woman, sit on the balcony of his house and sat at the entrance to the balcony, intending that if the enemy broke into the house she would push her daughter to her death. Challenged by Usama to explain her action, she declared: 'I would rather see her dead than a prisoner of peasants and wool-carders.' Usama and his sister thanked her for this.[145]

Narrative accounts of crusades tended to concentrate on how badly the religious enemy mistreated women and to brush over how their own side treated captured women. However, Fulcher of Chartres, who was on the First Crusade, stated that when the Turks fled after the Battle of Antioch (June 1098) the crusaders killed any women they found in the Turks' abandoned tents by stabbing them in the stomach with their lances. Describing the capture of the city of Caesarea by storm in 1101, he recorded that 'hardly any of the masculine sex were left alive, but they spared many women, to serve as maid-servants turning hand mills; both beautiful and ugly women were sold and bought as slaves, as were the men'.[146] Saladin's secretary 'Imād al-Dīn described a similar situation in more extravagant terms: exulting over the fate of Frankish women captured in Saladin's victories, he declared they would be stripped, raped and put to hard labour.[147]

In general, however, the capture and killing of enemy women and children was mentioned only in passing as part of normal procedure in a victory. After the Portuguese and Ethiopians killed Imam Ahmad ibn Ibrahim al-Ghazi and defeated his army at Wayna Daga in February 1543 the Ethiopians rejoiced over their sisters, daughters, and wives who were freed from captivity in the Muslim camp at the same time as they took the Muslim women captive.[148] Brother Peter von Dusburg of the Teutonic Order mentioned almost in passing in his description of a dawn raid by the Teutonic knights of Ragnit on Gediminas of Lithuania's fortress that everything in the castle was burned: 'with men, women, little ones, and all their coverings', with only twelve survivors from the conflagration.[149]

Killing pregnant women, carrying off women, girls, and children as captives and selling them into slavery was depicted as characteristic of a religious enemy—whether it be Muslims, Lithuanians, or Swantopolk II of Pomerania, who was a Christian but was allied with the pagan Prussians.[150] The acquisition of slaves for trading may have been a major incentive in the Baltic Crusades, but although contemporary Latin Christian sources depicted slave-raiding, particularly of women, as a widespread pagan Prussian activity which the crusaders set out to halt, there is no direct material evidence for a slave trade.[151]

Emphasizing the enemy's barbarity and the atrocities inflicted upon women and children encouraged one's own side to avenge them. The Mamluks' capture of the city of Tripoli in 1289 and the city of Acre in 1291 was reported to Latin Europe with these atrocities set out in detail. Writing in the first two decades of the fourteenth century, the former secretary of grand master William de Beaujeu of the Order of the Temple wrote as an eyewitness of the fall of Acre. He described 'the ladies and burgesses and the cloistered maidens and other lesser folk' fleeing through the streets of Acre to escape by ship as the Muslim troops flooded in, carrying children in their arms, but being intercepted by the Muslims: 'one seized the mother and another the child, and carried them from place to place and separated them from each other'. Two Muslims fought over a woman and killed her; a woman was led away and the child at her breast was thrown to the ground and trampled by a horse. Pregnant women were caught up in the crowd of people fleeing and smothered with their unborn children.[152] Similarly those preaching the crusade in the aftermath of the conquest of Constantinople by the Ottoman Turks in 1453 were instructed to dwell on (among other atrocities) how women were raped, babies murdered, and pregnant women ripped open.[153]

Occasionally such reports of suffering women allowed them some agency, to fight back against the religious enemy. Peter von Dusburg described how when the Teutonic Knights arrived to rescue some Christian women captured by the Lithuanians, killing some with their swords and drowning others, the women turned on their Lithuanian captors and killed them 'in whatever manner they could'. In contrast, in his fellow-brother Nicolaus von Jeroschin's translation of this episode the women did not fight the Lithuanians themselves but fell weeping at the Brothers' feet when they were freed.[154] Giving the victims some agency showed that they had deliberately chosen martyrdom rather than having it forced on them. When Nicosia, capital of Venetian-ruled Cyprus, fell to the Ottoman Turks in September 1570, a Turkish galleon carrying booty and hundreds of captives bound for Istanbul to be presented to the sultan exploded in Famagusta harbour, with a roar that shook the whole town, killing almost everyone on the galleon and two other ships. It was reported by Father Angelo Calepio and other contemporaries that the explosion was caused by a noble Cypriot lady who preferred death to slavery, but there was no agreement over which lady was responsible.[155]

In times of war, even peaceful pilgrims were not exempt from violence. In January 1366 the Englishwoman Isolda Parewastell informed Pope Urban V that while on pilgrimage to the Holy Land she had been imprisoned, hung upside down in a rack, and beaten half-dead: presumably she was caught up in the reprisals against Christians following King Peter I of Cyprus's attack on Alexandria in October 1365. She made her escape, she claimed, only by a miracle.[156] After Jerusalem fell to Saladin in 1187 Margaret of Beverley paid for her freedom and set off with a group of other refugees for Lachish, but the group was captured by Muslims, enslaved, and forced to labour in the heat. After fifteen months they were ransomed by a man from Tyre (now Sūr in Lebanon). After further dangers and narrow escapes Margaret finally reached Christian-held Acre and embarked for the West.[157]

Isolda and Margaret lived to tell their tales, but very little information is available about the lives of those women captured during the crusades who were not later ransomed or otherwise released. Ibn al-Athīr made a few comments, describing how while he was living in Aleppo he found one of his slaves weeping and tried to comfort her: she was a young woman who had been taken prisoner when Saladin's brother al-'Adil captured the city of Jaffa in the summer of 1187, and she had a baby boy around a year old. She told him she was weeping because she had had a husband, six brothers, and two sisters, and had no idea what had happened to any of them. He also reported seeing in Aleppo a Muslim walking with a Frankish woman up to a door, on which he knocked; the owner of the house came out and after some conversation went inside and brought out another Frankish woman. The two women embraced with screams and tears, and then sat on the ground and talked. They were sisters, but had no news of what had become of the rest of their family.[158] Usama ibn Munqidh was puzzled by captive Frankish women and men who were honoured and promoted in Muslim society but who then left the Muslim faith and went back to live much more lowly lives among the Franks. For him their refusal to integrate demonstrated that they were an accursed race who would not change their ways to mix with other races.[159]

The Cairo Geniza documents include some information in the context of attempts to ransom captives. A letter written in Ascalon after 1153 notes that following negotiations a Jewish girl captive had been permitted to travel with her brother to Egypt to raise her ransom, but she had not yet returned; her Frankish captor was becoming impatient and was demanding either the payment of the ransom or the return of the girl. After the fall of Acre to the Mamluks in 1291, a Jewish girl 'who had lost her virginity because she was captured in

Acre by Muslims' was redeemed from captivity by a man who intended to marry her as his second wife—so was presumably a Muslim himself. The draft marriage contract survives, but we may only speculate how free she was in fact and whether she was given any choice in this marriage.[160]

Even high-status women captives could be placed in this situation. For example, after capturing Cyprus in May 1191 en route to join the Third Crusade, King Richard I of England entrusted the young daughter of the captured Isaac Doukas Komnenos, emperor of Cyprus, to his wife Berengaria's care. This young Greek Orthodox woman, whose name was never recorded by contemporaries, was a valuable prize: she was a member of an eminent Byzantine noble family, the Komnenoi, and she retained a claim to the throne of Cyprus through her father. At the end of the Third Crusade she sailed to France with Queen Berengaria and Joanna, dowager queen of Sicily. After Richard himself was taken prisoner by Duke Leopold V of Austria during his journey home from the East, one of the terms of his release was that the former emperor of Cyprus and his daughter should be released. Duke Leopold planned her marriage to one of his sons, but this fell through and she returned to Normandy. According to the 'Chronicle of Ernoul', after the death of King Richard she married Count Raymond VI of Toulouse (Joanna's widower); he then divorced her and she married a Flemish knight, a relative of Count Baldwin IX of Flanders, who joined the Fourth Crusade and attempted unsuccessfully to claim the throne of Cyprus in her name.[161]

Even after she was freed, the emperor's daughter was too valuable to her captors to send back to the East. In this case her value was her claim to land, but a more common justification for retaining prisoners was that their captivity enabled their souls to be saved through religious conversion. In the 1270s Henry III Borwin of Mecklenburg entrusted 'a little maiden whom we snatched from the mouth of the sword in the midst of the slaughter of the pagans' to the monastery of Rehna in Mecklenburg-Vorpommern. He later referred to her as 'our beloved adopted daughter, born of pagan parents'. The child would have been brought up as a Christian and was destined to become a nun at Rehna.[162] This girl's parents had apparently been killed in the war, but children could be retained in this way even when they had a loving family waiting for them. In 1557 the Hospitallers' Grand Prior of France captured two young Turkish women and their brother who were en route to Mecca on pilgrimage. He presented the young women to Queen Catherine de' Medici of France and her sister-in-law Margaret of Valois, soon to be duchess of Savoy. Their new owners baptized the elder, Fati, as Catherine and the younger as Margaret. The two new converts married Frenchmen. Back in Istanbul their mother petitioned Sultan Suleiman to get them released, stating that they had been forced to convert to Christianity, and she enlisted the sultan's daughter and granddaughter in her support. The sultan accordingly refused to release any French prisoners until the two Turkish girls were freed, but the French refused to send them back to Turkey on the basis that they were now Christians and happily married in France. The younger woman, Margaret, had become lady of the bed-chamber to Catherine de' Medici. Their captors would not give up such high-profile Christian converts, royal protégées whose conversion bolstered French royal prestige.[163]

This case demonstrates that even high-status women, despite all their contacts and influence, could not necessarily obtain freedom for their loved ones. Overall, crusading and even coming into contact with crusaders was a dangerous business, and it is understandable that many women did not travel to the frontline but remained at home, supporting the crusade in other ways. These also had their perils, as we shall now see.

4

The Home Front

Supporting the Crusade

So far we have considered the role of women in starting crusades and within crusades. What about those women who were left behind while their menfolk were away?

It was little wonder that women and families grieved to see their husbands and loved ones depart on crusade. Although the 'women's farewell' was a standard scene in contemporary accounts of crusades, the scenes of keepsakes and vows exchanged, and weeping and refusing to let go of loved ones until the last possible moment, were repeated in every account because they were true.[1] We have already encountered Blanche of Castile, who lost her husband, King Louis VIII of France, in a crusade, and after her sons Louis and Robert set out on crusade to the eastern Mediterranean in 1248 she never saw them again. Contemporary writers—Matthew Paris in England and the 'Minstrel of Reims' in France—wrote that Blanche did all she could to dissuade her eldest son from going on crusade.[2] She was a deeply devout woman, but she knew what damage the crusade could do to a family and kingdom.

However, Blanche also supported her eldest son during his crusade. Louis appointed his mother regent just as she had been regent after his father's death, and she ruled the kingdom of France during his absence. She was supported by an informal group of higher clergy, but she held

executive power as queen of France by the grace of God. As regent
during her son's crusade she had to deal with religious fanatics (the
Pastoureaux), ensure the loyalty of the great noble families, keep the support of the Church while protecting royal rights, and raise money to
pay for Louis's crusade; all this from a woman who was over sixty, who
might otherwise have been thinking about retirement into a convent.[3]

Administering and protecting the family estates, and raising money
for crusaders, were the two most visible roles women played to support crusaders. As administrators for their family estates they came
under pressure from relatives or other rival claimants, although as
members of crusaders' families they were also under papal protection,
more or less enforced by both secular and ecclesiastical authorities.
Sometimes they had to raise the ransom for captive crusaders. They
also gave spiritual support for crusades: taking part in liturgies to support the crusade, making donations to religious houses, and venerating
saints; while holy women supported the crusade through prayer and
their writings.

The costs of crusading for those left behind

Blanche of Castile's grandmother Eleanor of Aquitaine, queen of
France and then queen of England, participated in the Second Crusade
and supported her eldest surviving son Richard through the Third.
Although she was never officially regent of England, Eleanor provided
the presence and continuity of legitimate royal authority in England
throughout the very difficult years of 1192–1193, when her youngest
son was threatening King Richard's government and the king was a
prisoner; she ensured that the king's ransom was paid and that he
returned safely to his kingdom.[4]

Three letters survive purportedly from Eleanor to Pope Celestine
III, asking for the pope's help in securing Richard's release, and also
pointing out that as a crusader he had been under papal protection
and the pope should now act to support him. These letters may or

may not be genuine, but the point they raised was a crucial one. In theory, crusaders, their wives, children, and possessions were under the protection of the Church during their absence. If the king of England's body and estates could not be protected by the Church when he was on crusade, whose could?[5] Crusaders much further down the social scale also had to worry about their lands being seized and their wives and families attacked, evicted by their neighbours, or even murdered during their absence or if they died on crusade, when papal protection would lapse.[6]

Records of English legal cases record some of the tragedies and crimes that took place during crusaders' absences. During the Fifth Crusade, Simon of Duffield was found guilty at York and hanged for strangling Hawisa, niece of Jordan the Tall and wife of Peter of Duffield, who had 'set out for the land of Jerusalem'; this was a premeditated attack with accomplices and theft involved, but Peter's absence would have given the criminals their opportunity.[7] In the same judicial eyre of 1218–1219, Alice of Goldsborough had accused Thomas le Dispenser of lying with her by force, but Thomas did not appear in court. The coroners gave evidence that she had not sued for rape because of the civil war in England, and Thomas had set out to the land of Jerusalem. The judgement was that she should await his return and then have the appropriate compensation.[8] In 1229 an Essex jury recalled that one Ralph Hodeng, returning from the Holy Land, had been furious (*iratus*) to find that his daughter Alditha had married one of his villeins, one Alward or Eywald, without his permission; however, it is not clear whether Alditha was forced into the marriage or took the opportunity of her father's absence to marry the man of her choice.[9] In 1222, in a dispute over land in Warwickshire, the jurors set out the case of William Trussel, who set out towards 'the land of Jerusalem' in 1190, having entrusted his wife to her father's care. Six weeks or more after his departure his wife was murdered in her father's house and her body thrown into a marl pit. William's illegitimate half-brother acknowledged that he and William's former squire were guilty of the murder and abjured the realm.[10]

William's wife should have been safe with her father, but her tragic death reminds us that even when departing crusaders made arrangements to protect their loved ones, these might not continue after their departure. The problem was greater when a crusader had died far away. When Landgrave Ludwig IV of Thuringia died on crusade in 1227, his brother Heinrich seized control of Thuringia and would not allow Ludwig's widow, Elizabeth of Hungary, her dower. The matter was not resolved until Ludwig's remains had been returned for burial.[11] Hamo LeStrange, a wealthy lord in the Anglo-Welsh March who set out in 1270 to accompany the Lord Edward on his crusade, assigned his manor of Stretton to his sister Hawise on condition that she relinquish it on his return, and assigned other manors to his brothers. But he failed to obtain the necessary royal licence to alienate his estates, which he held directly from the king. He died in the East, and his sister and brothers then had a legal battle to prove that they had been in possession of his estate; the case was not resolved until 1275.[12] When John de Verdun joined Lord Edward's crusade he arranged that his first, deceased wife Margery de Lacy's share of Ludlow would pass to his youngest son Theobald on his death, but when he died on crusade his second, surviving wife Eleanor opposed this arrangement.[13]

In November 1367 John de Moulton was in London preparing to set out on crusade to Prussia with Anthony II de Lucy. He wrote a letter to his wife Mary, his 'very dear and beloved wife', explaining the details of his departure and the money he had borrowed for the journey, and then set out the arrangements he was making for the protection of his estates during his absence, as he had previously promised her. He had invested six 'feoffees' or trustees with his estates until his return, with the intention that if he died the feoffees would ensure the estates passed smoothly to Mary for her lifetime, with their only child Maud as heir. He was sending Mary a sealed copy of his will; Mary would be one executor and John's friend John de Cobeldyke was the other. When John de Moulton and Anthony de Lucy died in Prussia the following summer these plans were put into operation, but problems arose when one of the feoffees, Richard de Welby, who had travelled to Prussia with John and returned alive, claimed that John had granted him an annuity. Mary disputed this, and the estate was only finally settled in 1384.[14]

The question remained, of course, whether John de Moulton had really gifted an annuity to Richard de Welby; as John had died, Richard's claim could not be checked. But even if it were genuine, his gift demonstrates how the rewards crusaders gave to those who had helped them on campaign could harm their family at home. In another example, Robert of Sablonnières, a knight of Champagne who died on the Third Crusade, made a bequest to the Templars without consulting his sister Luca or his wife Margaret, which dispossessed Luca of her inheritance and Margaret of her dower. The two women sued to recover their rights. Acting on behalf of her son Count Henry II, Marie of France, countess of Champagne, upheld Margaret's right to her dower (which the Templars later bought from her) and made the Templars pay Luca for her share of her brother's property.[15]

The difficulty of raising sufficient funds to pay for a crusade could also cause crusaders' families considerable problems later. For instance, in 1249 Christiana, widow of Walter le Tayllur who had died in the Holy Land, claimed from Matthew de Caddeleigh land in New Sarum (now Salisbury) as her dower, but he replied that Walter had sold it to him before he went to the East and Christiana had agreed to the sale. Hence Walter's attempt to raise money for his expedition by selling his wife's dower lands had serious results for her after his death.[16] Similarly Petronilla de Lacy, widow of Ralph de Teoni of Painscastle who died on crusade in 1239, was only partially successful in claiming her dower rights in a tenement which Ralph had leased out to a third party for six years.[17]

Crusaders who failed to make arrangements for the payment of their debts during their absence could also cause their loved ones much trouble. As a crusader's possessions were under papal protection, creditors should not be able to take them; and in 1146 Pope Eugenius III proclaimed that crusaders were also exempt from law suits against them.[18] But when a crusader died their debts were due for payment, and creditors did not wait for a bereaved relative's period of mourning to pass before seeking their dues. Earl Saher de Quenci died in 1220 on the Fifth Crusade: Saher had not assigned his wife Margery's dower to her before he set out, so royal bailiffs took chattels and grain from her lands as well as his to meet his debts.[19] Before joining the Fifth Crusade, John de Mares sold his and his wife's moveable property, leaving his wife nothing with which to pay his debts; in 1268 Margaret, widow of crusader Thomas of Dreuton, found that she did not have enough property to pay his outstanding debts.[20]

Women might also have to meet a late husband's legacies to the crusade cause. In 1222 Count Henry of Rodez, adding a codicil to his will at the Hospital of St John at Acre after the Fifth Crusade, instructed his 'lady countess' and son to 'make full repayment' to the Hospitallers for all the expenses their Order had met on his behalf; in 1364 Elizabeth Daneys, widow of one Henry Daneys, paid 12 florins he had left to the Holy Land.[21]

Unlike these two husbands Count Henry I 'the Liberal' of Champagne made it home from his crusade in 1181 after a traumatic journey—he had been captured by Turks in Anatolia and ransomed by the Byzantine emperor Manuel Komnenos—but died eight days later. His widow Marie of France made a donation to the church of St Mammès of Langres which Henry had vowed during his imprisonment to make if he was freed. She also made a donation from her dower lands on the day after his death to the Templars of Payns in Champagne, specifically for the repose of her husband's soul. It is likely that the Templars had helped Count Henry while he was overseas, perhaps helping to negotiate his ransom, and Marie was settling the debt.[22]

Sometimes women had to become prisoners themselves in order to obtain a captive relative's release. In the early 1160s the Frankish lord Walter of Beirut and two of his brothers were captured by the Muslims; his mother Maria, who was administering the lordship in their absence, negotiated their release and handed herself over as a hostage for the balance of the ransom. Walter tried to borrow money to meet it, but as no one would lend he had to sell Beirut to King Amaury of Jerusalem to obtain his mother's release.[23] In 1124 the four-year-old Iveta of Jerusalem became a prisoner in place of her father King Baldwin II of Jerusalem, who had been captured in battle in the previous year by the Turkish bey Belek Ghazi. She was freed in the following year, but as she never married later Frankish writers speculated that she had been raped, although no contemporaries said as much. In any case, she became a nun and her eldest sister Melisende, by this time queen of Jerusalem, founded an abbey at Bethany so that she could be its abbess.[24]

Administering estates

In effect, every wife who remained at home running the family estates or business while her husband was on crusade was supporting the crusade effort.[25] Women who did not accompany their husbands or menfolk on crusade were often, although not invariably, left as regents to run the family estates during the crusader's absence. Their responsibilities would depend on their social position. In the early fifteenth century the writer Christine de Pizan set out the duties that a woman entrusted with government by her absent husband should perform. A queen would preside over the royal council, listening to proposals and making decisions of government, and dealing with petitioners, while a baroness—a noblewoman below the rank of countess—would preside over her council and oversee the bailiffs, provosts, administrators and governors of her estates, working with her husband's counsellors and taking advice from wise and experienced people. She should also ensure that her fortresses were well garrisoned and know how to launch an attack and defend against one. All ladies and young women in charge of a manor should carefully administer their financial resources, be familiar with the laws relating to land holding, rents, and taxes, and oversee the management of the estate, going out in person to ensure that everything is being done as it should. They should also ensure that the household was run effectively and efficiently. Christine mentioned the Countess of Eu, 'mother of the fine young count who died on the way to Hungary' (in 1396 at the Battle of Nicopolis, on crusade against the Ottoman Turks) as a fine example of 'a wise estate manager'.[26]

There was nothing new in women acting as regents for their husbands or other male relatives when their menfolk were absent from their estates, but the crusade produced more occasions when regencies were required. We have already seen Blanche of Castile acting as official regent for her son Louis IX of France; her grandmother Eleanor of Aquitaine acted as representative of her son Richard I of England while he was absent on the Third Crusade.

Richard set out on his crusade in summer 1190. He did not appoint his mother or his younger brother John as his regent but established two leading clerics to lead the government, the bishops of Ely and Durham, but they soon quarrelled.[27] Meanwhile, Eleanor escorted Berengaria of Navarre to join Richard, who had reached Messina in Sicily.[28] She may have given Richard an update on events in England, and she then went on to see the pope on Richard's behalf. She arrived back in England from Normandy in February 1192 just in time to stop her youngest son John setting sail for France to join Philip II of France, newly returned from the East. She proceeded to take an active role in the government of England to restore the peace and prevent war breaking out between various interests.[29] This became an all but overwhelming task when news reached England in early 1193 that Richard had been captured on his way back from the crusade and was now in Duke Leopold V of Austria's prison, but Eleanor and the Great Council of England took steps for defence of the realm, repelling an attempted invasion by Eleanor's son John, and set about raising the enormous ransom demanded by the Emperor for Richard's release. Eleanor also intervened to resolve a dispute over the election of a new archbishop of Canterbury.[30] When Richard was at last released in 1194 Eleanor accompanied him back to England, then to France in 1194. Later that year she retired to the convent at Fontevrault; she would then have been aged around seventy-two.[31]

While Eleanor was protecting her son's interests in England, in France Adela of Champagne, dowager queen of France, was acting as regent for her son King Philip II, with her brother, Philip's uncle Archbishop William of Reims.[32] Two generations later, in January 1271 Edmund, son of King Henry III of England, appointed his mother Eleanor of Provence as his legal representative while he was absent on crusade with his older brother Edward, the future King Edward I of England: she would hold supreme authority over all his officials and carry out all the duties he would have performed.[33]

Mothers of crusaders held an advantage over wives as regents in that they were probably already experienced in administration of their own estates and were known and respected by officials and subordinates. Where wives acted as regents they needed to be associated with their husbands in government before the husband's departure: so Clemence of Burgundy, who acted as regent for her husband Count Robert II of Flanders during his absence on the First Crusade, had already been witnessing her husband's charters, indicating that she was involved in the process of government. She was also involved in Robert's arrangements for departure, witnessing his donations to religious houses, and settlements of outstanding disputes. This not only gave her experience of governing the county—if she was not already sufficiently experienced in administration—but also accustomed Robert's subjects to her taking a leading role in government and built up their confidence in her ability to act in a position of authority, which was essential to ensure the stability of the county during his absence.[34] Similarly, Adela of Normandy, daughter of King William I of England and Matilda of Flanders, had been associated for many years with the comital government of her husband Stephen of Blois before he set off on the First Crusade, gaining experience of the customs of the county and establishing herself in the eyes of the people of the county as a legitimate holder of authority over them.[35] Setting out on pilgrimage to the Holy Land in 1138, Count Thierry of Flanders appointed his wife Sybil of Anjou as regent: she had already acted jointly with him in his land grants, had been associated with his

government, and Thierry's own documents named her as his associate
and mentioned her prestigious lineage. Sybil's father, Count Fulk V of
Anjou, had married again after the death of her mother, Eremburge
of Maine; through this marriage to Melisende of Jerusalem he became
king of Jerusalem, so Sybil was the step-daughter of the rulers of
Jerusalem. Sybil acted as regent for her husband again when he took
part in the Second Crusade. By this time their son Baldwin was his
father's confirmed heir and his name was regularly included in his
father's documents as acting with his father. Sybil continued this practice as regent, mentioning the young Baldwin in her charters as giving
his authority to her actions.[36]

Marie of France (d. 1198), daughter of King Louis VII of France and
Eleanor of Aquitaine, and wife of Count Henry I 'the Liberal' of
Champagne, acted as regent for her husband's expedition to the East
in 1179–1181. She had managed her own dower lands before being
appointed as regent, although she had not played an overt role in his
government. But in the months just before he set out she played a
much larger role, being associated with his acts in preparation for acting as regent. As a daughter of the French king, Marie had a powerful
family network to call upon if needed to help meet any problems that
might occur during her husband's absence, but in fact she showed
herself to be a strong ruler who did not need any assistance.[37]

As regents, all these women acted with full comital authority and
with their husband's ongoing support. As regent of Flanders, Clemence
used her own seal and minted her own coins, as the counts of Flanders
normally did. She could simply have continued to issue coins in her
husband's name; the fact she produced her own indicates that her
position as ruler of the county was acknowledged by her subjects and
also suggests that she was laying the groundwork for a longer-term
political strategy in case Robert did not return from the East.[38]
Stephen of Blois's letters to his wife from the crusading field left his
audience in no doubt as to her rank and position, addressing her as
countess and instructing her to govern her lands well and deal
honourably with her children and people. In addition to the support

of her absent husband, Adela was supported as regent by leading ecclesiastics, notably her long-standing ally Bishop Ivo of Chartres.[39]

A regency should end with the successful return of the crusader. Clemence of Flanders's husband Robert returned safely and gloriously from the First Crusade as one of the conquerors of Jerusalem, and confirmed Clemence's actions during his absence.[40] Stephen of Blois returned without glory, having departed from the siege of Antioch pleading illness at a point when it appeared that the crusaders were about to be destroyed, only for their fortunes to improve after his departure and for them to capture Antioch and Jerusalem. Over three decades later, the Anglo-Norman monastic historian Orderic Vitalis imagined Adela pointing out to Stephen that it was beneath his dignity to allow people to mock him for abandoning the crusade and reminding him that it was his duty as a noble Christian warrior to take up arms as a crusader again, to save thousands and overthrow the infidel. Whether or not Adela used such words, the fact that Orderic gave her credit for inspiring her husband to take up the crusade again must have reflected her continuing reputation as a pious woman, conscious of her social and religious duty. In 1101 Stephen set out again for the East, with 100 knights equipped by Adela and again appointing Adela as his regent. Stephen died at the Battle of Ramla in 1102 and Adela continued to act as regent, but now in the name of her under-age son Stephen.[41]

Countess Marie of Champagne likewise acted as regent a second time from 1190 when her son Count Henry II set out on the Third Crusade. This was a joint regency, with Henry sending mandates from overseas for his mother to implement; Marie also associated her younger son Thibaut, Henry's heir, with her government, including his name after hers on documents she approved. This regency ended tragically with the news of Henry's death in 1197. Her son's death, added to the news of the death of her half-sister Margaret, dowager queen of Hungary, in the East, seems to have been too much for Marie to bear. She died in March 1198 and was succeeded by her second son as Thibaut III.[42]

Thibaut III took the cross to join the Fourth Crusade but then died in May 1201 before setting out. His widow Blanche of Navarre (d. 1229), younger sister of Richard I of England's wife Berengaria, would have acted as his regent during his absence on crusade; now she acted as regent for their posthumous son Thibaut IV until he came of age in 1222. In the course of her regency she successfully saw off a rival claim to the county from a crusader, her vassal Erard of Ramerupt who took the cross and went to the kingdom of Jerusalem to marry Count Henry II's daughter Philippa in order to challenge Blanche's and her son Thibaut's right to rule Champagne.[43]

As soon as Thibaut III died, his wife had lost the protection which the Church gave crusaders and hence she and her son could be threatened by a counter-claim to their county. But as we have already seen, Church protection for crusaders and their families was not always effective. During Countess Sybil of Flanders's second regency for her husband Thierry a challenge to comital authority arose when Baldwin, count of Hainaut, attacked Sybil's lands at a time when she was about to give birth and so could not retaliate. After giving birth she led an army into the count's lands 'like a lioness gnashing her teeth in wrath' as the contemporary commentator Lambert de Waterlos wrote, and 'curbed the count with her people and thrashed him in many ways', plundering and burning his villages and towns, and spreading 'her fame and glory far and wide'. Lambert depicted Sybil's actions as widely praised, and entirely justified: Count Baldwin had broken his peace treaty with Count Thierry, and attacked a crusader's wife and property during his absence. In the following year Pope Eugenius III summoned Count Baldwin and Countess Sybil, 'a woman of virtue' as Lambert described her, to a Church Council at Reims, where he made peace between them.[44]

Although papal protection and Church support for crusaders' wives, children, and property provided some protection to the women running crusaders' estates during their absence, it could not guard against the risks of crusading: the danger that a husband, brother, or son would be captured and need to be ransomed, or that he would die and leave the family to mourn—as well as possibly in financial straits. Or, perhaps, the crusader would eventually return when the family had given up all hope, bringing a different sort of problem.

After the crusade

One of the best-known images of the crusader wife, mother, or daughter is the bereaved woman mourning for the dead. By early twenty-first century standards, medieval literary depictions of grief displays by both men and women are overblown. Writers depicted grief following the literary tradition of *planctus* (lament or grieving), drawing on classical depictions of grief on the death of heroes. Descriptions of the grief expressed at the death of leading crusaders communicated to their audience the tragedy of heroic death in God's service or (conversely) the significance of a villain's death.[45]

Yet these descriptions also reflected the reality of grief and the devastating impact of death. Wives or mothers who had gone through great hardship during their husband's or son's absence, buoyed up by the hope of his return as a crusade hero, could have been utterly devastated at the news of his death. Robert of Auxerre recorded that Marie of France, countess of Champagne, who had 'ruled vigorously and courageously', grieved excessively (*nimis indoluit*) when she heard the news of the deaths in the Holy Land of her son Count Henry II and her half-sister Margaret, dowager queen of Hungary, and died soon afterwards (*nec multo post obit*).[46] The commentator and historian Philippe Mouskes wrote that Blanche of Castile was so heartbroken at the death of her husband Louis VIII (8 November 1226) 'that she would have killed herself for grief / if she had not been held back against her will'.[47] By demonstrating to his audience what a devoted wife Blanche had been, Philippe legitimized her subsequent role as regent for her eldest son Louis.

Dietrich von Apolda's late thirteenth-century *Vita* (Life) of Elizabeth of Hungary recorded that when her husband, Landgrave

Ludwig IV of Thuringia, set out on crusade he showed her a ring with the image of the lamb of God which, he said, was evidence of his life and death. When Ludwig did not return, Elizabeth worried whether her beloved husband was dead or captured, until pilgrims returning from the crusade presented her with the ring, proving his death. She cried out 'Dead! To me the world and everything that is sweet in the world is dead!'[48] Although Dietrich wrote two generations after the event, his description explained what Elizabeth did next. Although she had already been following a pious life and had founded a hospital for the poor at Eisenach, she now threw herself into a life of harsh self-denial under the direction of her confessor, Conrad of Marburg, in addition to continuing to care for the poor and sick, founding a hospital for them in Marburg. She died in 1231, aged twenty-four.[49] As with Philippe Mouskes's description of Blanche of Castile's grief, by stressing Elizabeth's devoted love for the husband she had lost, Dietrich legitimated her subsequent actions.

Over a century later, the biographer of Marshal Boucicaut reported that when the news of the crusaders' defeat at Nicopolis (25 September 1396) reached France, 'No one could describe the great grief' of those who heard that their relatives were alive in captivity and those who heard that they were dead. Fathers grieved, mothers were beside themselves. 'Nothing, however, could compare with the pitiful mourning of the wives. The countess of Nevers, that woman of virtue and prudence who loved her lord dearly, thought that her heart would break; she could entertain no hope of his return.' The countess of Eu 'thought she would die of grief', while 'the good, fair baroness of Coucy wept and lamented her good lord's death to such an extent that it was feared that heart and life would quit her; and ever afterwards, no matter who asked her, she refused to remarry. The grief never left her.'[50] This writer's description of grief brought home to his audience the significance of this defeat on individuals and on France as a whole.

It could be many months or even years before the fate of those who set out on the journey was known for certain. When Marie of France's

daughter, Marie of Champagne, set off from Flanders in 1204 to join
her husband Count Baldwin IX on the Fourth Crusade—her husband had set off in the previous year and had left her as temporary
regent, as she was pregnant with their second daughter—she headed
for Acre, expecting to find her husband there. When she arrived she
found out that Baldwin and the main body of the crusade had not
reached the Holy Land but had instead captured Constantinople,
Baldwin had been elected emperor, and she was now empress. She
died of illness before she could join him.[51]

According to the cleric Gilbert of Mons, writing his history of the
lords of Hainaut in 1197, in the early twelfth century Ida of Louvain,
countess of Hainaut, travelled to the Holy Land seeking news of her
husband Count Baldwin II, who had taken part in the First Crusade
but had vanished in 1098 after being ambushed by the Turks in the
course of a diplomatic mission to Byzantium. She was unable to dis-
cover whether he was dead or a prisoner, and after much work and
heavy expenses she returned home even more uncertain of his fate.[52]

Canon lawyers recommended that if a married person believed that
their partner was dead, they should wait a year before remarrying.[53] A
wife or husband who had remarried because they believed that their
spouse had died in the East but who later discovered that their original spouse had returned to the West would have to set aside their
second spouse, return to the first, and do penance for adultery.[54]
Noble widows who were heiresses would be pressured to remarry
quickly: for example, Robert V de Brus and Robert VI de Brus returned
safely from the Lord Edward's crusade of 1271–1272 and married the
widows of men who had died during the crusade or shortly after. On
3 May 1273 Robert V married as his second wife Christina of Ireby,
widow of Adam of Gesemuth or Jesmond (her second husband), who
had been on the crusade and died either on it or shortly afterwards;
she was heiress to estates in Cumberland and dower lands in
Northumberland. This was a highly desirable match for Robert in
terms of land, although not of status. His son Robert VI married
Marjorie, widow of Adam of Kilconquhar who had been killed at

Acre. As Marjorie was countess of Carrick in her own right, Robert now became earl of Carrick. The history of Scotland attributed to John of Fordun includes a story of Martha (sic), the daughter (sic) of Earl Adam of Carrick, meeting the young and handsome Robert when she was out hunting with her squires and maids, leading him to her castle of Turnberry, and marrying him clandestinely without King Alexander III's permission. When the king heard what had happened he confiscated the castle and its lands, but after the intervention of friends and the payment of an agreed sum of money he returned the lands and approved Robert in the lordship. Given that Marjorie was in fact not the young maiden implied by this tale but a widow, and that Earl Adam was not her father but her first husband, this story is probably a romantic invention intended to bolster the reputation of their son Robert Bruce, who was enthroned as king of Scotland in 1306.[55]

Doubts over whether or not a crusader had died had many ramifications, including land disputes and legal delays. For example, in Essex in 1229 William Luvel and his wife Cecilia lost a case over land which they claimed was Cecilia's dower (dos) when the defendants showed that they were not legally married: Cecilia's first husband was still alive in the Holy Land.[56] In 1219 at Lincoln, Muriel, widow of Adam of Croxby, sued William de Tilebroc for land which was hers but which her husband had sold. William replied that he was under no obligation to reply to the suit because he understood that Adam was safe and sound 'in the parts of Jerusalem', but Muriel declared that Adam was dead, and she had two men as witnesses who were present at his death and who witnessed his funeral.[57] The case could therefore go ahead, but only because Muriel could verify her husband's death.

Where a person's death remained unverified, imposters could take advantage of the uncertainty to claim valuable inheritances. Lambert of Ardres and Walter of Le Clud recorded an attempt to claim the lordship of Ardres in northern France almost thirty years after the reported death of Baldwin, lord of Ardres, during the Second Crusade. Walter of Le Clud, Baldwin of Ardres's illegitimate son, explained that his father had died of sickness on the way to the Holy Land and his body was buried at sea at his own request; but in 1176 some people said they had seen him at Douai. This man who claimed to be Baldwin of Ardres was dressed in sackcloth and a hair shirt, with a long white beard and white hair, followed a religious lifestyle, and engaged in good works. When the current lord of Ardres—Count Baldwin of Guines, who had married Baldwin of Ardres's niece and heiress Christine—was told that his wife's uncle had returned from the dead, he refused to believe the story. Walter of le Clud was also doubtful that his father was alive, but went to meet the claimant, taking with him some of his more senior friends who had once known his father well. Despite a long conversation, neither Walter nor the people with him could be certain whether this was the genuine Baldwin of Ardres or not. They had hardly got back to report to the count when they heard that the alleged Baldwin had left taking a great deal of money with him. So then, Walter said, they knew he was a vagabond and not the real Baldwin. As Countess Christine was young (*iuvencula*) at the time of her marriage and Count Baldwin was probably a teenager, it is unlikely that either of them could remember what the elder Baldwin looked like.[58]

Count Baldwin IX of Flanders, VI of Hainaut, and first Latin emperor of Constantinople, was captured by the Bulgarians in 1205 and never seen again by his people, having presumably died in a Bulgarian prison. Baldwin was succeeded in Flanders and Hainaut by his elder daughter Jeanne. In 1224 rumours spread in the Tournai region that Count Baldwin would return. The following year some of the Flemish nobles produced an old man who they said was Count Baldwin. They dressed him in royal robes and led him through all the towns of Flanders in triumph, as cheering crowds welcomed him. 1225 was a year of famine in Flanders and Hainaut, and it was largely the urban poor who supported the false Baldwin, although foreign princes, notably the government of King Henry III of England, also acknowledged him as genuine.[59] According to the Minstrel of Reims, writing some thirty-five years later, the false count tried to capture Countess Jeanne, but warned by a friend she escaped in the nick of time riding a baggage animal, and took refuge in Mons-en-Hainaut. She appealed to her cousin King Louis VIII of France for help and Louis summoned the pretended count to his court, where he was questioned by Brother Guérin the Hospitaller, bishop of Senlis and Louis's chief advisor. When the 'count' could not even remember in which town he had married his wife Marie of Champagne (Jeanne's mother), he was revealed as a fraud and fled from the court. Six months later he was recognized, arrested, and handed over to Countess Jeanne, who put him in the pillory and then hanged him. The Minstrel of Reims was convinced he was an imposter, but in Flanders many people continued to believe in him and called Jeanne a parricide.[60] Countess Jeanne was fortunate in having the support of a powerful relative, the king of France; without his support to challenge the claimant she might have been forced to surrender her county to the imposter.

Financing crusaders

In addition to indirectly supporting the crusade effort through supporting crusading members of their family and running family estates during their absence, women could make a significant direct contribution to the crusade effort through their financial resources. Experts in canon law assumed that a woman should normally redeem her crusading vow by paying a sum of money to purchase a crusade indulgence so that a man could go in her place, unless she was wealthy and could be accompanied on her crusade by a retinue of soldiers.[61] Alternatively she might equip armed men herself and send them to the Holy Land in her place, as in 1291 the bishop of Norwich instructed Eva, widow of Robert Tiptoft or Tibetot, to do as she was too ill to go in person.[62]

By the late twelfth century the ecclesiastical authorities followed up those who had taken crusade vows to ensure that they fulfilled them in one way or another. These enquiries revealed that both men and women took vows which they failed to complete or redeem. Only two of the reports ordered by Archbishop Hubert Walter of Canterbury (archbishop 1193–1205) of those with outstanding crusade vows survive, from Cornwall and Lincolnshire: no women were included in the list of twenty-nine with outstanding vows in Lincolnshire, but the forty-seven listed in Cornwall included at least two and possibly five women (including a 'wife of Portjoia' and a Hawis of Trevisac). Again, an English episcopal inquiry of the late thirteenth century asked whether any, male or female (*intestati vel intestate*), of those who had taken the cross had died intestate without carrying out their vow (as they should have left money in their will to redeem their vow), presuming that women as well as men would have taken the cross and made a financial contribution. The money raised from this investigation was intended to finance King Edward I's crusade plans.[63]

The bulk of money raised from the laity for the crusades was raised through the organised selling of crusade indulgences. This procedure was first described in detail by the English monk Matthew Paris in the 1240s. In around 1241 the Dominican and Franciscan friars came to England with papal authorization to preach the crusade for the liberation of the Holy Land. They promised complete remission of sins to everyone who took the cross (the indulgence), but on the next day or the day after the friars absolved them from their vow and in return they gave some money, according to their means, to help the Holy Land. Many people took the cross on these terms. To encourage the English to give, the friars said that this money would be taken to Earl Richard of Cornwall, who was in the Holy Land on crusade at that time, and they showed a charter from him stating this. Matthew wrote that the friars gave the cross to 'the old and sickly, women, the feeble, and little children' in return for cash, and 20,000 marks were raised for the earl's crusade, but whether the money ever reached the earl was not known. Matthew complained later that the same thing happened in 1249.[64]

Matthew's complaints suggest that women were eager to purchase these indulgences. The indulgences sold in 1383 to support the controversial proposed crusade of Henry Despenser, bishop of Norwich, in Flanders were certainly much sought after and the Leicester monk Henry Knighton recorded that many noble ladies and other women bought them. Some paid for them with jewellery; one lady contributed 100 pounds, others more, others less; and many paid more than they could afford to gain absolution from sin for themselves and their friends.[65] These indulgences could also offer additional spiritual benefits. During the campaign to raise money for the 1429 crusade against the Hussites, Stamford nunnery purchased a 'confessional letter', which authorised a priest of the buyer's own choice to give confession and absolution when the buyer wished.[66]

Crusade indulgences were also used to raise money for crusade-related projects which did not require additional personnel but did need money. Between 1409 and 1411 the Hospitallers built a fortress at Bodrum on the south-west coast of what is now Turkey. In 1409 the Pisan pope Alexander V issued an indulgence in support of this enterprise, which would be available for five years: anyone who purchased one of these indulgences would have the right to appoint a confessor who could grant plenary remission of sins at the hour of death—that is, cancelling all their debt due to God for their sins when they were on their deathbed. Purchasers were in effect purchasing insurance against Hell. His successor John XXIII renewed this offer in 1412. The sale of these indulgences was administered by the Hospitallers themselves, who gave purchasers a written and illuminated document with a special seal to record their contribution. Of the three surviving documents, two were purchased by married couples: one was bought by John and Agnes Groby and their three children in 1413; another was purchased in 1414 by Sir William Fitzhugh and his wife Margery.[67] Perhaps less showy documents were also available for those who made smaller contributions.

The popes continued to issue indulgences as a means of fundraising for crusades, and the fact that some of the sins which could be absolved were solely applicable to women suggests that women were eager to buy. Sixtus IV's indulgence for war against the Turks issued in

1476–1478 could among other things absolve women whose heirs were sons conceived in adultery, and give permission to pregnant women to eat milk products and eggs at times when they were normally prohibited for religious reasons, for example during Lent. From the 1470s printed indulgences were produced with blanks where the purchaser's details could be filled in, which may have made indulgences cheaper to produce and easier for would-be purchasers to buy. On 13 December 1376 Henry and Katherine Langley of London purchased one of the first of these printed in England; before the end of March 1480 Simon Mountfort and his wife Emma bought a printed indulgence to help finance the defence of Rhodes against the Turks, and on 18 April 1481 John and Katherine Frisden bought indulgences at Oxford to give financial help to the Hospitallers after their successful defence of Rhodes in the previous year.[68]

Women and men who had vowed to go on pilgrimage could also redeem their vow by making a donation to the Church, just as if they were redeeming a crusade vow, and some of these payments went to support crusades or Christians in the Holy Land. In 1275 Archbishop Walter of York allowed Helewyse Palmer and her daughter Isabel to commute a vow of pilgrimage to the shrine of St James of Compostela into a donation to aid the Holy Land. Bishops also imposed fines in aid of the Holy Land on those revealed to have committed sexual sins. In 1275 a knight in the diocese of York named as S. Constable who had committed adultery with Katherine wife of the knight John Danthorpe undertook to pay a hundred pounds sterling to aid the Holy Land if he did it again.[69] In the diocese of Rochester, Kent (England) in 1335, those guilty of sexual sins were given a choice between performing public penance in their local church or making a donation in aid of Jerusalem.[70]

Women also helped to finance crusades by buying or selling land, making loans to crusaders, or agreeing to sales to third parties. Saura de St Jean, a member of a noble family from Savenès in Gascony, helped to finance the journey of two of her brothers to Jerusalem: her brother Dodo sold his share of the family inheritance to her and her son Bertrand, while her brother Lanfranc pledged his land to her and her son in return for a loan.[71] At Lincoln in 1218 Edith of Navenby successfully defended her right to land she held in pledge from a crusader for as long as he was 'in the parts of Jerusalem'; presumably she had lent him money in return.[72] We have already seen that some of these land transactions worked out badly for the women who agreed to sell their land to finance a crusader, when wives were left without assets to support themselves and their families or to pay their husband's debts.

Women also made donations directly to the crusades. The women who enthusiastically took the cross at Genoa in 1216 in response to the preaching of James of Vitry would have had disposable income and liquid assets of their own: of the surviving wills from Genoa from the period of the Fifth Crusade, fifteen contain legacies for the crusade, and ten of these were women's wills.[73] In 1307, Doña Teresa Gil made her will in Valladolid in Castile, far from the frontier with the Muslims. In addition to other legacies, she left 100 *maravedés* to the crusade (*la crusada*), the same sum that she bequeathed to the poor of the city of Zamora and to some of her servants.[74] But such bequests were only possible for women who had control of their own resources, which in some regions of Catholic Europe was only the case for unmarried women and widows.

Financial support for the crusade could also take the form of donation to one of the military religious orders that supported the crusade, dedicated to the care of Christian pilgrims and defence of Christendom. The most famous and influential were the Templars and the Hospitallers, both originally set up in Jerusalem and with a property portfolio that spanned most of Latin Christian Europe; but from the time of the Third Crusade there was also the Teutonic Order, founded in the Holy Land but with the bulk of its lands in Germany and the Baltic region, and many regional orders founded to support regional crusading movements, especially in the Iberian Peninsula. There was also the Order of St Lazarus, which was founded in the Holy Land to care for lepers but took up a military role by the mid-thirteenth century.

Women gave valuable donations and patronage to these institutions. Queens Urraca of Castile and Teresa of Portugal endowed the Hospitallers and Templars, respectively. In 1229 Urraca's descendent Berenguela of Castile donated her castle and town of Bolaños to the Order of Calatrava.[75] In 1187 Queen Sancha of Aragon founded a house of Hospitaller sisters and brothers at Sigena, and chose it for her burial. Her husband King Alfonso II also endowed it, while acknowledging that the new monastery was under his wife's control, and three of their daughters were associated with the house, although only one, Dulce, took vows. The house became a royal mausoleum, with Sancha and her son Pere II buried there. The foundation demonstrated the commitment of the ruling family of Aragon to holy war against the Muslims in Spain and their interest in Jerusalem.[76] The donation of Aconbury Priory by Margaret de Lacy (née Braose) to the Hospitallers at some point between 1216 and 1233 may have been prompted by the de Lacy family interests in the crusades as well as the good relations between the Hospitallers and Margaret's husband Walter de Lacy in Ireland.[77]

The Templars' first substantial properties in England were given to them by a woman, Countess Matilda of Boulogne, wife of King Stephen of England and niece of the first two Latin rulers of Jerusalem, Godfrey de Bouillon and King Baldwin I. As a member of the ruling family of Jerusalem it was entirely appropriate that Matilda gave this Jerusalem-based order generous gifts of land, at Cressing in Essex and Cowley in Oxfordshire.[78] In 1156 Margaret, countess of Warwick, endowed the Templars with Llanmadoc in the Gower in Wales.[79] The list of the Hospitallers' and Templars' donors in England, Scotland and Wales, drawn up in 1434 by Brother John Stillingflete of the Hospital of St John in England included Countess Matilda and many other women donors.[80] Women could also become members or associates of these institutions. Although they did not fight, they provided a support role of prayer and sometimes nursing care.[81] The Templars and Hospitallers had an organized support group, the frary, whose members were exempted from a seventh of their penance in return for annual donations and included men, women and married couples. The Order of St Lazarus produced formal letters of confraternity (literally brotherhood, but including sisters) for its donors that set out the spiritual benefits they would receive in return for their donation; and by the early sixteenth century it was also producing printed versions. Like crusade indulgences, these attracted donations from men and women from all social classes, commonly by husbands and wives together.[82]

Women also donated to religious orders that gave charitable support to captives and former captives from the crusades and negotiated ransoms for those captured by the other side: such as the Trinitarian Order, which was founded at the end of the twelfth century and operated in the Iberian Peninsula as well as the Middle East.[83] In Scotland Cristiana de Brus, countess of Dunbar, donated to and may have been the founder of the Trinitarian house at Dunbar, between 1240 and 1248, while Cristiana widow of Roger Mubray founded the Trinitarian house at Houston in East Lothian around 1270.[84] The Hospitallers were also involved in the freeing of captives. In May 1201 in the kingdom of Jerusalem Christine, daughter of the late Roger of Haifa, gave a casal (a village) to the Order of the Hospital of St John of Jerusalem, noting as a motivation for her gift the fact that the Hospital gave immense benefits and alms to the sick, poor, and captives, and also that she would be made a *consoror* or associate sister of the Order in return for her gift.[85] In May 1212 Count Ferrand and Countess Jeanne of Flanders and Hainaut promised the Hospitallers 700 *livres* (pounds) of Valencinnes if Gerard de Mons, currently a captive 'of the pagans' (presumably the Muslims in the Holy Land) was freed by next Christmas.[86] In February 1214 Blanche of Navarre, countess of Champagne, in her own name as Countess Palatine of Troyes but with the approval of her son Count Thibaut IV, confirmed an agreement that her 'dear and faithful woman' Rosceline of La Ferté had made with the Hospitallers: if they could free her son Guiard, who was currently held captive by the Muslims, and bring him to the city of Acre, she would give the Hospital rents worth ten *livres* a year from land she held from the countess.[87]

Spiritual support: prayer, holy women, and saints

All women could offer spiritual support to crusaders through participation in organized prayers or liturgies, processions, and fasting in preparation for an expedition. When the news of the loss of the relic of the True Cross to Saladin at the Battle of Hattin on 4 July 1187 reached Pope Gregory VIII he not only issued a call to crusade but also ordered penance and fasting for five years, and set up a special Order of Mass to be recited at nones from Advent to Christmas. In the following year, after Saladin captured Jerusalem and conquered most of the crusader states in the East, Pope Clement III ordered fasting and instructed all churches, including parish churches, throughout Christendom to recite Psalm 78 (beginning: 'O God, the heathen have come into Your inheritance') after the Lord's Prayer, asking God to free Jerusalem and Christians who had been captured by the Muslims. Only the priests would perform the prayers, but the whole congregation would hear them; and everyone was enjoined to fast. There were further public displays of devotion and petition to God to help the Third Crusade: in the kingdom of France in August 1191 the regents, Adela of Champagne, the king's mother, and her brother the archbishop of Reims, the king's uncle, organized a ceremony at Saint-Denis to pray for the liberation of Jerusalem and the health of the king and his army—who by this time were on their way back from Acre, although this would not yet have been known in France. Holy relics were displayed on the altar while the Christian faithful watched, wept, raised hands to Heaven in supplication and prayed. Pope Celestine III and Pope Innocent III renewed their predecessors' instructions to include a *clamor* or appeal on behalf of the Holy Land daily during the mass, not only in religious houses but in all public churches, so that the whole Christian community took part: men, women, and children.[88]

In 1212, in preparation for King Alfonso VIII of Castile's expedition against the Muslims in Spain, Pope Innocent III commanded that there should be liturgical processions in which men and women formed separate contingents and prayed to God for His support for the campaign. Innocent's encyclical for the Fifth Crusade, *Quia Maior* (1213), ordered monthly liturgical processions on the same lines, in which men and women were to pray for God to liberate the Holy Land from the Muslims. Men and women would take part in daily prayers at mass and almsgiving for the crusade. Among the laity, women were given a distinct role from men, and while this separation was a symbol of the population's humility and penance, it also underlined that women had an equal role to play with men in spiritual purification of Christian society. In 1217, in support of the Fifth Crusade, Pope Honorius III repeated Innocent's instructions for monthly lay processions in France and Germany.[89] Such prayers and processions in support of crusades became the norm throughout Latin Christendom, for individual crusades and in response to any news of Muslim triumphs in the Holy Land, although different regions adopted slightly different wording and practices.

Even after the fall of Acre to the Mamluks in 1291, the papacy continued to call for special prayers to be said, to defend the kingdom of Armenia and to assist the Hospitallers fighting the Muslims. In 1309 Pope Clement V told the clergy to insert prayers asking God to defend Christians from pagans into every mass, so that every time a Catholic Christian attended mass they would be reminded that Christianity was under threat from non-Christians. In effect, Clement was making crusading and fighting against pagans an essential part of being a Christian.[90] This religious warfare through prayer intensified during the fifteenth century in the face of the growing threat from the Ottoman Turks in eastern Europe. New services of the mass were developed which focussed on saving Europe from non-Christians, with prayers begging God for help against the Turks and arguing why

God should help His people. These 'war masses' blamed the Turks' victories on the Christian people's sin, expressed penitence, pleaded with God for mercy, and asked God that the enemy might be vanquished in the power of His name. Much use was made of Old Testament narrative (including the story of Judith who slew the Assyrian general Holofernes with her own hand) and rhetoric against God's enemies. These masses also referred to the End Times and implied that the coming of the Turks was a sign of the beginning of the End. The effect was to impress on Catholic Christians that the war against the Ottomans was a spiritual war against evil.[91]

This daily repetition to ordinary Catholic Christians of the importance of the crusade was reflected in references to Jerusalem or the Holy Land in the regulations of charitable guilds (or gilds) in England. These were self-help societies founded for mutually beneficial purposes, such as supporting their members who fell on hard times and arranging the funerals of members who died. The ordinances of the gild of the Tailors of Lincoln, founded in 1328, stated that 'if anyone wishes to make pilgrimage to the Holy Land of Jerusalem each brother and sister shall give him a penny'. The Fraternity of St Christopher in Norwich, which was founded in 1384 and included both 'brothers' and 'sisters', began each meeting with a prayer for the state of the Holy Church, the peace of the land, the pope of Rome and his cardinals, for the patriarch of Jerusalem, for the Holy Land and the Holy Cross, and a prayer that God in His might and mercy would bring it out of heathen power and into the rule of the Holy Church. The Fraternity of the Assumption of the Blessed Virgin Mary at Wiggenhall on the Ouse, also founded in 1384, began meetings with similar prayers, beseeching God that Jesus Christ would bring the Holy Land into Christ's power. This fraternity also had both male and female members, with half the twenty-eight members listed at the end of the roll being women.[92]

Moving from the general to the particular: individual holy women also supported crusading, either by advising crusaders, as did Hildegard of Bingen or Birgitta of Sweden, or campaigning for a crusade, like

Catherine of Siena or Joan of Arc, or by donation or prayer support. Elizabeth of Hungary, wife of Ludwig IV (d. 1227), Landgrave of Thuringia, left the hospital that she had founded for the poor sick at Marburg to the Hospital of St John of Jerusalem. However, her brother-in-law Conrad, who succeeded Ludwig as Landgrave, had the hospital at Marburg transferred to the Teutonic Order, which he patronized and later joined. Conrad and the Grand Master of the Teutonic Order, Hermann von Salza, campaigned for Elizabeth's canonization, and the Teutonic Order venerated her as one of its patron saints, envisaging her supporting the Order in Heaven through her direct intercession with Christ.[93]

Over a century and a half later, Dorothea of Montau (d. 1394), recluse and mystic in the Teutonic Order's Prussian lands, had much in common with her near-contemporaries Birgitta of Sweden and Catherine of Siena, deploying her prophetic utterances to criticize eminent figures and promote the crusade, although unlike them she did not promote a specific campaign. Like Birgitta she was married, she gave birth to nine children, and she venerated Birgitta's example; like Catherine, she received communion daily and would have preferred to subsist solely on the wafer representing Christ's body. Like Catherine, her family was reasonably well off but not noble: her father was an engineer from Holland in the Netherlands who had emigrated to Prussia, probably in response to the generous conditions of settlement offered by the Teutonic Order in Prussia to farmers with experience of draining swamps and building dams, who could help to develop the territories the Order had won. Montau (now Mątowy Wielkie in Poland) was a new village in the Vistula Delta founded in the 1340s as part of the Order's development of the Vistula waterway.[94]

The seventh-born child of a large family, Dorothea was married at the age of 16 or 17 to a much older man, Adalbrecht of Gdansk, a skilled swordsmith. According to Brother Johannes von Marienwerder's biography—which set out to emphasize Dorothea's devotion to Christ and play down her worldly interests—Dorothea spent more time in church than caring for her husband or children, praying and hearing masses from early each morning until beyond noon.[95] After her husband's death she dedicated herself to a life of prayer in the parish church of Gdansk, where—according to testimonies taken during the canonization process following her death—her pious devotion attracted some hostile comment from two priests, who regarded Dorothea's spiritual experiences and visions as a sign of heresy. As one witness, Metza Hugische of Gdansk, later explained to the investigators gathering evidence for Dorothea's canonization as a saint: 'because the said Dorothea narrated things to the said priests in confession which were completely unknown to people, and also on account of Dorothea's excessive and unaccustomed devotion to divine offices and divine works which was beyond other people's, they believed she was off her head'.[96] Dorothea was investigated for heresy but cleared, and in 1391 she moved to the church at Marienwerder (now Kwidzyn), where with the support of a priest of the Teutonic Order, Johannes of Marienwerder, she was able to have a cell built where she lived as a hermit.

Although it was the support of the Teutonic Order which won her the hermit's cell at Marienwerder, Dorothea was very critical of one Grand Master of the Teutonic Order, Conrad von Wallenrot, who had tried to have her removed from the church at Marienwerder. Dorothea foretold his death 'and so, as she predicted, it came about', and stated after his death that she had seen his soul being tortured in hell.[97] On the other hand, she gave her spiritual support to the Teutonic Order's campaigns against the Lithuanians. Brother Conrad von Lichtenstein, Grand Commander of the Teutonic Order, explained to the canonization enquiry in June 1404 that she had foretold the success of a campaign by Brother Conrad von Jungingen Grand Master of the Order. According to the Grand Commander, she had foretold that the Grand Master would have to pass through four perils during that campaign: at sea, on an island, before a castle, and in a wood, and that if he trusted in his army he would not come through safely but if he trusted in God he would escape without loss. It had all come to pass as the Blessed Dorothea had said, and he believed that the Grand Master had escaped these perils through her intercession.[98]

Leading members of the Teutonic Order were well aware of the prestige that association with a holy woman could give to their Order and its vocation of holy war in Prussia—especially as that holy war was now of dubious validity since the 1386 marriage between Queen Jadwiga of Poland and King Jagiełło of Lithuania and the official conversion of Lithuania to Christianity. In September 1395, five leading officials of the Teutonic Order wrote to Pope Boniface IX in support of Dorothea's canonization. Beginning with a quotation from the Old Testament Song of Songs, they declared that holy women—wives, widows, and virgins—were a '*novus genus milicie*', a new sort of knighthood, ordained by the Lord Jesus. When male warriors were exhausted and defeated, these holy women, strengthened by the *stigmata* in imitation of Christ's death, formed a line of fortresses against 'flesh, blood, and the princes of shadows'—that is, demonic powers. Defended by her shield of suffering, stained by the blood of Christ, Dorothea was the Order's own 'strenuous knight' in this body of fellow-knights.[99] It would not have been lost on the pope that the 'new sort of knighthood' had been the description used by St Bernard of Clairvaux in the 1130s for the original military-religious Order, the Templars.[100]

As well as supporting living holy women, crusaders venerated female saints. First among them was Christ's mother the Blessed Virgin Mary, intercessor for all Christians. Mary was invoked as patron of Livonia and of the Teutonic Order, appearing as a 'warrior goddess' with the missionizing priest Henry of Livonia describing her as 'a cruel wreaker of vengeance on her enemies'.[101] Although elsewhere she was not usually depicted in such martial terms, nevertheless she was the outstanding female patron of the crusades. John of Joinville recorded that a squire who fell overboard during the voyage back to France after Louis IX's first crusade ascribed his survival to Our Lady of Vauvert: she had held him up by the shoulders until he was rescued. John had a picture of this miracle painted on to the walls of his chapel at Joinville and depicted in the windows of his chapel at Blécourt.[102] On a larger scale, the various accounts of the Hospitallers' defeat of the Ottoman siege of Rhodes in 1480 gave different versions of a vision of the Holy Cross, the Blessed Virgin Mary, and St John the Baptist (the Order's saintly patron), which brought the Hospitallers victory at a crucial point of the siege.[103] The story reinforced the Order's image as a holy order which fought God's wars, for the Virgin and the Baptist would not have helped them if their cause was not just and holy. Ironically, the Virgin Mary was also invoked by the crusaders' enemies, such as the Rus', opponents of the Teutonic Order in the Battle on Lake Chud in April 1242, which the *Chronicle of Novgorod* described as a victory 'to the glory of the Holy Mother of God', while the heretic Cathars also regarded Mary as having an important positive role.[104]

Mary was not the only female saint venerated by the crusaders. The military religious orders claimed a number of female saints as patrons, probably because they presented valuable spiritual examples of long suffering and martyrdom.[105] The Fourth Crusade's sack of Constantinople brought many saints' relics to Europe and into the hands of Latin Christians. It is possible that the Templars' relic of Saint Euphemia, held at their new fortress of Castle Pilgrim in the later thirteenth century, had been taken from Constantinople in 1204.[106] The relic of St Helen of Athyra, venerated at the cathedral of Troyes in Champagne in the thirteenth century, was certainly looted from Constantinople in 1204 by Garnier de Traînel, bishop of Troyes, and reached Troyes in 1215. Although Garnier had also acquired other relics of more famous saints for his cathedral, they were only portions of saints' bodies, whereas the body of St Helen of Athyar was complete. By introducing and promoting her cult as a miracle-working saint who worked cures among her devotees, Bishop Garnier was able to raise funds to rebuild and enlarge the cathedral after the fire of 1188 and storm damage of 1228.[107]

Female Biblical figures were also widely used to promote crusading. Pope Gregory IX's bull or decree of 1234 promoting the crusade began with the words '*Rachel suum videns*' (Rachel, beholding her [creator]), as Rachel was identified in the Old Testament prophecies of Jeremiah as a mother-figure for all Israel who weeps for her children's sufferings (Jeremiah 31:15). In Pope Gregory's bull, Rachel was the Church, weeping over the state of the Holy Land, which had been conquered by Muslims in 1187–1189 and not yet recovered by a crusade. The bull depicts the city of Jerusalem itself as a woman, not unreasonably as the image of Jerusalem as a woman with a relationship to God was familiar from the Old Testament. But here Jerusalem was a woman at her weakest, helpless among her enemies, to encourage Latin Christians to support the crusade in some way: through action, financial donation, or prayer.[108]

The intercession of holy women and other female figures was important for crusaders not only in life but also after death. Let us now consider women's support for crusading after the crusade was over.

5

After the Crusade

Memory and Imagination

After a crusade, crusaders and their families would certainly remember their own part in the crusade and the impact that the crusade had had on their lives; but they would also want to ensure that future generations would be aware of what had happened, either to glorify their deeds or as a warning for the future. Women certainly played a role in this, although in most cases we do not know who initiated an event or monument in memorial of the crusades.

For example, who decided that a performance of the *Pas Saladin*, a late thirteenth or early fourteenth century epic poem about a battle between the crusaders and Saladin during the Third Crusade, should be the subject of a performance in honour of Isabelle of Bavaria's arrival at Paris for her wedding to King Charles VI of France in 1389? Or, indeed, who chose the *Pas Saladin* as the subject of a mural at Valenciennes castle in Hainaut in 1375–1376, or the story of Godfrey de Bouillon, hero of the First Crusade, as the subject of the fifteen tapestries at Pleshey Castle in Essex in the late fourteenth century?[1] As the crusade became an integral part of chivalric culture, the choice of a crusading subject for a performance or for art need not have been a decision to actively remember crusading but simply an expression of interest in all things chivalric. That said, sometimes it is possible to identify the initiator of patronage or memorialization, and the fact that sometimes the initiator was a woman is yet further evidence that women formed an integral part of that chivalric culture and did not regard the crusade as something separate from their own life experience.

Memory and memorialization are different things. Memory is what we ourselves remember; memorialization is the means of commemorating events in the past which we ourselves did not necessarily experience, using ritual and objects to ensure that these events are not forgotten by society. What crusaders and their families actually remembered and what they memorialized would not necessarily be the same thing, as they might also choose to omit certain events from memorialization. In addition, future generations of family members and wider society would amend this 'memory' to meet new social and cultural expectations and needs.[2]

Memorials and foundations

As washing the body of the deceased and clothing it for burial was traditionally a woman's task, we could expect that women would be closely involved in the immediate commemoration of the crusader dead.[3] Occasionally the written record does indeed record that a woman organized the burial of a crusader, as John of Joinville recorded that the lady of Sidon (Margaret de Reynel) received the remains of her cousin Walter IV of Brienne when King Louis IX negotiated the release of his bones from the Egyptians. She then had them buried at the Hospital of St John in Acre at her own expense, in a grand ceremony at which she paid for each knight to present a candle and a silver *denier* (penny), and the king to offer a candle and a gold bezant.[4] John did not describe the tomb, but presumably the lady of Sidon also paid for a memorial for her cousin.

The nature and extent of such commemoration would depend on the woman's own resources. Royal and noble women founded and patronized religious houses where crusaders could be commemorated and also commissioned tombs or memorials for former crusaders within them. Such structures not only acted as a memorial for the family and enhanced family identity but also were valuable for the religious house where they were placed, exalting the house through glorifying past donors, and establishing a permanent connection between the family and the community of the house, with hopes of further benefits in the future. The memorials were a focus for commemorative acts to benefit the crusader, such as prayers and masses for the crusader's soul. For the greatest spiritual benefit they should be situated in the most holy part of the church, in the middle of the choir or in the sanctuary as close as possible to the altar, where they would be hallowed by priestly prayer and the offering of spiritual sacrifice in the mass.

In assessing women's contribution to these memorials, however, we have the problem that in most cases it is unclear who was responsible for their design. We might assume that family members paid for a tomb, perhaps with the assistance of the religious house where it was placed, but this was not always the case. In some of the cases set out below tombs were prepared in advance by the person who intended to be buried there, with the family then making a contribution to the decoration or inscription after the user's death.

For example, in the 1170s Count Henry I the Liberal of Champagne constructed his own memorial within his new basilica of St-Étienne in Troyes: a magnificent metalwork tomb in a private chapel which would be watched over by the secular canons or priests who served the basilica. Within the tomb lay a bronze effigy of the count, visible through open arches on each side and the ends of the tomb, as if the count were a saint whose body would be venerated by the faithful. This was the image of himself that Henry wished to project to the world and his successors. However, two of the inscriptions on the tomb were inscribed after Henry's death and were probably commissioned by his widow Countess Marie from Simon Aurea Capra, an eminent Latin poet from whom Henry had earlier commissioned epitaphs. They refer to his pilgrimage to Jerusalem, his foundation of the church, his faith, hope, devotion, and piety, and compare him to the sun, which shone over his realm but has now left it in darkness.[5]

Blanche of Navarre, widow of Henry I's younger son Count Thibaut III of Champagne, who died just as he was about to set out to join the Fourth Crusade, commissioned a metalwork tomb for her husband placed directly behind his father's tomb. Unlike his father, Thibaut's effigy lay on top of the tomb; he wore a pilgrim's satchel over his right shoulder, a crusader's cross on the right breast of his cloak, and carried a pilgrim's staff in his clasped hands, symbols of his crusader vow. Inscriptions around the tomb (presumably dictated by Blanche) declared that he had been 'intent on making amends for the injuries of the Cross and the land of the Crucified' and had been 'seeking the terrestrial city' but instead 'he finds the celestial one'. Statuettes of his closest relatives in silver or bronze stood below in the arches around the tomb: at the head stood Philip Augustus, king of France (Thibaut's cousin, son of his father's sister Adela of Champagne), with Thibaut's brother Count Henry II, ruler of Jerusalem, to the left of Thibaut's head and his wife's brother King Sancho VII of Navarre to the right. His own mother, father, and brother stood further down the left-hand side, while his children, wife, and sister were on the right. Blanche's statuette held a model of the tomb in its hand and faced Count Henry I's tomb; the inscription over the statuette declared her lineage from the kings of Navarre and her burning love for the dead count. At the foot of the tomb was a statuette of King Richard I of England, who was husband of Blanche's sister Berengaria and a son of Thibaut's grandmother Eleanor of Aquitaine. Through this tomb Blanche commemorated her own and her husband's family as well as her husband himself, reminding all who saw it of his legitimate title to the county and his glorious relations—most of whom were, like him, crusaders.[6]

Blanche's own tomb at her foundation at Argensolles near Soissons, dating from around 1252 (over twenty years after her death) and probably commissioned by her son Thibaut IV, was less visually stunning but possibly more durable, being constructed from limestone rather than metalwork, with a recumbent effigy wearing a veil on her head and a long dress belted with a bag hanging from the belt, her mantle visible over her shoulders, and hands folded in prayer. Figures (angels?) stood on either side of her head, while her feet rested on the end of the tomb without any of the small animals which sometimes appeared on contemporary tombs. In its material and design it was more like her sister Berengaria's tomb (of which more below) than her husband's.[7]

Daughters commissioned crusaders' tombs as well as wives. It was probably Jeanne of Mayenne, third daughter of Juhel III of Mayenne (d. 1220), who commissioned her father's tomb between 1258 and 1264. Juhel had taken part in the Third Crusade and in 1204 founded the Cistercian abbey of Fontaine-Daniel. The tomb, placed in the sanctuary of the church, represented a chest with a figure of Juhel lying recumbent on top with eyes closed and hands together in prayer. His sword and shield were at his side, and on the four sides of the chest were the shields of his family network. The whole was covered with enamelled copper plaques in bright colours. The epitaph on the tomb, written in fine Latin verse, asked those who read it to pray that on the Day of Judgement Juhel would reign with Christ, reminded readers that Juhel had founded the abbey, and set out his virtues of goodness, fame, and generosity. In commissioning this tomb of her crusader father, Jeanne glorified the legacy of her family, which by the time the tomb was created was in decline. The abbey also gained a prestigious monument to their founder, which emphasized and maintained the mutually beneficial connection between the patronal family and the abbey.[8]

Some queens and noblewomen involved in the crusades commissioned their own tombs before their death. Shajar al-Durr commissioned her own magnificent tomb in Cairo, which would have been paid for from the gifts she had received from her husband Sultan Ṣāliḥ and any bequests she received from him, as by rights as his widow she should have inherited a portion of his estate. The tomb was part of a larger complex including a mosque, madrasa, baths, palace, and garden, although the complex remained unfinished at the time of her murder in 1257. It was positioned just across the street from the tombs of revered members of the Prophet Muhammad's family and the twelfth-century shrine of one of the daughters of 'Ali, the Prophet's cousin; perhaps Shajar hoped to attract the attention of visitors to those holy places or that her tomb would benefit from their close vicinity. Within the tomb, the mihrab (the semi-circular niche indicating the direction of the Kaaba in Mecca, which Muslims should face when praying) is lined in golden mosaic with a tree of life in green, black, and red with mother of pearl, a reference to her own name, as Shajar al-Durr means 'tree of pearls'. Friezes with inscriptions included some Quranic inscriptions taken from abandoned Fatimid palaces, representing the triumph of orthodox Sunni Islam over the heretic Shi'ite branch of Islam which the Fatimids had followed. Other insciptions, newly commissioned, not only praised Shajar in traditional terms for her modesty and chastity and the fact she was the mother of Sultan Ṣāliḥ's son but also referred to her 'glory', her authority, and stated that she 'is assisted by God and victorious in the succession of nights and days, through Muhammad, his family and companions, the generous, the pure, and the honourable'.[9]

Before creating her own tomb, Shajar had commissioned a commemorative tomb for her late husband, Sultan Ṣāliḥ, who had died while opposing the invading crusaders. This must have been completed very quickly, as it was not begun until after the murder of Tūrān-Shāh on 2 May 1250, and Ṣāliḥ's body was interred there on 25 October 1250. It was attached to the madrasa that Ṣāliḥ had built in Cairo. Like Shajar's later tomb for herself, the building included material from older buildings including (probably) the palace which was previously on the site, built by the Fatimid dynasty which Ṣāliḥ's Ayyūbid dynasty had replaced; pre-Christian carved stones were also reused in the building. Interior floors and walls were covered in marble panels. Frieze inscriptions quoted the Quran and praised Ṣāliḥ, recording his piety and the fact he was a holy warrior. The inscription on the tomb itself declared that he was the son of al-Kāmil (who had defeated the Fifth Crusade) and recorded that 'by God's mercy he died on the battlefield of Mansura fighting the accursed Franks'. This was not true: Ṣāliḥ had died in camp before the battle, but it was a convenient fiction as his death had been kept a secret until Tūrān-Shāh could arrive in Egypt. In his magnificent tomb, Ṣāliḥ became a martyr and champion of Islam, and by extension his widow who constructed the tomb became a martyr's widow.[10] Shajar's building work was not unique in the Islamic world: female contemporaries of Shajar who exercised power also constructed fine buildings with inscriptions that stressed their piety, modesty, and chastity.[11]

Eleanor of Castile, queen of England and crusader, also made preparations for her own tomb during her lifetime, although the final monument was completed by her grieving husband, King Edward I of England, along with the 'Eleanor Crosses' he commissioned to mark the resting places of her body on its road to its final resting place at Westminster, her heart tomb at the Dominicans' London church at Blackfriars, and her viscera tomb at Lincoln. Her gilt bronze effigy at Westminster, created by William Torel between 1291 and 1293, shows her recumbent with a crown over her loose, flowing hair. She is wearing a long robe and a mantle, her left hand on her breast holds the string of her mantle, and her right is at her side and originally held a sceptre. The pillow under her head and her tomb slab are covered in castles and lions, representing her homeland of Castile and León. There was an echo of the crusade on the base of the tomb, which was painted with figures, including four pilgrims praying and a knight kneeling before the Virgin and Child. The knight wears an armorial surcoat with the arms of Otto de Grandison, who accompanied Edward and Eleanor to the Holy Land in 1270 and was in the Holy Land with a small group of knights at the fall of Acre in May 1291.[12]

For the most part, however, tombs of women who took part in the crusades made no obvious reference to their involvement in crusading, either in the inscription or in the iconography. Berengaria of Navarre (d. 1230) was buried at her own foundation, the Cistercian abbey of L'Épau near Le Mans. Her fine stone tomb effigy, placed near the altar, was created shortly after her death and shows her recumbent with her head resting on a cushion, a crown over her veil, and dressed in a long robe decorated with crosses (although the decoration may be modern rather than medieval), cinched at the waist with a small bag hanging from her belt. At her feet a lion crouches over a grey-hound. She looks up at the viewer, holding between her hands a closed book (its individual pages and clasp can be seen on one side) while on its cover is an image of a recumbent female effigy, crowned, with free-flowing hair under a veil and with hands together in prayer, set between tall candles. In its material—stone—dress, and book, the tomb echoes that of Berengaria's mother-in-law, Eleanor of Aquitaine, at Fontevrault; but unlike Eleanor she holds her book closed, as if she were holding an icon or reliquary in her hands.[13] The brass tomb slab of Margaret of Provence, wife of Louis IX, in the middle of the choir at Saint-Denis, showed her wearing a long dress and mantle with a wimple, veil, and crown on her head. Her head was laid on a pillow (supported by angels), and she held a sceptre, with a little dog at her feet. The inscription described her as the noble queen of France and wife of Lord Saint Louis formerly king of France, gave her date of death (1285) and asked the reader to pray for her soul.[14] Nothing in this design specifically recalled the crusade.

Some of the crusading queens discussed earlier in this book were buried within family mausoleums, where they were remembered as pious patronesses, governors, and mothers, but not for their involvement in the crusade. Eleanor of Aquitaine was buried in the abbey church in the double monastery of Fontevrault, founded by the reformer Robert of Arbrissel in 1101 and patronized by the counts of Anjou, alongside her second husband, King Henry II of England, and with her crusader son Richard and her youngest daughter Joanna who had joined him on his crusade; they were later joined by Eleanor's daughter-in-law Isabelle d'Angoulême (d. 1246). Eleanor's stone effigy shows her recumbent, dressed as a noblewoman, with a wimple, veil, and crown on her head, holding an open book in her hands—perhaps to depict her piety. In contrast, the effigies of her husband and son carry sceptres, while her daughter-in-law Isabelle has her hands crossed on her breast. Eleanor may have commissioned her husband's and son's tombs, but it is not known whether she planned her own.[15] Joanna's effigy does not survive.

Although Blanche of Castile never went on crusade herself, her role in supporting crusading and crusaders was reflected in the gathering of her crusading family about her grave. She probably could have been buried with her husband in the choir of the abbey of Saint-Denis, the mausoleum of the Capetians, as her daughter-in-law Isabelle of Aragon would be; but instead she was buried in the centre of the choir of her most important religious foundation, the Cistercian nunnery at Maubuisson. Her tomb was destroyed during the French Revolution, but a seventeenth-century description recorded that it was huge, made of copper and supported on a base of copper with columns. Her copper effigy showed her dressed in a nun's habit but with a crown on her head, and the inscription described her as daughter of King Alfonso, wife of King Louis, and princess of Castile who governed France and lay here as a poor nun. Several of her descendants and relatives and others connected to the crusader states were also buried at Maubuisson. The heart and entrails of her son Alfonse of Poitiers (who died on his return from crusade in 1271) were buried there, as were her grandson Robert II of Artois, born during Louis IX's first crusade, and her great-granddaughter Catherine I de Courtenay, titular Latin Empress of Constantinople. More distant relatives whose graves were at Maubuisson included two of the children of her niece Berenguela of Castile and John de Brienne—Empress Marie of Constantinople and John count of Montfort—and a grandchild of Berenguela and John de Brienne: Empress Marie's niece Margaret, who was widow of Bohemond VII, prince of Antioch and count of Tripoli. There was also Philippa of Champagne, daughter of Count Henry II of Champagne and Isabel I of Jerusalem, and unsuccessful claimant to the county of Champagne. Another descendant of Berenguela and John, Blanche of Eu (daughter of their eldest son Alfonso) entered Maubuisson as a nun and rose to be its third abbess. A black marble effigy of a crowned woman, brought to the abbey of Saint-Denis from Maubuisson after 1815, has been supposed to represent Empress Marie de Brienne, although there are also other possibilities.[16]

The symbolism on and within tombs can be difficult to interpret. When Anthony II de Lucy, lord of Cockermouth and Egremont, died on crusade in Prussia in 1368, his body was wrapped in lead, sealed in a wooden coffin, and returned for burial in the church of St Bees Priory in Cumberland. When his coffin was opened in 1981 his corpse was found to be intact, with a wreath of hair on his chest. This may have been the hair of his wife Joan that he had taken on crusade with him as a keepsake; and it is likely that Joan commissioned his effigy. The sculpture is of a recumbent knight in full plate armour holding an object on his chest, now so damaged that it cannot be definitely identified, but which has been interpreted as either a chalice or a heart casket: either could be a reference to his status as a crusader.[17] Damaged tombs have sometimes inspired local myths about crusaders which have no verifiable historical basis, such as the story from Crickhowell and Much Cowarne in the Welsh Marches of a wife who gave up her hand to ransom her husband from the Muslims after he was captured on crusade, which is still told by local people. The story, which appears to be an early nineteenth-century invention, apparently arose because the woman's effigy on a joint tomb of husband and wife had lost one hand.[18]

There were forms of building other than tombs which could commemorate involvement in the crusades. Countess Aigeline of Burgundy may have been responsible for commissioning a sculpture formerly in Belval Priory which shows a bearded figure with staff and cross on his breast, with a female figure at his left side embracing him. The sculpture may represent Count Hugh of Vaudémont, who accompanied King Louis VII of France on the Second Crusade, returned safely, and died in around 1155. The sculpture could represent his return from crusade, being greeted by his loving wife, and was commissioned after his death as a memorial to him and his pious journey.[19]

After the Fifth Crusade, Matilda de Courtenay, countess of Nevers, widow of Hervé de Donzy, commissioned sculpted images on the west façade of the church of Saint-Adrien in Mailly-le-Château (a property of her family). The central figure is a noblewoman holding a cross in her hand, with four serfs (wearing short tunics) on her right and left. The central figure could represent Matilda de Courtenay herself as a returning crusader, conferring franchises on her burghers and serfs.[20] Mosaic panels at the church of S. Giovanni Evangelista in Ravenna, dating from 1213 and depicting scenes from the Fourth Crusade, may have been donated by a woman in honour of her husband who had been on the Fourth Crusade, probably after his death to commemorate his deeds in Zara and Constantinople and his safe return.[21] As none of these installations include the donor's name, this can only be deduced from the form and content of the work.

A new church might form a memorial of a crusade or pilgrimage to the Holy Land. On 15 January 1366 the Englishwoman Isolda Parewastell petitioned Pope Urban V for permission to found, in thanks for her miraculous escape from torture while on pilgrimage to the Holy Land, a chapel in Bridgewater, Somerset, and endow it with a perpetual annual income of thirty-six florins, 'to the honour and praise of the glorious Blessed Virgin Mary and for the salvation of her soul and the souls of her progenitors'. Instead of founding a new chapel, the pope allowed her to endow a new altar in Bridgewater parish church. Isolda also asked that all those who, having repented and confessed, devoutly visited the altar once a year at specified holy festivals would have one year and forty days of their penance remitted, and this the pope agreed.[22] There is a tradition that St Catherine's church at Eyton on the Weald Moors in Shropshire was founded by Catherine de Eyton in gratitude for her husband's safe return from the crusades.[23]

Noble crusaders also founded and supported religious institutions on land conquered during crusades, which performed the dual function of thanking God for divine aid during the campaign and ongoing prayer support for the new settlers and Christian converts. These new religious houses could be for either women or men: Cistercian nunneries were founded in Reval (now Tallinn) and in Dorpat (now Tartu) in Estonia, and a Birgittine nunnery, following the monastic rule drawn up by St Birgitta of Sweden, was established at Reval. Riga in

Livonia had several religious houses for women.[24] Wealthy and influential nunneries were established and developed within the kingdom of Jerusalem, including the abbey founded at Bethany by Queen Melisende of Jerusalem, where her young sister Iveta became abbess. In addition, the crusaders and Frankish settlers in the crusader states patronized Greek Orthodox monasteries in the region, including women's communities.[25]

On a smaller scale, John of Joinville recalled how King Louis IX's ship was caught in a terrible storm off the coast of Cyprus during his voyage back to France in late spring 1254. When the sailors told Queen Margaret that they were all in danger of drowning she went in search of the king to ask him to make a vow of pilgrimage to God or His saints so that God would deliver them from their danger, but could not find him. Joinville advised her to promise to make a pilgrimage to the shrine of St Nicholas at Varangeville, but the queen said she dared not make such a promise without consulting the king first. So Joinville advised her to promise to donate a silver ship to the chapel of St Nicholas, worth five marks, for the king, herself, and their three children. Having made the promise, the wind fell. When they got back to France the queen had the ship made in Paris, with figures of herself, the king, and the children all in silver, at a cost of a hundred *livres*. She sent it to Joinville, who took it to the chapel of St Nicholas on his own vowed pilgrimage.[26]

There were other material objects which maintained memory of past crusades and crusaders, in the form of relics. When Mary de St Pol, countess of Pembroke, made her will on 13 March 1376 she noted that her body was to be buried in her pre-prepared tomb in the church of the sisters of Denny in Cambridgeshire—which she had founded in the site of a former Templar house—and she left to the church of Westminster Abbey 'a cross with a foot of gold and emeralds, which Sir William de Valence, knight, brought from the Holy Land'. William de Valence, father of Mary's late husband Aymer de Valence, had accompanied the Lord Edward on his crusade of 1270–1272.[27]

Liturgy and ritual

Liturgy and ritual drew both laymen and laywomen into spiritual warfare in support of the crusades, as successive popes ordered congregations to say prayers in support of the crusades and prescribed special masses to support crusaders and war against non-Christians. Liturgy also played a role in commemoration: masses were said for the souls of the dead and liturgies were adapted or drawn up to commemorate significant events. Just as every saint has their holy day within the sanctoral cycle of the liturgical year, significant events during the crusades were also commemorated. The date of the conquest of Jerusalem by the First Crusade on 15 July 1099 was remembered by many Benedictine religious houses across Latin Christendom, including the double abbey for nuns and monks at Fontevrault, where the date was noted on the liturgical calendar as 'Sepulchri Domini', the day the Holy Sepulchre was liberated by the Christians.[28]

All religious houses would have followed papal instructions to fast and do penance after Saladin's capture of the True Cross and of Jerusalem in 1187, and incorporated the *clamor* or appeal to God to aid the Holy Land into their masses as ordered by the pope, and in the early fourteenth century they would have incorporated the prayers set down by Pope Clement V asking for God's protection against pagans. Likewise, individuals would have commissioned religious houses to perform memorial masses and chantries for the souls of crusaders. Historian Theodore Evergates noted that Count Henry I the Liberal of Champagne 'was remembered in many monastic obituaries. For the nuns of the ancient Benedictine abbey of Faremoutiers he was a "venerable count".'[29] Boucicaut's biographer recorded that after news of the disaster at Nicopolis on 25 September 1396 reached France: 'all our lords had the mass for the dead chanted and had the service solemnly done in their chapels for the good lords, knights and squires, and all the Christians who died there'.[30] Presumably the mothers and wives who were bereaved were included in the 'lords' who ordered masses said.

Written record

As well as commissioning memorials, prayers, and masses in commemoration of the crusader dead, women could also ensure their memorialization through the written word, although they did not necessarily do the writing themselves.[31] It may have been William Longespee II's wife Idonea de Camville who ensured that the date of her husband's death at the Battle of Mansura in February 1250 was inserted into the chronicle of Barlings Abbey, a Premonstratensian house in the Isle of Oxeney in Lincolnshire. His death was inserted under 1252 rather than 1250.[32] Lacock Abbey, founded by Countess Ela of Salisbury, William Longespee II's mother, also recorded his death, in terms similar to Matthew Paris's account of Countess Ela's reaction to her son's death. Having explained that the countess was 'unwomanishly' (i.e., efficiently) governing the 'convent of religious ladies' at Lacock (which she had founded), Matthew recorded that when she heard the news of her son's death she remembered that at the time that he fell as a martyr she had had a glorious vision of him. Thereupon she clasped her hands, bent her knees, and gave thanks to God that He had willed that she should bring forth such a son, who was worthy to receive a martyr's crown. Those who related these things, Matthew wrote, were full of admiration for her reaction, because she exalted in spiritual joy rather than collapsing in grief. The account of the history of Lacock Abbey in the abbey's register noted that William Longespee II, son of William Longespee I and Ela:

> Manfully fighting against the enemies of Christ in the Holy Land, suffering insult there for Jesus' name, ending temporal life, to conquer in Christ without end, as it is said, ascended as an athlete of God to the palace of Heaven in A.D. 1249, whose soul Lady Ela his mother, then

abbess of Lacock, saw in her cell entering Heaven, and told the hour to the rest of the sisters.[33]

Like Mary Magdalene at the Holy Sepulchre on Easter morning, Countess Ela gave an oral testimony which gained permanency by being written down by a man (Matthew Paris).[34]

Women also wrote personally about the events of the crusades. A letter survives which purports to have been sent by Berenguela of Castile to her sister Blanche in 1212 reporting their father King Alfonso VIII of Castile's victory over the Almohad caliph at Las Navas de Tolosa. The letter was sent 'with sisterly love' and includes many references to 'the king our father' but the style of address is odd (in this letter Berenguela calls herself queen of Castile, but she normally called herself queen of León) and the details in the letter are different from those in Alfonso VIII's own letters reporting the victory. In fact this letter was probably a forgery composed by Blanche of Castile for her great niece Marie de Brienne on her marriage to Baldwin II of Constantinople in 1234. The letter was evidence of Marie's family's crusading credentials: it would have demonstrated that not only was Marie the daughter of a king of Jerusalem but also the great-granddaughter of the hero of Las Navas. That said, the fact that such a letter was considered credible suggests that Berenguela *could* have written to her sister—but her original letter no longer survives.[35]

Blanche of Castile may also have written a letter to her first cousin once removed Blanche of Navarre, countess of Champagne, incorporating a copy of a letter about the victory at Las Navas de Tolosa brought to her by 'a messenger from Spain'. The letter that survives under her name describes the discussions between the Christian kings of Castile, Navarre, and Aragon before the battle, the opposing armies, the course of the battle, and the Christians' pursuit of the defeated Muslim army, but again the details of the battle differ from Alfonso VIII's own letters. The leading figure in the letter is King Sancho VII of Navarre, brother of Countess Blanche of Champagne, rather than King Alfonso VIII, suggesting that this letter actually originated from the Navarrese court, not from Castile. The address on the letter is also incorrect, as it calls Blanche queen of France; she did not become queen until 1223.[36] Whether or not these letters were genuine reports or created later, they demonstrated the family's crusading credentials.

Some genuine letters survive or are known to have been written. Blanche of Castile kept her cousin King Henry III of England informed on the progress of her son Louis IX's first crusade, and Louis's wife Margaret of Provence wrote from the East to her sister Eleanor of Provence and husband Henry III in 1252 on 'the state of the Holy Land'.[37] Beatrice of Vienne, wife of Count Amaury of Montfort (son of Simon de Montfort and Alice of Montmorency) sent on to Earl Richard of Cornwall a letter she had received from the east about Count Amaury's capture at the Battle of Gaza in 1239.[38] Marie des Baux wrote to Pope Clement VI during her crusade with her husband Humbert II of Viennois with news of events.[39]

But when it came to writing history, few women authors are known by name.[40] That said, one of the best-known female historians of the period included a crusade in her work: Anna Komnene, in her biography of her father, the *Alexiad*. Anna explains that her book was based on notes made by her husband Nikephorus Bryennius, who died in 1137 before he could complete it. As her husband was involved in some of the military events of the First Crusade, this gave Anna's work eye-witness authority. Anna herself may have witnessed some of what she describes, such as the arrival of the western armies at Constantinople and the arrival of the crusade leader Bohemond at her father's court; and she could have consulted others who were directly involved. She also recorded that later in her father's reign, she, her sister Maria, and their mother often travelled with the Emperor when he led the Byzantine army and were present in his tent when he made government decisions, so that she had an understanding of military campaigns and their organization.[41]

Anna's account of the crusaders was written four decades after events, and as its primary aim was to praise Alexios it could not be an

objective record. However, it provides a unique interpretation of the
First Crusade from the viewpoint of the Byzantine court: a Christian
account by a non-Latin Christian who regarded the Latin Christians
as cultural inferiors. The fact that Anna calls the crusaders 'Keltoi' or
Celts, the name of the Romans' ancient barbarian enemies, is indica-
tive of her attitude towards them. She described their 'countless'
armies moving across Europe and into Asia with a plague of locusts
before them which destroyed the vines, 'and with these warriors came
a host of civilians, outnumbering the sand of the sea shore or the stars
of heaven': as if they were a mindless mass of destruction, rather than
human beings. She famously declared that a charging 'Kelt' on horseback could go right through the wall of ancient Babylon, and was
shocked that a Frankish priest took part in military violence by shoot-
ing a bow, comparing him to 'a wild animal'. She admitted that the
Kelts were 'indomitable in the opening cavalry charge' but because
they lacked discipline they could easily be defeated, and as soon as
they dismounted they were helpless. She also set out a lively description of Bohemond, one of the leaders of the Sicilian Normans in the
First Crusade, who appears as a physical giant, impressive to look at,
dangerous to know:

> There was a hard, savage quality about his whole aspect, due, I suppose,
> to his great stature and his eyes; even his laugh sounded like a threat
> to others.

She depicted him as essentially a barbarian who—although he was
cunning and indefatigable—was only one step up from an intelligent
animal. For a real man Anna would look to her husband Nicephorus
Bryennius, physically perfect, intellectually outstanding, a magnificent
soldier, learned, and a fine writer. Her attitude to the crusaders in
general and Bohemond in particular was shaped by decades of conflict between the Normans, who had invaded and conquered Sicily,
and the Byzantines, who claimed Sicily and saw the Normans as a
dangerous threat to their control of the west Balkans.[42]

At the other end of the Mediterranean, the Occitan troubadour Gormonda de Monpeslier also wrote about the crusades, in this case in defence of the Albigensian Crusade. Troubadours (in Occitania) or trouvères (in northern France) composed songs and poems for public performance, specializing in satires and debate poems as well as love songs. Most of their compositions are anonymous, and most of the named authors were male, but Gormonda's name has survived on this example of her work. Early in 1229, just before the treaty which ended the war, she composed a *sirventes*, or political satire, defending papal policy in the crusade and replying to a *sirventes* by the male trouba-dour Guilhem Figueira. Figueira had attacked the papacy, accused the papacy of being the root of all evil, criticized papal policy against King John of England and the Greeks, blamed the papacy for the failure of the Fifth Crusade, and condemned it for promoting the Albigensian crusades and the killing of Christians. Responding stanza by stanza to Guilhem's song, Gormonda defended the papacy over the Fifth Crusade and the Albigensian crusades, arguing that the heretics were worse than Saracens. She criticized Count Raymond VII of Toulouse, calling him a traitor and condemning him for 'suspect faith', and urged her listeners to take up the cross against the 'false heretics'— that is, to join the crusade:

> Anyone who wishes to be saved
> should at once take the cross
> in order to crush and wreck
> the false heretics,
> for the Heavenly One
> came here to open his arms
> entirely to his friends;
> and since He took on such sufferings,
> anyone who is unwilling to hear Him
> or believe His teachings is assuredly wicked.

Gormonda's song may have been written to be performed to a monastic audience or another religious community, such as the Dominicans. These were sentiments which the Dominicans could have used in preaching the crusade against the heretics.[43]

Cultural patronage

Women also patronized writings and art which reflected the crusades. For example, Blanche of Castile, queen of France, commissioned up to four 'moralized' Bibles, for her husband, her son, and her daughter-in-law Margaret of Provence. 'Moralized' Bibles included alongside the Bible text a commentary interpreting the text for its readers, with sumptuous illuminations; the commentary and illuminations in Blanche's moralized Bibles depict the Old Testament wars between the Israelites and their enemies as if they were the Albigensian Crusade between the French and the Cathar heretics, and the illustrations show the French fighting Cathar perfects (sometimes holding a white cat, as Cathars were alleged to be cat-worshippers) and Arab Muslims.[44] In these bibles, the Capetians' wars in defence of the faith became a continuation of God's wars in the ancient past.

Literary patronage by female crusaders did not always promote the crusades so overtly. The French translation of Vegetius's military manual *De re militari* which Eleanor of Castile commissioned for her husband Edward was probably produced while they were at Acre during Edward's crusade, as its illustrations appear to be products of the workshop of manuscript illuminators at Acre; although apart from its subject, warfare, it has no direct link to the crusades.[45] It has been suggested that an *Histoire Universelle* or 'History of the World' produced at Acre in 1287, which depicts the Amazons in very positive roles 'as defenders of the social order', was commissioned by a female patron: possibly Countess Alice of Blois, who as we have already seen arrived in Acre in 1286 or 1287 and died there the following year.[46] But even where a female donor is illustrated in a work of art (as in the icon of Saint Sergios at the Monastery of St Catherine in Sinai, with a female supplicant kneeling at his foot), the identity of the donor is not always known.[47]

Although a woman might not be the named patron of a work she could nevertheless have a role in influencing its development.[48]

Scholars agree that the so-called Melisende Psalter was produced for Queen Melisende of Jerusalem. The intricately carved ivory covers are almost certainly the original covers for the volume. The front cover shows the story of King David through images in six medallions, with between them images of the virtues such as humility and fortitude: as the Latin terms for these virtues are female nouns, these are shown as female figures, and it is tempting to see Melisende herself in the crowned female image of humility in the centre. The six medallions on the back cover show a king in contemporary Byzantine-style dress, performing the acts of mercy set out in Matthew 25:35–36: feeding the hungry, giving drink to the thirsty, taking the homeless into his home, clothing the naked, helping the sick and visiting a prisoner. The images between the medallions are of animals fighting and of birds, with at top centre a bird labelled 'Herodius', a gerfalcon, also called in Latin a *falco* or *fauco*. This may represent Melisende's husband Fulk of Anjou, and hence the volume may have been commissioned for Melisende by Fulk.[49]

The calendar of holy days in the psalter includes some dates significant to the queen of Jerusalem: the date of the capture of Jerusalem by the First Crusade, and the dates of the deaths of Melisende's parents (Morphia of Melitene and King Baldwin II), but no later rulers of Jerusalem. However, it is not based on the calendar produced for the Augustinian canons of Jerusalem but appears to be secular and based on an English model, indicating that it was not commissioned by Melisende or by a native of the kingdom of Jerusalem. Fulk could have been the source through his connections with England: his son Geoffrey had married Matilda of England and their eldest son Henry became King Henry II of England. Yet as Fulk himself was not from England it is not clear why he would have used an English calendar for this psalter. The text of the psalms, with a liturgical calendar, the creeds, canticles, and other prayers and offices, are prefaced by beautiful illustrations in the style of contemporary Byzantine art, each with a background of gold leaf. The whole combined a variety of cultural traditions in art, including French, English, and Italian characteristics as well as Byzantine, which would reflect the multicultural society of the crusader kingdom. Overall, the illuminations and contents of the psalter are consistent with its having been produced between 1131 and 1143 in the scriptorium of the Church of the Holy Sepulchre in Jerusalem. The private prayers and addition of her parents' dates of death to the calendar indicate that Melisende had considerable input to the contents of this psalter, although her husband Fulk may have paid for it.[50] Its engagement with the crusades themselves, however, is limited to the inclusion in its calendar of the date of the conquest of Jerusalem by the First Crusade.

Queen Charlotte of Cyprus, whose sad history was told in Chapter Two, owned a beautifully illuminated Greek-Latin psalter, which asserts on the verso of folio 1 that 'this book belongs to Queen Charlotte of Jerusalem of Cyprus and Armenia'. This may have been one of the books which she gave to Pope Innocent VIII when she was trying to get military support to help her recover her kingdom in 1474–1475. The manuscript predated Charlotte, being produced (judging from its palaeography and style) around 1300. Its contents and workmanship indicate that in the scriptorium where it was produced Latin and Greek scribes and rubricators worked alongside each other. It demonstrates the multi-cultural nature of Cypriot society at the beginning of the fourteenth century but does not reflect the holy war of the crusades in the same way as, for example, Blanche of Castile's moralizing bibles.[51]

It has been suggested that the thirteenth-century Riccardiana Psalter, with many illuminations showing images of Jerusalem, was commissioned by Emperor Frederick II for his third wife, Isabel of England (d. 1241), younger sister of King Henry III and Earl Richard of Cornwall; or that the recipient was Frederick's second wife Queen Isabel II of Jerusalem (d. 1228), daughter of John de Brienne and Maria of Montferrat. It is more likely, however, that it was commissioned by a noble or other wealthy person who had no personal link to Jerusalem. Its calendar includes bishops and saints associated with Jerusalem and the Holy Land, with the dates of the First Crusade's

capture of Jerusalem in 1099 and the re-dedication of the church of
the Holy Sepulchre in 1149, but its litany of saints includes Italian,
English, and northern French saints, which could suggest it was produced in Normandy or Sicily, while the inclusion of St Benedict and
his sister Scholastica might indicate it was produced for a Benedictine
nun. Possibly it was commissioned by a noble nun who was interested
in Jerusalem and wanted a connection to the city through the illuminations in the psalter, so that through contemplating them she
could imagine herself in the city, in a virtual pilgrimage. The reader
might have been 'in an institution that had ties to or once was in
Jerusalem but had to leave' after Saladin captured the city in 1187.[52]

Nuns did have access to a range of religious and historical works
related to the crusades. Three nunneries in England (Swine, Syon, and
Thetford) probably had a copy of the 'revelations' of St Birgitta in
English, and one (Swine) in Latin; Syon may also have had a copy in
Latin. As we have seen, Birgitta's visions included revelations about
crusading in the east Baltic. As Syon was a Bridgettine house, following
the rule established by St Birgitta for the religious houses she founded
in 1346, it is not surprising that the nuns there had a copy of St
Birgitta's work, but her revelations would have been profitable reading for any religious. Barking Abbey's books included a volume of
devotional and moral works in French, including a French account of
the death of King Louis IX on crusade, as well as Louis's instructions
from his camp at Carthage (Tunis) to his daughter Isabelle and his son
Philip. Polsloe Priory had a copy of the *Liber gestorum Karoli, regis
Franciae* ('Book of the deeds of Charles, king of France': presumably a
version of the Latin history of Charlemagne ascribed to Charlemagne's
Archbishop Turpin), which described Charlemagne's holy wars against
the Muslims. Syon had a copy of William of Tripoli's *De statu
Saracenorum*, 'on the condition of the Saracens', a description of the
Middle East and how the Holy Land could be reconquered. This last
formed part of a manuscript which probably originally belonged to
the brothers' library at Syon, but later came into the sisters'
possession.[53]

The house of Augustinian canonesses at Campsey in Suffolk owned an early-fourteenth-century volume of saints' lives that opened with Nicolas de Bozon's 'Life' of St Elizabeth of Hungary in French octo-syllabic rhyming couplets. This 'Life' presents the crusade as a pious undertaking with a divine reward, stating that St Elizabeth many times preached to her husband that he should go to the Holy Land to serve God and gain Heaven. The noble duke believed her advice, went there and died, as a result of which one of her relatives blamed her for his death, threw her out of the country and took all she had (in fact a contemporary witness, Elizabeth's maid Guda, indicated that Elizabeth's husband Ludwig had gone on crusade of his own will, and she had consented to it, rather than her urging him to go). The story ends with her husband's bones being returned to the land where she went; she 'did the honour that she could' and then went to a private place to serve God. At the end of the volume is a statement that it was for reading aloud at meal times.[54] Even where we have no direct evidence that the nuns read these books or heard them read, as nunneries did have procedures for the issue and return of books for reading by the sisters presumably all the books in their collections would have been read at some point.[55]

Individual royal and noble women also owned books about crusades, suggesting that they were interested in crusading. In 1250 King Henry III of England requested Brother Roger de Sandford, master of the Templars in England, to let one Henry of the Wardrobe have 'for the queen's use' (or work) 'a certain large book which is in his house at London, written in the Gallic language, in which are contained the deeds of Antioch and of other kings, etc.'. Possibly the queen, Eleanor of Provence, wished to consult the book to assist in the design of a mural painting of 'the history of Antioch' produced in her apartment at Westminster; possibly she simply wanted to read it as preparation for the crusade. Henry had already taken crusade vows, and took new vows in 1250 when news reached England of Louis IX's capture in Egypt, although it is not clear when Eleanor took the cross herself. As it was 'Henry of the Wardrobe' (one of the king's officials) who took the message, and as the book was not in the English Templars' possession when they were arrested in 1308, it was probably royal property, stored for safe keeping in the king's storage at the New Temple. The identity of the book is unclear from the description: the crusade epic *La Chanson d'Antioche* would fit, but it could have been the 'History of Eracles', the French translation of Archbishop William of Tyre's History.[56] Whatever the identity and ownership of the book, the fact that Eleanor of Provence wished to consult it indicates she was interested in the crusades.

Isabel Bruce, sister of King Robert Bruce of Scotland and queen of Norway from 1293, owned a copy of the 'History of Eracles'. Her name and her ownership are recorded on the first and last leaves of the volume. There are several routes by which this book could have reached Isabel: brought back from the Holy Land by a pilgrim or crusaders, carried by ambassadors or merchants, or sent as a gift from France either to Scotland or to Norway—the numerous possibilities demonstrate the very extensive connections between Norway, the rest of Latin Europe, and the eastern Mediterranean in the late thirteenth century. We do not know how far Isabel read the book, but she could have used it as the basis of a virtual pilgrimage to the East, and as a mirror for queens, with its stories of how good queens should act.[57]

Duchess Eleanor of Gloucester, Countess of Essex, making her will at Pleshey Castle on 9 August 1399, left, among other legacies, to her son Humphrey (who would in fact predecease her) a poem of the *Historie de Chivaler a Cigne* ('History of the Knight of the Swan'), a coat of mail, and a brass cross which had belonged to her husband, Humphrey's father. The Old French crusade epic poem about the Knight of the Swan was part of a series of stories praising the lineage of Godfrey de Bouillon, hero of the First Crusade, and Eleanor's family were crusaders. Eleanor was the daughter and co-heir of Humphrey V de Bohun earl of Hereford, Essex, and Northampton, who had joined King Peter of Cyprus's crusade to Alexandria in 1365; she was sister of Mary, wife of Henry Bolingbroke, crusader and later King Henry IV of England, and her husband was Thomas of Woodstock, seventh son of King Edward III, who had planned a crusade to Prussia. The coat of mail which Eleanor left to her son could have been made for her husband's crusade.[58]

At some point Joan Beaufort, Countess of Westmorland and half-sister of the crusader Henry Bolingbroke, lent her brother's son, King Henry V of England, a copy of *Les Cronikels de Jerusalem et de Viage de Godfray de Boylion* (the Chronicles of Jerusalem and the journey of Godfrey de Bouillon), a variation on the book which Duchess Eleanor de Bohun had owned. Young Henry failed to return the book and in 1424 Joan petitioned the royal Council to order the king's clerk of the Wardrobe to return it.[59]

In around 1170 one Konrad the Priest composed the *Ruolantes Liet* (Song of Roland), a German version of the legend of Charlemagne's nephew Roland. Although set long before the First Crusade, the story of Roland's death at Muslim hands as part of the struggle between Islam and Christianity for control of the Iberian Peninsula has obvious links to crusading. Konrad's book ends with the statement that a Duke Henry had the original brought from France, where it was written, 'because the noble duchess wished it'. The duke was probably Henry the Lion, duke of Saxony and husband of Matilda of England (d. 1189), daughter of King Henry II and Eleanor of Aquitaine. Given King Henry II's family connections to the kingdom of Jerusalem it would not be surprising if Matilda were involved in commissioning Konrad's work.[60]

But the fact that a noble patroness's family was involved in the crusades did not necessarily mean that it was her main interest. The opening lines of Chrétien de Troyes's romance *Le Chevalier de la Charrette* ('the Knight of the Cart', also known as *Lancelot*), praise 'My lady of Champagne' and explain that she had commissioned the work and given Chrétien its matter and sense, so that he could not have done it without her pains and attention. The countess in question was clearly Marie of France, and given her parents', husband's, and sons' interest in crusading, we might expect some references to the Holy Land or Jerusalem in this romance. In fact there is just one mention of crusading, where the poet states that knights who had taken the cross (*croisié se erent*) did not take part in a tournament. In Chrétien's imagined world crusading was a knightly activity but it did not impinge greatly on the lives of individual knights unless they chose to take the cross. *Le Chevalier de la Charrette* was written before or around the same time as Chrétien's work *Le Chevalier au Lion* ('The Knight of the Lion', also known as *Yvain*), in which Kay mentions Nūr al-Dīn, son of Zengī and conqueror of Damascus (d. 1174), as someone who is still alive and whom every drunkard boasts he will kill. This comment suggests the poem was written around the mid-1170s, when Nūr al-Dīn's death was recent news and the knights of the region around Troyes were preparing to accompany their lords to the Holy Land: either Philip of Alsace, count of Flanders, who was overseas 1177–1178, or Count Henry I the Liberal, overseas 1179–1181. Chrétien's earlier poem *Cligés* largely focussed on the eastern Mediterranean, but the focus was Christian Constantinople rather than Jerusalem and war with the Muslims.[61] Of Chrétien's work, only *Le Chevalier de la Charrette* was definitely influenced by Countess Marie, and does not suggest that the crusade was her major interest. The work had considerable impact on the development of the Arthurian legends, setting up Lancelot as the ideal self-sacrificing lover who risks his honour and his life to rescue his kidnapped beloved, but does not go on crusade.

We might expect the *Lais* of the poet Marie de France, dedicated to a 'noble king' who was probably King Henry II of England, to refer specifically to the crusades, as Henry supported the Holy Land financially from 1166, made regular donations to the Templars and to the Order of St Lazarus in the Holy Land, and from 1172 transferred large sums of money to the Holy Land each year; he also took the cross in 1188. Marie's work only suggests an awareness of the proximity of the East, in a single reference to the father of the heroine Le Fresne having brought a cloth from Constantinople, 'where he was'.[62] Other writers—usually anonymous—drew on women who had been involved in crusade history to provide a factual basis for their fictional imaginings about the crusades. As we have seen, women were seldom involved in military action in crusades, but as romantic love interest, wronged heroine, pitiful victim, or treacherous jezebel their inclusion made stories more appealing to the audience—which would include many women.[63]

For example, the thirteenth-century biography of the twelfth-century troubadour Jaufré Rudel claimed that the poet had been infatuated with a countess of the crusader county of Tripoli: the biographer was possibly referring to Countess Hodierna, younger sister of Queen Melisende of Jerusalem, who was involved in the government of the County of Tripoli and the kingdom of Jerusalem but not known as a patron of the arts.[64] In around 1260 the so-called Minstrel of Reims re-imagined Queen Sybil's role in the Third Crusade, depicting the Frankish nobility of the Latin East as traitors to her, and Saladin as defending her interests.[65] During 1392 and 1393 the French writer Jean d'Arras composed a story of Mélusine, legendary fairy ancestress of the Lusignans, in which her sons are involved in wars against 'Saracens' (here meaning Muslims) in the eastern Mediterranean and eastern Europe, giving a pseudo-historical justification for contemporary French military involvement against the Ottoman Turks.[66] Latin Christian writers also developed legends around Saladin, opponent of the Third Crusade, giving him a Christian noblewoman as mother or ancestress, and claiming that he had an affair with Eleanor of Aquitaine (who, of course, took part in the Second Crusade, not the Third). The fifteenth-century French romance *Saladin* adjusted this story to give Saladin a romantic relationship with the wife of King Philip II of France, who is here a daughter of the king of Aragon. When she discovers Saladin is a pagan (in this context meaning a Muslim) she is dismayed, but then—unlike Dowager Queen Joanna of Sicily in the Muslim accounts of the Third Crusade—decides that the difference in religion is not important. She attempts to elope with Saladin and is only prevented by the heroic French knight Andrew de Chavigny.[67]

These stories would have been read and listened to by women as well as men, and although they were created as entertainment rather than as serious history they suggest that audiences continued to be fascinated by the crusades to the Holy Land—even after crusades to Jerusalem had ceased and the Ottoman Turks were a greater threat to Latin Christendom than Saladin had ever been. Women and men still purchased indulgences to support wars against the Turks and took part in religious rituals which begged God to assist Christians against the Turks, but few of them would ever travel to Jerusalem, let alone take part in a crusade.

Summing Up

As crusading became an integral part of medieval Latin Christian society, women could not avoid being drawn into it in one way or another. Even those who never physically took part in a crusade supported them financially by purchasing indulgences, and in prayer and ritual whenever they attended a mass. Even female saints were co-opted as supporters of the crusade. For most women, however, as for most men, the crusade was an expression of faith which they supported but in which they were not personally involved.

The most significant determining factor in the nature and extent of a woman's involvement in crusading was her social status and economic position in society.[1] Women of high social status had more opportunity to play a significant role in organization and recruitment to crusades than those of lower classes, as they had the resources and the authority to initiate crusades and to influence others to become involved. Their extensive family networks gave them a broad range of influence and also drew them into crusade involvement which they could otherwise have avoided. Mothers brought up their children to believe that crusading was part of their family tradition and a duty to God, and siblings kept each other informed of their involvement in crusading. That said, many of the campaigns considered here, although they were wars against Muslims or other non-Christians, were more about control of territory than defending the Christian faith. The crusade provided a useful framework to justify a campaign and to raise troops, money, and other resources, but the Portuguese attack on

Ceuta in 1415, for example, aimed to control territory and trade as much as waging holy war. Again, Queen Johanna of Naples's professed interest in the crusades appears to have been more about establishing a reputation as a pious queen and faithful supporter of the papacy than in providing any material aid for the Christians of the eastern Mediterranean.

Exactly what women did during crusades and their motivations can be difficult to ascertain. Contemporary commentators framed women's involvement in these campaigns within society's expectations of women and did not always fully explain a woman's role. The same can be said of depictions of men: they also had their stereotypical roles. The narrative sources give the impression that women and children suffered the most in these wars, as they were taken captive and enslaved: they did not emphasize that men also suffered, as male captives were routinely killed, sometimes after horrific tortures. It is a moot point whether it is better to die in agony or live as a slave.

We have seen that most of the evidence for women's active involvement in crusading relates to women acting with their menfolk: father, uncle, husband, brothers, and sons, implying that most women who became involved in crusading did so as part of their wider family group. This impression may be a trick of the surviving evidence. The fact that women were less likely to be publicly involved in high-level strategic decision making during a campaign meant that they were less likely than men to be mentioned by narrative commentators. With very few exceptions, only the very highest-status women were mentioned by name in narrative accounts, and then usually in connection with their male relatives. Commentators did not always record the involvement of even high-status women: very often our only evidence of a woman's involvement in a campaign is a passing reference in a papal letter or a legal document. Most of these legal documents mentioning women crusaders concern married women acting with their husbands: they would make their will with their husband, witness their husband's will, or make a donation with their husband. Hence the creation of evidence was skewed towards the married woman travelling with her husband. Although many women would have travelled as servants, they left virtually no evidence behind them. Perhaps Johannina, beneficiary of Count Henry of Rodez's will at Acre in 1221, was the count's female servant; perhaps the six women named as beneficiaries in the will of Isabelle of Aragon, queen of France, in 1271 had been with her at Tunis; but we do not know.[2] As for all the anonymous women mentioned in passing as bringing food and water to the warriors or throwing stones at the enemy, we do not know whether they travelled alone or with their menfolk. Of course, the same is the case for the bulk of male participants.

Modern scholars have sometimes deduced women's influence although it is not explicitly expressed in the surviving evidence. For example, scholars have suggested that Duchess Isabel of Burgundy had considerable influence over her husband Philip the Good's crusading plans and gave them a practical edge which Philip's plans lacked; but, although this makes good sense, by its very nature such hidden 'soft power' is more difficult to prove than visible 'hard power'.[3]

Nevertheless, it is likely that some of the women depicted in the narrative sources as weak and unable to go to war themselves, encouraging their menfolk to fight in on their behalf, were deliberately working around cultural norms in order to achieve their aims. When in 1224 Queen Berenguela of Castile enthusiastically supported her son Fernando III's plans to make war on the 'enemies of the Christian faith', we may ask whether the initiative was actually hers rather than her son's, but contemporaries presented it as her son's to bolster his prestige and encourage the nobility and clergy to support him. In April 1250 when Margaret of Provence was trying to persuade the members of the Italian Communes in Damietta not to abandon the city, she took practical steps to retain them, by purchasing all the available food to ensure that they had a reliable supply, but she also appealed to their mercy and charity, begging them not to abandon the city and at least to stay until her lying-in was complete. This combined approach was successful in persuading them not to desert. When in 1414–1415 Yūsuf III of Granada used his own wife to make diplomatic approaches to Queen Philippa of Portugal, hoping to avert a Portuguese invasion, he did not realize that Philippa's own family crusading traditions would have underlain the attack; unsurprisingly, the queen rebuffed the attempt. Like the women who historian Joan Ferrante suggested adopted 'public postures and private maneuvers' to achieve their aims, noblewomen involved in crusading could exercise 'powerful influence from positions of apparent weakness', adopting a public posture of frailty and humility while exercising influence out of the public gaze.[4]

Despite these problems of evidence, when the surviving evidence is assembled it shows that women were actively involved in crusading, either accompanying their husbands or as sole pilgrims, sometimes as tradespeople, merchants, or women serving the army in other ways, and that they were involved on all crusading fronts in one way or another. They occasionally appear in the sources communicating with external groups, either as diplomats or passing on intelligence. After the loss of Acre in 1291, crusades to the eastern Mediterranean were on a smaller scale, so that there were fewer opportunities for noblewomen to take part in person, but they still took the cross: for instance, when King Philip IV of France took the cross in a grand ceremony at Paris in 1313, his three sons and his son-in-law King Edward II of England, his daughter Queen Isabelle of England and his sons' wives also took it. Such public demonstrations by prominent and powerful women encouraged wide recruitment and donation of resources, even if (as in Isabelle's case) she never set out on crusade and was later absolved of her vow.[5] Some noblewomen did set out on these later expeditions (as did Marie des Baux in 1345 and Constanza of Castile in 1386), and presumably women continued to accompany crusade armies as providers of essential services, as Philippe de Mézières envisaged in his crusade plan. Women also played a role in military action (for example, during the crusades against the Albigensians and against the Hussites) although the tasks they performed were not those requiring extensive military training: gathering stones for ammunition, building siege defences, or operating a simple stonethrowing machine.

Women also played a background support role in crusades. They took part in liturgies and ritual processions, joined guilds which prayed for the Holy Land, and purchased crusade indulgences. They cared for crusaders' property and families during their absence. Holy women and the hosts of Heaven were also enlisted to support the crusades, and female saints were as supportive as male: women could fight with spiritual arms as well as men, and sometimes it seems that a female saint was preferable to a male one. Holy women's promotion of the crusade and campaigns against non-Christians both expressed and bolstered their sanctity. Supporting the crusade could involve considerable personal suffering, as in the cases of women who lost their lives or their lands during crusaders' absence, or who lost their dower lands in the course of raising funds for a family member going on crusade. For many there was the personal tragedy of family members who departed on crusade and never returned, or the anxiety and financial trials of those who had to negotiate for the release of captive family members. A crusader's return could bring other problems, especially when the crusader had been away so long that their spouse had remarried.

Women were widely involved in commemorating crusaders and the crusades, in physical structures, ritual, and writing. Although it is not always possible to work out who was responsible for commissioning a work of memorialization, women's role in memorializing the crusades seems to have followed the same paths as men's. As in other aspects of women's involvement in crusading, wealthy and influential women could ensure that their piety was recorded more effectively than non-noble women. Shajar al-Durr's tomb and the tomb she commissioned for her late husband stress her victory and his holy war, and Matilda de Courtenay's image on the west façade of the church of Saint-Adrien in Mailly-le-Château holds a cross, emphasizing that she was a former crusader.

This book has concentrated on women who took part in crusading in one way or another: initiating campaigns, joining crusades, buying indulgences to support crusades, and so on. Not all women promoted crusading all the time. Blanche of Castile tried to stop her son Louis IX from taking the cross, although she could not prevent his doing so. Elizabeth of Hungary abandoned the world after losing her husband Ludwig IV on a crusade. Some holy women saw that the crusade could be a distraction from true piety or a screen to hide less honourable motivations. Weighing up the costs of crusading, some feared losing loved ones, personal suffering and family ruin, and as we have seen the event often justified their fears.

But as fourteenth-century crusade theorists Marino Sanudo and Philippe de Mézières realized, women would always accompany crusaders, and indeed they should go with the crusade to support the men and help their husbands to avoid the sin of adultery. No matter what moralizing commentators might claim, the crusade movement needed women: their money, their prayer support, their active participation and their inspiration.

Chronology of the Crusades

This list includes the major campaigns and a selection of smaller expeditions and important events in the history of crusading during the period covered by this book, from the mid-eleventh century to the Ottoman capture of Cyprus in 1570.

1064	Barbastro (Iberian Peninsula) is captured by a combined Christian force.
1074	Pope Gregory VII proposes a campaign to aid the Byzantine Greeks against the Seljuk Turks.
1085	Toledo (Iberian Peninsula) is captured by King Alfonso VI of Castile.
1086	Alfonso VI of Castile is defeated by the Almoravids at Sagrajas.
1087	A Latin Christian naval force from Italy attacks and plunders al-Mahdiya (North Africa).
1095	Pope Urban II calls the First Crusade at the Church Council of Clermont.
1099	The First Crusade captures Jerusalem. The Latin kingdom of Jerusalem is founded.
1100–1101	A follow-up expedition to the East is defeated by the Turks.
1108	Castilians defeated by Almoravids at Battle of Uclés.
1116–1117	Almoravids raid Coimbra region and besiege Coimbra.
1119	Battle 'of the Field of Blood': Prince Roger of Antioch is defeated by Il-ghazi ibn Artuk of Mardin.
1120	The military religious order of the Temple is founded in Jerusalem.
1122–1124	A Venetian naval expedition to the Holy Land: Tyre is captured.
1123–1124	A Castilian campaign captures the city of Sigüenza (between Toledo and Zaragoza).

1129	A Frankish (Latin Christian) expedition sets out from Jerusalem to attack Damascus but is unsuccessful.
1136	King Fulk of Jerusalem entrusts Beit Jibrin castle to the Hospital of St John of Jerusalem.
1138–1139	Count Thierry of Flanders goes on pilgrimage to the Holy Land.
1144	Zengī, ruler of Mosul and Aleppo, captures Edessa.
1146	Death of Zengī.
1147	Lisbon is captured by King Alfonso Henriques I of Portugal and crusading forces.
1147–1148	The Second Crusade. The crusaders besiege Damascus, but fail to capture it.
1153	The forces of King Baldwin III of Jerusalem capture Ascalon.
1154	Nūr al-Dīn (Zengī's son) captures Damascus.
	The Almohads win control of Granada.
1158	Count Thierry of Flanders goes on pilgrimage to the Holy Land.
1163–1169	King Amaury (Amalric) of Jerusalem campaigns against Egypt.
1169	Saladin becomes vizier of Egypt.
1172	Duke Henry the Lion of Saxony goes on pilgrimage to the Holy Land.
	The Almohads take control of Seville.
1174	Death of Nūr al-Dīn. Saladin seizes Damascus.
1177	Count Philip of Flanders goes on pilgrimage to the Holy Land. The forces of King Baldwin IV of Jerusalem defeat Saladin's army at Montgisard.
1179–1181	Crusade of Count Henry I 'the Liberal' of Champagne.
1187	Saladin defeats the army of the kingdom of Jerusalem at the Battle of Hattin (4 July). He captures Jerusalem (2 October).
1189–1192	The Third Crusade. Aim: to recover Jerusalem. It fails, but recovers some territory.
1191	King Richard I of England captures Cyprus from Emperor Isaac Doukas Komnenos.
1197–1198	The German crusade conquers some territory and converts the Teutonic Hospital at Acre into a military religious order, the Hospital of St Mary of the Teutons ('the Teutonic Order').

1202–1204   The Fourth Crusade. Aim: to assist Christians in the Holy Land. It captures Constantinople and sets up the Latin Empire of Constantinople.

1209–1226   The Albigensian Crusades.

1212   The Children's Crusade. It breaks up before it leaves Europe. Battle of Las Navas de Tolosa: the Almohads are defeated by a combined Christian force.

1213   Battle of Muret. The Albigensian crusaders under Simon de Montfort defeat King Pere (Peter) II of Aragon.

1218–1221   The Fifth Crusade. Aim: to conquer Egypt. Captures Damietta but defeated by Ayyūbid sultan Al-Kāmil.

1224   Fernando III of Castile begins his campaign against al-Andalus (Muslim Spain).

1228–1229   Crusade of Emperor Frederick II. He recovers Jerusalem for the kingdom of Jerusalem through a treaty with Sultan Al-Kāmil.

1229   King James I of Aragon captures the Balearic Islands.

1230s   The Teutonic Order begins military operations in Prussia.

1233   King James I of Aragon invades the kingdom of Valencia.

1236   Fernando III of Castile captures Cordoba.

1237   The Teutonic Order takes over the Order of Swordbrothers in Livonia (now Latvia).

1238   King James I of Aragon captures the city of Valencia.

1239–1240   Crusade of Thibaut IV, count of Champagne and king of Navarre, to Acre. Thibaut negotiates a peace treaty with al-Sālih Ismā'īl, Ayyūbid ruler of Damascus.

1240–1241   Crusade of Earl Richard of Cornwall, to Acre. Richard recovers territory for the kingdom of Jerusalem by negotiation with al-Sālih Ayyūb, sultan of Cairo.

1242   The Livonian branch of the Teutonic Order is defeated at Lake Chud (Peipus) by a Russian force led by Prince Alexander Nevsky.

1244   The Franks finally lose Jerusalem.

1248   Fernando III of Castile captures Seville.

1248–1254   First crusade of King Louis IX of France: to Egypt. The crusade captures the port of Damietta, but suffers losses at Mansura in February 1250. Louis is captured, released in May, then goes to Acre.

1250	A Mamluk coup in Egypt overthrows the Ayyūbids.
1251	First 'Shepherds' Crusade': a popular religious movement to help King Louis. The crusaders attack clergy and Jews and their movement is crushed.
1258	The Mongols capture Baghdad.
1260	Battle of 'Ain Jālūt (Ayn Jalut). The Mamluks of Egypt defeat the Mongols.
	Baybars becomes sultan of Egypt.
1261	Michael Palaeologos recaptures Constantinople from the Franks.
1263–1271	Sultan Baybars campaigns in Syria and Palestine.
1266	Count Charles of Anjou conquers Sicily in a crusade.
1269	The princes of Aragon go to Acre on crusade.
1269–1270	A Frisian crusade arrives in Acre.
1270	The second crusade of King Louis IX of France besieges Tunis. Failure.
1271–1272	The crusade of the Lord Edward of England (later King Edward I of England) to Acre: ends with a truce.
1274	The Second Church Council of Lyons discusses plans for recovering the Holy Land. No decision reached.
1277	Death of Baybars.
1282	The Sicilian Vespers: the Sicilians revolt against Charles of Anjou, king of Naples and Sicily.
1285	The French launch a crusade against Aragon, in revenge for the Aragonese assisting the Sicilian revolt.
1287–1288	Expedition of Countess Alice of Blois to the Holy Land.
1291	Acre is captured by al-Ashraf Khalīl, sultan of Egypt. The remaining Frankish territories in the Holy Land fall to the Mamluks soon afterwards.
1300	The Mongol il-Khan Ghazan campaigns in the Holy Land and defeats the Mamluks.
1301	A group of leading Genoese noblewomen plan a crusade, but drop their plans when Pope Boniface VIII will not allow them to conquer and fortify lands for their own benefit.
1306	The Hospital of St John of Jerusalem begins the conquest of the Greek Orthodox Christian island of Rhodes.

1309	The Teutonic Order moves its headquarters to Marienburg in Prussia. The Hospital of St John moves its headquarters to Rhodes.
1312	Pope Clement V dissolves the Order of the Temple.
1320	The second 'Shepherds' Crusade': the crusaders kill Jews and attack the clergy; their movement is crushed.
1332–1334	The first naval crusading league established, to fight Muslims at sea.
1343	Pope Clement VI asks Queen Johanna of Naples for her help in a naval expedition against the Turks.
1344	A naval crusading league captures Smyrna (now Izmir).
1345–1347	Humbert II, Dauphin of Viennois, leads a crusading expedition against the Turks.
1348–1351	King Magnus IV of Sweden's crusades to Finland and Russia.
1365	Peter I of Cyprus's crusade captures Alexandria, but withdraws soon afterwards.
1369	Assassination of King Peter I of Cyprus.
1373	Death of Birgitta of Sweden.
1372	Queen Margaret of Cilician Armenia appeals to Pope Gregory XI for aid against the Turks.
1373	The Genoese invade Cyprus.
1374	Pope Gregory XI entrusts the defence of Smyrna to the Hospitallers of St John.
1374–1380	Catherine of Siena campaigns for a crusade.
1375	Cilician Armenia is conquered by the Mamluks.
1378	Start of the Great Schism.
1383	Crusade of Henry Despenser, bishop of Norwich, to Flanders.
1386–1387	John of Gaunt's crusade to Castile.
1386	Queen Jadwiga of Poland marries Jagiełło of Lithuania. Lithuania accepts Christianity.
1389	Battle of Kosovo Polje: the Ottoman Turks claim victory.
1390	A French expedition sets out to capture al-Mahdiya (North Africa). The siege ends with a peace treaty and the French withdraw peacefully.
1394	Death of Dorothea of Montau.

1396	Battle of Nicopolis: the western European crusaders are defeated by the Ottoman Turks under Bayezid I.
1399–1404	Boucicaut, marshal of France, raids Turkish settlements in eastern Mediterranean.
1402	'Tamerlane' (Timur the Lame) captures Symrna.
1410	The Teutonic Order is defeated by a combined Latin Christian Lithuanian-Polish force at Tannenberg/Grunwald/Žalgiris.
1415	A Portuguese army led by King João I and his sons captures Ceuta in North Africa.
1420–1431	Crusades against the Hussite heretics of Bohemia.
1429	Joan of Arc declares her intention of leading a crusade.
1434	Battle of Lipany: the Hussite moderates defeat the radicals.
1444	The crusade of Varna: defeated by the Ottoman Turks.
1453	Constantinople is conquered by the Ottoman Turks under Mehmed II.
1456	Crusaders led by John Hunyadi defend Belgrade against the Ottoman Turks.
1463	Charlotte de Lusignan, queen of Cyprus and titular queen of Jerusalem, is driven out of Cyprus by her half-brother James, allied with the Mamluks of Egypt. Venice gains control of Cyprus.
1480	The Hospital of St John successfully defends Rhodes against the Ottoman Turks. The Ottomans capture Otranto in Italy, but lose it the following year.
1492	The Muslim city of Granada falls to the forces of Isabel and Ferdinand of Castile-Aragon.
	Christopher Columbus's first voyage to the Indies.
	Alonso de Lugo's crusade in La Palma, Canary Islands.
1497	The Spanish capture Melilla in North Africa.
1501–1502	A Venetian-Hungarian naval crusading league ravages Turkish bases in the Ionian islands.
1505–1510	The Spanish wage a crusading war of conquest in North Africa.
1509	Queen Eleni of Ethiopia proposes an alliance against the Muslims to King Manuel of Portugal.
1516–1517	The Ottoman sultan Selim I defeats the Mamluks and conquers Egypt.

1518	Martin Luther's *Explanations of the Ninety-Five Theses* state that Ottoman attacks on Europe are God's punishment for Christians' sins and so the Church authorities should not resist them with arms, only with prayer.
1519–1521	Hernán Cortés and a Spanish force conquer the Aztecs of Mexico.
1522–1523	Rhodes falls to the Ottoman Turks, commanded by Süleyman the Magnificent.
1529	The first Ottoman siege of Vienna. The Ottomans are repulsed.
1530	The Hospital of St John moves to Malta.
1541–1543	A Portuguese force led by Cristóvão da Gama assists Queen Säblä Wängel of Ethiopia and her son King Gälawdewos against a Muslim invasion led by Imam Ahmad ibn Ibrahim al-Ghazi.
1551	The Turks recapture Tripoli (North Africa).
1565	The Hospital of St John defends Malta against the forces of Süleyman the Magnificent.
1570	Cyprus is conquered by the Ottoman Turks.
1571	Battle of Lepanto: a victory for the Catholic Christian Holy League against the Ottoman Turks, but Cyprus is not recaptured.

List of Popes

Antipopes (those not acknowledged by the Catholic Church as legitimately elected) are generally omitted from this list, as they were not associated with the crusades discussed in this book. However, the rival popes during the Great Schism of 1378 to 1417 have been included with their location in Rome, Avignon, or Pisa in parentheses.

1061–1073	Alexander II
1073–1085	Gregory VII
1086–1087	Victor III
1088–1099	Urban II
1099–1118	Paschal II
1118–1119	Gelasius II
1119–1124	Calixtus II
1124–1130	Honorius II
1130–1143	Innocent II
1143–1144	Celestine II
1144–1145	Lucius II
1145–1153	Eugenius III
1153–1154	Anastasius IV
1154–1159	Adrian IV
1159–1181	Alexander III
1181–1185	Lucius III
1185–1187	Urban III
1187	Gregory VIII
1187–1191	Clement III
1191–1198	Celestine III
1198–1216	Innocent III

1216–1227	Honorius III
1227–1241	Gregory IX
1241	Celestine IV
1243–1254	Innocent IV
1254–1261	Alexander IV
1261–1264	Urban IV
1265–1268	Clement IV
1271–1276	Gregory X
1276	Innocent V
1276	Adrian V
1276–1277	John XXI
1277–1280	Nicholas III
1281–1285	Martin IV
1285–1287	Honorius IV
1288–1292	Nicholas IV
1294	Celestine V
1294–1303	Boniface VIII
1303–1304	Benedict XI
1305–1314	Clement V
1316–1334	John XXII
1334–1342	Benedict XII
1342–1352	Clement VI
1352–1362	Innocent VI
1362–1370	Urban V
1370–1378	Gregory XI
1378–1389	Urban VI (Rome)
1378–1394	Clement VII (Avignon)
1389–1404	Boniface IX (Rome)
1393–1423	Benedict XIII (Avignon) (deposed 1417)
1404–1406	Innocent VII (Rome)
1406–1415	Gregory XII (Rome)
1409–1410	Alexander V (Pisa)
1410–1415	John XXIII (Pisa)

1417–1431	Martin V
1431–1447	Eugenius IV
1447–1455	Nicholas V
1455–1458	Calixtus III
1458–1464	Pius II
1464–1471	Paul II
1471–1484	Sixtus IV
1484–1492	Innocent VIII
1492–1503	Alexander VI
1503	Pius III
1503–1513	Julius II
1513–1521	Leo X
1522–1523	Adrian VI
1523–1534	Clement VII
1534–1549	Paul III
1550–1555	Julius III
1555	Marcellus II
1555–1559	Paul IV
1559–1565	Pius IV
1566–1572	Pius V

Family Trees

These family trees show the family relationships between various individuals discussed in this book.

1. The descendants of Eleanor of Aquitaine, queen of France and of England.
2. The descendants of King Alfonso VI of León and Castile.
3. The family of Blanche of Castile, queen of France.
4. The daughters of John of Gaunt.

Abbreviations used

m married.

m 1, m 2 married first, married second.

m (2) married X: this was spouse's second marriage.

q.v. appears elsewhere on this family tree with further detail.

→ additional siblings omitted.

↓ family line continues.

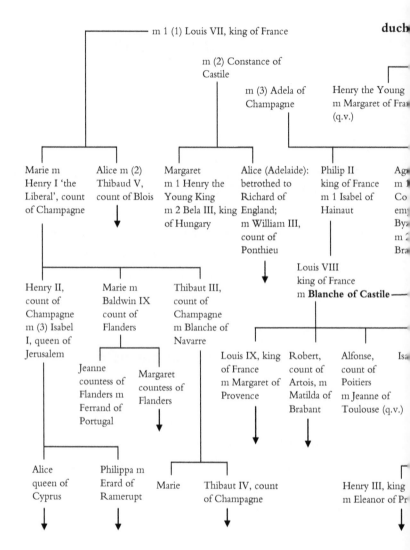

duch

m 1 (1) Louis VII, king of France

m (2) Constance of Castile

m (3) Adela of Champagne

Henry the Young m Margaret of Fran (q.v.)

Marie m Henry I 'the Liberal', count of Champagne	Alice m (2) Thibaud V, count of Blois	Margaret m 1 Henry the Young King m 2 Bela III, king of Hungary	Alice (Adelaide): betrothed to Richard of England; m William III, count of Ponthieu	Philip II king of France m 1 Isabel of Hainaut	Ag m 1 Co em Byz m 2 Bra

Henry II, count of Champagne m (3) Isabel I, queen of Jerusalem

Marie m Baldwin IX count of Flanders

Thibaut III, count of Champagne m Blanche of Navarre

Louis VIII king of France m **Blanche of Castile** ——

Jeanne countess of Flanders m Ferrand of Portugal

Margaret countess of Flanders

Louis IX, king of France m Margaret of Provence

Robert, count of Artois, m Matilda of Brabant

Alfonse, count of Poitiers m Jeanne of Toulouse (q.v.)

Isa

Alice queen of Cyprus

Philippa m Erard of Ramerupt

Marie

Thibaut IV, count of Champagne

Henry III, king m Eleanor of Pr

1. The descendants of Eleanor of Aquitaine, queen of France and of England

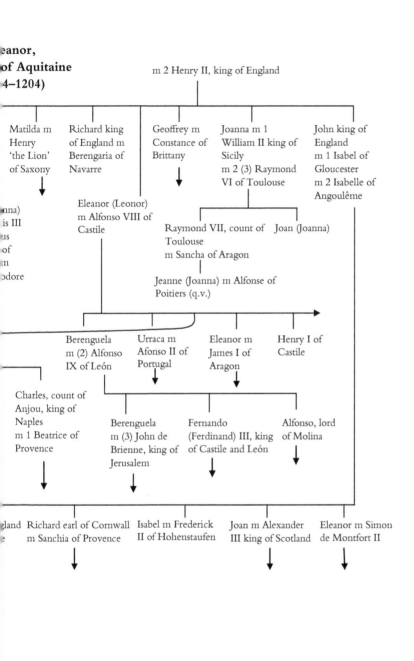

**eanor,
of Aquitaine
4–1204)**

m 2 Henry II, king of England

Matilda m
Henry
'the Lion'
of Saxony

Richard king
of England m
Berengaria of
Navarre

Geoffrey m
Constance of
Brittany

Joanna m 1
William II king of
Sicily
m 2 (3) Raymond
VI of Toulouse

John king of
England
m 1 Isabel of
Gloucester
m 2 Isabelle of
Angoulême

nna)
is III
us
of
m
odore

Eleanor (Leonor)
m Alfonso VIII of
Castile

Raymond VII, count of   Joan (Joanna)
Toulouse
m Sancha of Aragon

Jeanne (Joanna) m Alfonse of
Poitiers (q.v.)

Berenguela
m (2) Alfonso
IX of León

Urraca m
Afonso II of
Portugal

Eleanor m
James I of
Aragon

Henry I of
Castile

Charles, count of
Anjou, king of
Naples
m 1 Beatrice of
Provence

Berenguela
m (3) John de
Brienne, king of
Jerusalem

Fernando
(Ferdinand) III, king
of Castile and León

Alfonso, lord
of Molina

land
e

Richard earl of Cornwall
m Sanchia of Provence

Isabel m Frederick
II of Hohenstaufen

Joan m Alexander
III king of Scotland

Eleanor m Simon
de Montfort II

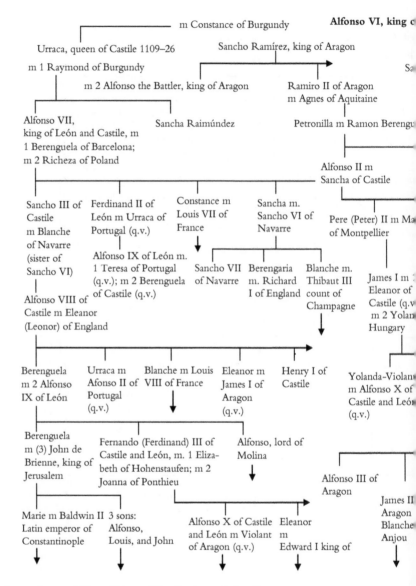

2. The descendants of King Alfonso VI of León and Castile

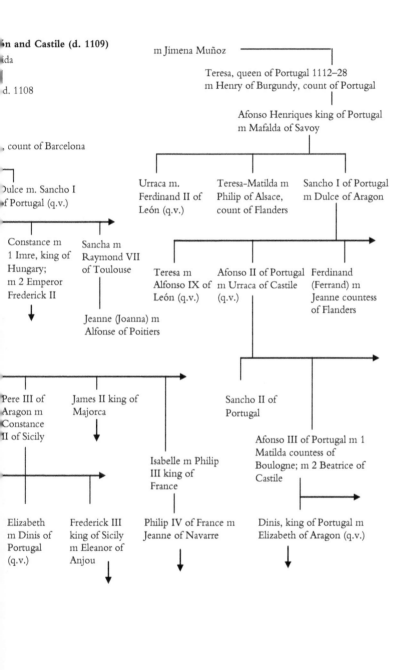

n and Castile (d. 1109)

ida

d. 1108

m Jimena Muñoz

Teresa, queen of Portugal 1112–28
m Henry of Burgundy, count of Portugal

Afonso Henriques king of Portugal
m Mafalda of Savoy

, count of Barcelona

Dulce m. Sancho I
of Portugal (q.v.)

Urraca m.
Ferdinand II of
León (q.v.)

Teresa-Matilda m
Philip of Alsace,
count of Flanders

Sancho I of Portugal
m Dulce of Aragon

Constance m
1 Imre, king of
Hungary;
m 2 Emperor
Frederick II

Sancha m
Raymond VII
of Toulouse

Jeanne (Joanna) m
Alfonse of Poitiers

Teresa m
Alfonso IX of
León (q.v.)

Afonso II of Portugal
m Urraca of Castile
(q.v.)

Ferdinand
(Ferrand) m
Jeanne countess
of Flanders

Pere III of
Aragon m
Constance
II of Sicily

James II king of
Majorca

Sancho II of
Portugal

Isabelle m Philip
III king of
France

Afonso III of Portugal m 1
Matilda countess of
Boulogne; m 2 Beatrice of
Castile

Elizabeth
m Dinis of
Portugal
(q.v.)

Frederick III
king of Sicily
m Eleanor of
Anjou

Philip IV of France m
Jeanne of Navarre

Dinis, king of Portugal m
Elizabeth of Aragon (q.v.)

Alfonso VII, king of León and Castile, m 1 Berenguela of Barcelona; m 2 Richeza of Poland

Sancho III of Castile
m Blanche of Navarre (q.v.)

Ferdinand II of León m
Urraca of Portugal

Constance m (2) Lo■
VII of France

Alfonso VIII, king of Castile m
Eleanor (Leonor) of
England

Alfonso IX of León m. 1 Teresa of
Portgual; m 2 Berenguela of Castile
(q.v.)

Berenguela
m (2) Alfonso IX
of León

Urraca m Afonso II of
Portugal

**Blanche o■
queen of Frar
Died 1**

m. Louis VIII, king ■

Berenguela
m (3) John de
Brienne, king of
Jerusalem

Fernando
(Ferdinand) III, king
of Castile and León

Alfonso,
lord of
Molina

Louis IX (Saint Louis), king
of France m Margaret of
Provence

R■
of
M
Br

Marie m Baldwin
II Latin emperor
of Constantinople

Alfonso, m
Mary
countess
of Eu

Louis m
Agnes of
Beaumont

John, count
of Montfort

Isabelle m
Thibaut V
of Cham-
pagne
(q.v.)

Philip III m 1
Isabelle of
Aragon;
m 2 Maria of
Brabant

Philip de
Courtenay m
Beatrice of
Naples (q.v.)

John
count
of Eu

Blanche
of Eu

Blanche

Margaret
countess of
Tripoli

Philip IV of France m
Jeanne I of Navarre (q.v.)

Charles of Valo■
Catherine I de ■

Catherine I de Courtenay m (2)
Charles of Valois (q.v.)

Louis X of France
and I of Navarre
d. 1316

Isabelle m
Edward II of
England

Philip VI of
France

Cather
m (2)
Taran■

Catherine II de Courtenay m
(2) Philip, prince of Taranto
(q.v.)

Jeanne II of Navarre

Louis of T■
d 1362

3. The family of Blanche of Castile, queen of France

García Ramírez, king of Navarre m Margaret of L'Aigle

Sancha m Alfonso
II of Aragon

Sancha m. Sancho VI of Navarre

Blanche of Navarre m
Sancho III of Castile (q.v.)

Sancho VII
of Navarre

Berengaria
m. Richard I
of England

Blanche m. Thibaut III
count of Champagne

tile
223–26

Eleanor m
James I of
Aragon

Henry I of Castile

Marie

nce, d. 1226

Thibaut IV count of
Champagne, I king of
Navarre m 2 Margaret of
Bourbon

count
s, m
of

Alfonse,
count of
Poitiers
m Jeanne of
Toulouse

Isabelle

Charles, count of Anjou,
king of Naples; m 1 Beatrice
of Provence; m 2 Margaret
of Burgundy

e m
of
e (q.v.)

Robert
II of
Artois

Charles II of Naples m
Maria of Hungary

Robert I of Naples m
1 Yolanda of Aragon

Beatrice m
Philip de
Courtenay
(q.v.)

Thibaud V of
Champagne,
II of Navarre:
m Isabelle of
France (q.v.)

Henry, king of
Navarre m
Blanche of
Artois (q.v.)

enay (q.v.)

Charles duke of
Calabria m 2
Marie of Valois

Charles of Artois

Jeanne I m Philip
IV of France (q.v.)

de Courtenay
prince of

Johanna queen of
Naples: d. 1382

king of Naples:

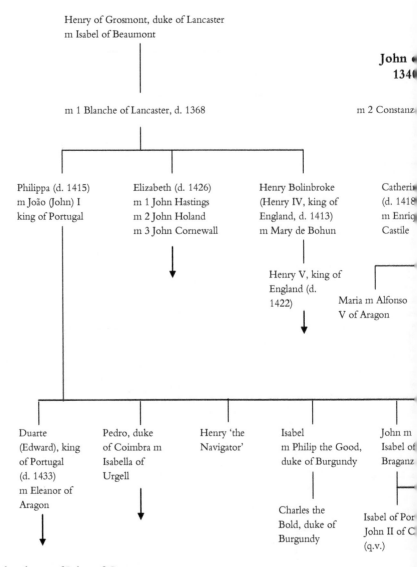

Henry of Grosmont, duke of Lancaster
m Isabel of Beaumont

John o
1340

m 1 Blanche of Lancaster, d. 1368   m 2 Constanz

Philippa (d. 1415)   Elizabeth (d. 1426)   Henry Bolinbroke   Catheri
m João (John) I   m 1 John Hastings   (Henry IV, king of   (d. 1418
king of Portugal   m 2 John Holand   England, d. 1413)   m Enriq
    m 3 John Cornewall   m Mary de Bohun   Castile

Henry V, king of
England (d.
1422)   Maria m Alfonso
    V of Aragon

Duarte   Pedro, duke   Henry 'the   Isabel   John m
(Edward), king   of Coimbra m   Navigator'   m Philip the Good,   Isabel of
of Portugal   Isabella of   duke of Burgundy   Braganz
(d. 1433)   Urgell
m Eleanor of
Aragon

                                    Charles the   Isabel of Por
                                    Bold, duke of   John II of C
                                    Burgundy   (q.v.)

4. The daughters of John of Gaunt
From Anthony Goodman, *John of Gaunt: The Exercise of Princely Power in fourteenth-century Europe* (London: Longman, 1992), pp. 408–409, with additions

Gaunt
399

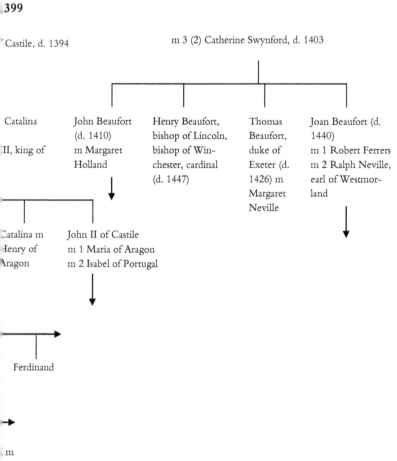

Castile, d. 1394   m 3 (2) Catherine Swynford, d. 1403

Catalina   John Beaufort   Henry Beaufort,   Thomas   Joan Beaufort (d.
                  (d. 1410)   bishop of Lincoln,   Beaufort,   1440)
II, king of   m Margaret   bishop of Win–   duke of   m 1 Robert Ferrers
                  Holland   chester, cardinal   Exeter (d.   m 2 Ralph Neville,
                                       (d. 1447)   1426) m   earl of Westmor-
                                                             Margaret   land
                                                             Neville

Catalina m   John II of Castile
Henry of   m 1 Maria of Aragon
Aragon   m 2 Isabel of Portugal

Ferdinand

m

Endnotes

PREFACE

1. As Helen Solterer wrote in 1991: 'It is interesting to note that modern readers in the past have been inspired by the figure of the female Crusader', but 'much of this work is romanticized for one reason or another': Helen Solterer, 'Figures of Female Militancy in Medieval France', *Signs* 16.3 (1991): pp. 522–549, at p. 549 note 63.

2. Attitudes towards women's involvement in the crusades mirror attitudes to medieval women's exercise of power, depicting it as exceptional, rare, and somehow shocking. For the 'Beyond Exceptionalism' movement, seeking 'the acceptance of female agency, authority, and power as a "non story" in medieval society, without losing sight of the predominance [of] patriarchy and accepted misogyny', see Heather J. Tanner, Laura L. Gathagan and Lois L. Huneycutt, 'Introduction', in *Medieval Elite Women and the Exercise of Power, 1100–1400: Moving beyond the Exceptionalist Debate*, edited by Heather J. Tanner (Cham: Palgrave Macmillan, 2019), pp. 1–18, at p. 15.

3. Sabine Geldsetzer, *Frauen auf Kreuzzügen, 1096–1291* (Darmstadt: Wissenschaftliche Buchgesellschaft, 2003), pp. 181–215, identified and listed women who had taken a crusade vow, women who took part in crusade campaigns but do not appear to have taken a vow, women who were pilgrims or travellers rather than crusaders, and those whose status is unclear; but many of those she listed are anonymous figures and subsequent research has shown that a few of the named crusaders listed did not exist.

CHAPTER 1

1. See, for example, James A. Brundage, 'The Votive Obligations of Crusaders: The Development of a Canonistic Doctrine', *Traditio* 24 (1968): pp. 77–118, at pp. 106, 112–14; Maureen Purcell, 'Women

Crusaders: a Temporary Canonical Aberration?' in *Principalities, Powers and Estates. Studies in Medieval and Early Modern Government and Society*, edited by L. O. Frappell (Adelaide: Adelaide University Union Press, 1979), pp. 57–64; Walter Porges, 'The Clergy, the Poor, and Non-combatants on the First Crusade', *Speculum* 21.1 (1946): pp. 1–23, at pp. 13–15.

2. Alan Murray, 'Sex, Death and the Problem of Single Women in the Armies of the First Crusade', in *Shipping, Trade and Crusade in the Medieval Mediterranean: Studies in Honour of John Pryor*, edited by Ruthy Gertwagen and Elizabeth Jeffreys (Farnham: Ashgate, 2012), pp. 255–70, at pp. 263–4; Fulcher of Chartres in *Fulcheri Carnotensis Historia Hierosolymitana (1095–1127). Mit Erläuterungen und einem Anhange*, edited by Heinrich Hagenmeyer (Heidelberg: Carl Winters, 1913), p. 223 (Book 1 chapter 15). See also James A. Brundage, 'Prostitution, Miscegenation and Sexual Purity in the First Crusade', in *Crusade and Settlement: Papers read at the First Conference of the Society for the Study of the Crusades and the Latin East and presented to R. C. Smail*, edited by Peter W. Edbury (Cardiff: University College Cardiff Press, 1985), pp. 57–65; Andrew Holt, 'Feminine Sexuality and the Crusades: Clerical Opposition to Women as a Strategy for Crusading Success', in *Sexuality in the Middle Ages and Early Modern Times: New Approaches to a Fundamental Cultural-Historical and Literary-Anthropological Theme*, edited by Albrecht Classen (Berlin: De Gruyter, 2008), pp. 449–69.

3. *Itinerarium peregrinorum et gesta regis Ricardi; auctore, ut videtur, Ricardo, canonico Sanctæ Trinitatis Londoniensis*, in *Chronicles and Memorials of the Reign of Richard I*, edited by William Stubbs, Rolls Series 38, vol. 1 (London: Longman, 1864), p. 440 (Book 6 chapter 35); *Chronicle of the Third Crusade, A Translation of the* Itinerarium peregrinorum et gesta regis Ricardi, trans. Helen J. Nicholson, Crusade Texts in Translation 3 (Aldershot: Ashgate, 1997), pp. 379–80; *The History of the Holy War: Ambroise's* Estoire de la Guerre Sainte, edited by Marianne Ailes and Malcolm Barber, 2 vols (Woodbridge: Boydell, 2003), lines 12,201–12,206 (vol. 1, p. 197; vol. 2, p. 192); *L'Estoire de la Guerre Sainte*, edited by Catherine Croizy-Naquet, Classiques français du Moyen Âge 174 (Paris: Honoré Champion, 2014), lines 12,235–12,240, p. 721. For the view that sexual activity is essential to male and female health, see Joan Cadden, *Meanings of Sex Difference in the Middle Ages: Medicine, Science, and Culture* (Cambridge: Cambridge University Press, 1993), pp. 273–6.

4. For example, Christine de Pisan, *The Treasure of the City of Ladies, or the Book of the Three Virtues*, trans. Sarah Lawson (Harmondsworth: Penguin, 1985), p. 129 (Part 2, chapter 9).

5. See, for instance, David J. Hay, *The Military Leadership of Matilda of Canossa, 1046–1115* (Manchester: Manchester University Press, 2008), pp. 247–54; Patrick Corbet, 'Entre Aliénor d'Aquitaine et Blanche de Castille. Les princesses au pouvoir dans la France de l'Est', in *Mächtige Frauen? Königinnen und Fürstinnen im europäischen Mittelalter (11.–14. Jahrhundert)*, edited by Claudia Zey with Sophie Caflisch and Philippe Goridis, Vorträge und Forschungen 81 (Ostfildern: Jan Thorbecke, 2015), pp. 225–47, at 239–40; Geldsetzer, *Frauen auf Kreuzzügen*, pp. 123, 256 note 13; Helen Nicholson, *Medieval Warfare: Theory and Practice of War in Europe, 300–1500* (Basingstoke: Palgrave Macmillan, 2004), pp. 61–3; Katrin E. Sjursen, 'Pirate, Traitor, Wife: Jeanne of Belleville and the Categories of Fourteenth-Century French Noblewomen', in *Medieval Elite Women and the Exercise of Power, 1100–1400: Moving beyond the Exceptionalist Debate*, edited by Heather J. Tanner (Cham: Palgrave Macmillan, 2019), pp. 135–56, at p. 136; Katrin E. Sjursen, 'The War of the Two Jeannes and the Role of the Duchess in Lordship in the Fourteenth Century', *Medieval Feminist Forum* 51.1 (2015): pp. 4–40; Justine Firnhaber-Baker, 'The Social Constituency of the Jacquerie Revolt of 1358', *Speculum* 95.3 (2020): pp. 689–715, at p. 711; Jean A. Truax, 'Anglo-Norman Women at War: Valiant Soldiers, Prudent Strategists or Charismatic Leaders?' in *The Circle of War in the Middle Ages: Essays on Medieval Military and Naval History*, edited by Donald J. Kagay and L. J. Andrew Villalon (Woodbridge: Boydell, 1999), pp. 111–25; James E. Gilbert, 'A Medieval "Rosie the Riveter"? Women in France and Southern England during the Hundred Years War', in *The Hundred Years War: A Wider Focus*, edited by L. J. Andrew Villalon and Donald J. Kagay, History of Warfare 25 (Leiden: Brill, 2005), pp. 333–63.

6. Simon Lloyd, *English Society and the Crusade, 1216–1307* (Oxford: Oxford University Press, 1988), pp. 77–8, 168–9, 173–5, 260, 268; Christopher Tyerman, *England and the Crusades, 1095–1588* (Chicago, IL: University of Chicago Press, 1988), pp. 171, 209–11, 221, 283–5; Jonathan Riley-Smith, 'Family Traditions and Participation in the Second Crusade', in *The Second Crusade and the Cistercians*, edited by Michael Gervers (New York: St Martin's Press, 1992), pp. 101–8; James M. Powell, 'The Role of Women in the Fifth Crusade', in *The Horns of Ḥaṭṭīn*, edited by B. Z. Kedar (Jerusalem: Yad Izhak Ben-Zvi, 1992), pp. 294–301; Helen Nicholson, 'Women on the Third Crusade', *Journal of Medieval History* 23.4 (1997): pp. 335–49; *Gendering the Crusades*, edited by Susan B. Edgington and Sarah Lambert (Cardiff: University of Wales Press, 2001); Stephen Bennett, *Elite Participation in the Third Crusade* (Woodbridge: Boydell, 2021), pp. 109–14.

7. Geldsetzer, *Frauen auf Kreuzzügen*, pp. 181–213.

8. Christoph T. Maier, 'The Roles of Women in the Crusade Movement: A Survey', *Journal of Medieval History* 30.1 (2004): pp. 61–82, at pp. 69–70.

9. Conor Kostick, 'Women and the First Crusade: prostitutes or pilgrims?' in *Studies on Medieval and Early Modern Women 4: Victims or Viragos?* edited by Christine Meek and Catherine Lawless (Dublin: Four Courts Press, 2005), pp. 57–68; Conor Kostick, *The Social Structure of the First Crusade* (Leiden: Brill, 2008), pp. 271–85; Murray, 'Sex, Death and the Problem of Single Women', pp. 255–70.

10. Geldsetzer, *Frauen auf Kreuzzügen*, pp. 157–62; Yvonne Friedman, *Encounter between Enemies: Captivity and Ransom in the Latin Kingdom of Jerusalem* (Leiden: Brill, 2002), pp. 162–86; Yvonne Friedman, 'Captivity and Ransom: the Experience of Women', in *Gendering the Crusades*, edited by Susan B. Edgington and Sarah Lambert (Cardiff: University of Wales Press, 2001), pp. 121–39.

11. Gilbert, 'A Medieval "Rosie the Riveter"?' pp. 345, 348–9, 351; see also Firnhaber-Baker, 'The Social Constituency of the Jacquerie Revolt', p. 711.

12. On the problem of impurity see Leigh Ann Craig '"Stronger than Men and braver than Knights": Women and the Pilgrimages to Jerusalem and Rome in the Later Middle Ages', *Journal of Medieval History* 29.3 (2003): pp. 153–75, at pp. 166–7.

13. Geldsetzer, *Frauen auf Kreuzzügen*, pp. 95–103; Albert of Aachen, *Historia Ierosolimitana: History of the Journey to Jerusalem*, edited and translated by Susan B. Edgington (Oxford: Oxford University Press, 2007), pp. 138–41 (Book 3, section 2).

14. Johannes de Tulbia, 'De Domino Iohanne, rege Ierusalem', in *Quinti Belli Sacri Scriptores Minores*, edited by Reinhold Röhricht, Publications de la Société de l'Orient Latin, Série historique 2 (Geneva: J.-G. Fick, 1879), pp. 119–40, at p. 139; Oliver of Paderborn in Jessalynn Bird, Edward Peters, and James M. Powell, eds and trans., *Crusade and Christendom: Annotated Documents in Translation from Innocent III to the Fall of Acre, 1187–1291* (Philadelphia, PA: University of Pennsylvania Press, 2013), pp. 193, 221.

15. Jessalynn Bird, 'Indulgences and Penance', in *The Crusades: An Encyclopedia*, ed. Alan V. Murray, 4 vols (Santa Barbara, CA: ABC Clio, 2006), vol. 2, pp. 633–7.

16. Matthew E. Parker, '*Papa et pecunia*: Innocent III's combination of Reform and Fiscal Policy to Finance Crusades', *Mediterranean Historical Review* 32.1 (2017): pp. 1–23, at pp. 6–7, 13; James A. Brundage, *Medieval*

Canon Law and the Crusader (Madison, WI: University of Wisconsin Press, 1969), p. 77; Geldsetzer, *Frauen auf Kreuzzügen*, pp. 34–41.

17. Maier, 'The Roles of Women in the Crusade Movement', citing (for instance), Constance M. Rousseau, 'Home Front and Battlefield: The Gendering of Papal Crusading Policy (1095–1221)', in *Gendering the Crusades*, edited by Susan B. Edgington and Sarah Lambert (Cardiff: University of Wales Press, 2001), pp. 31–44; Thérèse de Hemptinne, 'Les épouses de croisés et pèlerins flamandes aux XIᵉ et XIIᵉ siècles: L'exemple des comtesses de Flandre Clémence et Sybille', in *Autour de la première Croisade. Actes du colloque de la Society for the Study of the Crusades and the Latin East, Clermont-Ferrand, 22–25 juin 1995*, edited by Michel Balard (Paris: Publications de la Sorbonne, 1996), pp. 83–95.

18. Recent scholarship on some of these broader aspects includes: M. Cecilia Gaposchkin, *Invisible Weapons: Liturgy and the Making of Crusade Ideology* (Ithaca, NY: Cornell University Press, 2017); Amnon Linder, *Raising Arms: Liturgy in the Struggle to Liberate Jerusalem in the Late Middle Ages* (Turnhout: Brepols, 2003); Megan Cassidy-Welch, ed., *Remembering the Crusades and Crusading* (London: Routledge, 2017); Danielle E. A. Park, *Papal Protection and the Crusader: Flanders, Champagne, and the Kingdom of France, 1095–1222* (Woodbridge: Boydell, 2018); Simon Thomas Parsons and Linda M. Paterson, eds, *Literature of the Crusades* (Cambridge: D. S. Brewer, 2018); Christopher Tyerman, *How to Plan a Crusade: Reason and Religious War in the High Middle Ages* (London: Allen Lane, 2015).

19. Giles Constable, 'The Historiography of the Crusades', in *The Crusades from the Perspective of Byzantium and the Muslim World*, edited by Angeliki E. Laiou and Roy Parviz Mottahedeh (Dumbarton Oaks: Dumbarton Oaks Research Library, 2001), pp. 1–22, at p. 12. For the term 'crusader states', see Andrew D. Buck, 'Settlement, Identity, and Memory in the Latin East: An Examination of the Term "Crusader States"', *English Historical Review* 135/573 (2020): pp. 271–302.

20. Constable, 'Historiography', pp. 12–14.

21. Norman Housley, *The Later Crusades: From Lyons to Alcazar, 1274–1580* (Oxford: Oxford University Press, 1992), pp. 2–6, 47–8, 389–91.

22. Taddesse Tamrat, 'Ethiopia, the Red Sea and the Horn', in *The Cambridge History of Africa, volume 3: from c. 1050 to c. 1600*, edited by Roland Oliver (Cambridge: Cambridge University Press, 1977), pp. 98–182, at pp. 169–77, 181–2; Verena Krebs, *Medieval Ethiopian Kingship, Craft, and Diplomacy with Latin Europe* (Cham: Palgrave Macmillan, 2021), p. 154; Margaux Herman, 'Towards a History of Women in Medieval Ethiopia', in

A Companion to Medieval Ethiopia and Eritrea, edited by Samantha Kelly (Leiden: Brill, 2020), pp. 365–94, at pp. 393–4.

23. [Miguel de Castanhoso] *The Portuguese expedition to Abyssinia in 1541–1543, as narrated by Castanhoso*, trans. R. S. Whiteway, Hakluyt Society second series vol. 10 (London: Hakluyt Society, 1902), pp. 4, 6, 7, 8, 19–20, 68–9, 72.

24. *The True History of the Conquest of New Spain by Bernal Díaz del Castillo, one of its conquerors, from the only exact copy made of the Original Manuscript*, edited by Genaro García, translated with introduction and notes by Alfred Percival Maudslay, Hakluyt Society second series 23 (London: Hakluyt Society, 1908), pp. 7, 13–14, 26, 97–9, 111, 121, 127, 128–130, 231, 244, 256, 269, 280 (Book 1, chapters 1–2, 5, Book 2, chapters 27–28, 31, 34, 36, Book 4, chapters 63, 66, 69, 73, 77).

25. For a survey, see: Sylvia Schein, 'Bridget of Sweden, Margery Kempe and Women's Jerusalem Pilgrimages in the Middle Ages', *Mediterranean Historical Review* 14:1 (1999): pp. 44–58.

26. Second Crusade: *The Conquest of Lisbon: De expugnatione Lyxbonense*, translated by Charles Wendell David, foreword and bibliography by Jonathan Phillips (New York: Columbia University Press, 2001), pp. 70, 108, 120; Odo of Deuil, *De Profectione Ludovici VII in Orientem; The Journey of Louis VII to the East*, edited and translated by Virginia Gingerick Berry (New York: Columbia University Press, 1948), pp. 16, 22, 34, 38, 40, 44, 76; Third Crusade: *Das Itinerarium peregrinorum: eine zeitgenössische englische Chronik zum dritten Kreuzzug in ursprünglicher Gestalt*, edited by Hans Eberhard Mayer, Schriften der Monumenta Germaniae historica (Deutsches Institut für Erforschung des Mittelalters) 18 (Stuttgart: Anton Hiersemann, 1962), p. 277 line 12, p. 278 line 17, p. 309 line 5; 'Narratio de Itinere Navali Peregrinorum Hierosolymam Tendentium et Silviam Capientium, A. D. 1189', edited by Charles Wendell David, *Proceedings of the American Philosophical Society* 81.5 (1939): pp. 591–676, at pp. 610, 636; for Louis IX's first crusade as a pilgrimage, see Caroline Smith, *Crusading in the Age of Joinville* (Aldershot: Ashgate, 2006), pp. 109–17; for the link between crusades and pilgrimage in the fourteenth century see Timothy Guard, *Chivalry, Kingship and Crusade: The English Experience in the Fourteenth Century* (Woodbridge: Boydell, 2013), pp. 21, 28, 73–4, 95–6, 101–2, 120, 156; in the 1350s Geoffroi de Charny equated 'voiages et pelerinages' (journeys and pilgrimages) as undertakings in which young warriors may make their reputation: *The Book of Chivalry of Geoffroi de Charny: Text, Context, and Translation*, edited and translated by Richard W. Kaeuper and Elspeth Kennedy (Philadelphia: University of

Pennsylvania Press, 1996), p. 90, section 9; Philippe de Mézières, Chancellor of the Frankish kingdom of Cyprus, entitled his book urging Christians to unite in a new crusade 'The Dream of the old pilgrim': Philippe de Mézières, Chancellor of Cyprus, *Le Songe du vieil pelerin*, edited by G. W. Coopland, 2 vols (Cambridge: Cambridge University Press, 1969); Henry Despenser's crusade of 1383, in *Documents on the Later Crusades, 1274–1580*, edited and translated by Norman Housley (Basingstoke: Macmillan, 1996), p. 96.

27. Jonathan Riley-Smith, *The First Crusade and the Idea of Crusading* (London: Athlone Press, 1986), p. 22; James Muldoon, 'Crusading and Canon Law', in *Palgrave Advances in the Crusades*, edited by Helen J. Nicholson (Basingstoke: Palgrave Macmillan, 2005), pp. 37–57, at p. 46.

28. Christopher Tyerman, *The Debate on the Crusades* (Manchester: Manchester University Press, 2011), p. 23; Christopher Tyerman, *The Invention of the Crusades* (Basingstoke: Macmillan, 1998), pp. 20–4, 27–8; Gaposchkin, *Invisible Weapons*, pp. 65–91.

29. Gaposchkin, *Invisible Weapons*, pp. 230–2.

30. Bird, Peters, and Powell, eds and trans., *Crusade and Christendom*, p. 447; I. L. Bass, 'The Crozier and the Cross: Crusading and the English Episcopate, *c.* 1170–1313' (PhD thesis, Manchester Metropolitan University, 2019), p. 148.

31. Craig, '"Stronger than Men and Braver than Knights"', pp. 153–75.

32. Angela E. Bailey, 'Women Pilgrims and their Travelling Companions in twelfth-century England', *Viator* 46.1 (2015): pp. 115–34; Bailey's study relates to pilgrimages within England, but the cases of Margery Kempe and Isabel Parewastell, both lone female pilgrims, suggest that her findings could also apply to pilgrimages abroad.

33. Felicity Riddy, 'Kempe [*née* Brunham], Margery (*b. c.* 1373, *d.* in or after 1438)', in *Oxford Dictionary of National Biography*, edited by H. C. G. Matthew and Brian Harrison (Oxford: Oxford University Press, 2004), online edition accessed 28 September 2020. https://doi-org.abc.cardiff.ac.uk/10.1093/ref:odnb/15337; Anthony Goodman, *Margery Kempe and her World* (Harlow: Longman, 2002), pp. 185–95; *The Book of Margery Kempe*, translated by Anthony Bale (Oxford: Oxford University Press, 2015), pp. 57–72 (chapters 26–30).

34. Anthony Luttrell, 'Chaucer's English Knight and his Holy War', in *Tribute to Alain Blondy* (Valetta: Fondation de Malte, 2017), pp. 211–25, at p. 213.

35. All these examples are from Tyerman, *England and the Crusades*, p. 283; citing *Calendar of the Close Rolls Preserved in the Public Record Office, Edward*

III, vol. VIII: *A.D. 1346–1349* (London: HMSO, 1905), p. 501; *Calendar of Inquisitions Post Mortem and other Analogous Documents Preserved in the Public Record Office*, vol. 14: *Edward III* (London: HMSO, 1952), p. 248, no. 234; *Calendar of the Close Rolls Preserved in the Public Record Office, Richard II*, vol. V: *A.D. 1392–1396* (London: HMSO, 1925), p. 523.

36. Craig, '"Stronger than Men and Braver than Knights"', pp. 158, 162–4, 167, 170–1 173–5; *Felix Fabri (circa 1480–1383 A.D.)*, vol. 1 (part 1), trans. Aubrey Stewart (London: Palestine Pilgrims' Text Society, 1896), p. 11.

37. Susan B. Edgington, 'Crusading Chronicles', in *Encyclopedia of the Medieval Chronicle*, edited by Graeme Dunphy, 2 vols (Leiden: Brill, 2010), vol. 1, pp. 499–500.

38. *The History of the Holy War: Ambroise's* Estoire de la Guerre Sainte, edited by Marianne Ailes and Malcolm Barber; *L'Estoire de la Guerre Sainte*, edited by Catherine Croizy-Naquet; *Itinerarium peregrinorum et gesta regis Ricardi*, edited by William Stubbs; *Chronicle of the Third Crusade: A Translation of the* Itinerarium Peregrinorum et Gesta Regis Ricardi, trans. Helen J. Nicholson.

39. Both translated in [John of] Joinville and [Geoffrey de] Villehardouin, *Chronicles of the Crusades*, translated by M. R. B. Shaw (Harmondsworth: Penguin, 1963).

40. Lisa M. Ruch, 'Matthew Paris', in *Encyclopedia of the Medieval Chronicle*, edited by Graeme Dunphy, 2 vols (Leiden: Brill, 2010), vol. 2, pp. 1093–5.

41. Peter W. Edbury and John Gordon Rowe, *William of Tyre: Historian of the Latin East* (Cambridge: Cambridge University Press, 1988); Peter W. Edbury, 'Ernoul, *Eracles*, and the Collapse of the Kingdom of Jerusalem', in *The French of Outremer: Communities and Communications in the Crusading Mediterranean*, edited by Laura K. Morreale and Nicholas L. Paul (New York: Fordham University Press, 2018), pp. 44–67.

42. Lindy Grant, 'Récit d'un ménestrel de Reims', in *Encyclopedia of the Medieval Chronicle*, edited by Graeme Dunphy, 2 vols (Leiden: Brill, 2010), vol. 2, p. 1265.

43. *The Alexiad of Anna Comnena*, translated by E. R. A. Sewter (Harmondsworth: Penguin, 1969); Jakov Ljubarskij, 'Why is the *Alexiad* a Masterpiece of Byzantine Literature?' in *Anna Komnene and her Times*, edited by Thalia Gouma-Peterson (New York: Garland, 2000), pp. 169–85, quotation at p. 170.

44. ʿImād al-Dīn al-Iṣfahānī, *Conquête de la Syrie et de la Palestine par Saladin (al-Fatḥ al-qussī fī l-fatḥ al-qudsī)*, translated by Henri Massé, Documents relatifs à l'histoire des Croisades 10 (Paris: Paul Geuthner, 1972); *The Rare*

and Excellent History of Saladin or al-Nawādir al-Sulṭāniyya wa'l-Maḥāsin al-Yūsufiyya by Bahā' al-Dīn Ibn Shaddād, translated by D. S. Richards, Crusade Texts in Translation 7 (Aldershot: Ashgate, 2002).

45. *The Chronicle of Ibn al-Athīr for the Crusading Period from al-Kāmil fī'l-ta'rīkh. Part 2: The Years 541–589/1146–1193: The Age of Nur al-Din and Saladin*, trans. D. S. Richards, Crusade Texts in Translation 15 (Farnham: Ashgate, 2007).

46. Usama ibn Munqidh, *The Book of Contemplation: Islam and the Crusades*, translated by Paul M. Cobb (London: Penguin, 2008), pp. xxxiv–xxxv.

47. For an analysis of the problems see Natasha Hodgson, 'Nobility, Women and Historical Narratives of the Crusades and the Latin East', *Al-Masāq: Islam and the Medieval Mediterranean* 17.1 (2005): pp. 61–85; Natasha R. Hodgson, *Women, Crusading and the Holy Land in Historical Narrative* (Woodbridge: Boydell, 2007). On clerics' anxiety about women as sexual temptresses see also, for example, Holt, 'Feminine Sexuality', pp. 456–58, 461–7.

48. *Gesta Francorum et Aliorum Hierosolimitanorum: The Deeds of the Franks and the other Pilgrims to Jerusalem*, edited and translated by Rosalind Hill (Edinburgh: Thomas Nelson, 1962), pp. 53–4.

49. Natasha Hodgson, 'The Role of Kerbogha's Mother in the *Gesta Francorum* and Selected Chronicles of the First Crusade', in *Gendering the Crusades*, edited by Susan B. Edgington and Sarah Lambert (Cardiff: University of Wales Press, 2001), pp. 163–76.

50. Ralph V. Turner, *Eleanor of Aquitaine: Queen of France, Queen of England* (New Haven, CT: Yale University Press, 2009), pp. 81, 86, 88; Geldsetzer, *Frauen auf Kreuzzügen*, pp. 122, 124–5; Hodgson, *Women, Crusading and the Holy Land*, pp. 131–4; Jonathan Phillips, *The Second Crusade: Extending the Frontiers of Christendom* (New Haven, CT: Yale University Press, 2007), pp. 210–12; Thomas Fuller, *The Historie of the Holy Warre*, 3rd ed. (Cambridge: John Williams, 1640), p. 80 (Book 2 chapter 28); Odo of Deuil, *De Profectione Ludovici VII in Orientem*, pp. 56–7; *O City of Byzantium, Annals of Niketas Choniatēs*, trans. Harry J. Magoulias (Detroit: Wayne State University, 1984), p. 35 (section 60).

51. Sarah Lambert, 'Crusading or Spinning', in *Gendering the Crusades*, edited by Susan B. Edgington and Sarah Lambert (Cardiff: University of Wales Press, 2001), pp. 1–15, at p. 9.

52. *La Continuation de Guillaume de Tyr (1184–1197)*, edited by Margaret Ruth Morgan, Documents relatifs à l'histoire des Croisades 14 (Paris: Paul Geuthner, 1982), p. 36 (section 22); *Die lateinische Fortsetzung Wilhelms von Tyrus*, edited by Marianne Salloch (Leipzig: H. Eichblatt, 1934), p. 58

(Book 1 chapter 6); Jonathan Phillips, *The Life and Legend of the Sultan Saladin* (London: Bodley Head, 2019), p. 168.

53. Francesco Balbi di Correggio, *The Siege of Malta 1565*, trans. Henry Alexander Balbi (Copenhagen: Dr h. c. Ole Rostock, 1961), pp. 31–2.

54. *The Chronicle of Muntaner*, trans. Lady Goodenough, vol. 1, Hakluyt Society 2nd series 47 (London: Hakluyt Society, 1920), pp. 82–6 (chapters 32–3); new online edn at: Ramon Muntaner, *Chronicle*, trans. Lady Goodenough (Cambridge Ontario: Parentheses, 2000), pp. 69–72, at: www.yorku.ca/inpar/muntaner_goodenough.pdf, accessed 7 December 2020. For the crusade see Norman Housley, *The Italian Crusades: The Papal-Angevin Alliance and the Crusades against Christian Lay Powers, 1254–1343* (Oxford: Oxford University Press, 1982), pp. 18–19.

55. Albert of Aachen, the Anonymous of Mainz, and Solomon ben Simson, in *The First Crusade: The Chronicle of Fulcher of Chartres and Other Source Materials*, edited by Edward Peters, 2nd ed. (Philadelphia, PA: University of Pennsylvania Press, 1998), pp. 111, 118–19, 130; Guibert of Nogent, translated in *The Deeds of God through the Franks: a translation of Guibert de Nogent's* Gesta Dei per Francos, trans. Robert Levine (Woodbridge: Boydell, 1997), p. 156.

56. Hilary Rhodes, *The Crown and the Cross: Burgundy, France, and the Crusades, 1095–1223*, Outremer: Studies in the Crusades and the Latin East 9 (Turnhout: Brepols, 2020), pp. 80–7.

57. Rhodes, *The Crown and the Cross*, p. 85, note 133.

58. Rhodes, *The Crown and the Cross*, pp. 80–7; Hodgson, *Women, Crusading and the Holy Land*, pp. 100, 215.

59. Geldsetzer, *Frauen auf Kreuzzügen*, pp. 191–2; Valette is listed as an individual who took crusade vows by Reinhold Röhricht, *Studien zur Geschichte des fünften Kreuzzuges* (Innsbruck: Wagner'schen Universitäts-Buchhandlung, 1891), p. 132; followed by James M. Powell, *Anatomy of a Crusade, 1213–1221* (Philadelphia, PA: University of Pennsylvania Press, 1986), p. 245. Röhricht's source of reference was M. Guirondet, 'Les Croisiés de Saint-Antonin', in *Bulletin Archéologique et Historique publié sous la direction de la Société Archéologique de Tarn-et-Garonne*, 5 (1877): pp. 113–24, at pp. 122–3, which gives the crusader's name as Jordan Valette.

60. *Itinerarium peregrinorum et gesta regis Ricardi*, p. 101 (Book 1, chapter 50); *Chronicle of the Third Crusade*, p. 106; *The History of the Holy War*, lines 3622–3655 (vol. 1, pp. 58–9, vol. 2, p. 83); *L'Estoire de la Guerre Sainte*, lines 3627–3660, pp. 441–2.

61. *The Alexiad of Anna Comnena*, p. 309.

62. For example, the translator of the 'Itinerary of Richard I and others to the Holy Land', in *Chronicles of the Crusades* (London: George Bell and Sons, 1882), pp. 65–339, rendered the terms 'suis' and 'gens' as 'his men' when 'his people' would be equally or more appropriate, at pp. 142, 171, 195, 220, 285, 303, 311, 335; for the Latin text see the *Itinerarium peregrinorum et gesta regis Ricardi*, pp. 123, 167, 203, 239, 384, 398, 437 (Book 1, chapter 64, Book 2, Chapters 19, 40, 41, Book 3, chapter 23, Book 5, chapter 39, Book 6, Chapters 3, 9, 34).

63. Bernold of St Blasien (Constance) and the Annals of Disibodenberg described women joining the First Crusade wearing men's clothing: quoted by Kostick, 'Women and the First Crusade: prostitutes or pilgrims?' pp. 67–8; Kostick, *The Social Structure of the First Crusade*, pp. 283–4; according to one 'life' of St Hildegund von Schönau her father dressed her in male clothing in order to go on pilgrimage to Jerusalem before the Third Crusade: Valerie R. Hotchkiss, *Clothes make the Man: Female Cross Dressing in Medieval Europe*, new ed. (New York: Routledge, 2012), p. 36; Muslim accounts of Frankish crusader women dressed in male armour on the battlefield: 'Imād al-Dīn quoted by Abū Shāma in 'Le Livre des deux jardins', in *Recueil des Historiens des Croisades, Historiens Orientaux*, edited by l'Académie des Inscriptions et Belles-Lettres, vol. 4 (Paris: Imprimerie nationale, 1898), p. 434; *The Chronicle of Ibn al-Athīr*, p. 368.

64. Nicholson, 'Women on the Third Crusade', pp. 337–42, 348–9.

65. Hotchkiss, *Clothes make the Man*, pp. 42–7.

66. Geldsetzer, *Frauen auf Kreuzzügen*, pp. 196–8, citing and amending Benjamin Z. Kedar, 'The Passenger List of a Crusader Ship, 1250: Towards the History of the Popular Element on the Seventh Crusade', *Studi Medievali* 3rd series 13.1 (1972): pp. 267–79.

67. Jonathan Riley-Smith, *The First Crusaders, 1095–1131* (Cambridge: Cambridge University Press, 1997), pp. 28–9; Christoph T. Maier, *Preaching the Crusades: Mendicant Friars and the Cross in the Thirteenth Century* (Cambridge: Cambridge University Press, 1994), pp. 116–22.

68. Geldsetzer, *Frauen auf Kreuzzügen*, pp. 63–7.

69. Riley-Smith, *The First Crusaders*, pp. 109–18 (quotation at p. 112), 124–130, 149; Riley-Smith, *The First Crusade and the Idea of Crusading*, pp. 41–7.

70. Maier, 'The Roles of Women in the Crusade Movement', pp. 70–1; Geldsetzer, *Frauen auf Kreuzzügen*, pp. 45–67.

71. On this motivation see Firnhaber-Baker, 'The Social Constituency of the Jacquerie Revolt', p. 714.

CHAPTER 2

1. 'Chanson de croisade', in *Songs of the Women* Trouvères, edited by, translated and introduced by Eglal Doss-Quinby, Joan Tasker Grimbert, Wendy Pfeffer, and Elizabeth Aubrey (New Haven, CT: Yale University Press, 2001), p. 146, no. 28 lines 1–2; for another song from the point of view of the abandoned woman see pp. 141–6.

2. Luca Barbieri, 'Crusade Songs and the Old French Literary Canon', in *Literature of the Crusades*, edited by Simon Thomas Parsons and Linda M. Paterson (Cambridge: D. S. Brewer, 2018), pp. 75–95, especially pp. 77–83.

3. James A. Brundage, 'The Crusader's Wife: A Canonistic Quandary', *Studia Gratiana* 12 (1967): pp. 425–41; Brundage, 'The Votive Obligations of Crusaders', pp. 80–81, 100–101, 103–104, 107, 109, 110, 113; Maier, 'The Roles of Women in the Crusade Movement', pp. 71–2.

4. Gerald of Wales, *The Journey through Wales and The Description of Wales*, trans Lewis Thorpe (Harmondsworth: Penguin, 1978), p. 172 (Book 2 Chapter 2); Ironically in view of Gerald's enthusiasm for the crusade, he had to abandon his own plans to join the Third Crusade because of lack of funds: *The Autobiography of Gerald of Wales*, edited and translated by H. E. Butler, new ed. (Woodbridge: Boydell, 2005), pp. 116–17 (Book 2, Chapters 21–22).

5. *Das Itinerarium peregrinorum*, p. 277, lines 17–19 (my translation). On this work, see Hannes Möhring, 'Joseph Iscanus, Neffe Balduins von Canterbury, und eine anonyme englische Chronik des Dritten Kreuzzugs: Versuch einer Identifikation', *Mittellateinisches Jahrbuch* 19 (1984): pp. 184–90; Helen J. Nicholson, 'The Construction of a Primary Source. The Creation of *Itinerarium Peregrinorum* 1', *Cahiers de recherches médiévales et humanistes / Journal of Medieval and Humanistic Studies* 37 (2019): pp. 143–65.

6. Nicholson, 'Women on the Third Crusade', p. 339; *The Chronicle of Ibn al-Athīr*, p. 364.

7. Antoine de la Sale, *Jehan de Saintré*, edited by Jean Misrahi and Charles A. Knudson, Textes Littéraires Français 117 (Geneva: Droz, 1978), p. 187, lines 28–32. For a comparison of women's roles in war in Old French literature and in historical actuality see Sophie Harwood, *Medieval Women and War: Female Roles in the Old French Tradition* (London: Bloomsbury Academic, 2020).

8. See Hay, *The Military Leadership of Matilda of Canossa*.

9. Hay, *The Military Leadership of Matilda of Canossa*, pp. 48–50.

10. Hay, *The Military Leadership of Matilda of Canossa*, pp. 15–16, 121–3; H. E. J. Cowdrey, 'The Mahdia Campaign of 1087', *The English Historical Review* 92/362 (1977): pp. 1–29.

11. Steve Tibble, *The Crusader Armies 1099–1187* (New Haven, CT: Yale University Press, 2018), pp. 10–19; Peter Frankopan, *The First Crusade: The Call from the East* (London: Bodley Head, 2012), pp. 43–70, 87–100. For a discussion of the wider context see, for example, Robert Bartlett, *The Making of Europe. Conquest, Colonization and Cultural Change, 950–1350* (Harmondsworth: Penguin, 1993); Ronnie Ellenblum, *The Collapse of the Eastern Mediterranean: Climate Change and the Decline of the East, 950–1072* (Cambridge: Cambridge University Press, 2012).

12. For the background see Angus MacKay, *Spain in the Middle Ages: From Frontier to Empire, 1000–1500* (Basingstoke: Macmillan, 1977); Bernard F. Reilly, *The Kingdom of León-Castilla under Queen Urraca, 1109–1126* (Princeton, NJ: Princeton University Press, 1982), pp. 3–44. For Alfonso VI and Urraca as successor to the Visigoths, see for example Therese Martin, 'The Art of a Reigning Queen as Dynastic Propaganda in Twelfth-Century Spain', *Speculum* 80.4 (2005): pp. 1134–1171, at pp. 1149–1152, 1156.

13. For a discussion of the relationship and the difference between the 'reconquest' and crusade, see Luis García-Guijarro Ramos, '*Reconquista* and Crusade in the Central Middle Ages. A Conceptual and Historiographical Survey', in *Crusading on the Edge: Ideas and Practice of Crusading in Iberia and the Baltic Region, 1100–1500*, edited by Torben Kjersgaard Nielsen and Iben Fonnesberg-Schmidt, Outremer: Studies in the Crusades and the Latin East 4 (Turnhout: Brepols, 2016), pp. 55–88, at pp. 86–7.

14. Reilly, *The Kingdom of León-Castilla under Queen Urraca*, pp. 26, 44, 50, 55. Alfonso's son Sancho, son of the Muslim Zaida, had died in battle in 1108 fighting the Almoravids.

15. Reilly, *The Kingdom of León-Castilla under Queen Urraca*, pp. 64–65, 67, 73, 91–92, 105, 106, 130.

16. Martin, 'The Art of a Reigning Queen', pp. 1160–3; Angel G. Gordo Molina, 'Urraca I de León y Teresa de Portugal. Las Relaciones de Fronteras y el Ejercicio de la Potestad Femenina en la Primera Mitad del Siglo XII. Jurisdicción, *Imperium* y Linaje', *Intus-Legere Historia* 2.1 (2008): pp. 9–23, at p. 17.

17. Reilly, *The Kingdom of León-Castilla under Queen Urraca*, pp. 111–112, 169.

18. Reilly, *The Kingdom of León-Castilla under Queen Urraca*, pp. 93, 105, 130, 279, 295–297, 309, 316–319, 366.

19. Reilly, *The Kingdom of León-Castilla under Queen Urraca*, pp. 178–179, 326, 355.

20. Marquis d'Albon, ed., *Cartulaire général du l'ordre du Temple 1119?–1150* (Paris: Librairie Ancienne, Honoré Champion, 1913), pp. 7–8, nos 10–11; Marsilio Cassotti, *D. Teresa: A Primeira Rainha de Portugal*, trans. Ana Isabel Ruiz Barata (Lisbon: A Esfera dos Livros, 2008), p. 208. Teresa has been largely overlooked by scholars: see Gordo Molina, 'Urraca I de León y Teresa de Portugal', pp. 13–14; for a more recent assessment of Teresa as queen and hereditary bearer of royal authority see Miriam Shadis, 'Unexceptional Women: Power, Authority, and Queenship in Early Portugal', in *Medieval Elite Women and the Exercise of Power, 1100–1400: Moving beyond the Exceptionalist Debate*, edited by Heather J. Tanner (Cham: Palgrave Macmillan, 2019), pp. 247–70, at pp. 247, 250–8.

21. Reilly, *The Kingdom of León-Castilla under Queen Urraca*, pp. 320, 339, 353, 355, 357, 359, 361, 370; Gordo Molina, 'Urraca I de León y Teresa de Portugal', pp. 15–16 and note 19; Torquato de Sousa Soares, 'O governo de Portugal pela Infanta-Rainha D. Teresa (1112–1128)', in *Colectânea de Estudos em Honra do Professor Doutor Damião Peres* (Lisbon: Academia Portuguesa de História, 1974), pp. 95–119, at pp. 101–3, 106, 107; Carl Erdmann, *Papsturkunden in Portugal*, Abhandlungen der Gesellschaft der Wissenschaften zu Göttingen, Philologisch-Historische Klasse Neue Folge 20 (Berlin: Weidmannsche Buchhandlung, 1927), digitalised version created as part of the project 'Papsturkunden des frühen und hohen Mittelalters', digitised by Matthias Witzleb, edited by Daniel Berger (Göttingen: Akademie der Wissenschaften zu Göttingen, 2009), no. 18, p. 172.

22. *The Latin Chronicle of the Kings of Castile*, translated by Joseph F. O'Callaghan (Tempe AZ: Arizona Center for Medieval and Renaissance Studies, 2002), pp. 30–31, 88–90 (quotation at p. 88); Miriam Shadis, *Berenguela of Castile (1180–1246) and Political Women in the High Middle Ages* (New York: Palgrave Macmillan, 2009), pp. 125, 135–7.

23. *The Latin Chronicle of the Kings of Castile*, pp. 96, 101–102, 134, 143; Shadis, *Berenguela of Castile (1180–1246)*, pp. 133–47.

24. *Chronica Adefonsi Imperatoris*, Book 2 chapter 12, translated as *The Chronicle of Alfonso the Emperor* by Glenn Edward Lipskey (PhD thesis, Northwestern University, 1972), [131]–[132], paragraph 150, online at https://libro.uca.edu/lipskey/chronicle.htm, accessed 13 October 2020. For this story see also Heath Dillard, *Daughters of the Reconquest: Women in Castilian Town Society, 1100–1300* (Cambridge: Cambridge University Press, 1984), p. 15.

25. Martin Aurell, 'Les femmes guerrières (XIe et XIIe siècles)', in *Famille, violence et christianisation au Moyen Âge: mélanges offerts à Michel Rouche*, edited by Martin Aurell and Thomas Deswarte (Paris: Presses universitaires de Paris-Sorbonne, 2005), pp. 319–30, p. 324.

26. Joseph F. O'Callaghan, *The Last Crusade in the West: Castile and the Conquest of Granada* (Philadelphia, PA: University of Pennsylvania Press, 2014), pp. 42, 46–51 (quotations on p. 47).

27. O'Callaghan, *The Last Crusade in the West*, pp. 63–66, 69.

28. Guard, *Chivalry, Kingship and Crusade*, pp. 53–55, 74–75, 95–6; Tyerman, *England and the Crusades*, pp. 275–276, 303.

29. Guard, *Chivalry, Kingship and Crusade*, pp. 57, 58, 62, 64–65, 67, 80–82, 85, 111–112, 133; Tyerman, *England and the Crusades*, pp. 123, 259, 266, 270, 279, 282, 296, 334, 338–9; Anthony Goodman, *John of Gaunt: The Exercise of Princely Power in Fourteenth-Century Europe* (Harlow: Longman, 1992), pp. 43, 94, 111–143, 147–148, 175, 200–3; William E. Lunt, *Financial Relations of the Papacy with England* [vol. 2]: *1327–1534* (Cambridge, MA: Medieval Academy of America, 1962), pp. 544–8.

30. Jennifer R. Goodman, 'The Lady with the Sword: Philippa of Lancaster and the Chivalry of the Infante Dom Henrique (Prince Henry the Navigator)', in *Queens, Regents and Potentates*, edited by Theresa M. Vann (Dallas, TX: Academia Press, 1993), pp. 149–165, quotation at p. 159; P. E. Russell, 'Prince Henry the Navigator', *Diamente* 11 (1960): pp. 3–30, at pp. 27–8; reprinted in P. E. Russell, ed., *Portugal, Spain and the African Atlantic, 1343–1490: Chivalry and Crusade from John of Gaunt to Henry the Navigator* (London: Variorum, 1995), article XI; Housley, *The Later Crusades*, pp. 287–8.

31. Niniane teaches the young Lancelot, in *Lancelot: Roman en prose du XIIIᵉ siècle*, edited by Alexandre Micha, vol. 7, Textes Littéraires Français 288 (Geneva: Droz, 1980), pp. 248–59 (XXIa, 10–24); the damsel presents Arthur with the sword from the lake: *La Suite du Roman de Merlin*, edited by Gilles Roussineau, Textes Littéraires Français 472 (Geneva: Droz, 1996), vol. 1, pp. 50–2, sections 63–65.

32. Felipe Fernández-Armesto, *Before Columbus: Exploration and Colonisation from the Mediterranean to the Atlantic, 1229–1492* (Basingstoke: Macmillan, 1987), pp. 186–92; Housley, *The Later Crusades*, pp. 310–11.

33. O'Callaghan, *The Last Crusade in the West*, p. 123.

34. O'Callaghan, *The Last Crusade in the West*, pp. 125–8; Housley, *The Later Crusades*, p. 297; for Sixtus's grant of crusade taxes see *Documents on the Later Crusades*, pp. 156–62.

35. Fernando del Pulgar, *Crónica de los reyes católicos*, vol. 2, *Guerra de Granada*, edited by Juan de Mata Carriazo (Madrid: Espasa-Calpe, 1943), pp. 418–19, chapter 250.

36. O'Callaghan, *The Last Crusade in the West*, pp. 122–96 (especially 142, 144, 147, 177, 183), 233, 248; Housley, *The Later Crusades*, pp. 296, 306.

37. *Documents on the Later Crusades*, pp. 169–72; Housley, *The Later Crusades*, pp. 311–12; [Bernal Díaz del Castillo], *The True History of the Conquest of New Spain*, pp. 132–135, quotation at p. 133 (Book 2, chapter 37). On Muslim noblewomen assisting the crusaders in fiction, see Hodgson, *Women, Crusading and the Holy Land*, pp. 68–70; Helen J. Nicholson, 'Love in a Hot Climate: Gender Relations in *Florent et Octavien*', in *Languages of Love and Hate: Conflict, Communication, and Identity in the Medieval Mediterranean*, edited by Sarah Lambert and Helen Nicholson, International Medieval Research 15 (Turnhout: Brepols, 2012), pp. 21–36; Jacqueline de Weever, *Sheba's Daughters: Whitening and Demonizing the Saracen Woman in Medieval French Epic* (New York: Garland, 1998).

38. Krebs, *Medieval Ethiopian Kingship*, pp. 143–51; Tamrat, 'Ethiopia, the Red Sea and the Horn', pp. 180–181, quotation at p. 181; Herman, 'Towards a History of Women in Medieval Ethiopia', pp. 391, 393–4; [Miguel de Castanhoso] *The Portuguese expedition to Abyssinia in 1541–1543*, quotation at p. 6.

39. *Willelmi Tyrensis Archiepiscopi Chronicon*/Guillaume de Tyr, *Chronique*, edited by R. B. C. Huygens, vol. 2, Corpus Christianorum Continuatio Mediaeualis 63A (Turnhout: Brepols, 1986), p. 720 (Book 16, Chapter 4, lines 73–82).

40. *Willelmi Tyrensis Archiepiscopi Chronicon*, vol. 2, p. 761 (Book 17, Chapter 1, lines 38–41); Phillips, *The Second Crusade*, pp. 216–18.

41. *Willelmi Tyrensis Archiepiscopi Chronicon*, vol. 2, pp. 768–9 (Book 17, Chapter 7); Phillips, *The Second Crusade*, pp. 221–6.

42. Helen J. Nicholson, 'Queen Sybil of Jerusalem as a Military Leader', in *Von Hamburg nach Java. Studien zur mittelalterlichen, neuen und digitalen Geschichte. Festschrift zu Ehren von Jürgen Sarnowsky*, edited by Jochen Burgtorf, Christian Hoffarth, and Sebastian Kubon (Göttingen: Vandenhoeck & Ruprecht, 2020), pp. 265–76.

43. Housley, *The Later Crusades*, pp. 43, 196–7; George Hill, *A History of Cyprus, volume 3: The Frankish Period, 1432–1571* (Cambridge: Cambridge University Press, 1948), pp. 553–616, 679 (p. 607 on the Hospitallers' right to give asylum).

44. Housley, *The Later Crusades*, pp. 197–9; Hill, *A History of Cyprus, volume 3: 1432–1571*, pp. 657–764, esp. 706.

45. Riley-Smith, 'Family Traditions and Participation in the Second Crusade'; Riley-Smith, *The First Crusaders*, pp. 98–100, 171.

46. Powell, 'The Role of Women in the Fifth Crusade', p. 294.

47. Housley, *The Later Crusades*, p. 92; Charity Cannon Willard, 'Isabel of Portugal and the fifteenth-century Burgundian Crusade', in *Journeys Toward God: Pilgrimage and Crusade*, edited by Barbara N. Sargent-Baur (Kalamazoo, MI: Medieval Institute Publications, 1992), pp. 205–214, at p. 206; Richard Vaughan, *Philip the Good: The Apogee of Burgundy* (London: Longman, 1970), p. 270; Hill, *A History of Cyprus, volume 3: 1432–1571*, pp. 531–6; Richard J. Walsh, 'Charles the Bold and the Crusade: Politics and Propaganda', *Journal of Medieval History* 3.1 (1977): pp. 53–86; Charity Cannon Willard, 'The Patronage of Isabel of Portugal', in *The Cultural Patronage of Medieval Women*, edited by June Hall McCash (Athens, GA: University of Georgia Press, 1996), pp. 306–20, at p. 308.

48. Guy Perry, *John of Brienne: King of Jerusalem, Emperor of Constantinople, c. 1175–1237* (Cambridge: Cambridge University Press, 2013), pp. 128–9, 131, 164–5.

49. Theresa M. Vann, ' "Our father has won a great victory": the Authorship of Berenguela's Account of the Battle of Las Navas de Tolosa, 1212', *Journal of Medieval Iberian Studies* 3.1 (2011): pp. 79–92.

50. Elizabeth M. Hallam and Judith Everard, *Capetian France 987–1328*, 2nd ed. (Harlow: Longman, 2001), pp. 267–70; Lindy Grant, *Blanche of Castile, Queen of France* (New Haven: Yale University Press, 2016), pp. 78–105; André Poulet, 'Capetian Women and the Regency: The Genesis of a Vocation', in *Medieval Queenship*, edited by John Carmi Parsons (Stroud: Alan Sutton, 1994), pp. 93–116, at pp. 108–10.

51. M. C. Gaposchkin, 'Kingship and Crusade in the First Four Moralized Bibles', in *The Capetian Century, 1214–1314*, edited by William Chester Jordan and Jenna Rebecca Phillips (Turnhout: Brepols, 2017), pp. 71–112; Christoph T. Maier, 'The *bible moralisée* and the Crusades', in *The Experience of Crusading, volume one: Western Approaches*, edited by Marcus Bull and Norman Housley (Cambridge: Cambridge University Press, 2003), pp. 209–22; Sean L. Field, *Courting Sanctity: Holy Women and the Capetians* (Ithaca, NY: Cornell University Press, 2019), pp. 1–2, 19–20, 24.

52. John of Joinville, 'The Life of Saint Louis', in Joinville and Villehardouin, *Chronicles of the Crusades*, trans. M. R. B. Shaw (Harmondsworth: Penguin, 1963), pp. 191, 315; Jean Sire de Joinville, *Histoire de Saint Louis, Credo et Lettre à Louis X*, edited by Natalis de Wailly (Paris: Firmin Didot, 1874), pp. 62–3, 330–1, sections 107, 603; Matthew Paris, *Chronica Majora*, edited by Henry Richards Luard, Rolls Series 57, 7 vols (London:

Longman, 1872–1883), vol. 5, pp. 3–5; *Récits d'un ménestrel de Reims au treizième siècle*, edited by Natalis de Wailly (Paris: Renouard, 1876), pp. 191–2 (sections 370–371); Hallam and Everard, *Capetian France*, pp. 275, 279, 281; William Chester Jordan, *Louis IX and the Challenge of the Crusade: A Study in Rulership* (Princeton, NJ: Princeton University Press, 1979), pp. 7–8, 70, 80, 110–24; Grant, *Blanche of Castile*, esp. pp. 130–45 on her regency during Louis IX's crusade.

53. Matthew Paris, *Chronica Majora*, vol. 5, pp. 248–53 (quotations pp. 248, 251); Hallam and Everard, *Capetian France*, pp. 281–2; Grant, *Blanche of Castile*, pp. 141–2.

54. Agnes of Harcourt, 'The Life of Isabelle of France', in *The Writings of Agnes of Harcourt*, edited by Sean L. Field (Notre Dame, IN: University of Notre Dame Press, 2003), pp. 64, 65. For a recent analysis of Agnes and her work see Sean L. Field, 'Agnes of Harcourt as Intellectual: New Evidence for the Composition and Circulation of the *Vie d'Isabelle de France*', in *Women Intellectuals and Leaders in the Middle Ages*, edited by Kathryn Kerby-Fulton, Katie Ann-Marie Bugyis, and John van Engen (Cambridge: D. S. Brewer, 2020), pp. 79–95.

55. Elizabeth Casteen, 'Sex and Politics in Naples: The Regnant Queenship of Johanna I', *Journal of the Historical Society* 11.2 (2011): pp. 183–210; Elizabeth Casteen, *From She-Wolf to Martyr: The Reign and Disputed Reputation of Johanna I of Naples* (Ithaca, NY: Cornell University Press, 2016), pp. 162–95. The Great Schism of 1378–1417 should not be confused with the schism between the Greek Orthodox and the Latin Christian Churches, which began in 1054 when the leaders of the two Churches excommunicated each other, but which never prevented the secular leaders on each side from working together or Latin Christians responding to appeals for aid from Greek Christians: Jonathan Harris, *Byzantium and the Crusades*, 2nd ed. (London: Bloomsbury, 2014), pp. 51, 119, 191, 202–4.

56. Kenneth Setton, *The Papacy and the Levant (1204–1571)*, 4 vols (Philadelphia: American Philosophical Society, 1976–1984), vol. 1: *The Thirteenth and Fourteenth Centuries*, p. 188. Clement VI wrote also to Catherine II of Valois-Courtenay (d. 1346), titular Latin empress (as great granddaughter of Baldwin II of Constantinople and Marie de Brienne) and widow of Philip of Taranto (grandson of Charles I of Anjou and prince of Achaea), noting that she had promised to contribute two galleys to this naval expedition: Setton, *The Papacy and the Levant*, vol. 1, pp. 153, 159–160, 187–8.

57. Anthony T. Luttrell, 'The Hospitallers' Interventions in Cilician Armenia: 1291–1375', in *The Cilician Kingdom of Armenia*, edited by

T. S. R. Boase (Edinburgh: Scottish Academic Press, 1978), pp. 118–44, at p. 131; Setton, *The Papacy and the Levant*, vol. 1, p. 328; Charles Kohler, 'Lettres pontificales concernant l'histoire de la Petite Arménie au XIVᵉ siècle', in *Florilegium ou, Recueil de Travaux d'Érudition dédiés à Monsieur le Marquis Melchior de Vogüé à l'Occasion du quatre-vingtième Anniversaire de sa Naissance, 18 Octobre 1909* (Paris: Imprimerie nationale, 1909), pp. 303–27, at pp. 324–6.

58. Peter W. Edbury, *The Kingdom of Cyprus and the Crusades, 1191–1374* (Cambridge: Cambridge University Press, 1991), pp. 174, 201 note 17, 202; Luttrell, 'The Hospitallers' Interventions', pp. 131–2.

59. Norman Housley, *The Avignon Papacy and the Crusades, 1305–1378* (Oxford: Oxford University Press, 1986), p. 117; F. Cerasoli, 'Gregorio XI e Giovanna I di Napoli. Documenti inediti dell'Archivio segreto Vaticano. Continuazione e fine', *Archivio Storico per le Province Napoletane* 25.1 (1900): pp. 3–26, at pp. 6–8, no. 167; Casteen, 'Sex and Politics in Naples', pp. 201–202, 204–6.

60. Paul Rousset, 'Sainte Catherine de Sienne et le problème de la croisade', *Schweizerische Zeitschrift für Geschichte* 25 (1975): pp. 499–513, at p. 505; Casteen, *From She-Wolf to Martyr*, pp. 189–93.

61. Donald E. Queller, *The Fourth Crusade: The Conquest of Constantinople, 1201–1204* (Leicester: Leicester University Press, 1978), pp. 30–3; Michael Angold, *The Fourth Crusade: Event and Context* (Harlow: Pearson Longman, 2003), p. 40; Harris, *Byzantium and the Crusades*, p. 163; *O City of Byzantium, Annals of Niketas Choniatēs*, pp. 294–5.

62. Peter of les Vaux-de-Cernay, *The History of the Albigensian Crusade*, trans. W. A. Sibly and M. D. Sibly (Woodbridge: Boydell, 1998), p. 59 (section 107), p. 78 (section 141), p. 96 (section 181), p. 132 (section 258), p. 134 (section 265), p. 161 (section 339), p. 205 (section 449), p. 270 (section 600), p. 272 n. 99, p. 273 (section 606B), p. 278 (sections 617–618), p. 296, pp. 294–8; Laurence W. Marvin, *The Occitan War: A Military and Political History of the Albigensian Crusade, 1209–1218* (Cambridge: Cambridge University Press, 2008), pp. 71, 74, 81, 89, 148, 178, 271, 280, 282, 297; Monique Zerner, 'L'épouse de Simon de Montfort et la croisade albigeoise', in *Femmes, mariages, lignages: XIIe–XIVe siècles. Mélanges offerts à Georges Duby* (Brussels: De Boeck-Wesmael, 1992), pp. 449–70: for consideration of Alice's date of death, see Zerner, p. 466.

63. John of Joinville, 'The Life of Saint Louis', pp. 198–9; Jean Sire de Joinville, *Histoire de Saint Louis*, pp. 76–79, sections 137–140.

64. Benjamin Hendrickx, 'The Visit of Marie de Brienne to Cyprus in the Context of her Quest for Assistance to the Latin Empire of

Constantinople', in *Cyprus and the Crusades*, edited by Nicholas Coureas and Jonathan Riley-Smith (Nicosia: Society for the Study of the Crusades and the Latin East and the Cyprus Research Centre, 1995), pp. 59–67; Guy Perry, *The Briennes: The Rise and Fall of a Champenois Dynasty in the Age of the Crusades, c. 950–1356* (Cambridge: Cambridge University Press, 2018), pp. 76, 78, 84–9, 122–5; for the context, see: David Jacoby, 'The Latin Empire of Constantinople and the Frankish States in Greece', in *The New Cambridge Medieval History, volume 5: c.1198–c.1300*, edited by David Abulafia (Cambridge: Cambridge University Press, 1999), pp. 523–42; for Charles's Byzantine policy see also Jean Dunbabin, *Charles I of Anjou: Power, Kingship and State-Making in Thirteenth-Century Europe* (London: Longman, 1998), pp. 93–8; Michael Lower, *The Tunis Crusade of 1270: A Mediterranean History* (Oxford: Oxford University Press, 2018), pp. 92–4.

65. Anthony Luttrell, 'Englishwomen as Pilgrims to Jerusalem: Isolda Parewastell, 1365', in *Equally in God's Image: Women in the Middle Ages*, edited by Julia Bolton Holloway, Constance S. Wright, and Joan Bechtold (New York: Peter Lang, 1990), pp. 184–97, at p. 187; *Les Registres de Boniface VIII*, edited by Georges Digard, Maurice Faucon, Antoine Thomas, and Robert Fawtier (Paris: Ernest Thorin and E. de Boccard, 1884–1935), vol. 3, pp. 290–294, nos. 4380–4386 (quotations from nos. 4380 and 4382); Sylvia Schein, *Fideles Crucis: The Papacy, the West, and the Recovery of the Holy Land 1274–1314* (Oxford: Oxford University Press, 1991), pp. 162–6.

66. Fernández-Armesto, *Before Columbus*, pp. 210–211, 237.

67. Barbara Newman, 'Possessed by the Spirit: Devout Women, Demoniacs, and the Apostolic Life in the Thirteenth Century', *Speculum* 73.3 (1998): pp. 733–70, at p. 762; *Die Fragmente der Libri VIII Miraculorum des Caesarius von Heisterbach*, edited by Aloys Meister (Rome: Herder'schen Verlagshandlung zu Freiburg im Breisgau and Buchhandlung Spithöver, 1901), pp. 88–9 (Book 2, Chapter 16).

68. Jessalynn Bird, 'Preaching and Crusading Memory', in *Remembering the Crusades and Crusading*, edited by Megan Cassidy-Welch (London: Routledge, 2017), pp. 13–33, at p. 25; James of Vitry, 'The Life of Mary of Oignies', translated by Margot H. King, in *Mary of Oignies, Mother of Salvation*, edited by Anneke B. Mulder-Bakker (Turnhout: Brepols, 2006), pp. 33–127, at p. 107 (Book 2, chapter 9, section 82). For the battle of Montgey see Marvin, *The Occitan War*, pp. 105–8.

69. Bridget Morris, *St Birgitta of Sweden* (Woodbridge: Boydell, 1999), pp. 1–2; *The Revelations of St. Birgitta of Sweden*, translated by Denis Searby,

introduction and notes by Bridget Morris, 4 volumes (Oxford: Oxford University Press, 2006–2015).

70. Morris, *St Birgitta of Sweden*, pp. 83–6; *The Revelations of St. Birgitta of Sweden*, volume 2: *Liber Caelestis, Books IV–V*, Book 4 chapter 129, quotation at verse 57; Claire L. Sahlin, 'Holy Women of Scandinavia: A Survey', in *Medieval Holy Women in the Christian Tradition, c. 1100–c. 1500*, edited by A. J. Minnis and Rosalynn Voaden (Turnhout: Brepols, 2010), pp. 689–713, at pp. 697–703.

71. *The Revelations of St. Birgitta of Sweden*, volume 3: *Liber Caelestis, Books VI–VII*, Book 7 chapter 11, quotations at verses 17, 20.

72. *The Revelations of St. Birgitta of Sweden*, volume 2: *Liber Caelestis, Books IV–V*, Book IV chapter 4, verses 38–39, Book IV chapter 1, verse 6.

73. Morris, *St Birgitta of Sweden*, pp. 93, 122–129, 139–41; Casteen, *From She-Wolf to Martyr*, pp. 162–87.

74. Morris, *St Birgitta of Sweden*, pp. 83–4.

75. For Catherine and the crusade, see: *A Companion to Catherine of Siena*, edited by Carolyn Muessig, George Ferzoco, and Beverly Mayne Kienzle (Leiden: Brill, 2012), pp. 5; 30, 31, 35, 39, 82; Suzanne Noffke, 'Catherine of Siena', in *Medieval Holy Women in the Christian Tradition, c. 1100–c. 1500*, edited by A. J. Minnis and Rosalynn Voaden (Turnhout: Brepols, 2010), pp. 601–22, at p. 603; Rousset, 'Sainte Catherine de Sienne et le problème de la croisade'; F. Thomas Luongo, *The Saintly Politics of Catherine of Siena*(Ithaca NY: Cornell University Press, 2006), pp. 83–89, 157–9, 171–2, 204–5; Luttrell, 'Englishwomen as Pilgrims to Jerusalem', pp. 187–8.

76. Morris, *St Birgitta of Sweden*, p. 1 n. 2; Luongo, *The Saintly Politics of Catherine of Siena*, p. 56 (incorrectly calling Birgitta 'queen'), pp. 57–58, 73.

77. Luongo, *The Saintly Politics of Catherine of Siena*, pp. 30–32, 38–40, 44–48, 59, 70 (quotation).

78. Luongo, *The Saintly Politics of Catherine of Siena*, pp. 82–5; see a translation in Vida D. Scudder, *Saint Catherine of Siena as seen in her Letters* (London: Dent, 1911), p. 102.

79. Luongo, *The Saintly Politics of Catherine of Siena*, pp. 85–7 (quotation on p. 86).

80. Luongo, *The Saintly Politics of Catherine of Siena*, pp. 76, 163, 165; Nancy Goldstone, *The Lady Queen: The Notorious Reign of Joanna I, Queen of Naples, Jerusalem, and Sicily* (New York: Walker, 2009), pp. 264–6.

81. Luongo, *The Saintly Politics of Catherine of Siena*, pp. 165–7; see Scudder, *Saint Catherine of Siena*, pp. 121–122, 127–128, 132–133, 184, 234.

82. Luongo, *The Saintly Politics of Catherine of Siena*, pp. 162, 170, 173, 179; see Scudder, *Saint Catherine of Siena*, pp. 170–171, 178–9.

83. Luttrell, 'Englishwomen as Pilgrims to Jerusalem', pp. 187–8.

84. *Procès de Condamnation de Jeanne d'Arc*, edited by Pierre Champion, vol. 1 (Paris: Champion, 1920), p. 199; Christine de Pizan, 'The Tale of Joan of Arc', in *The Selected Writings of Christine de Pizan*, translated by Renate Blumenfeld-Kosinski and Kevin Brownlee (New York: W. W. Norton, 1997), pp. 259–60, stanzas 42–43, 48; Kelly DeVries, *Joan of Arc: A Military Leader* (Stroud: History Press, new edition 2011), pp. vii, 63–5; Jane Marie Pinzino, 'Just War, Joan of Arc, and the Politics of Salvation', in *Hundred Years War: A Wider Focus*, edited by L. J. Andrew Villalon and Donald J Kagay, History of Warfare 25 (Leiden: Brill, 2005), pp. 365–98, at pp. 389–91.

85. Miriam Rita Tessera, 'Philip count of Flanders and Hildegard of Bingen: Crusading against the Saracens or Crusading against Deadly Sin?' in *Gendering the Crusades*, edited by Susan B. Edgington and Susan Lambert (Cardiff: University of Wales Press, 2001), pp. 77–93.

CHAPTER 3

1. *Die Akten des Kanonisationsprozesses Dorotheas von Montau von 1394 bis 1521*, edited by Richard Stachnik with Anneliese Triller and Hans Westpfahl, Forschungen und Quellen Zur Kirchen- und Kulturgeschichte Ostdeutschlands 15 (Cologne: Böhlau, 1978), p. 517.

2. For details of how women lived on crusade and what they did, from active participation in combat to cooking, laundry and childcare, see Geldsetzer, *Frauen auf Kreuzzügen*, pp. 68–176.

3. Riley-Smith, *The First Crusade and the Idea of Crusading*, p. 35.

4. '*Via ad Terram Sanctam* (1289–1293)', in *Projets de Croisade (v. 1290–v. 1330)*, edited by Jacques Paviot, Documents relatifs à l'histoire des croisades 20 (Paris: L'Académie des Inscriptions et Belles-Lettres, 2008), pp. 19, 179.

5. Marino Sanudo Torsello, *The Book of the Secrets of the Faithful of the Cross: Liber Secretorum Fidelium Crucis*, trans. Peter Lock, Crusade Texts in Translation 21 (Farnham: Ashgate, 2011), pp. 121–2, 213, 215–16, 225, 229, 253 (Book 2 chapter 16, Book 3 part 4 chapters 2, 4, 5, 14, part 5 chapter 4, part 6 chapter 11).

6. Philippe de Mézières, *Le Songe du Vieil Pelerin*, vol. 2, pp. 101–2, 437–9 (Book 3, fo. 339r2, 339v2–340r1: my translations); Guard, *Chivalry, Kingship and Crusade*, p. 140; for another analysis see Renate Blumenfeld-Kosinski, 'Roles for Women in Colonial Fantasies of Fourteenth-Century France: Pierre Dubois and Philippe de Mézières', in *The French of Outremer: Communities and Communications in the Crusading*

Mediterranean, edited by Laura K. Morreale and Nicholas L. Paul (New York: Fordham University Press, 2018), pp. 247–81, at pp. 266–70.

7. Cadden, *Meanings of Sex Difference in the Middle Ages*, pp. 273–6; Bernard Hamilton, 'Eleanor of Castile and the Crusading Movement', *Mediterranean Historical Review* 10 (1995): pp. 92–103, at pp. 96–7.

8. Pierre Dubois, *The Recovery of the Holy Land*, trans. Walther I. Brandt (New York: Columbia University Press, 1956), pp. 83, 117–20, 124, 138–9 (sections 16, 60–63, 69, 85); see also Blumenfeld-Kosinski, 'Roles for Women', pp. 247–66.

9. Park, *Papal Protection and the Crusader*, pp. 42–63; Kostick, *The Social Structure of the First Crusade*, pp. 276–8; Murray, 'Sex, Death and the Problem of Single Women', p. 256; Geldsetzer, *Frauen auf Kreuzzügen*, pp. 53–61, 185–6.

10. Park, *Papal Protection and the Crusader*, pp. 143–51; Geldsetzer, *Frauen auf Kreuzzügen*, pp. 51–2, 188–90.

11. [Roger of Howden] *Gesta regis Henrici secundi: The Chronicle of the Reigns of Henry II and Richard I, A.D. 1169–1192*, edited by William Stubbs, Rolls Series 49, vol. 2 (London: Longman, 1867), p. 149.

12. Gregory Leighton, 'Written and Visual Expressions of Authority of Female Monastic Institutions in medieval Livonia: 13th to 15th centuries', *Studia Slavica et Balcanica Petropolitana* 1 (2021): pp. 15–35, at pp. 18–19.

13. Geldsetzer, *Frauen auf Kreuzzügen*, pp. 54–5, 193–5.

14. Jordan, *Louis IX and the Challenge of the Crusade*, p. 216 and note 16; Geldsetzer, *Frauen auf Kreuzzügen*, pp. 56, 57–60, 74, 95, 98, 199–200; Joseph Strayer, 'The Crusades of Louis IX', in *A History of the Crusades*, edited by Kenneth M. Setton, vol. 2, *The Later Crusades, 1189–1311*, edited by Robert Lee Wolff and Harry W. Hazard (Madison: University of Wisconsin Press, 1969), pp. 486–518, at p. 517; Lower, *The Tunis Crusade of 1270*, pp. 120–2, 175–6.

15. Setton, *The Papacy and the Levant*, vol. 1, pp. 196, 197, 200, 209–10.

16. Geldsetzer, *Frauen auf Kreuzzügen*, pp. 51–2.

17. Goodman, *John of Gaunt*, pp. 118, 119, 123.

18. Geldsetzer, *Frauen auf Kreuzzügen*, p. 191; *L'Estoire de Eracles Empereur et la Conqueste de la Terre d'Outremer*, in *Recueil des historiens des Croisades, Historiens Occidentaux*, edited by l'Académie des Inscriptions et Belles-Lettres, vol. 2 (Paris: Imprimerie Impériale, 1859), p. 332 (Book 32 chapter 3).

19. Adnan A. Husain and Margaret Aziza Pappano, 'The One Kingdom Solution?: Diplomacy, Marriage, and Sovereignty in the Third Crusade',

in *Cosmopolitanism and the Middle Ages*, edited by John M. Ganim and Shayne Aaron Legassie (New York: Palgrave Macmillan, 2013), pp. 121–40.

20. Ibn Ḥawqal recorded that Muslim men of rural Sicily married Christian women; sons were raised as Muslims and daughters as Christian: Alex Metcalfe, *Muslims and Christians in Norman Sicily: Arabic Speakers and the end of Islam* (London: Routledge, 2013), pp. 16–17; Sarah C. Davis-Secord, *Where Three Worlds Met: Sicily in the early medieval Mediterranean* (Ithaca, NY: Cornell University Press, 2017), pp. 133–4.

21. Antony Eastmond, *Tamta's World: The Life and Encounters of a Medieval Noblewoman from the Middle East to Mongolia* (Cambridge: Cambridge University Press, 2017), pp. 1, 5–7, 9–14, 133; Zaroui Pogossian, 'Women, Identity, and Power: A Review Essay of Antony Eastmond, *Tamta's World*', *Al-ʿUṣūr al-Wusṭā: The Journal of Middle East Medievalists* 27 (2019): pp. 233–66. For some further examples of marriage between Armenians and Muslims see Eastmond, *Tamta's World*, pp. 196–202; A. C. S. Peacock, 'Georgia and the Anatolian Turks in the 12th and 13th Centuries', *Anatolian Studies* 56 (2006): pp. 127–46, at pp. 138–41.

22. For a brief introduction to Nubian relations with Egypt in this period see David N. Edwards, *The Nubian Past: An Archaeology of the Sudan* (London: Routledge, 2004), pp. 248–50; Giovanni R. Ruffini, 'The History of Medieval Nubia', in *The Oxford Handbook of Ancient Nubia*, edited by Geoff Emberling and Bruce Beyer Williams (Oxford: Oxford University Press, 2021), pp. 750–71; for Ibn Khaldūn see Ivan Hrbek, 'Egypt, Nubia and the Eastern Deserts', in *The Cambridge History of Africa, volume 3: from c. 1050 to c. 1600*, edited by Roland Oliver (Cambridge: Cambridge University Press, 1977), pp. 10–97, at p. 77.

23. Krebs, *Medieval Ethiopian Kingship*, p. 175 note 171; Herman, 'Towards a History of Women in Medieval Ethiopia', pp. 382, 388–9, 391.

24. Peter Jackson, *The Seventh Crusade, 1244–1254: Sources and Documents*, Crusade Texts in Translation 16 (Farnham: Ashgate, 2009), p. 105.

25. John of Joinville, 'The Life of Saint Louis', pp. 262–3; Jean Sire de Joinville, *Histoire de Saint Louis*, pp. 216–18, sections 397–400.

26. D. Fairchild Ruggles, *Tree of Pearls: The Extraordinary Architectural Patronage of the 13th-Century Egyptian Slave-Queen Shajar al-Durr* (Oxford: Oxford University Press, 2020), pp. 60–3, 66–9, 78, 102–11; Jackson, *The Seventh Crusade*, pp. 125–63; Eastmond, *Tamta's World*, pp. 117–19.

27. On this point see the extract from the *Mirāt al-zamān* written by the Sibt Ibn al-Jawzī translated in Jackson, *The Seventh Crusade*, p. 161 (and see pp. 5–6 on the Sibt).

28. For discussion of Shajar's power as sultan and comparison to other female rulers in the Muslim world in the thirteenth century see: Ruggles, *Tree of Pearls*, pp. 2, 68–77 (quotation on p. 69); Eastmond, *Tamta's World*, pp. 110–11, 117–21, 197–205; Niall Christie, 'Fighting Women in the Crusading Period through Muslim Eyes: Transgressing Expectations and Facing Realities?' in *Crusading and Masculinities*, edited by Natasha R. Hodgson, Katherine J. Lewis and Matthew M. Mesley, Crusades Subsidia 13 (London: Routledge, 2019), pp. 183–95, at p. 189.

29. Geldsetzer, *Frauen auf Kreuzzügen*, pp. 193, 201.

30. Matilda de Courtenay: Nurith Kenaan-Kedar, 'Pictorial and Sculptural Commemoration of Returning or Departing Crusaders', in *The Crusades and Visual Culture*, edited by Elizabeth Lapina, April Jehan Morris, Susanna A. Throop, and Laura J. Whatley (Farnham: Ashgate, 2015), pp. 91–104, at p. 98; René de Lespinasse, *Hervé de Donzy, Comte de Nevers* (Nevers: P. Fay, 1868), p. 67; Edmond Martène and Ursini Durand, eds, *Thesaurus Novus Anecdotorum*, vol. 1 (Paris: Florentinus Delaulne et al., 1717), pp. 867–9. Catherine: Geldsetzer, *Frauen auf Kreuzzügen*, p. 192; Christophre Butkens, *Trophées tant sacrés que prophanes du Duché de Brabant*, vol. 2 (The Hague: Chrétien van Lom, 1724), p. 177, cited by Reinhold Röhricht, *Studien zur Geschichte des fünften Kreuzzuges* (Innsbruck: Wagner'schen Universitäts-Buchhandlung, 1891), p. 87.

31. Geldsetzer, *Frauen auf Kreuzzügen*, pp. 76, 104, 192; Anne E. Lester, 'Remembrance of Things Past: Memory and Material Objects in the time of the Crusades, 1095–1291', in *Remembering the Crusades and Crusading*, edited by Megan Cassidy-Welch (London: Routledge, 2017), pp. 73–94, at p. 80; Bird, Peters, and Powell, eds and trans., *Crusade and Christendom*, pp. 439–42, at p. 441.

32. Geldsetzer, *Frauen auf Kreuzzügen*, pp. 196–8, citing Kedar, 'The Passenger List of a Crusader Ship'.

33. Geldsetzer, *Frauen auf Kreuzzügen*, p. 202; *Close Rolls of the Reign of Henry III Preserved in the Public Record Office, A.D. 1268–1272* (London: HMSO, 1938), pp. 288–9.

34. Tyerman, *England and the Crusades*, p. 242; *Calendar of the Patent Rolls preserved in the Public Record Office, Edward II, A.D. 1307–1313* (London: HMSO, 1894), p. 233.

35. Gavin Fort, '"Make a Pilgrimage for Me": The Role of Place in Late Medieval Proxy Pilgrimage', in *Travel, Time and Space in the Middle Ages and Early Modern Time: Explorations of World Perceptions and Processes of Identity Formation*, edited by Albrecht Classen (Berlin: De Gruyter, 2018), pp. 424–45.

36. Hodgson, *Women, Crusading and the Holy Land*, pp. 117–18; citing *Curia Regis Rolls of the reign of Henry III, preserved in the Public Record Office*, vol. 12, *9–10 Henry III* (London: HMSO, 1957), p. 12, no. 69.

37. Geldsetzer, *Frauen auf Kreuzzügen*, p. 187; Hodgson, Women, *Crusading and the Holy Land*, 211–12; Rhodes, *The Crown and the Cross*, p. 85 n. 133.

38. Roger of Howden, *Chronica*, edited by William Stubbs, Rolls Series 51, vol. 4 (London: Longman, 1871), p. 14.

39. Hodgson, Women, *Crusading and the Holy Land*, p. 118; Geldsetzer, *Frauen auf Kreuzzügen*, pp. 181–2; 'Annales de Terre Sancte', edited by Reinhold Röhricht and Gaston Raynaud, *Archives de l'Orient Latin* 2 (1884): documents, pp. 427–61, at pp. 459–60; Marino Sanudo, *The Book of the Secrets of the Faithful of the Cross*, p. 365 (Book 3, part 12, chapter 20); Jaroslav Folda, *Crusader Art: The Art of the Crusaders in the Holy Land, 1099–1291* (Aldershot: Lund Humphries, 2008), p. 151; Anne Derbes and Mark Sandona, 'Amazons and Crusaders: The *Histoire Universelle* in Flanders and the Holy Land', in *France and the Holy Land: Frankish Culture at the End of the Crusades*, edited by Daniel H. Weiss and Lisa Mahoney (Baltimore: Johns Hopkins University Press, 2004), pp. 187–229, at pp. 214–15 (but note that the 'Knights' at the tournament mentioned here were in fact the king's knights, not the Knights Hospitaller).

40. Purcell, 'Women Crusaders?' p. 60.

41. Geldsetzer, *Frauen auf Kreuzzügen*, pp. 135–6; Michael Prestwich, *Edward I* (London: Methuen, 1988), p. 78; Hamilton, 'Eleanor of Castile and the Crusading Movement', pp. 100, 103; *Chronicon domini Walteri de Hemingburgh, vulgo Hemingford nuncupati, ordinia sancti Augustini canonici regularis, in coenobio beate Mariæ de Gisburn, de gestis regum Angliæ*, edited by Hans Claude Hamilton, vol. 1 (London: English Historical Society, 1848), p. 336; Ptolemy of Lucca, *Historia Ecclesiastica*, Book 23, chapter 6, in *Rerum Italicarum Scriptores*, edited by Lodovico Antonio Muratori, vol. 11 (Milan: Stamperia della Società Palatina, 1727), cols 742–1242, at col. 1168.

42. [Miguel de Castanhoso] *The Portuguese expedition to Abyssinia in 1541–1543*, pp. 47, 62.

43. Geldsetzer, *Frauen auf Kreuzzügen*, pp. 137–40, 193–4; summarised by Hodgson, Women, *Crusading and the Holy Land*, p. 42; John of Joinville, 'The Life of Saint Louis', p. 241; Jean Sire de Joinville, *Histoire de Saint Louis*, p. 170, section 310.

44. For a supposed woman medical practitioner on the Fourth Crusade who did not, in fact, join that crusade, see Susan B. Edgington, 'A female

physician on the Fourth Crusade?: Laurette de Saint-Valéry', in *Knighthoods of Christ: Essays on the History of the Crusades and the Knights Templar Presented to Malcolm Barber*, edited by Norman Housley (Aldershot: Ashgate, 2007), pp. 77–85.

45. Geldsetzer, *Frauen auf Kreuzzügen*, pp. 97–8.

46. Geldsetzer, *Frauen auf Kreuzzügen*, p. 185. On the professionalization of midwifery in the second half of the thirteenth century see Geldsetzer, *Frauen auf Kreuzzügen, 1096–1291*, p. 98, citing Michel Salvat, 'L'accouchement dans la littérature scientifique médiévale', *Senefiance* 9 (1980): 87–106.

47. Geldsetzer, *Frauen auf Kreuzzügen*, pp. 98, 195, 203, 213–14.

48. Albert of Aachen, *Historia Ierosolimitana*, pp. 344–7 (Book 5, sections 5–7); Yvonne Friedman, 'Gestures of Conciliation: Peacemaking Endeavors in the Latin East', in *In Laudem Hierosolymitani: Studies in Crusades and Medieval Culture in Honour of Benjamin Z. Kedar*, edited by Iris Shagrir, Ronnie Ellenblum, and Jonathan Riley-Smith, Crusades Subsidia 1 (Aldershot: Ashgate, 2007), pp. 31–48, at pp. 34–5.

49. In many Old French romance epics of the twelfth, thirteenth and four-teenth centuries a Muslim noblewoman converts to Christianity, mar-ries a Christian knight and then acts as a mediator with the Muslims. For further discussion see, for example, Sarah-Grace Heller, 'Surprisingly historical women in the Old French Crusade Cycle', in *Women and Medieval Epic: Gender, Genre, and the Limits of Epic Masculinity*, edited by Sara S. Poor and Jana K. Schulman (New York: Palgrave Macmillan, 2007), pp. 41–66, at pp. 51–3.

50. *Livländische Reimchronik*, ed. Franz Pfeiffer, Bibliothek des literarischen Vereins in Stuttgart 7 (Stuttgart: Literarischen Vereins, 1844), pp. 174–5, 176–9, lines 6439–6463, 6525–6585; Leighton, 'Written and Visual Expressions of Authority', p. 18.

51. Nora Berend, 'Hungary, "the Gate of Christendom"', in *Medieval Frontiers: Concepts and Practices*, edited by David Abulafia and Nora Berend (Aldershot: Ashgate, 2002), pp. 195–215, at p. 209.

52. Colin Imber, *The Crusade of Varna, 1443–45*, Crusade Texts in Translation 14 (Aldershot: Ashgate, 2006), pp. 6, 10, 23–4.

53. Odo of Deuil, *De Profectione Ludovici VII in Orientem*, pp. 56–7; Phillips, *The Second Crusade*, pp. 174, 190, 276; 'Annales Herbipolenses', in *Monumenta Germaniae Historica Scriptores in Folio*, edited by George Heinrich Pertz, vol. 16 (Hanover: Aulic Hahn, 1859), pp. 1–12, at p. 4, lines 33–36.

54. Robert of Clari, *The Conquest of Constantinople*, trans. Edgar Holmes McNeal (New York: Columbia University Press, 1936, reprinted Toronto: University of Toronto Press, 1996), p. 79.

55. Ewan Short, 'The Agency and Authority of Agnes of France and Margaret of Hungary in the Aftermath of the Fall of Constantinople (1204–1206)', *Question* 3 (2019): pp. 28–37, 96–101, at pp. 32–3, 35–6.

56. Short, 'The Agency and Authority of Agnes of France and Margaret of Hungary', pp. 33–5; Geoffrey de Villehardouin, 'The Conquest of Constantinople', in Joinville and Villehardouin, *Chronicles of the Crusades*, translated by M. R. B. Shaw (Harmondsworth: Penguin, 1963), pp. 29–160, at p. 74. Margaret of Hungary was cousin-in-law to Agnes of France: Maria of Antioch, mother of Agnes's first husband, was the step-sister of Margaret's mother.

57. Geldsetzer, *Frauen auf Kreuzzügen*, pp. 140–1; *The Chronicle of Ibn al-Athīr*, p. 352; *Radulphi de Coggeshall Chronicon Anglicanum*, edited by Joseph Stevenson, Rolls Series 66 (London: Longman, 1875), pp. 38–9, 45; story retold by Roger of Wendover, *The Flowers of History*, edited by Henry G. Hewlett, Rolls Series 84 (London: Longman, 1886–1889), vol. 1 pp. 209–10; Matthew Paris, *Chronica Majora*, vol. 2, p. 385; Matthew Paris, *Historia Anglorum sive, ut vulgo dicitur, Historia Minor, item, ejusdem Abbreviatio Chronicorum Angliæ*, edited by Frederic Madden, Rolls Series 44 (London: Longman, 1866–1869), vol. 2, p. 31.

58. Rasa Mazeika, ' "Nowhere was the Fragility of their Sex Apparent": Women Warriors in the Baltic Crusade Chronicles', in *From Clermont to Jerusalem: The Crusades and Crusader Societies 1095–1500. Selected Proceedings of the International Medieval Congress, University of Leeds, 10–13 July 1995*, edited by Alan V. Murray, International Medieval Research 3 (Turnhout: Brepols, 1998), pp. 229–48, at p. 239 and note 24; Peter von Dusburg, *Chronicon Terre Prussie*, edited by Max Toeppen, in *Scriptores rerum Prussicarum*, vol. 1 (Leipzig: S. Hirzel, 1861), p. 115; see also the retelling of this event in *The Chronicle of Prussia by Nicolaus von Jeroschin: A History of the Teutonic Knights in Prussia, 1190–1331*, trans. Mary Fischer, Crusade Texts in Translation 20 (Farnham: Ashgate, 2010), p. 157.

59. *La Continuation de Guillaume de Tyr*, pp. 47–8, section 35; *Chronique d'Ernoul et de Bernard le trésorier*, ed. L. de Mas Latrie (Paris: Jules Renouard, 1871), pp. 163–4; Edbury, 'Ernoul, *Eracles*, and the Collapse of the Kingdom of Jerusalem', p. 53.

60. O'Callaghan, *The Last Crusade in the West*, p. 64; Gomes Eannes de Zurara, *Crónica da Tomada de Ceuta*, edited by Francisco Maria Esteves

Pereira (Lisbon: Academia das Sciências de Lisboa, 1915), pp. 107–8 (chapter 34).

61. Fernández-Armesto, *Before Columbus*, pp. 210–11, 237.

62. [Bernal Díaz del Castillo], *The True History of the Conquest of New Spain*, pp. 126–35, 170, 235, 244, 249, 273, 280, quotation at p. 135 (Book 2, chapters 36–37, Book 3, chapter 46, Book 4, chapters 64, 66, 68, 74, 77).

63. Frederic L. Cheyette, *Ermengard of Narbonne and the World of the Troubadours* (Ithaca NY: Cornell University Press, 2001), pp. 86–7, 251; Matthew Bennett, 'Virile Latins, Effeminate Greeks and Strong Women: Gender Definitions on Crusade?' in *Gendering the Crusades*, edited by Susan B. Edgington and Sarah Lambert (Cardiff: University of Wales Press, 2001), pp. 16–30, at pp. 26–7; Jacqueline Caille, 'Les Seigneurs de Narbonne dans le conflit Toulouse-Barcelone au XIIe siècle', *Annales du Midi: revue archéologique, historique et philologique de la France méridionale* 97/171 (1985): pp. 227–44, at p. 232; Claude de Vic and Joseph Vaissete, *Histoire générale de Languedoc*, vol. 3 (Toulouse: Édouard Privat, 1872), p. 739 (Book 17, chapter 72).

64. Geldsetzer, *Frauen auf Kreuzzügen*, pp. 196–8; Murray, 'Sex, Death and the Problem of Single Women,' pp. 266–70.

65. *The History of the Holy War*, lines 5688–5689 (vol. 1, p. 92, vol. 2, p. 110); *L'Estoire de la Guerre Sainte*, lines 5695–5696, p. 508; *Itinerarium peregrinorum et gesta regis Ricardi*, p. 248 (Book 4, chapter 9); *Chronicle of the Third Crusade*, p. 235.

66. ʿImād al-Dīn in Abū Shāma, 'Le Livre des Deux Jardins', p. 434.

67. Mazeika, '"Nowhere was the Fragility of their Sex Apparent"', pp. 241–3; *The Chronicle of Prussia by Nicolaus von Jeroschin*, p. 70.

68. Bernard Hamilton, 'Women in the Crusader States: the Queens of Jerusalem, 1100–1190', in *Medieval Women*, edited by Derek Baker, Studies in Church History Subsidia 1 (Oxford: Basil Blackwell, 1978), pp. 143–74, at p. 155; see also Hans Eberhard Mayer, 'Studies in the History of Queen Melisende of Jerusalem', *Dumbarton Oaks Papers* 26 (1972): pp. 93, 95–182 at p. 174.

69. Thomas Asbridge, 'Alice of Antioch: A Case Study of Female Power in the Twelfth Century', in *The Experience of Crusading, volume two: Defining the Crusader Kingdom*, edited by Peter Edbury and Jonathan Phillips (Cambridge: Cambridge University Press, 2003), pp. 29–47, at pp. 34–5; Andrew D. Buck, 'Women in the Principality of Antioch: Power, Status and Social Agency', *Haskins Society Journal* 31 (2019): 95–132, at p. 101.

70. Nicholson, 'Queen Sybil of Jerusalem as a Military Leader'.

71. *Itinerarium peregrinorum et gesta regis Ricardi*, pp. 342–3, 348 (Book 5, chapters 28, 35); *Chronicle of the Third Crusade*, pp. 308–9, 312–13; *The History of the Holy War*, lines 8887–8903, 9000–9022 (vol. 1, pp. 144–6, vol. 2, pp. 152–4); *L'Estoire de la Guerre Sainte*, lines 8909–8924, 9024–9047, pp. 613, 617.

72. Peter W. Edbury, 'Women and the Customs of the High Court of Jerusalem according to John of Ibelin', in *Chemins d'outre mer. Études d'histoire sur la Méditerranée médiévale offertes à Michel Balard*, edited by Damien Coulon, Catherine Otten-Froux, Paul Pagès, and Dominque Valérian (Paris: Publications de la Sorbonne, 2004), pp. 285–92, at p. 286.

73. Asbridge, 'Alice of Antioch', p. 31.

74. Malcolm Barber, *The Crusader States* (New Haven: Yale University Press, 2012), pp. 299, 301, 307.

75. For the experiences of Stephanie de Milly and Isabel de Ibelin see Helen J. Nicholson, 'The True Gentleman? Correct Behaviour towards Women according to Christian and Muslim Writers: From the Third Crusade to Sultan Baybars', in *Crusading and Masculinities*, edited by Natasha R. Hodgson, Katherine J. Lewis, and Matthew M. Mesley, Crusades Subsidia 13 (London: Routledge, 2019), pp. 100–12, at pp. 102–3, 106–7. After the fall of Tripoli in 1289 to the Mamluks, the conquerors allowed Lucy, countess regnant of Tripoli, to keep some of her estates: Robert Irwin, 'The Mamlūk Conquest of the County of Tripoli', in *Crusade and Settlement: Papers read at the First Conference of the Society for the Study of the Crusades and the Latin East and presented to R. C. Smail*, edited by Peter W. Edbury (Cardiff: University College of Cardiff Press, 1985), pp. 246–50, at p. 249.

76. 'Song of the battle of Ústí', translated in Thomas A. Fudge, *The Crusade against Heretics in Bohemia, 1418–1437*, Crusade Texts in Translation 9 (Aldershot: Ashgate, 2002), pp. 200–7, at p. 201.

77. 'Song of the battle of Ústí', pp. 206–7.

78. Geldsetzer, *Frauen auf Kreuzzügen*, pp. 24–5, 202; 'Codicillus Henrici comitis Ruthensis' in *Veterum scriptorum et monumentorum historicorum, dogmaticorum, moralium, amplissima collectio*, edited by Edmond Martène and Ursin Durand, vol. 1 (Paris: Montalant, 1724), cols 1168–1172, at col. 1170B. On the bezant, see Robert Kool, 'Finding French Deniers in the Latin Kingdom of Jerusalem. The Archaeological and Cultural Perspective', in *Transferts culturels entre France et Orient latin (XIIe-XIIIe siècles)*, edited by Martin Aurell, Marisa Galvez, and Estelle Ingrand-Varenne (Paris: Classiques Garnier, 2021), pp. 101–28, at p. 110.

79. Geldsetzer, *Frauen auf Kreuzzügen*, pp. 52, 201; Doris Mary Stenton, ed., *Rolls of the Justices in Eyre, Being the Rolls of Pleas and Assizes for Yorkshire in 3 Henry III (1218–1219)*, Selden Society, 56 (1937), p. 384, no. 1072.

80. Geldsetzer, *Frauen auf Kreuzzügen*, pp. 52–3, 202; Tyerman, *England and the Crusades*, p. 218; Stenton, ed., *Rolls of the Justices in Eyre, Being the Rolls of Pleas and Assizes for Yorkshire in 3 Henry III*, p. 297, no. 818.

81. Geldsetzer, *Frauen auf Kreuzzügen*, pp. 52, 202; Stenton, ed., *Rolls of the Justices in Eyre, Being the Rolls of Pleas and Assizes for Yorkshire in 3 Henry III*, p. 183, no. 431; Fort, ' "Make a Pilgrimage for Me" '.

82. Geldsetzer, *Frauen auf Kreuzzügen*, pp. 23–4, 201; Doris M. Stenton, ed., *Rolls of the Justices in Eyre for Gloucestershire, Warwickshire, and Shropshire, 1221, 1222*, Selden Society, 59 (1940), pp. 643–4, no. 1520.

83. 'Chronicon Ebersheimense', edited by K. Weidland, in *Monumenta Germaniae Historica Scriptores* (henceforth *MGH SS*) 23, edited by George Heinrich Pertz (Hanover: Aulic Hahn, 1874), p. 450, lines 6–17; 'Annales Marbacenses', edited by R. Wilmans, in *MGH SS* 17, p. 172, lines 19–43 (translated in Bird, Peters, and Powell, eds and trans., *Crusade and Christendom*, pp. 101–2); 'Annales Colonienses maximi: recensio secunda et tertia', edited by Karl Pertz, in *MGH SS* 17, p. 826 line 38 – p. 827 line 4; 'Chronica Sigeberti auctarium Mortui Maris' [Mortemer], edited by D. L. C. Bethmann, in *MGH SS* 6, edited by George Heinrich Pertz (Hanover: Aulic Hahn, 1844), p. 467, lines 22–29; 'Annales Admuntenses: continuatio Admuntensis', edited by D. Wilhelm Wattenbach, in *MGH SS* 9, edited by George Heinrich Pertz (Hanover: Aulic Hahn, 1851), p. 592, lines 20–25; 'Annales Placentini Guelfi' in *MGH SS* 18, edited by George Heinrich Pertz (Hanover: Aulic Hahn, 1863), p. 426, lines 47–52; 'Ogerii Panis Annales' [of Genoa], in *MGH SS* 18, p. 131, lines 38–43; 'Annales de Waverleia', in *Annales Monastici*, vol. 2, edited by Henry Richards Luard, Rolls Series 36 (London: Longman, 1865), p. 281: under 1214; Dana Munro, 'The Children's Crusade', *American Historical Review* 19.3 (1914): pp. 516–24; Joseph E. Hansbery, 'The Children's Crusade', *Catholic Historical Review* 24.1 (1938): pp. 30–8; Norman P. Zacour, 'The Children's Crusade', in *A History of the Crusades*, edited by Kenneth M. Setton, vol. 2, *The Later Crusades, 1189–1311*, edited by Robert Lee Wolff and Harry W. Hazard (Madison, WI: University of Wisconsin Press, 1969), pp. 325–42; Gary Dickson, *The Children's Crusade: Medieval History, Modern Mythistory* (Basingstoke: Palgrave Macmillan, 2008), esp. pp. 33–5.

84. Jackson, *The Seventh Crusade*, pp. 181–93, especially pp. 182, 186, 187 (quotation).

85. Malcolm Barber, 'The Pastoureaux of 1320', *Journal of Ecclesiastical History* 32 (1981): pp. 143–66, esp. pp. 163–4.

86. Mazeika, ' "Nowhere was the Fragility of their Sex Apparent" ', pp. 240–1 and note 26.

87. 'Imād al-Dīn al-Isfahānī, *Conquête de la Syrie*, pp. 202–3; Cadden, *Meanings of Sex Difference in the Middle Ages*, pp. 273–6.

88. Philippe de Mézières, *Le Songe du Vieil Pelerin*, vol. 2, pp. 438–9.

89. *The History of the Holy War*, lines 5690–5691 (vol. 1, p. 92, vol. 2, p. 110); *L'Estoire de la Guerre Sainte*, lines 5697–5698, p. 508.

90. Geldsetzer, *Frauen auf Kreuzzügen*, pp. 162–7.

91. William Camden, *Remaines of a Greater Worke Concerning Britain* (London: Simon Waterson, 1605), p. 219 ('Grave speeches and witty apothegmes'); quoted by Fuller, *The Historie of the Holy Warre*, p. 275 (Book 5, chapter 26).

92. Geldsetzer, *Frauen auf Kreuzzügen*, pp. 155–6; 'Gesta Obsidionis Damiate', in *Quinti belli sacri scriptores minores*, edited by Reinhold Röhricht, Publications de la Société de l'Orient Latin, Série historique 2 (Geneva: J.-G. Fick, 1879), pp. 71–115, at p. 111; John of Joinville, 'The Life of Saint Louis', p. 233; Jean Sire de Joinville, *Histoire de Saint Louis*, pp. 150–1, section 274.

93. Geldsetzer, *Frauen auf Kreuzzügen*, pp. 157–62, 203; *Itinerarium peregrinorum et gesta regis Ricardi*, pp. 176, 234, 286 (Book 2, chapter 26, Book 3, chapter 18, Book 4, chapter 27); *Chronicle of the Third Crusade*, pp. 174, 221, 265; *The History of the Holy War*, lines 7062–7063 (vol. 1, p. 114, vol. 2, p. 127); *L'Estoire de la Guerre Sainte*, lines 7073–7074, p. 553; John of Joinville 'The Life of Saint Louis', p. 325; Jean Sire de Joinville, *Histoire de Saint Louis*, pp. 354–5, section 645.

94. Geldsetzer, *Frauen auf Kreuzzügen*, pp. 74–8. For Joanna and Berengaria in the Holy Land see *Itinerarium peregrinorum et gesta regis Ricardi*, pp. 234, 286, 441 (Book 3, chapter 18, Book 4, chapter 27, Book 6, chapter 37); *Chronicle of the Third Crusade*, pp. 221, 265, 381. Ambroise mentions the two queens only once after they left Cyprus: *The History of the Holy War*, lines 7062–7063 (vol. 1, p. 114, vol. 2, p. 127); *L'Estoire de la Guerre Sainte*, lines 7073–7074, p. 553.

95. Herman, 'Towards a History of Women in Medieval Ethiopia', p. 393; [Miguel de Castanhoso] *The Portuguese expedition to Abyssinia in 1541–1543*, pp. 4, 6, 10–76.

96. Guillaume Caoursin, 'Descriptio obsidionis Rhodiae', in Theresa M. Vann and Donald J. Kagay, *Hospitaller Piety and Crusader Propaganda: Guillaume Caoursin's Description of the Ottoman Siege of Rhodes, 1480* (Farnham: Ashgate, 2015), pp. 86–147, at pp. 112–13; Francesco Balbi di Correggio, *The Siege of Malta 1565*, pp. 128, 131.

97. *Chronica Adefonsi Imperatoris*, Book 2 chapter 12, translated in *The Chronicle of Alfonso the Emperor*, [131]–[132], paragraph 150.

98. O'Callaghan, *The Last Crusade in the West*, pp. 102–3.

99. Alan V. Murray, 'Contrasting Masculinities in the Baltic Crusades: Teutonic Knights and Secular Crusaders at War and Peace in Late Medieval Prussia', in *Crusading and Masculinities*, edited by Natasha R. Hodgson, Katherine J. Lewis, and Matthew M. Mesley, Crusades Subsidia 13 (London: Routledge, 2019), pp. 113–28, at pp. 115–23.

100. William of Tudela and Anonymous Successor, *The Song of the Cathar Wars: A History of the Albigensian Crusade*, trans. Janet Shirley, Crusade Texts in Translation 2 (Aldershot: Ashgate, 1996), pp. 122–4, 128, 129, and note 3 on p. 123; Peter of Les Vaux-de-Cernay, *The History of the Albigensian Crusade*, pp. 270, 273, paragraphs 600, 606B.

101. Lambert, 'Crusading or Spinning', pp. 8–9.

102. Nicholson, 'Women on the Third Crusade', pp. 337–9.

103. *The Chronicle of Ibn al-Athīr*, p. 350.

104. Nicholson, 'Women on the Third Crusade', pp. 340–2, 348; Maier, 'The Roles of Women in the Crusade Movement', p. 69; Michael R. Evans, '"Unfit to Bear Arms": The Gendering of Arms and Armour in Accounts of Women on Crusade', in *Gendering the Crusades*, edited by Susan B. Edgington and Sarah Lambert (Cardiff: University of Wales Press, 2001), pp. 45–58, at pp. 45–6, 52; Christie, 'Fighting women in the Crusading Period'.

105. Bennett, 'Virile Latins, Effeminate Greeks and Strong Women', pp. 24–5.

106. Quotation translated from *Gesta Francorum*, p. 19; see also 'Fragmentum de captione Damiatæ', edited by Paul Meyer, in *Quinti belli sacri scriptores minores*, edited by Reinhold Röhricht, Publications de la Société de l'Orient Latin, Série historique 2 (Geneva: J.-G. Fick, 1879), pp. 166–202, at p. 187; Oliver of Paderborn in Bird, Peters, and Powell, eds and trans., *Crusade and Christendom*), pp. 179, 206; Lambert, 'Crusading or Spinning', p. 9.

107. William of Tudela and Anonymous Successor, *The Song of the Cathar Wars*, pp. 132 (quotation), 174; Fudge, *The Crusade against Heretics in Bohemia*, p. 73.

108. William of Tudela and Anonymous Successor, *The Song of the Cathar Wars*, pp. 124, 167, 191.

109. Fudge, *The Crusade against Heretics in Bohemia*, p. 38; Frederick G. Heymann, *John Žižka and the Hussite Revolution* (Princeton NJ: Princeton University Press, 1955), pp. 82–3.

110. Guillaume Caoursin, '*Descriptio obsidionis Rhodiae*', pp. 110–11.

111. Francesco Balbi di Correggio, *The Siege of Malta 1565*, p. 53.

112. *Itinerarium peregrinorum et gesta regis Ricardi*, p. 101 (Book 1, chapter 50); *Chronicle of the Third Crusade*, p. 106; *The History of the Holy War*, lines

3622–3655 (vol. 1, pp. 58–9, vol. 2, p. 83); *L'Estoire de la Guerre Sainte*, lines 3627–3660, pp. 441–2.

113. William of Tudela and Anonymous Successor, *The Song of the Cathar Wars*, p. 156; *La Continuation de Guillaume de Tyr*, p. 67, section 54. For women involved in prayer and ritual but not taking the lead, see for example Francesco Balbi di Correggio, *The Siege of Malta 1565*, pp. 109–10, 145.

114. Tyerman, *How to Plan a Crusade*, p. 166; Johannes de Tulbia, 'De Domino Iohanne', p. 139; Oliver of Paderborn in Bird, Peters, and Powell, eds and trans., *Crusade and Christendom*, pp. 193, 221, implies that the women and children received the same as the fighting men.

115. Mazeika, '"Nowhere was the Fragility of their Sex Apparent"', pp. 229–30 and note 1. Brother Nicolaus von Jeroschin's German translation of Brother Peter's Latin, produced between 1331 and 1341, also recounts this story: *The Chronicle of Prussia by Nicolaus von Jeroschin*, p. 106.

116. Guard, *Chivalry, Kingship and Crusade*, p. 140.

117. William of Tudela and Anonymous Successor, *The Song of the Cathar Wars*, p. 172.

118. Heymann, *John Žižka*, pp. 59, 138 (quotation); Fudge, *The Crusade against Heretics in Bohemia*, pp. 77–8, and see pp. 31, 39, 40, 79, 95, 105, 124, 138 and 170 for other references to women in the Taborite army. For the chronicle, see now Thomas A. Fudge, *Origins of the Hussite Uprising: the Chronicle of Laurence of Březová (1414–1421)* (London: Routledge, 2020).

119. Heymann, *John Žižka*, p. 138 note 7; Fudge, *The Crusade against Heretics in Bohemia*, p. 73.

120. *The History of the Holy War*, lines 3304–3309 (vol. 1, p. 53, vol. 2, p. 79); *L'Estoire de la Guerre Sainte*, lines 3309–3314, p. 431; *Itinerarium peregrinorum et gesta regis Ricardi*, p. 82 (Book 1, chapter 34); *Chronicle of the Third Crusade*, p. 89; Evans, '"Unfit to Bear Arms"', pp. 52–3.

121. Luttrell, 'Englishwomen as Pilgrims to Jerusalem', pp. 187, 194 note 20, citing Ludolphus de Sudheim, 'De Itinere Terre Sancte', edited by G. A. Neumann, in *Archives de l'Orient Latin* 2 (1884), Documents: III Voyages, pp. 305–77, at p. 334.

122. Maier, 'The Roles of Women in the Crusade Movement', pp. 64–7; Hodgson, *Women, Crusading and the Holy Land*, p. 48; Thomas's life of Margaret is printed in Paul Gerhard Schmidt, '"Peregrinatio periculosa". Thomas von Froidmont über die Jerusalemfahrten seiner Schwester Margareta', in *Kontinuität und Wandel: Lateinische Poesie von Naevius bis Baudelaire. Franco Munari zum 65. Geburtstag*, edited by

Ulrich Justus Stache, Wolfgang Maaz, and Fritz Wagner (Hildesheim: Weidemann, 1986), pp. 461–85. For a translation see Julia Bolton Holloway, 'Margaret of Jerusalem/Beverley and Thomas of Beverley/ Froidmont, her brother, her biographer', at www.umilta.net/jerusalem. html, accessed 23 December 2020.

123. *An Arab-Syrian Gentleman and Warrior in the Period of the Crusades: Memoirs of Usāmah ibn-Munqidh,* trans. Philip K. Hitti (repr. Princeton NJ: Princeton University Press, 1987), pp. 153–4, 157–8; Usama ibn Munqidh, *The Book of Contemplation: Islam and the Crusades,* trans. Paul M. Cobb (London: Penguin, 2008), pp. 135–7, 139–41; Christie, 'Fighting Women', pp. 186–9. Usama set out to record the unusual and bizarre; most Muslim and Christian women in Palestine and Syria would have continued their normal lives under Frankish rule and seen little change from before the Frankish invasion: Daniella Talmon-Heller, 'Arabic Sources on Muslim Villagers under Frankish Rule', in *From Clermont to Jerusalem: The Crusades and Crusader Societies 1095–1500. Selected Proceedings of the International Medieval Congress, University of Leeds, 10–13 July 1995,* edited by Alan V. Murray, International Medieval Research 3 (Turnhout: Brepols, 1998), pp. 103–17.

124. *An Arab-Syrian gentleman,* pp. 158–9; Usama ibn Munqidh, *The Book of Contemplation,* pp. 141–2.

125. Ramon Muntaner, *Chronicle,* translated by Lady Goodenough, vol. 1, pp. 311–12 (chapter 124); online edn, www.yorku.ca/inpar/muntaner_goodenough.pdf, pp. 260–1.

126. Mazeika, ' "Nowhere was the Fragility of their Sex Apparent" ', pp. 236–7 and note 17; see also *The Chronicle of Prussia by Nicolaus von Jeroschin,* p. 173.

127. *An Arab-Syrian gentleman,* p. 158; Usama ibn Munqidh, *The Book of Contemplation,* p. 141.

128. L'Abbé René Aubert de Vertot, *Histoire des Chevaliers Hospitaliers de S. Jean de Jerusalem, appellez depuis Chevaliers de Rhodes, et aujourd'hui Chevaliers de Malthe* (Paris: Rollin, Quillau and Desaint, 1726), vol. 3, pp. 342–3 (Book 8): quotations from p. 342, note.

129. G. W. Coopland, *The Tree of Battles of Honoré Bonet: An English Version* (Liverpool: Liverpool University Press, 1949), pp. 168, 185 (Part 4 chapters 70, 94).

130. Phillips, *The Second Crusade,* p. 227; *Itinerarium peregrinorum et gesta regis Ricardi,* pp. 186–8, 191 (Book 2 chapters 30–32); *Chronicle of the Third Crusade,* pp. 182–3, 185.

131. Friedman, *Encounter Between Enemies*, p. 173; ʿImād al-Dīn al-Isfahānī, *Conquête de la Syrie*, pp. 294–5; *The Rare and Excellent History of Saladin*, pp. 37, 147–8.

132. Friedman, *Encounter Between Enemies*, pp. 169–72, 174, 177, 179, 181–6.

133. *An Arab-Syrian gentleman*, p. 179; Usama ibn Munqidh, *The Book of Contemplation*, p. 162; discussion in Friedman, *Encounter Between Enemies*, pp. 170–1.

134. David J. Hay, ' "Collateral Damage?" Civilian Casualties in the Early Ideologies of Chivalry and Crusade', in *Noble Ideals and Bloody Realities, Warfare in the Middle Ages*, edited by Niall Christie and Maya Yazigi (Leiden: Brill, 2006), pp. 3–25, at pp. 19–21; Friedman, 'Captivity and Ransom', pp. 127–8; Penny J. Cole, ' "O God, the Heathen have Come into Your Inheritance" (Ps. 78.1): The Theme of Religious Pollution in Crusade Documents, 1095–1188', in *Crusaders and Muslims in Twelfth-Century Syria*, edited by Maya Shatzmiller (Leiden: Brill, 1993), pp. 84–111, at pp. 89–100; *Gesta Francorum*, pp. 8 ('Palagonia'), 47–8 (Antioch), 75 (al-Bara), 80 (Marra), 91–2 (Jerusalem); Joshua 6:21, 8:24–26, 10:29–30, 32, 35, 37, 39, 40, 11:10–11, 21–2.

135. *Gesta Francorum*, pp. 58 (women of the city still alive at Antioch) 80 (prisoners sold as slaves).

136. Friedman, 'Captivity and Ransom', p. 128; S. D. Goitein, 'Geniza Sources for the Crusader Period: A Survey', in *Outremer: Studies in the history of the Crusading Kingdom of Jerusalem presented to Joshua Prawer*, edited by B. Z. Kedar, H. E. Mayer, and R. C. Smail (Jerusalem: Yad Izhak Ben-Zvi Institute, 1982), pp. 306–22, at p. 312.

137. *The Chronicle of Ibn al-Athīr*, p. 135.

138. Fudge, *The Crusade against Heretics in Bohemia*, pp. 104–5. For further accounts of Hussite atrocities against Catholics see pp. 142, 179 and note 179.

139. Fudge, *The Crusade against Heretics in Bohemia*, pp. 63, 72, 104, 121, 131, 139, 145, 188.

140. Malcolm Barber, 'The Albigensian Crusades: Wars Like any Other?', in *Dei Gesta per Francos: Études sur les croisades dédiées à Jean Richard; Crusade Studies in Honour of Jean Richard*, edited by Michel Balard, Benjamin Z. Kedar, and Jonathan Riley-Smith (Aldershot: Ashgate, 2001), pp. 45–55, at p. 48; William of Tudela and Anonymous Successor, *The Song of the Cathar Wars*, pp. 21 (Béziers), 33 (Minerve), 41, 42 (Lavaur and Lady Girauda). Peter of Les Vaux-de-Cernay, *The History of the Albigensian Crusade*, p. 85 (burning of heretics at Minerve), 117 (death of Lady Giraude of Lavaur).

141. Robert Chazan, *European Jewry and the First Crusade* (Berkeley: University of California Press, 1987), pp. 6–7; Chaviva Levin, 'Constructing Memories of Martyrdom: Contrasting Portrayals of Martyrdom in the Hebrew Narratives of the First and Second Crusade', in *Remembering the Crusades: Myth, Image, and Identity*, edited by Nicholas Paul and Suzanne M. Yeager (Baltimore: Johns Hopkins University Press, 2012), pp. 50–68, at p. 51.

142. Chazan, *European Jewry*, pp. 111–13, 121, 122, 127–8, 129, 228–39, 244, 253–9, 263–6, 270, 276–7; 'The Version of the Anonymous of Mainz' and 'The Version of Solomon ben Simson' in *The First Crusade*, edited by Peters, pp. 115–25, 127–38: Minna at pp. 117–18, Rachel at pp. 122–3, 137–8. For an analysis of the story of Isaac son of David see Hannah Johnson, 'Massacre and Memory: Ethics and Method in Recent Scholarship on Jewish Martyrdom', in *Christians and Jews in Angevin England: The York Massacre of 1190, Narratives and Contexts*, edited by Sarah Rees Jones and Sethina C. Watson (Woodbridge: Boydell, 2013), pp. 261–77, at pp. 270–5. See also: Anna Sapir Abulafia, 'Invectives against Christianity in the Hebrew Chronicles of the First Crusade', in *Crusade and Settlement: Papers read at the First Conference of the Society for the Study of the Crusades and the Latin East and presented to R. C. Smail*, edited by Peter W. Edbury (Cardiff: University College Cardiff Press, 1985), pp. 66–72; Anna Sapir Abulafia, *Christian-Jewish Relations 1000–1300: Jews in the Service of Medieval Christendom* (Harlow: Longman, 2011), esp. pp. 135–66.

143. Levin, 'Constructing Memories of Martyrdom', pp. 55–7, 59.

144. John T. Appleby, *England without Richard, 1189–1199* (London: G. Bell, 1965), pp. 43–6; for analysis and context, see *Christians and Jews in Angevin England: The York Massacre of 1190, Narratives and Contexts*, edited by Sarah Rees Jones and Sethina C. Watson (Woodbridge: Boydell, 2013).

145. *An Arab-Syrian gentleman*, p. 154; Usama ibn Munqidh, *The Book of Contemplation*, pp. 136–7: quotation from p. 137.

146. *Fulcheri Carnotensis Historia*, pp. 257, 403 (Book 1 chapter 23, Book 2 chapter 9); discussion by Friedman, *Encounter Between Enemies*, pp. 164, 167, 171.

147. 'Imād al-Dīn al-Iṣfahānī, *Conquête de la Syrie*, p. 50; see also the discussion in Friedman, *Encounter Between Enemies*, pp. 169–70.

148. [Miguel de Castanhoso] *The Portuguese expedition to Abyssinia in 1541–1543*, p. 81.

149. 'Cum hominibus, mulieribus et parvulis e omni supellectili': Peter von Dusburg, *Chronicon Terre Prussie*, p. 217; *The Chronicle of Prussia by*

Nicolaus von Jeroschin, p. 291; for another example of the Brothers killing everyone, young and old, men and women, in a raid see p. 261.

150. Peter von Dusburg, *Chronicon Terre Prussie*, pp. 69, 72–4 (Swantopolk), 187 (Lithuanian attack on Revel, killing or capturing 5,000 noble Christian men, married women and virgins), 188 (in the Wehlau regin the Lithuanians kill 36 men and capture women and children, they then kill more than six thousand people of both sexes in the Dobrin area and carry thousands of Christians away to slavery); *The Chronicle of Prussia by Nicolaus von Jeroschin*, pp. 92, 98–100, 114 (Swantopolk), 257, 267, 277, 278 (Lithuanians capture or kill women and children).

151. For the lack of archaeological evidence for Prussian slave-raiding, see Aleksander Pluskowski, *The Archaeology of the Prussian Crusade: Holy War and Colonisation* (London: Routledge, 2013), pp. 63, 65, 87; for the debate over the existence or not of a widespread slave trade in the Baltic area see Magdelana Naum, 'Ambiguous Pots: Everyday Practice, Migration and Materiality. The Case of medieval Baltic Ware on the Island of Bornholm (Denmark)', *Journal of Social Archaeology* 12.1 (2012): pp. 92–119, at pp. 99–100, 107–8, 110.

152. *The 'Templar of Tyre', Part III of the 'Deeds of the Cypriots'*, trans. Paul Crawford, Crusade Texts in Translation 6 (Aldershot: Ashgate, 2003), pp. 113, 116–17.

153. Gaposchkin, *Invisible Weapons*, p. 239.

154. Mazeika, ' "Nowhere was the Fragility of their Sex Apparent" ', pp. 237–8 and note 20; Peter von Dusburg, *Chronicon Terre Prussie*, pp. 176–7. *The Chronicle of Prussia by Nicolaus von Jeroschin*, p. 259.

155. Hill, *A History of Cyprus, volume 3: 1432–1571*, pp. 983–7; citing (for example) Father Angelo Calepio in Fr. Steffano Lusignano di Cipro, *Chorograffia et Breve Historia Universale dell'isola de Cipro principiando al tempo di Noè per insino al 1572* (Bologna: Alessandro Benaccio, 1573), fols 106r, 109.

156. Luttrell, 'Englishwomen as Pilgrims to Jerusalem', p. 189.

157. Schmidt, ' "Peregrinatio periculosa". Thomas von Froidmont über die Jerusalemfahrten seiner Schwester Margareta', pp. 461–85; translated by Holloway, 'Margaret of Jerusalem/Beverley and Thomas of Beverley/Froidmont, her brother, her biographer', at www.umilta.net/jerusalem.html, accessed 23 December 2020.

158. *The Chronicle of Ibn al-Athīr*, p. 326.

159. *An Arab-Syrian gentleman*, pp. 159–60; Usama ibn Munqidh, *The Book of Contemplation*, pp. 142–3.

160. Goitein, 'Geniza Sources for the Crusader Period', pp. 315, 321.

161. W. H. Rudt de Collenberg, 'L'Empereur Isaac de Chypre et sa fille (1155–1207)', *Byzantion* 38.1 (1968): pp. 123–79, at pp. 155–77; *Chronique d'Ernoul et de Bernard le trésorier*, pp. 352–3.

162. Leighton, 'Written and Visual Expressions of Authority', p. 20. During the crusades in Prussia and Livonia the crusaders and the Teutonic Order regularly took the children of the local nobility as hostages for their parents' good behaviour and sent them to Germany to be educated in Christianity and Latin Christian culture, but this child represented spoils of war rather than being a hostage.

163. Setton, *The Papacy and the Levant*, vol. 4: *The Sixteenth Century from Julius III to Pius V*, pp. 835–41.

CHAPTER 4

1. Lambert, 'Crusading or Spinning', p. 5. For a possible keepsake of his wife's hair carried by a crusader see Alexander Grant, 'The St Bees Lord and Lady, and their Lineage', in *North-West England from the Romans to the Tudors: essays in memory of John Macnair Todd*, edited by Keith J. Stringer, *Cumberland and Westmorland Antiquarian and Archaeological Society Extra series* 41 (2014): pp. 171–200, at p. 191; for the later story of Landgrave Ludwig IV of Thuringia showing his wife Elizabeth his ring as he departed on crusade see Nicholas Paul, *To Follow in their Footsteps: The Crusades and Family Memory in the High Middle Ages* (Ithaca NY: Cornell University Press, 2012), pp. 108, 167.

2. Matthew Paris, *Chronica Majora*, vol. 5, pp. 3–5; *Récits d'un ménestrel de Reims*, pp. 191–2 (sections 370–1).

3. Grant, *Blanche of Castile*, pp. 131–42, 281–2.

4. Turner, *Eleanor of Aquitaine*, pp. 256–79; John Gillingham, *Richard I* (New Haven: Yale University Press, 1999), pp. 125–6, 140–3, 222–53.

5. Muldoon, 'Crusading and Canon Law', p. 46; Beatrice A. Lees, 'The Letters of Queen Eleanor of Aquitaine to Pope Celestine III', *English Historical Review* 21/81 (1906): pp. 78–93; Park, *Papal Protection and the Crusader, passim* (for crusader protection) and especially p. 187 on the letters; H. G. Richardson, 'The Letters and Charters of Eleanor of Aquitaine', *English Historical Review* 74/291 (1959): pp. 193–213, at p. 202; for the text of the letters see *Foedera, conventiones, literæ, et cujuscunque generis acta publica, inter reges Angliæ et alios quosvis imperatores…*, edited by Thomas Rymer and Robert Sanderson, 3rd edn revised by George Holmes (London: John Neaulme, 1745), vol. 1 part 1, pp. 23–5.

6. Tyerman, *England and the Crusades*, p. 210.

7. Tyerman, *England and the Crusades*, p. 211; Kathryn Hurlock, *Britain, Ireland & the Crusades, c. 1000–1300* (Basingstoke: Palgrave Macmillan, 2013), p. 118; Stenton, ed., *Rolls of the Justices in Eyre, Being the Rolls of Pleas and Assizes for Yorkshire in 3 Henry III*, pp. 298–301, no. 823.

8. Stenton, ed., *Rolls of the Justices in Eyre, Being the Rolls of Pleas and Assizes for Yorkshire in 3 Henry III*, p. 275, no. 740.

9. Tyerman, *England and the Crusades*, p. 211; *Curia Regis Rolls of the Reign of Henry III preserved in the Public Record Office*, vol. 13, *11–14 Henry III (1227–1230)* (London: HMSO, 1959), p. 370, no. 1760.

10. Hurlock, *Britain, Ireland & the Crusades*, p. 118; *Curia Regis Rolls of the Reign of Henry III preserved in the Public Record Office*, vol. 10, *5–6 Henry III* (London: HMSO, 1949), p. 293; Stenton, ed., *Rolls of the Justices in Eyre for Gloucestershire, Warwickshire, and Shropshire, 1221, 1222*, p. 258, no. 582.

11. Paul, *To Follow in their Footsteps*, pp. 161, 166.

12. Lloyd, *English Society and the Crusade*, p. 174; Tyerman, *England and the Crusades*, p. 196.

13. Kathryn Hurlock, *Wales and the Crusades, c. 1095–1291* (Cardiff: University of Wales Press, 2011), p. 126.

14. Peter Coss, *The Foundations of Gentry Life: The Multons of Frampton and their World, 1270–1370* (Oxford: Oxford University Press, 2010), pp. 199–204, 207–8.

15. Theodore Evergates, *Marie of France: Countess of Champagne, 1145–1198* (Philadelphia, PA: University of Pennsylvania Press, 2019), p. 84.

16. Lloyd, *English Society and the Crusade*, p. 175.

17. Lloyd, *English Society and the Crusade*, p. 175 note 104; Hurlock, *Wales and the Crusades*, pp. 125; *Curia Regis Rolls of the Reign of Henry III*, vol. 16: *21 to 26 Henry III (1237–1242)*, edited by L. C. Hector (London: HMSO, 1979), p. 320, no. 1625.

18. Park, *Papal Protection and the Crusader*, p. 81.

19. Lloyd, *English Society and the Crusade*, pp. 174–5.

20. Tyerman, *England and the Crusades*, p. 210.

21. Bird, Peters, and Powell, eds and trans., *Crusade and Christendom*, p. 444; Lunt, *Financial Relations of the Papacy with England, 1327–1534*, p. 534.

22. Evergates, *Marie of France*, pp. 33, 37; Theodore Evergates, *Henry the Liberal: Count of Champagne, 1127–1181* (Philadelphia, PA: University of Pennsylvania Press, 2016), pp. 22–4, 162–3; Evergates (*Marie of France*, p. 129 note 2) notes that Marie's donation to the Templars was cited by A. Pétel, 'La Commanderie de Payns et ses dépendances à Savières, à Saint-Mesmin, à Messon, et au Pavillon', *Revue Champenoise et Bourguignon* 1 (July 1904): pp. 25–54 at p. 40, but without details of the source.

23. Friedman, *Encounter Between Enemies*, pp. 82–3; Hans Eberhard Mayer, 'The Wheel of Fortune: Seignorial Vicissitudes under Kings Fulk and Baldwin III of Jerusalem', *Speculum* 65.4 (1990): pp. 860–77, at p. 867.

24. Friedman, *Encounter Between Enemies*, p. 183; Erin L. Jordan, 'Hostage, Sister, Abbess: The Life of Iveta of Jerusalem', *Medieval Prosopography* 32 (2017): 66–86; Barber, *The Crusader States*, pp. 138, 143, 157; Hamilton, 'Women in the Crusader States', p. 151; Adam J. Kosto, *Hostages in the Middle Ages* (Oxford: Oxford University Press, 2012), pp. 85–6, 166–7.

25. Maier, 'The Roles of Women in the Crusade Movement', pp. 75–7.

26. Christine de Pisan, *The Treasure of the City of Ladies*, pp. 59–61, 128–33 (Part 1, chapter 11, Part 2, chapters 9–10).

27. Appleby, *England without Richard*, pp. 1–3, 18–20, 48–50, 82–93.

28. Gillingham, *Richard I*, pp. 125–6.

29. Appleby, *England without Richard*, pp. 59, 101–4.

30. Appleby, *England without Richard*, pp. 107–9, 112–15.

31. Appleby, *England without Richard*, pp. 119–21, 123, 127, 136, 138, 142, 231; Turner, *Eleanor of Aquitaine*, pp. 275–6.

32. Poulet, 'Capetian Women and the Regency', at p. 108.

33. Lloyd, *English Society and the Crusade*, p. 169.

34. Park, *Papal Protection and the Crusader*, pp. 48–50; Karen S. Nicholas, 'Countesses as Rulers in Flanders', in *Aristocratic Women in Medieval France*, edited by Theodore Evergates (Philadelphia, PA: University of Pennsylvania Press, 1999), pp. 111–37, at pp. 117–20; Hemptinne, 'Les épouses des croisés et pèlerins flamands'.

35. Park, *Papal Protection and the Crusader*, pp. 51–2: Kimberly A. LoPrete, 'Adela of Blois: Familial Alliances and Female Lordship', in *Aristocratic Women in Medieval France*, edited by Theodore Evergates (Philadelphia, PA: University of Pennsylvania Press, 1999), pp. 7–43, at pp. 17–22; see also Kimberly A. LoPrete, *Adela of Blois: Countess and Lord (c. 1067–1137)* (Dublin: Four Courts, 2007).

36. Park, *Papal Protection and the Crusader*, pp. 137–9, 144–5: Nicholas, 'Countesses as Rulers in Flanders', pp. 121–3.

37. Park, *Papal Protection and the Crusader*, pp. 165–7; Evergates, *Marie of France*, pp. 5–6, 18, 22, 26–7, 28–9, 30.

38. Park, *Papal Protection and the Crusader*, pp. 58–9; Nicholas, 'Countesses as Rulers in Flanders', p. 117.

39. Park, *Papal Protection and the Crusader*, pp. 59–63; LoPrete, 'Adela of Blois', pp. 20, 22.

40. Park, *Papal Protection and the Crusader*, pp. 57–9, 64–5; Nicholas, 'Countesses as Rulers in Flanders', pp. 117–20.

41. Park, *Papal Protection and the Crusader*, pp. 65–7, 73; LoPrete, 'Adela of Blois', pp. 24–6.

42. Evergates, *Marie of France*, pp. 67–85, 89–90.

43. Park, *Papal Protection and the Crusader*, pp. 196–202; Theodore Evergates, 'Aristocratic Women in the County of Champagne', in *Aristocratic Women in Medieval France*, edited by Theodore Evergates (Philadelphia, PA: University of Pennsylvania Press, 1999), pp. 74–110, at pp. 81–5; Perry, *The Briennes*, pp. 58–63.

44. Park, *Papal Protection and the Crusader*, pp. 147–51; Nicholas, 'Countesses as Rulers in Flanders', p. 123; Lambert de Waterlos, 'Annales Cameracenses', in *Monumenta Germaniae Historica Scriptores in Folio*, vol. 16, edited by George Heinrich Pertz (Hanover: Aulic Hahn, 1859), pp. 509–54, at pp. 516–17.

45. On the literary functions of descriptions of grief see, for instance, Leslie Abend Callahan, 'The Widow's Tears: the Pedagogy of Grief in Medieval France and the Image of the Grieving Widow', in *Constructions of Widowhood and Virginity in the Middle Ages*, edited by Cindy L. Carlson and Angela Jane Weisl (Basingstoke: Macmillan, 1999), pp. 245–63.

46. Evergates, *Marie of France*, p. 90, citing Robert, canon of Saint-Marien of Auxerre, *Chronicon*, edited by O. Holder-Egger, in *Monumenta Germaniae Historica Scriptores in Folio*, vol. 26, edited by Societas Aperiendis Fontibus rerum Germanicarum Medii Aevi (Hanover: Hahn, 1882), pp. 219–76, at p. 257, lines 38–40.

47. Grant, *Blanche of Castile*, pp. 78, 347 n. 1; Philippe Mousket, *Chronique rimée*, edited by F. de Reiffenberg, 2 vols (Brussels: 1836–1838), vol. 2, p. 554, lines 27,303–27,304 (Ki se fust ocise de duel/S'on n'el tenist outre son voel).

48. Paul, *To Follow in their Footsteps*, pp. 108, 166–8 and note 134.

49. *The Life and Afterlife of St. Elizabeth of Hungary: Testimony from her Canonization Hearings*, translated with notes by Kenneth Baxter Wolf (New York: Oxford University Press, 2011), pp. ix–x.

50. *Le Livre des Fais du bon Messire Jehan le Maingre, dit Bouciquaut, Mareschal de France et Gouverneur de Jennes*, edited by Denis Lalande, Textes Littéraires Français 331 (Geneva: Droz, 1985), pp. 118–20 (Book 1, chapter 27); translation in *Documents on the Later Crusades*, p. 107.

51. Park, *Papal Protection and the Crusader*, pp. 193–6; Nicholas, 'Countesses as Rulers in Flanders', pp. 128–9.

52. Paul, *To Follow in their Footsteps*, pp. 151–3; *La Chronique de Gislebert de Mons*, edited by Léon Vanderkindere (Brussels: Kiessling, 1904), p. 45;

Gilbert of Mons, *Chronicle of Hainaut*, trans. Laura Napran (Woodbridge: Boydell, 2005), p. 30.

53. James A. Brundage, 'The Crusader's Wife Revisited', *Studia Gratiana* 14 (1967): pp. 243–51, at pp. 245–50.

54. Danielle Park gives two examples: Stephen Aicaphit went to Jerusalem for seven years and his wife remarried, thinking him dead, but he returned and forced her to give up her second husband and return to him; when an unnamed woman went to Jerusalem and stayed there her husband remarried, but she then returned and he was forced to return to her: Park, *Papal Protection and the Crusader*, pp. 7–8.

55. Ruth M. Blakely, *The Brus Family in England and Scotland 1100–1295* (Woodbridge: Boydell, 2005), pp. 82–3; Johannes de Fordun, 'Gesta Annalia', in *Johannis de Fordun, Chronica Gentis Scotorum*, edited by William F. Skene (Edinburgh: Edmonston and Douglas, 1871), pp. 254–383, at p. 304; Hurlock, *Britain, Ireland & the Crusades*, p. 119.

56. Tyerman, *England and the Crusades*, p. 211; *Curia Regis Rolls of the Reign of Henry III*, vol. 13, p. 347, no. 1636.

57. Doris Mary Stenton, ed., *Rolls of the Justices in Eyre for Lincolnshire (1218–1219) and Worcestershire (1221)*, Selden Society 53 (1934), p. 315, no. 655.

58. Paul, *To Follow in their Footsteps*, pp. 155–7; *Lamberti Ardensis Historia Comitum Ghisnensium*, edited by I. Heller, in *Monumenta Germaniae Historica Scriptores in Folio*, vol. 24, edited by Societas Aperiendis Fontibus rerum Germanicarum Medii Aevi (Hanover: Hahn, 1879), pp. 593–4, 633–4 (chapters 65–67, 141–3); Lambert of Ardres, *The History of the Counts of Guines and Lords of Ardres*, trans. Leah Shopkow (Philadelphia, PA: University of Pennsylvania Press, 2001), pp. 13, 104–6, 177–80. For another imposter claiming (in 1178–1179) to have returned alive from wars against Muslims, this time not involving an heiress, see the pseudo-Alfonso I the Battler of Aragon in Paul, *To Follow in their Footsteps*, pp. 284–5.

59. Norman Cohn, *The Pursuit of the Millennium: Revolutionary Millenarians and Mystical Anarchists of the Middle Ages*, revised ed. (London: Pimlico, 1993), pp. 90–3.

60. Peter Lock, *The Franks in the Aegean, 1204–1500* (Harlow: Longman, 1995), p. 53; *Récits d'un Ménestrel de Reims*, pp. 164–71 (sections 314–329); and see Robert Bartlett, 'Pretenders and Returners: Dynastic Imposters in the Middle Ages', in *Blood Royal: Dynastic Politics in Medieval Europe*, edited by Robert Bartlett (Cambridge: Cambridge University Press, 2020), pp. 360–78; Nicholas, 'Countesses as Rulers in Flanders', pp. 129–33.

61. Brundage, *Medieval Canon Law and the Crusader*, p. 77.

62. Geldsetzer, *Frauen auf Kreuzzügen*, p. 182; Ian Bass, '"Articuli Inquisicionis de crucesignatis": Late Thirteenth-Century Inquiry into English Crusaders', *Crusades* 17 (2018): pp. 171–94, at 183 and note 67.

63. Tyerman, *England and the Crusades*, pp. 170–1; Geldsetzer, *Frauen auf Kreuzzügen*, pp. 39, 42, 182; Bass, '"Articuli Inquisicionis de crucesignatis"', p. 191.

64. Geldsetzer, *Frauen auf Kreuzzügen* p. 40; Matthew Paris, *Chronica Majora*, vol. 4, pp. 133–4; vol. 5, p. 73; for the background to the collection of 1241 see Michael Lower, *The Barons' Crusade: A Call to Arms and its Consequences* (Philadelphia, PA: University of Pennsylvania Press, 2005), pp. 31–6. A mark, a unit of account commonly used in England at this time, was two thirds of a pound, so in 1241 the friars raised £13,333 pounds, six shillings and eightpence for the crusade through the sale of indulgences.

65. Lunt, *Financial Relations of the Papacy with England, 1327–1534*, p. 541; *Chronicon Henrici Knighton vel Cnitthon Monarchi Leycestrensis*, edited by Joseph Rawson Lumby, vol. 2 (1337–1395) (London: HMSO, 1893), p. 198.

66. R. N. Swanson, 'Preaching Crusade in Fifteenth-Century England: Instructions for the Administration of the anti-Hussite Crusade of 1429 in the Diocese of Canterbury', *Crusades* 12 (2013): pp. 175–96, at p. 181.

67. Tyerman, *England and the Crusades*, pp. 313–15; Anthony Luttrell, 'English Contributions to the Hospitaller Castle at Bodrum in Turkey: 1407–1437', in *The Military Orders*, vol. 2: *Welfare and Warfare*, edited by Helen Nicholson (Aldershot: Ashgate, 1998), pp. 163–72, at pp. 165, 167; Lunt, *Financial Relations of the Papacy with England, 1327–1534*, pp. 558–9.

68. Tyerman, *England and the Crusades*, p. 316; citing E. Gordon Duff, *Fifteenth century English books: a bibliography of books and documents printed in England and of books for the English market printed abroad* (Oxford: Bibliographical Society, 1917), pp. 54–5, nos 204, 208; Lunt, *Financial Relations of the Papacy with England, 1327–1534*, pp. 586–7, 589; R. N. Swanson, 'Crusade Administration in Fifteenth-Century England: Regulations for the Distribution of Indulgences in 1489', *Historical Research* 84/223 (2011): pp. 183–8, at p. 186; Karl Borchardt, 'Late Medieval Indulgences for the Hospitallers and the Teutonic Order', in *Ablasskampagnen des Spätmittelalters: Luthers Thesen von 1517 im Kontext*, edited by Andreas Rehberg, Bibliothek des Deutschen Historischen Instituts in Rom 132 (Berlin: De Gruyter, 2017), pp. 195–18.

69. Bird, Peters, and Powell, eds and trans., *Crusade and Christendom*, p. 447.

70. Guard, *Chivalry, Kingship and Crusade*, p. 121.

71. *Cartulaires du Chapitre de l'église métropolitaine Sainte-Marie d'Auch*, vol. 1: *Cartulaire noir*, edited by C. Lacave La Plagne Barris, Société historique de Gascogne (Paris: Honoré Champion, 1988), pp. 65–66, no. 64; discussed by Maier, 'The Roles of Women in the Crusade Movement', pp. 75–6; Riley-Smith, *The First Crusaders*, pp. 129–30.

72. Stenton, ed., *Rolls of the Justices in Eyre for Lincolnshire (1218–1219) and Worcestershire (1221)*, p. 70, no. 159.

73. Powell, 'The Role of Women in the Fifth Crusade', pp. 296–8.

74. Ana Rodríguez, 'Remembering the Crusades while living the Reconquest: Iberia, twelfth to fourteenth centuries', in *Remembering the Crusades and Crusading*, edited by Megan Cassidy-Welch (London: Routledge, 2017), pp. 202–15, at p. 204.

75. Shadis, *Berenguela of Castile (1180–1246)*, p. 142.

76. Luis García-Guijarro Ramos, 'The Aragonese Hospitaller Monastery of Sigena: its Early Stages, 1188–*c*. 1210', in *Hospitaller Women in the Middle Ages*, edited by Anthony Luttrell and Helen J. Nicholson (Aldershot: Ashgate, 2006), pp. 113–51.

77. Helen J. Nicholson, 'Margaret de Lacy and the Hospital of Saint John at Aconbury, Herefordshire', *Journal of Ecclesiastical History* 50 (1999): pp. 629–51; reprinted in *Hospitaller Women in the Middle Ages*, edited by Anthony Luttrell and Helen J. Nicholson (Aldershot: Ashgate, 2006), pp. 153–77.

78. Beatrice A. Lees, ed., *Records of the Templars in England in the Twelfth Century: The Inquest of 1185 with Illustrative Charters and Documents* (London: Oxford University Press, 1935), pp. 145–6, 176–8; Michael Gervers, ed., *The Cartulary of the Knights of St. John of Jerusalem in England. Secunda Camera, Essex* (Oxford: Oxford University Press, 1982), nos 1 and 2, pp. 1–2.

79. *Monasticon anglicanum: A History of the abbies and other monasteries, hospitals, friaries, and cathedral and collegiate churches, with their dependencies, in England and Wales...*, edited by William Dugdale; revised by John Caley, Henry Ellis, and Bulkeley Bandinel, 6 vols in 8 (London: Harding, Harding and Lepard, 1830), vol. 6.2, p. 841 no. 32.

80. John Stillingflete, 'Liber Johannis Stillingflete de nominibus fundatorum Hosp. S. Johannis Jerusalem in Anglia', in *Monasticon anglicanum*, vol. 6.2, pp. 831–9.

81. *Hospitaller Women in the Middle Ages*, edited by Anthony Luttrell and Helen J. Nicholson (Aldershot: Ashgate, 2006); Udo Arnold, 'Die Frau im Deutschen Orden', in *Stationen Einer Hochschullaufbahn: Festschrift für Annette Kuhn zum 65. Geburtstag*, edited by Udo Arnold, Peter Meyers,

and Uta C. Schmidt (Dortmund: Ebersbach 1999), pp. 261–76; Myra Miranda Bom, *Women in the Military Orders of the Crusades* (New York: Palgrave Macmillan, 2012).

82. Lees, ed., *Records of the Templars in England*, pp. 38–9; Rory MacLellan, 'Hospitaller Confraternity Scripts, Crusading and the English Reformation, *c.* 1440–537', *Historical Research* 92/256 (2019): pp. 445–57, especially p. 450; David Marcombe, *Leper Knights: The Order of St Lazarus of Jerusalem in England, c.1150–1544* (Woodbridge: Boydell, 2003), pp. 189–94, 256–7.

83. Friedman, *Encounter Between Enemies*, pp. 187–211; Alan Forey, 'The Military Orders and the Ransoming of Captives from Islam (Twelfth to Early Fourteenth Centuries)', *Studia Monastica* 33 (1991): pp. 259–79.

84. Ian B. Cowan and David E. Easson, *Medieval Religious Houses: Scotland*, 2nd ed. (London: Longman, 1976), pp. 108, 109.

85. Forey, 'The Military Orders and the Ransoming of Captives', p. 276; Friedman, *Encounter Between Enemies*, p. 200; *Cartulaire général de l'ordre des Hospitaliers de S. Jean de Jérusalem (1100–1310)*, edited by Joseph Delaville le Roulx, vol. 2 (Paris: Ernest Leroux, 1897), p. 8, no. 1146.

86. Friedman, *Encounter Between Enemies*, p. 204; *Cartulaire général de l'ordre des Hospitaliers*, vol. 2, p. 142, no. 1385.

87. Forey, 'The Military Orders and the Ransoming of Captives', p. 277; *Cartulaire général de l'ordre des Hospitaliers*, vol. 2, p. 171, no. 1434.

88. Gaposchkin, *Invisible Weapons*, pp. 194–202; Linder, *Raising Arms*, pp. 1–3.

89. Rousseau, 'Home Front and Battlefield', pp. 36–7; Gaposchkin, *Invisible Weapons*, pp. 204–206, 217–19; Bird, Peters, and Powell, eds and trans., *Crusade and Christendom*, pp. 82–85, 111–12.

90. Gaposchkin, *Invisible Weapons*, pp. 221–5; Linder, *Raising Arms*, pp. 118–21.

91. Gaposchkin, *Invisible Weapons*, pp. 226–55. On dedicated war masses against the Turks see also Linder, pp. 186–90.

92. Tyerman, *England and the Crusades*, pp. 260–61, citing Toulmin Smith, *English Gilds*, Early English Text Society, 40 (London: Oxford University Press, 1870), pp. 22–4 (no. 8: St Christopher, Norwich), 111–13 (no. 43: Wiggenhall), 182 (Tailors of Lincoln).

93. *The Life and Afterlife of St. Elizabeth of Hungary*, pp. 11–12, 20, 72 note 149, 177; *Cartulaire général de l'ordre des*, vol. 2, p. 432, no. 2008; Axel Ehlers, *Die Ablasspraxis des Deutschen Ordens im Mittelalter*, Quellen und Studien zur Geschichte des Deutschen Ordens 64 (Marburg: N. G. Elwert, 2007), pp. 120–2, 397.

94. Johannes von Marienwerder, *The Life of Dorothea von Montau, a fourteenth-century Recluse*, trans. Ute Stargardt (Lewiston: Edwin Mellen, 1997), pp. 5–6, 12, 22, 113.

95. Johannes von Marienwerder, *The Life of Dorothea von Montau*, pp. 61–52, 66, 68–9 (Book 1, Chapters 25, 28, 30).

96. *Die Akten des Kanonisationsprozesses Dorotheas von Montau*, pp. 108–9 (quotation at p. 108).

97. *Die Akten des Kanonisationsprozesses Dorotheas von Montau*, pp. 212–13, 265–6, 413 (quotation).

98. *Die Akten des Kanonisationsprozesses Dorotheas von Montau*, p. 66. By the date of these campaigns Lithuania had officially converted to Christianity.

99. *Die Akten des Kanonisationsprozesses Dorotheas von Montau*, p. 517.

100. Bernard of Clairvaux, *In Praise of the New Knighthood: A Treatise on the Knights Templar and the Holy Places of Jerusalem*, trans. M. Conrad Greenia, Cistercian Fathers Series 19B (Kalamazoo: Cistercian Publications, 2000).

101. Eric Christiansen, *The Northern Crusades*, 2nd edn (London: Penguin, 1997), p. 222; Mazeika, '"Nowhere was the Fragility of their Sex Apparent"', pp. 244–7.

102. John of Joinville, 'The Life of Saint Louis', p. 326; Jean Sire de Joinville, *Histoire de Saint Louis*, pp. 356–357, sections 650–1.

103. Theresa M. Vann and Donald J. Kagay, *Hospitaller Piety and Crusader Propaganda: Guillaume Caoursin's Description of the Ottoman Siege of Rhodes, 1480* (Farnham: Ashgate, 2015), pp. 140–1, 203, 276–7, 308–9.

104. *The Chronicle of Novgorod 1016–1471*, trans. Robert Michell and Nevill Forbes, *Camden Third Series*, 25 (1914), p. 87; Sarah Hamilton, 'The Virgin Mary in Cathar Thought', *The Journal of Ecclesiastical History* 56.1 (2005): pp. 24–49.

105. Helen J. Nicholson, 'Saints venerated in the Military Orders', in *Selbstbild und Selbstverständnis der geistlichen Ritterorden*, edited by Roman Czaja and Jürgen Sarnowsky, Ordines Militares: Colloquia Torunensia Historica XIII (Toruń: Uniwersytetu Mikołaja Kopernika, 2005), pp. 91–113.

106. 'The Ways and Pilgrimages of the Holy Land', text A (1261–65), and Philip of Savona, 'Description of the Holy Land (1285–89)', in *Pilgrimage to Jerusalem and the Holy Land, 1187–1291*, trans. Denys Pringle, Crusade Texts in Translation 23 (Farnham: Ashgate, 2012), pp. 209–28 and 321–59, at pp. 211, 352–3.

107. Patrick J. Geary, *Living with the Dead in the Middle Ages* (Ithaca, NY: Cornell University Press, 1994), pp. 221–42.

108. Lower, *The Barons' Crusade*, pp. 25–9; David Morris, 'The Servile Mother: Jerusalem as Woman in the Era of the Crusades', in *Remembering the Crusades: Myth, Image, and Identity*, edited by Nicholas Paul and Suzanne Yeager (Baltimore, MD: Johns Hopkins University Press, 2012), pp. 174–94.

CHAPTER 5

1. Richard A. Leson, 'Chivalry and Alterity: Saladin and the Remembrance of Crusade in a Walters *Histoire d'Outremer*', *Journal of the Walters Art Museum* 68/69 (2011–2012): pp. 87–96, at p. 92; Laura Hibbard Loomis, 'Secular Dramatics in the Royal Palace, Paris, 1378, 1389, and Chaucer's "Tregetoures"', *Speculum* 33.2 (1958): pp. 242–55, at pp. 251–2; Roger Sherman Loomis, '*Richard Cœur de Lion* and the *Pas Saladin* in Medieval Art', *PMLA* 30.3 (1915): pp. 509–28, at p. 525.

2. Megan Cassidy-Welch and Anne E. Lester, 'Memory and Interpretation: new Approaches to the Study of the Crusades', in *Crusades and Memory: Journal of Medieval History* 40.3 (2014): pp. 225–36, at p. 226 (volume republished as: *Crusades and Memory: Rethinking Past and Present* (London: Routledge, 2015). For further discussion of how individuals and society memorialised the past in medieval Europe see, for example, *Memory and the Medieval Tomb*, edited by Elizabeth Valdez del Alamo and Carol Stamatis Pendergast (Aldershot: Ashgate, 2000); *Medieval Memories: Men, Women and the Past, 700–1300*, edited by Elisabeth van Houts (Harlow: Longman, 2001); *Medieval Concepts of the Past: Ritual, Memory, Historiography*, edited by Gerd Althoff, Johannes Fried, and Patrick J Geary (Cambridge: Cambridge University Press, 2002). For memory and the crusades, see also: Nicholas Paul and Suzanne Yeager, eds, *Remembering the Crusades: Myth, Image, and Identity* (Baltimore: Johns Hopkins University Press, 2012); Paul, *To Follow in their Footsteps*; Cassidy-Welch, ed., *Remembering the Crusades and Crusading*.

3. For instance, it was assumed in some of the stories told against the Templars during the trial of 1307–11 that a woman would wash her male relative's body at his death: *The Proceedings Against the Templars in the British Isles*, edited by and trans. Helen J. Nicholson, vol. 2 (Farnham: Ashgate, 2011), pp. 438 and note 32, 440, 441. For examples of women's roles in dealing with the bodies of their menfolk after death, see Elisabeth van Houts, *Memory and Gender in Medieval Europe, 900–1200* (Basingstoke: Macmillan, 1999), pp. 94–5; Elisabeth van Houts, 'Introduction: Medieval Memories', in *Medieval Memories: Men, Women and the Past, 700–1300*, edited by Elisabeth van Houts (Harlow: Longman, 2001), pp. 1–16, at pp. 8–10.

4. Perry, *The Briennes*, p. 95; John of Joinville, 'The Life of Saint Louis', p. 281; Jean Sire de Joinville, *Histoire de Saint Louis*, pp. 254–5, sections 466–467. On the *denier* in the crusader states see Robert Kool, 'Finding French Deniers in the Latin Kingdom of Jerusalem. The Archaeological

and Cultural Perspective', in *Transferts culturels entre France et Orient latin (XII–XIII siècles)*, edited by Martin Aurell, Marisa Galvez, and Estelle Ingrand-Varenne (Paris: Classiques Garnier, 2021), pp. 101–28.

5. Evergates, *Henry the Liberal*, pp. 140–5, 166–9. For a drawing and a plan of the chapel, see Evergates, *Marie of France*, pp. 12, 15.

6. Evergates, *Henry the Liberal*, p. 182; Evergates, *Marie of France*, pp. 95–6; Kenaan-Kedar, 'Pictorial and Sculptural Commemoration', p. 97; Nurith Kenaan-Kedar, 'The Enigmatic Sepulchral Monument of Berengaria (CA. 1170–1230), Queen of England (1191–1199)', *Assahp. Section B, Studies in art history* 12 (2007): pp. 49–61, at pp. 52–56, figures 3 and 4.

7. Kathleen Nolan, 'Symbolic Geography in the Tomb and Seal of Berengaria of Navarre, Queen of England', in *Moving Women Moving Objects (400–1500)*, edited by Tracy Chapman Hamilton and Mariah Proctor-Tiffany (Leiden: Brill, 2019), pp. 59–85, at p. 75 and note 48.

8. Robert Marcoux, 'Memory, Presence and the Medieval Tomb', in *Revisiting the Monument: Fifty Years Since Panofsky's* Tomb Sculpture, edited by Ann Adams and Jessica Barker (London: Courtauld Institute of Art, 2016), pp. 49–67, at pp. 56–8.

9. Ruggles, *Tree of Pearls*, pp. 111–40, quotation at p. 123; Eastmond, *Tamta's World*, pp. 120–1.

10. Ruggles, *Tree of Pearls*, pp. 78–101; Eastmond, *Tamta's World*, p. 120.

11. Eastmond, *Tamta's World*, pp. 111, 196–204.

12. Loveday Lewes Gee, *Women, Art and Patronage from Henry III to Edward III, 1216–1377* (Woodbridge: Boydell, 2002), pp. 1, 30, 112; description of Eleanor's tomb from 'Edward I and Eleanor of Castile', online at www.westminster-abbey.org/abbey-commemorations/royals/edward-i-and-eleanor-of-castile, accessed 24 November 2020; John Maddicott, 'Grandson [Grandison], Sir Otto de (*c.* 1238–1328)', in *Oxford Dictionary of National Biography*, edited by H. C. G. Matthew and Brian Harrison (Oxford: Oxford University Press, 2004, online version 23 September 2004), accessed 24 November 2020: from https://doi-org.abc.cardiff.ac.uk/10.1093/ref:odnb/37827.

13. Elizabeth Hallam, 'Berengaria [Berengaria of Navarre] (*c.* 1165–1230)', in *Oxford Dictionary of National Biography*, edited by H. C. G. Matthew and Brian Harrison (Oxford: Oxford University Press, 2004, online version 23 September 2004), accessed 24 November 2020: https://doi-org.abc.cardiff.ac.uk/10.1093/ref:odnb/2192; Nolan, 'Symbolic Geography', pp. 59–85; Kenaan-Kedar, 'The Enigmatic Sepulchral Monument of Berengaria', pp. 49–61.

14. 'Tombeaux des rois et reines de France', drawings prepared for Roger de Gaignières, c. 1700, Oxford, Bodleian Library MS. Gough Drawings Gaignières 2, image 24, online at: https://digital.bodleian.ox.ac.uk/object s/17fc19da-984d-414e-8475-2225eb3d041b, accessed 24 November 2020.

15. Jane Martindale, 'Eleanor [Eleanor of Aquitaine], *suo jure* duchess of Aquitaine (*c.* 1122–1204)', in *Oxford Dictionary of National Biography*, edited by H. C. G. Matthew and Brian Harrison (Oxford: Oxford University Press, 2004, *online version* 23 September 2004), accessed 24 November 2020: https://doi-org.abc.cardiff.ac.uk/10.1093/ref:odnb/8618; Paul, *To Follow in their Footsteps*, pp. 219–20; Nolan, 'Symbolic Geography', pp. 59–85, at pp. 72–3 and notes 39, 41; Kenaan-Kedar, 'The Enigmatic Sepulchral Monument of Berengaria', pp. 49–61, at p. 57. At the time of writing images of the four effigies were online at: https://artsandculture.google.com/exhibit/a-royal-family-on-the-move-abbaye-royale-de-fontevraud/gQLCb3VjN4p7JA?hl=en, accessed 24 November 2020.

16. Grant, *Blanche of Castile*, pp. 225, 228–9; Perry, *The Briennes*, pp. 64, 104–5, 115, 125. For other possible 'owners' of the black marble effigy from Maubuisson see Elizabeth A. R. Brown, 'The Oxford Collection of the Drawings of Roger de Gaignières and the Royal Tombs of Saint-Denis', *Transactions of the American Philosophical Society* 78.5 (1988): pp. i–viii+1–74 at p. 15, suggesting Catherine de Courtenay.

17. Christopher J. Knüsel, Catherine M. Batt, Gordon Cook, Janet Montgomery, Gundula Müldner, Alan R. Ogden, Carol Palmer, Ben Stern, John Todd, and Andrew S. Wilson, 'The Identity of the St Bees Lady, Cumbria: An Osteobiographical Approach', *Medieval Archaeology* 54:1 (2010): pp. 271–311, at pp. 294, 301, 302; Grant, 'The St Bees Lord and Lady, and their Lineage', at pp. 191, 198–9; Canon Bower, 'On a Brass found in Arthuret Church', *Transactions of the Cumberland and Westmorland Antiquarian and Archaeological Society, new series* 1 (1901): pp. 114–15, at p. 115.

18. Elizabeth Siberry, 'A Crickhowell Crusader: The Case of the Missing Hands', *Brycheiniog: Cyfnodolyn Cymdeithas Brycheiniog, The Journal of the Brecknock Society* 46 (2015): pp. 101–8. I heard a version of the story from a member of the public at Hereford in 2013.

19. Nurith Kenaan-Kedar and Benjamin Z. Kedar, 'The Significance of a Twelfth-Century Sculptural Group: *Le Retour du Croisé*', in *Dei gesta per Francos: Études sur les croisades dédiées à Jean Richard; Crusade Studies in Honour of Jean Richard*, edited by Michel Balard, Benjamin Z. Kedar,

and Jonathan Riley-Smith (Aldershot: Ashgate, 2001), pp. 29–44; Kenaan-Kedar, 'Pictorial and Sculptural Commemoration', pp. 94–7.

20. Kenaan-Kedar, 'Pictorial and Sculptural Commemoration', pp. 98–9.

21. Kenaan-Kedar, 'Pictorial and Sculptural Commemoration', pp. 98, 100–2.

22. Luttrell, 'Englishwomen as Pilgrims to Jerusalem', pp. 189–92, 197 note 46.

23. Hurlock, *Wales and the Crusades*, p. 130.

24. Leighton, 'Written and Visual Expressions of Authority', pp. 19–28.

25. Bernard Hamilton and Andrew Jotischky, *Latin and Greek Monasticism in the Crusader States* (Cambridge: Cambridge University Press, 2020), pp. 220–41, 336.

26. John of Joinville, 'The Life of Saint Louis', pp. 321–2; Jean Sire de Joinville, *Histoire de Saint Louis*, pp. 346–7, sections 630–633.

27. Tyerman, *England and the Crusades*, p. 261; *Testamenta Vetusta, being Illustrations from Wills, of Manners, Customs, &c., as well as of the Descents and Possessions of many distinguished Families, from the reign of Henry the Second to the accession of Queen Elizabeth*, edited by Nicholas Harris Nicolas (London: Nichols and Son, 1826), vol. 1, p. 100.

28. M. Cecilia Gaposchkin, 'The Liturgical Memory of July 15, 1099: Between History, Memory, and Eschatology', in *Remembering the Crusades and Crusading*, edited by Megan Cassidy-Welch (London: Routledge, 2017), pp. 34–48, at p. 41; Gaposchkin, *Invisible Weapons*, p. 168.

29. Evergates, *Henry the Liberal*, p. 165.

30. *Le Livre des Fais*, p. 120 (Book 1, chapter 27); translation in *Documents on the Later Crusades*, p. 107.

31. Graeme Dunphy, 'Women chroniclers and chronicles for women', in *The Encyclopedia of the Medieval Chronicle*, edited by Graeme Dunphy (Leiden: Brill, 2010), vol. 2, pp. 1521–4.

32. Simon Lloyd, 'William Longespée II: The Making of an English Crusading Hero', *Nottingham Medieval Studies* 35 (1991): pp. 41–69 and 36 (1992): pp. 79–125, at p. 86; citing William Stubbs, 'Introduction', in *Chronicles of the Reigns of Edward I and Edward II*, Rolls Series 76, vol. 2 (London: Longman, 1883), pp. vii–cix, at p. xli.

33. Lloyd, 'William Longespée II', pp. 79–125, at pp. 86–7; Paul, *To Follow in their Footsteps*, p. 164; Matthew Paris, *Chronica Majora*, vol. 5, p. 173; 'Fundatorum Historia' in 'Cartae ad Prioratum de Lacock, in agro Wiltoniensi, spectantes', in *Monasticon anglicanum*, vol. 6.1, pp. 501–10, at p. 501 (no. 2).

34. For women as a source of oral testimony in written male histories see Van Houts, *Memory and Gender in Medieval Europe*, pp. 25, 51–3, 55–6.

35. Vann, ' "Our father has won a great victory" ', pp. 79–92, esp. p. 88. Many scholars, including Shadis, *Berenguela of Castile (1180–1246)*, pp. 129–33, have accepted the letter as genuine; but Vann's analysis is meticulous and her arguments against authenticity are convincing. See also Grant, *Blanche of Castile*, pp. 165–6.

36. 'Carissimæ sorori suæ B. illustri Trecensi Palatinæ', in *Recueil des Historiens des Gaules et de la France*, vol. 19, edited by Michel-Jean-Joseph Brial, new edition edited by Léopold Delisle (Paris: Victor Palmé, 1880), pp. 255–6; Vann, ' "Our father has won a great victory" ', p. 87.

37. Jackson, *The Seventh Crusade*, pp. 92–3; Laura Julinda Whatley, 'Romance, Crusade, and the Orient in King Henry III of England's Royal Chambers', *Viator* 44.3 (2013): pp. 175–98, at p. 178.

38. Lloyd, *English Society and the Crusade*, p. 260; Matthew Paris, *Chronica Majora*, vol. 4, p. 25.

39. Setton, *The Papacy and the Levant*, vol. 1, p. 209.

40. Van Houts, *Memory and Gender in Medieval*, pp. 12–13, 38–9, 141; for a list of twenty-five European women who composed in Latin between the twelfth and the mid-sixteenth century see David N. Bell, *What Nuns Read: Books & Libraries in Medieval English Nunneries* (Kalamazoo: Cistercian Publications, 1995), p. 67; and of course there were more who composed in the vernacular.

41. Ewan Short, 'The Socioemotional Labour Performed by Women in the Medieval Byzantine *oikos* (1000–1118)', *Gendered Voices* 4 (2019): pp. 19–22, at p. 21.

42. *The Alexiad of Anna Comnena*, pp. 308–10, 317–18, 349, 416, 422–3 (Book 10 chapters 5, 8, Book 11 chapter 6, Book 13 chapters 8, 10: quotations at pp. 308, 309, 318, 349, 422); Bennett, 'Virile Latins, Effeminate Greeks and Strong Women', pp. 17–18.

43. The translation of verse XVII of Gormonda's 'Greu m'es a durar' is taken from Linda Paterson's online edition, part of her project 'Troubadours, Trouvères and the Crusades', under 'Troubadour Texts', www.rialto.unina.it/Gorm/177.1%28Paterson%29.htm, accessed 26 October 2020; see also Katharina Städtler, 'The Sirventes by Gormonda de Monpeslier', in *The Voice of the Trobairitz: Perspectives on the Women Troubadours*, edited by William D. Paden (Philadelphia, PA: University of Philadelphia Press, 1989), pp. 129–55.

44. Gaposchkin, 'Kingship and Crusade in the First Four Moralized Bibles', pp. 79, 95–108; Maier, 'The *bible moralisée* and the Crusades'. For a description of the *Bible moralisée* produced for Margaret of Provence,

see the British Library's description of Harley MS 1526: www.bl.uk/manuscripts/FullDisplay.aspx?ref=Harley_MS_1526.

45. Hamilton, 'Eleanor of Castile and the Crusading Movement', at p. 101; Gee, *Women, Art and Patronage*, p. 9.

46. Folda, *Crusader Art*, p. 151; Derbes and Sandona, 'Amazons and Crusaders', pp. 214–15.

47. Folda, *Crusader Art*, pp. 124–5, 127.

48. See the essays in June Hall McCash, *The Cultural Patronage of Medieval Women* (Athens, GA: University of Georgia Press, 1996). For an overview of medieval women's ownership of books see Susan Groag Bell, 'Medieval Women Book Owners: Arbiters of Lay Piety and Ambassadors of Culture' in *Women and Power in the Middle Ages*, edited by Mary Erler and Maryanne Kowaleski (Athens, GA: University of Georgia Press, 1988), pp. 149–87.

49. Folda, *Crusader Art*, pp. 32–6; Jaroslav Folda, 'Melisende of Jerusalem: Queen and Patron of Art and Architecture in the Crusader Kingdom', in *Reassessing the Roles of Women as 'Makers' of Medieval Art and Architecture*, edited by Therese Martin (Leiden: Brill, 2012), pp. 429–77, at 449–58; British Library description of Egerton MS 1139, online at: www.bl.uk/manuscripts/FullDisplay.aspx?ref=Egerton_MS_1139.

50. Folda, *Crusader Art*, pp. 32–6; Folda, 'Melisende of Jerusalem', pp. 449–58.

51. Christine Havice, 'The Marginal Miniatures in the Hamilton Psalter (Kupferstichkabinett 78.A.9.)', *Jahrbuch Der Berliner Museen* 26 (1984): pp. 79–142, at pp. 79–80.

52. Cathleen A. Fleck, 'The Luxury Riccardiana Psalter in the Thirteenth Century: A Nun's Prayerbook?' *Viator* 46.1 (2015): pp. 135–60, quotation at p. 152; Fleck, 'The Crusader Loss of Jerusalem'.

53. Bell, *What Nuns Read*, pp. 113–14, 160, 170, 171, 174, 182, 209, 212, 223, 233, 235, 238, 242; David Knowles and R. Neville Hadcock, *Medieval Religious Houses, England and Wales*, 2nd ed. (Harlow: Longman, 1971), p. 202.

54. Bell, *What Nuns Read*, pp. 124, 231; Louis Karl, 'Vie de sainte Elisabeth de Hongrie par Nicolas Bozon', *Zeitschrift für romanische Philologie* 34 (1910): pp. 295–314, at pp. 312, 314, lines 317–28, 400–6; *The Life and Afterlife of St. Elizabeth of Hungary*, p. 204; S. Arthur Strong, *A Catalogue of Letters and Other Historical Documents Exhibited in the Library at Welbeck* (London: John Murray, 1903), p. 5.

55. Bell, *What Nuns Read*, pp. 41–5, 75–8.

56. Whatley, 'Romance, Crusade, and the Orient', pp. 177–80, 185–6, quotation at p. 180 note 27; Bjørn Bandlien, 'A Manuscript of the Old French

William of Tyre (Pal. Lat. 1963) in Norway', *Studi mediolatini e volgari* 62 (2016): pp. 21–80, at p. 45; Agnes Sandys, 'The Financial and Administrative Importance of the London Temple in the Thirteenth Century', in *Essays in Medieval History presented to Thomas Frederick Tout*, edited by A. G. Little and F. M. Powicke (Manchester: Manchester University Press, 1925; repr. Freeport, NY: Books for Libraries, 1967), pp. 147–62. For a recent assessment of Henry III's crusade plans and Henry's attempts to implement them see David Carpenter, *Henry III: The Rise to Power and Personal Rule, 1207–1258* (New Haven, CT: Yale University Press, 2020), pp. 512–67.

57. Bandlien, 'A Manuscript of the Old French William of Tyre'.

58. Tyerman, *England and the Crusades*, p. 261; *Testamenta Vetusta*, vol. 1, p. 148; *A Collection of all the Wills, now known to be extant, of the Kings and Queens of England, Princes and Princesses of Wales, and every branch of the Blood Royal, from the reign of William the Conqueror to that of Henry the Seventh* [ed. J. Nichols] (London: J. Nichols, 1780), p. 181.

59. Tyerman, *England and the Crusades*, p. 303.

60. Rita Lejeune and Jacques Stiennon, *The Legend of Roland in the Middle Ages*, trans. Christine Trollope, 2 vols (New York: Phaidon, 1971), vol. 1, pp. 112–15; Rita Lejeune, 'Rôle littéraire de la famille d'Aliénor d'Aquitaine', *Cahiers de Civilisation médiévale* 1.3 (1958): pp. 319–37: at pp. 328–9.

61. Evergates, *Marie of France*, pp. 34–5; *Les Romans de Chrétien de Troyes édités d'après la copie de Guiot (Bibl. nat. fr. 794) III: Le Chevalier de la Charrette*, edited by Mario Roques, Classiques Français du Moyen Âge 86 (Paris: Honoré Champion, 1975), lines 1–29, 5769–5770, pp. vii–ix, 1–2, 176; Chrestien de Troyes, *Yvain, Le Chevalier au Lion*, edited by Wendelin Foerster, Intro and notes T. B. W. Reid (Manchester: Manchester University Press, repr. 1984), lines 595–596, pp. ix–xi, 17; *Les Romans de Chrétien de Troyes édités d'après la copie de Guiot (Bibl. nat. fr. 794) II: Cligés*, edited by Alexandre Micha, Classiques Français du Moyen Âge 84 (Paris: Honoré Champion, 1982).

62. Marie de France, 'Le Fresne', in *Lais*, edited by A. Ewert (Oxford: Basil Blackwell, 1978), pp. 35–48, at line 125; Hans Eberhard Mayer, 'Henry II of England and the Holy Land', *The English Historical Review* 97/385 (1982): pp. 721–39, at pp. 722–4; for Henry's donations to the Templars and Order of St Lazarus see Helen Nicholson, *Templars, Hospitallers and Teutonic Knights: Images of the Military Orders, 1128–1291* (Leicester: Leicester University Press, 1993), pp. 16–17.

63. On this topic generally see Harwood, *Medieval Women and War*.

64. Kevin James Lewis, 'Countess Hodierna of Tripoli: From Crusader Politician to "Princesse Lointaine"', *Assuming Gender* 3.1 (2013): pp. 1–26.

65. Helen J. Nicholson, '"La roine preude femme et bonne dame": Queen Sybil of Jerusalem (1186–1190) in History and Legend, 1186–1300', *The Haskins Society Journal* 15 (2004): pp. 110–24.

66. Discussed in Helen J. Nicholson, 'Remembering the Crusaders in Cyprus: the Lusignans, the Hospitallers and the 1191 Conquest of Cyprus in Jean d'Arras's *Mélusine*', in *Literature of the Crusades*, edited by Simon Thomas Parsons and Linda M. Paterson (Cambridge: D. S. Brewer, 2018), pp. 158–72.

67. *Saladin. Suite et fin du deuxième Cycle de Croisade*, edited by Larry S. Crist, Textes littéraires français 185 (Geneva: Droz, 1972), pp. 94–7, 108–9, 148–56. For a comprehensive study of these legends see Margaret Jubb, *The Legend of Saladin in Western Literature and Historiography* (Lewiston: Edwin Mellen, 2000).

SUMMING UP

1. Geldsetzer, *Frauen auf Kreuzzügen*, pp. 177–9.

2. Geldsetzer, *Frauen auf Kreuzzügen*, pp. 24–5, 202–3.

3. Housley, *The Later Crusades*, p. 92.

4. Joan Ferrante, 'Public Postures and Private Maneuvers: Roles Medieval Women Play', in *Women and Power in the Middle Ages*, edited by Mary Erler and Maryanne Kowaleski (Athens, GA: University of Georgia Press, 1988), pp. 213–29, at p. 227.

5. Guard, *Chivalry, Kingship and Crusade*, p. 139.

Bibliography

PRIMARY SOURCES

Abū Shāma. 'Le Livre des deux jardins'. In *Recueil des Historiens des Croisades, Historiens Orientaux*, edited by l'Académie des Inscriptions, Belles-Lettres, vol. 4 (Paris: Imprimerie nationale, 1898).

Agnes of Harcourt, *The Writings of Agnes of Harcourt*, edited by Sean L. Field (Notre Dame, IN: University of Notre Dame Press, 2003).

Die Akten des Kanonisationsprozesses Dorotheas von Montau von 1394 bis 1521, edited by Richard Stachnik with Anneliese Triller and Hans Westpfahl. Forschungen und Quellen Zur Kirchen- und Kulturgeschichte Ostdeutschlands 15 (Cologne: Böhlau, 1978).

Albert of Aachen, *Historia Ierosolimitana: History of the Journey to Jerusalem*, edited and translated by Susan B. Edgington (Oxford: Oxford University Press, 2007).

[Ambroise] *L'Estoire de la Guerre Sainte*, edited by Catherine Croizy-Naquet. Classiques français du Moyen Âge 174 (Paris: Honoré Champion, 2014).

[Ambroise] *The History of the Holy War: Ambroise's Estoire de la Guerre Sainte*, edited by Marianne Ailes and Malcolm Barber, 2 vols (Woodbridge: Boydell, 2003).

[Anna Komnene] *The Alexiad of Anna Comnena*, translated by E. R. A. Sewter (Harmondsworth: Penguin, 1969).

'Annales Admuntenses: continuatio Admuntensis', edited by D. Wilhelm Wattenbach. In *Monumenta Germaniae Historica Scriptores in Folio*, vol. 9, edited by George Heinrich Pertz (Hanover: Aulic Hahn, 1851), pp. 579–93.

'Annales Colonienses maximi: recensio secunda et tertia', edited by Karl Pertz. In *Monumenta Germaniae Historica Scriptores in Folio*, vol. 17, edited by George Heinrich Pertz (Hanover: Aulic Hahn, 1861), pp. 729–847.

'Annales Herbipolenses'. In *Monumenta Germaniae Historica Scriptores in Folio*, vol. 16, edited by George Heinrich Pertz (Hanover: Aulic Hahn, 1859), pp. 1–12.

'Annales Marbacenses', edited by R. Wilmans. In *Monumenta Germaniae Historica Scriptores in Folio*, vol. 17, edited by George Heinrich Pertz (Hanover: Aulic Hahn, 1861), pp. 142–80.

'Annales Placentini Guelfi'. In *Monumenta Germaniae Historica Scriptores in Folio*, vol. 18, edited by George Heinrich Pertz (Hanover: Aulic Hahn, 1863), pp. 411–57.

'Annales de Terre Sancte', edited by Reinhold Röhricht and Gaston Raynaud. *Archives de l'Orient Latin* 2 (1884): Documents, pp. 427–61.

'Annales de Waverleia'. In *Annales Monastici*, vol. 2, edited by Henry Richards Luard. Rolls Series 36 (London: Longman, 1865), pp. 129–411.

'Anonymous of Mainz'. In *The First Crusade: The Chronicle of Fulcher of Chartres and Other Source Materials*, edited by Edward Peters, 2nd ed. (Philadelphia, PA: University of Pennsylvania Press, 1998), pp. 115–25.

Antoine de la Sale, *Jehan de Saintré*, edited by Jean Misrahi and Charles A. Knudson. Textes Littéraires Français 117 (Geneva: Droz, 1978).

[Baha' al-Dīn Ibn Shaddād] *The Rare and Excellent History of Saladin or al-Nawādir al-Sulṭāniyya wa'l-Maḥāsin al-Yusufiyya by Bahā' al-Dīn Ibn Shaddād*, translated by D. S. Richards. Crusade Texts in Translation 7 (Aldershot: Ashgate, 2002).

[Bernal Díaz del Castillo] *The True History of the Conquest of New Spain by Bernal Díaz del Castillo, one of its conquerors, from the only exact copy made of the Original Manuscript*, edited by Genaro García, translated with introduction and notes by Alfred Percival Maudslay. Hakluyt Society second series 23 (London: Hakluyt Society, 1908).

Bernard of Clairvaux, *In Praise of the New Knighthood: A Treatise on the Knights Templar and the Holy Places of Jerusalem*, translated by M. Conrad Greenia, Cistercian Fathers Series 19B (Kalamazoo, MI: Cistercian Publications, 2000).

Bird, Jessalynn, Edward Peters, and James M. Powell, editors and translators. *Crusade and Christendom: Annotated Documents in Translation from Innocent III to the Fall of Acre, 1187–1291* (Philadelphia, PA: University of Pennsylvania Press, 2013).

[Boniface VIII] *Les Registres de Boniface VIII*, edited by Georges Digard, Maurice Faucon, Antoine Thomas, and Robert Fawtier (Paris: Ernest Thorin and E. de Boccard, 1884–1935).

Boucicaut, see *Le Livre des Fais*.

[Birgitta of Sweden] *The Revelations of St. Birgitta of Sweden*, translated by Denis Searby, introduction and notes by Bridget Morris, 4 volumes (Oxford: Oxford University Press, 2006–2015).

[Caesarius of Heisterbach] *Die Fragmente der Libri VIII Miraculorum des Caesarius von Heisterbach*, edited by Aloys Meister (Rome: Herder'schen Verlagshandlung zu Freiburg im Breisgau and Buchhandlung Spithöver, 1901).

Calendar of the Close Rolls Preserved in the Public Record Office, Edward III, vol. VIII: *A.D. 1346–1349* (London: HMSO, 1905).

Calendar of the Close Rolls Preserved in the Public Record Office, Richard II, vol. V: *A.D. 1392–1396* (London: HMSO, 1925).

Calendar of Inquisitions Post Mortem and other Analogous Documents Preserved in the Public Record Office, vol. 14: Edward III (London: HMSO, 1952).

Calendar of the Patent Rolls preserved in the Public Record Office, Edward II, A.D. 1307–1313 (London: HMSO, 1894).

'Carissimæ sorori suæ B. illustri Trecensi Palatinæ'. In *Recueil des Historiens des Gaules et de la France*, vol. 19, edited by Michel-Jean-Joseph Brial, new edition edited by Léopold Delisle (Paris: Victor Palmé, 1880), pp. 255–6.

Cartulaire général de l'ordre des Hospitaliers de S. Jean de Jérusalem (1100–1310), edited by Joseph Delaville le Roulx, 4 vols (Paris: Ernest Leroux, 1894–1905).

Cartulaire général de l'ordre du Temple 1119?–1150, edited by the Marquis d'Albon (Paris: Librairie Ancienne, Honoré Champion, 1913).

Cartulaires du Chapitre de l'église métropolitaine Sainte-Marie d'Auch, vol. 1: *Cartulaire noir*, edited by C. Lacave La Plagne Barris, Société historique de Gascogne (Paris: Honoré Champion, 1988).

The Cartulary of the Knights of St. John of Jerusalem in England. Secunda Camera, Essex, edited by Michael Gervers (Oxford: Oxford University Press, 1982).

[Catherine of Siena] *Saint Catherine of Siena as seen in her Letters*, translated by Vida D. Scudder (London: Dent, 1911).

Celestine III, Pope, 'Epistolae et Privilegia'. In *Patrologia Latina*, edited by Jacques-Paul Migne (Paris: Migne, 1844–1864), vol. 202, cols 867–1248.

Cerasoli, F., editor. 'Gregorio XI e Giovanna I di Napoli. Documenti inediti dell'Archivio segreto Vaticano. Continuazione e fine'. *Archivio Storico per le Province Napoletane* 25.1 (1900): pp. 3–26.

Chrestien de Troyes, *Yvain, Le Chevalier au Lion*, edited by Wendelin Foerster. Introduction and notes by T. B. W. Reid (Manchester: Manchester University Press, repr. 1984).

Chrétien de Troyes. *Les Romans de Chrétien de Troyes édités d'après la copie de Guiot (Bibl. nat. fr. 794) II: Cligés*, edited by Alexandre Micha. Classiques français du Moyen Âge 84 (Paris: Honoré Champion, 1982).

Chrétien de Troyes. *Les Romans de Chrétien de Troyes édités d'après la copie de Guiot (Bibl. nat. fr. 794) III: Le Chevalier de la Charrette*, edited by Mario Roques. Classiques français du Moyen Âge 86 (Paris: Honoré Champion, 1975).

Chrétien de Troyes. *Les Romans de Chrétien de Troyes édités d'après la copie de Guiot (Bibl. nat. fr. 794) V: Le Conte du Graal (Perceval)*, edited by Félix Lecoy. 2 vols. Classiques français du Moyen Âge 100, 103 (Paris: Honoré Champion, 1981).

Christine de Pisan. *The Treasure of the City of Ladies, or the Book of the Three Virtues*, translated by Sarah Lawson (Harmondsworth: Penguin, 1985).

Christine de Pizan, 'The Tale of Joan of Arc'. In *The Selected Writings of Christine de Pizan*, translated by Renate Blumenfeld-Kosinski and Kevin Brownlee (New York: W. W. Norton, 1997).

Chronica Adefonsi Imperatoris, translated as *The Chronicle of Alfonso the Emperor* by Glenn Edward Lipskey (PhD thesis, Northwestern University, 1972), online at https://libro.uca.edu/lipskey/chronicle.htm.

'Chronica Sigeberti auctarium Mortui Maris', edited by D. L. C. Bethman. In *Monumenta Germaniae Historica Scriptores in Folio*, vol. 6, edited by George Heinrich Pertz (Hanover: Aulic Hahn, 1844), pp. 463–9.

The Chronicle of Novgorod 1016–1471, translated by Robert Michell and Nevill Forbes. *Camden Third Series* 25 (1914).

'Chronicon Ebersheimense', edited by K. Weidland. In *Monumenta Germaniae Historica Scriptores in Folio*, vol. 23, edited by George Heinrich Pertz (Hanover: Aulic Hahn, 1874), pp. 429–53.

Chronique d'Ernoul et de Bernard le trésorier, ed. L. de Mas Latrie (Paris: Jules Renouard, 1871).

Close Rolls of the Reign of Henry III Preserved in the Public Record Office, A.D. 1268–1272 (London: HMSO, 1938).

'Codicillus Henrici comitis Ruthensis'. In *Veterum scriptorum et monumentorum historicorum, dogmaticorum, moralium, amplissima collectio*, edited by Edmond Martène and Ursin Durand, vol. 1 (Paris: Montalant, 1724), cols 1168–1172.

A Collection of all the Wills, now known to be extant, of the Kings and Queens of England, Princes and Princesses of Wales, and every branch of the Blood Royal, from the reign of William the Conqueror to that of Henry the Seventh [ed. J. Nichols] (London: J. Nichols, 1780).

The Conquest of Lisbon: De expugnatione Lyxbonense, translated by Charles Wendell David, foreword and bibliography by Jonathan Phillips (New York: Columbia University Press, 2001).

La Continuation de Guillaume de Tyr (1184–1197), edited by Margaret Ruth Morgan. Documents relatifs à l'histoire des Croisades 14 (Paris: Paul Geuthner, 1982).

Curia Regis Rolls of the Reign of Henry III preserved in the Public Record Office, vol. 10, *5–6 Henry III (1221–1222)* (London: HMSO, 1949).

Curia Regis Rolls of the reign of Henry III preserved in the Public Record Office, vol. 12, *9–10 Henry III (1225–1226)* (London: HMSO, 1957).

Curia Regis Rolls of the Reign of Henry III preserved in the Public Record Office, vol. 13, *11–14 Henry III (1227–1230)* (London: HMSO, 1959).

Curia Regis Rolls of the Reign of Henry III preserved in the Public Record Office, vol. 16, *21 to 26 Henry III (1237–1242)*, edited by L. C. Hector (London: HMSO, 1979).

L'Estoire de Eracles Empereur et la Conqueste de la Terre d'Outremer. In *Recueil des historiens des Croisades, Historiens Occidentaux*, edited by l'Académie des Inscriptions et Belles-Lettres, vol. 2 (Paris: Imprimerie Impériale, 1859).

Felix Fabri (circa 1480–1383 A.D.), vol. 1 (part 1), translated by Aubrey Stewart (London: Palestine Pilgrims' Text Society, 1896).

Fernando del Pulgar, *Crónica de los reyes católicos*, vol. 2, *Guerra de Granada*, edited by Juan de Mata Carriazo (Madrid: Espasa-Calpe, 1943).

Foedera, conventiones, literæ, et cujuscunque generis acta publica, inter reges Angliæ et alios quosvis imperatores..., edited by Thomas Rymer and Robert Sanderson, 3rd ed. revised by George Holmes (London: John Neaulme, 1745).

'Fragmentum de captione Damiatæ', edited by Paul Meyer. In *Quinti Belli Sacri Scriptores Minores*, edited by Reinhold Röhricht. Publications de la Société de l'Orient Latin, Série historique 2 (Geneva: J.-G. Fick, 1879), pp. 166–202.

Francesco Balbi di Correggio, *The Siege of Malta 1565*, translated by Henry Alexander Balbi (Copenhagen: Dr. h. c. Ole Rostock, 1961).

Fudge, Thomas A., editor and translator. *The Crusade against Heretics in Bohemia, 1418–1437*. Crusade Texts in Translation 9 (Aldershot:Ashgate,2002).

[Fulcher of Chartres] *Fulcheri Carnotensis Historia Hierosolymitana (1095–1127). Mit Erläuterungen und einem Anhange*, edited by Heinrich Hagenmeyer (Heidelberg: Carl Winters, 1913).

[Geoffrey de Charny] *The Book of Chivalry of Geoffroi de Charny: Text, Context, and Translation*, edited and translated by Richard W. Kaeuper and Elspeth Kennedy (Philadelphia, PA: University of Pennsylvania Press, 1996).

Geoffrey de Villehardouin, 'The Conquest of Constantinople'. In Joinville and Villehardouin, *Chronicles of the Crusades*, translated by M. R. B. Shaw (Harmondsworth: Penguin, 1963), pp. 29–160.

[Gerald of Wales] *The Autobiography of Gerald of Wales*, edited and translated by H. E. Butler, new ed. (Woodbridge: Boydell, 2005).

Gerald of Wales. *The Journey through Wales and The Description of Wales*, translated by Lewis Thorpe (Harmondsworth: Penguin, 1978).

Gesta Francorum et Aliorum Hierosolimitanorum: The Deeds of the Franks and the other Pilgrims to Jerusalem, edited and translated by Rosalind Hill (Edinburgh: Thomas Nelson, 1962).

'Gesta Obsidionis Damiate'. In *Quinti Belli Sacri Scriptores Minores,* edited by Reinhold Röhricht. Publications de la Société de l'Orient Latin, Série historique 2 (Geneva: J.-G. Fick, 1879), pp. 71–115.

[Gislebert de Mons] *La Chronique de Gislebert de Mons,* edited by Léon Vanderkindere (Brussels: Kiessling, 1904); translated as Gilbert of Mons, *Chronicle of Hainaut,* translated by Laura Napran (Woodbridge: Boydell, 2005).

Gomes Eannes de Zurara, *Crónica da Tomada de Ceuta,* edited by Francisco Maria Esteves Pereira (Lisbon: Academia das Sciências de Lisboa, 1915).

[Guibert of Nogent] *The Deeds of God through the Franks: a translation of Guibert de Nogent's* Gesta Dei per Francos, translated by Robert Levine (Woodbridge: Boydell, 1997).

Guillaume Caoursin, '*Descriptio obsidionis Rhodiae*'. In Theresa M. Vann and Donald J. Kagay, *Hospitaller Piety and Crusader Propaganda: Guillaume Caoursin's Description of the Ottoman Siege of Rhodes, 1480* (Farnham: Ashgate, 2015), pp. 86–147.

[Henry Knighton] *Chronicon Henrici Knighton vel Cnitthon Monarchi Leycestrensis,* edited by Joseph Rawson Lumby, vol. 2 (1337–1395) (London: HMSO, 1893).

[Honoré Bonet] *The Tree of Battles of Honoré Bonet: An English Version,* translated by G. W. Coopland (Liverpool: Liverpool University Press, 1949).

Housley, Norman, editor and translator. *Documents on the Later Crusades, 1274–1580* (Basingstoke: Macmillan, 1996).

[Ibn al-Athīr] *The Chronicle of Ibn al-Athīr for the Crusading Period from* al-Kamil fi'l-Ta'rikh, part 2: *The Years 541–589/1146–1193: The Age of Nur al-Din and Saladin,* translated by D. S. Richards. Crusade Texts in Translation 15 (Farnham: Ashgate, 2007).

'Imād al-Dīn al-Iṣfahānī, *Conquête de la Syrie et de la Palestine par Saladin (al-Fatḥ al-qussî fî l-fatḥ al-qudsî),* translated by Henri Massé, Documents relatifs à l'histoire des Croisades 10 (Paris: Paul Geuthner, 1972).

Imber, Colin, editor and translator. *The Crusade of Varna, 1443–45.* Crusade Texts in Translation 14 (Aldershot: Ashgate, 2006).

Das Itinerarium peregrinorum: eine zeitgenössische englische Chronik zum dritten Kreuzzug in ursprünglicher Gestalt, edited by Hans Eberhard Mayer, Schriften der Monumenta Germaniae historica (Deutsches Institut für Erforschung des Mittelalters) 18 (Stuttgart: Anton Hiersemann, 1962).

Itinerarium peregrinorum et gesta regis Ricardi, see Richard de Templo.

Jackson, Peter, editor and translator. *The Seventh Crusade, 1244–1254: Sources and Documents.* Crusade Texts in Translation 16 (Farnham: Ashgate, 2009).

James of Vitry, 'The Life of Mary of Oignies', translated by Margot H. King. In *Mary of Oignies, Mother of Salvation,* edited by Anneke B. Mulder-Bakker (Turnhout: Brepols, 2006), pp. 33–127.

Jean Sire de Joinville, *Histoire de Saint Louis, Credo et Lettre à Louis X,* edited by Natalis de Wailly (Paris: Firmin Didot, 1874); translated as 'The Life of Saint Louis', in Joinville and Villehardouin, *Chronicles of the Crusades,* translated by M. R. B. Shaw (Harmondsworth: Penguin, 1963), pp. 161–353.

Johannes de Fordun, 'Gesta Annalia'. In *Johannis de Fordun, Chronica Gentis Scotorum,* edited by William F. Skene (Edinburgh: Edmonston and Douglas, 1871).

Johannes von Marienwerder, *The Life of Dorothea von Montau, a fourteenth-century Recluse,* translated by Ute Stargardt (Lewiston: Edwin Mellen, 1997).

Johannes de Tulbia, 'De Domino Iohanne, rege Ierusalem'. In *Quinti Belli Sacri Scriptores Minores,* edited by Reinhold Röhricht. Publications de la Société de l'Orient Latin, Série historique 2 (Geneva: J.-G. Fick, 1879), pp. 119–40.

John Stillingflete, 'Liber Johannis Stillingflete de nominibus fundatorum Hosp. S. Johannis Jerusalem in Anglia'. In *Monasticon anglicanum: A History of the abbies and other monasteries, hospitals, frieries, and cathedral and collegiate churches, with their dependencies, in England and Wales ...,* edited by William Dugdale; revised by John Caley, Henry Ellis, and Bulkeley Bandinel, 6 vols in 8 (London: Harding, Harding and Lepard, 1830), vol. 6.2, pp. 831–9.

Kohler, Charles, editor. 'Lettres pontificales concernant l'histoire de la Petite Arménie au XIVe siècle'. In *Florilegium ou, Recueil de Travaux d'Érudition dédiés à Monsieur le Marquis Melchior de Vogüé à l'Occasion du quatre-vingtième Anniversaire de sa Naissance, 18 Octobre 1909* (Paris: Imprimerie nationale, 1909), pp. 303–27.

[Lambert of Ardres] *Lamberti Ardensis Historia Comitum Ghisnensium,* edited by I. Heller. In *Monumenta Germaniae Historica Scriptores in Folio,* vol. 24, edited by Societas Aperiendis Fontibus rerum Germanicarum Medii Aevi (Hanover: Hahn, 1879), pp. 550–642, translated as: Lambert of Ardres, *The History of the Counts of Guines and Lords of Ardres,* translated by Leah Shopkow (Philadelphia, PA: University of Pennsylvania Press, 2001).

Lambert de Waterlos, 'Annales Cameracenses'. In *Monumenta Germaniae Historica Scriptores in Folio,* vol. 16, edited by George Heinrich Pertz (Hanover: Aulic Hahn, 1859), pp. 509–54.

Lancelot: Roman en prose du XIIIe siècle, edited by Alexandre Micha, vol. 7. Textes Littéraires Français 288 (Geneva: Droz, 1980).

Die lateinische Fortsetzung Wilhelms von Tyrus, edited by Marianne Salloch (Leipzig: H. Eichblatt, 1934).

The Latin Chronicle of the Kings of Castile, translated by Joseph F. O'Callaghan (Tempe, AZ: Arizona Center for Medieval and Renaissance Studies, 2002).

Livländische Reimchronik, ed. Franz Pfeiffer, Bibliothek des literarischen Vereins in Stuttgart 7 (Stuttgart: Literarischen Vereins, 1844).

Le Livre des Fais du bon Messire Jehan le Maingre, dit Bouciquaut, Mareschal de France et Gouverneur de Jennes, edited by Denis Lalande. Textes Littéraires Français 331 (Geneva: Droz, 1985).

Ludolphus de Sudheim, 'De Itinere Terre Sancte', edited by G. A. Neumann. In *Archives de l'Orient Latin* 2 (1884), Documents: III Voyages, pp. 305–77.

[Margery Kempe] *The Book of Margery Kempe*, translated by Anthony Bale (Oxford: Oxford University Press, 2015).

Marie de France, 'Le Fresne'. In *Lais*, edited by A. Ewert (Oxford: Basil Blackwell, 1978), pp. 35–48.

Marino Sanudo Torsello, *The Book of the Secrets of the Faithful of the Cross: Liber Secretorum Fidelium Crucis*, translated by Peter Lock. Crusade Texts in Translation 21 (Farnham: Ashgate, 2011).

Martène Edmond, and Ursini Durand, editors. *Thesaurus Novus Anecdotorum*, vol. 1 (Paris: Florentinus Delaulne et al., 1717).

Matthew Paris, *Chronica Majora*, edited by Henry Richards Luard. Rolls Series 57 (London: Longman, 1872–1883).

Matthew Paris, *Historia Anglorum sive, ut vulgo dicitur, Historia Minor, item, ejusdem Abbreviatio Chronicorum Angliæ*, edited by Frederic Madden. Rolls Series 44 (London: Longman, 1866–1869).

[Miguel de Castanhoso] *The Portuguese expedition to Abyssinia in 1541–1543, as narrated by Castanhoso*, translated by R. S. Whiteway. Hakluyt Society second series vol. 10 (London: Hakluyt Society, 1902).

[Minstrel of Reims] *Récits d'un ménestrel de Reims au treizième siècle*, edited by Natalis de Wailly (Paris: Renouard, 1876).

Monasticon anglicanum: A History of the abbies and other monasteries, hospitals, frieries, and cathedral and collegiate churches, with their dependencies, in England and Wales..., edited by William Dugdale; revised by John Caley, Henry Ellis, and Bulkeley Bandinel, 6 vols in 8 (London: Harding, Harding and Lepard, 1830).

'Narratio de Itinere Navali Peregrinorum Hierosolymam Tendentium et Silviam Capientium, A. D. 1189', edited by Charles Wendell David. *Proceedings of the American Philosophical Society* 81.5 (1939): pp. 591–676.

[Nicolaus von Jeroschin] *The Chronicle of Prussia by Nicolaus von Jeroschin: A History of the Teutonic Knights in Prussia, 1190–1331*, translated by Mary Fischer. Crusade Texts in Translation 20 (Farnham: Ashgate, 2010).

[Niketas Choniatēs] *O City of Byzantium, Annals of Niketas Choniatēs*, translated by Harry J. Magoulias (Detroit, MI: Wayne State University, 1984).

Odo of Deuil. *De Profectione Ludovici VII in Orientem; The Journey of Louis VII to the East*, edited and translated by Virginia Gingerick Berry (New York: Columbia University Press, 1948).

'Ogerii Panis Annales'. In *Monumenta Germaniae Historica Scriptores in Folio*, edited by George Heinrich Pertz, vol. 18 (Hanover: Aulic Hahn, 1863), pp. 115–42.

Papsturkunden in Portugal, edited by Carl Erdmann, Abhandlungen der Gesellschaft der Wissenschaften zu Göttingen, Philologisch-Historische Klasse Neue Folge 20 (Berlin: Weidmannsche Buchhandlung, 1927).

Peter von Dusburg, *Chronicon Terre Prussie*, edited by Max Toeppen. In *Scriptores rerum Prussicarum*, vol. 1 (Leipzig: S. Hirzel, 1861).

Peter of les Vaux-de-Cernay, *The History of the Albigensian Crusade*, translated by W. A. Sibly and M. D. Sibly (Woodbridge: Boydell, 1998).

Peters, Edward, editor and translator. *The First Crusade: The Chronicle of Fulcher of Chartres and Other Source Materials*, 2nd ed. (Philadelphia, PA: University of Pennsylvania Press, 1998).

Philippe de Mézières, Chancellor of Cyprus. *Le Songe du vieil pelerin*, edited by G. W. Coopland, 2 vols (Cambridge: Cambridge University Press, 1969).

Philippe Mousket, *Chronique rimée*, edited by F. de Reiffenberg, 2 vols (Brussels: 1836–1838).

Pierre Dubois, *The Recovery of the Holy Land*, translated by Walther I. Brandt (New York: Columbia University Press, 1956).

Pringle, Denys, editor and translator. *Pilgrimage to Jerusalem and the Holy Land, 1187–1291*. Crusade Texts in Translation 23 (Farnham: Ashgate, 2012).

The Proceedings Against the Templars in the British Isles, edited and translated by Helen J. Nicholson, 2 vols (Farnham: Ashgate, 2011).

Procès de Condamnation de Jeanne d'Arc, edited by Pierre Champion, vol. 1 (Paris: Champion, 1920).

Ptolemy of Lucca, *Historia Ecclesiastica*. In *Rerum Italicarum Scriptores*, edited by Ludovico Antonio Muratori, 25 vols (Milan: Stamperia della Società Palatina, 1723–1751), vol. 11 (1727), cols 742–1242.

Radulphi de Coggeshall Chronicon Anglicanum, edited by Joseph Stevenson. Rolls Series 66 (London: Longman, 1875).

[Ramon Muntaner] *The Chronicle of Muntaner*, translated by Lady Goodenough. Hakluyt Society 2nd series 47, 50 (London: Hakluyt Society, 1920, 1921); new online edition: Ramon Muntaner, *Chronicle*, translated by Lady Goodenough (Cambridge Ontario: Parentheses, 2000), at: http://www.yorku.ca/inpar/muntaner_goodenough.pdf.

Records of the Templars in England in the Twelfth Century: The Inquest of 1185 with Illustrative Charters and Documents, edited by Beatrice A. Lees (London: Oxford University Press, 1935).

[Richard de Templo] *Itinerarium peregrinorum et gesta regis Ricardi; auctore, ut videtur, Ricardo, canonico Sanctæ Trinitatis Londoniensis*, edited by William Stubbs, vol. 1 of *Chronicles and Memorials of the Reign of Richard I*. Rolls Series 38 (London: Longman, 1864), pp. 1–450. Translated as: 'Itinerary of Richard I and others to the Holy Land', in *Chronicles of the Crusades* (London: George Bell and Sons, 1882), pp. 65–339; and as *Chronicle of the Third Crusade: A Translation of the* Itinerarium Peregrinorum et Gesta Regis Ricardi, translated by Helen J. Nicholson. Crusade Texts in Translation 3 (Aldershot: Ashgate, 1997).

Robert, canon of Saint-Marien of Auxerre, *Chronicon*, edited by O. Holder-Egger. In *Monumenta Germaniae Historica Scriptores in Folio*, vol. 26, edited by Societas Aperiendis Fontibus rerum Germanicarum Medii Aevi (Hanover: Hahn, 1882), pp. 219–76.

Robert of Clari. *The Conquest of Constantinople*, translated by Edgar Holmes McNeal (New York: Columbia University Press, 1936, reprinted Toronto: University of Toronto Press, 1996).

Roger of Howden, *Chronica*, edited by William Stubbs. Rolls Series 51, 4 vols (London: Longman, 1868–1871).

[Roger of Howden] *Gesta regis Henrici secundi: The Chronicle of the Reigns of Henry II and Richard I, A.D. 1169–1192*, edited by William Stubbs. Rolls Series 49 (London: Longman, 1867).

Roger of Wendover, *The Flowers of History*, edited by Henry G. Hewlett. Rolls Series 84 (London: Longman, 1886–1889).

Rolls of the Justices in Eyre for Gloucestershire, Warwickshire, and Shropshire, 1221, 1222, edited by Doris M. Stenton. Selden Society 59 (1940).

Rolls of the Justices in Eyre for Lincolnshire (1218–1219) and Worcestershire (1221), edited Doris Mary Stenton, Selden Society 53 (1934).

Rolls of the Justices in Eyre, Being the Rolls of Pleas and Assizes for Yorkshire in 3 Henry III (1218–1219), edited by Doris Mary Stenton. Selden Society 56 (1937).

Saladin. Suite et fin du deuxième Cycle de Croisade, edited by Larry S. Crist. Textes Littéraires Français 185 (Geneva: Droz, 1972).

'Solomon ben Simson'. In *The First Crusade: The Chronicle of Fulcher of Chartres and Other Source Materials*, edited by Edward Peters, 2nd ed. (Philadelphia, PA: University of Pennsylvania Press, 1998), pp. 127–37.

Songs of the Women Trouvères, edited, translated, and introduced by Eglal Doss-Quinby, Joan Tasker Grimbert, Wendy Pfeffer and Elizabeth Aubrey (New Haven, CT: Yale University Press, 2001).

La Suite du Roman de Merlin, edited by Gilles Roussineau. Textes Littéraires Français 472 (Geneva: Droz, 1996).

The 'Templar of Tyre', Part III of the 'Deeds of the Cypriots', translated by Paul Crawford. Crusade Texts in Translation 6 (Aldershot: Ashgate, 2003).

Testamenta Vetusta, being Illustrations from Wills, of Manners, Customs, &c., as well as of the Descents and Possessions of many distinguished Families, from the reign of Henry the Second to the accession of Queen Elizabeth, edited by Nicholas Harris Nicolas (London: Nichols and Son, 1826).

Usama ibn Munqid. *The Book of Contemplation: Islam and the Crusades*, translated by Paul M. Cobb (London: Penguin, 2008).

[Usāmah ibn-Munqidh] *An Arab-Syrian Gentleman and Warrior in the Period of the Crusades: Memoirs of Usāmah ibn-Munqidh*, translated by Philip K. Hitti (repr. Princeton, NJ: Princeton University Press, 1987).

'Via ad Terram Sanctam (1289–1293)'. In *Projets de Croisade (v. 1290–v. 1330)*, edited by Jacques Paviot, Documents relatifs à l'histoire des croisades 20 (Paris: L'Académie des Inscriptions et Belles-Lettres, 2008), pp. 171–81.

[Walter of Guisborough] *Chronicon domini Walteri de Hemingburgh, vulgo Hemingford nuncupati, ordinia sancti Augustini canonici regularis, in coenobio beate Mariæ de Gisburn, de gestis regum Angliæ*, edited by Hans Claude Hamilton, vol. 1 (London: English Historical Society, 1848).

William of Tudela and Anonymous Successor, *The Song of the Cathar Wars: A History of the Albigensian Crusade*, translated by Janet Shirley. Crusade Texts in Translation 2 (Aldershot: Ashgate, 1996).

Willelmi Tyrensis Archiepiscopi Chronicon/Guillaume de Tyr, *Chronique*, edited by R. B. C. Huygens, 2 vols, Corpus Christianorum Continuatio Mediaeualis 63, 63A (Turnhout: Brepols, 1986).

Wolf, Kenneth Baxter, editor and translator. *The Life and Afterlife of St. Elizabeth of Hungary: Testimony from her Canonization Hearing* (Oxford: Oxford University Press, 2011).

SECONDARY WORKS

Abulafia, Anna Sapir. 'Invectives against Christianity in the Hebrew Chronicles of the First Crusade'. In *Crusade and Settlement: Papers read at the First Conference of the Society for the Study of the Crusades and the Latin East and presented to R. C. Smail*, edited by Peter W. Edbury (Cardiff: University College Cardiff Press, 1985), pp. 66–72.

Abulafia, Anna Sapir. *Christian-Jewish Relations 1000–1300: Jews in the Service of Medieval Christendom* (Harlow: Longman, 2011).

Angold, Michael. *The Fourth Crusade: Event and Context* (Harlow: Pearson Longman, 2003).

Appleby, John T. *England without Richard, 1189–1199* (London: G. Bell, 1965).

Arnold, Udo. 'Die Frau im Deutschen Orden'. In *Stationen Einer Hochschullaufbahn: Festschrift für Annette Kuhn zum 65. Geburtstag*, edited by Udo Arnold, Peter Meyers, and Uta C. Schmidt (Dortmund: Ebersbach 1999), pp. 261–76.

Asbridge, Thomas. 'Alice of Antioch: A Case Study of Female Power in the Twelfth Century'. In *The Experience of Crusading, volume two: Defining the Crusader Kingdom*, edited by Peter Edbury and Jonathan Phillips (Cambridge: Cambridge University Press, 2003), pp. 29–47.

Aurell, Martin. 'Les femmes guerrières (XIe et XIIe siècles)'. In *Famille, violence et christianisation au Moyen Âge: mélanges offerts à Michel Rouche*, edited by Martin Aurell and Thomas Deswarte (Paris: Presses universitaires de Paris-Sorbonne, 2005), pp. 319–30.

Bailey, Angela E. 'Women Pilgrims and their Travelling Companions in twelfth-century England'. *Viator* 46.1 (2015): pp. 115–34.

Bandlien, Bjørn. 'A Manuscript of the Old French William of Tyre (Pal. Lat. 1963) in Norway'. *Studi mediolatini e volgari* 62 (2016): pp. 21–80.

Barber, Malcolm. 'The Pastoureaux of 1320'. *Journal of Ecclesiastical History* 32 (1981): pp. 143–66.

Barber, Malcolm. 'The Albigensian Crusades: Wars Like any Other?' In *Dei Gesta per Francos: Études sur les croisades dédiées à Jean Richard; Crusade Studies in Honour of Jean Richard*, edited by Michel Balard, Benjamin Z. Kedar, and Jonathan Riley-Smith (Aldershot: Ashgate, 2001), pp. 45–55.

Barber, Malcolm. *The Crusader States* (New Haven, CT: Yale University Press, 2012).

Barbieri, Luca. 'Crusade Songs and the Old French Literary Canon'. In *Literature of the Crusades*, edited by Simon Thomas Parsons and Linda M. Paterson (Cambridge: D. S. Brewer, 2018), pp. 75–95.

Bartlett, Robert. *The Making of Europe. Conquest, Colonization and Cultural Change, 950–1350* (Harmondsworth: Penguin, 1993).

Bartlett, Robert. 'Pretenders and Returners: Dynastic Imposters in the Middle Ages'. In *Blood Royal: Dynastic Politics in Medieval Europe*, edited by Robert Bartlett (Cambridge: Cambridge University Press, 2020), pp. 360–78.

Bass, Ian. ' "Articuli Inquisicionis de crucesignatis": Late Thirteenth-Century Inquiry into English Crusaders'. *Crusades* 17 (2018): pp. 171–94.

Bass, I. L. 'The Crozier and the Cross: Crusading and the English Episcopate, *c*. 1170–1313' (PhD thesis, Manchester Metropolitan University, 2019).

Bell, David N. *What Nuns Read: Books & Libraries in Medieval English Nunneries* (Kalamazoo, MI: Cistercian Publications, 1995).

Bell, Susan Groag. 'Medieval Women Book Owners: Arbiters of Lay Piety and Ambassadors of Culture'. In *Women and Power in the Middle Ages*, edited by Mary Erler and Maryanne Kowaleski (Athens, GA: University of Georgia Press, 1988), pp. 149–87.

Bennett, Matthew. 'Virile Latins, Effeminate Greeks and Strong Women: Gender Definitions on Crusade?' In *Gendering the Crusades*, edited by Susan B. Edgington and Sarah Lambert (Cardiff: University of Wales Press, 2001), pp. 16–30.

Bennett, Stephen. *Elite Participation in the Third Crusade* (Woodbridge: Boydell, 2021).

Berend, Nora, 'Hungary, "The Gate of Christendom" '. In *Medieval Frontiers: Concepts and Practices*, edited by David Abulafia and Nora Berend (Aldershot: Ashgate, 2002), pp. 195–215.

Bird, Jessalynn. 'Indulgences and Penance'. In *The Crusades: An Encyclopedia*, ed. Alan V. Murray, 4 vols (Santa Barbara, CA: ABC Clio, 2006), vol. 2, pp. 633–7.

Bird, Jessalynn. 'Preaching and Crusading Memory'. In *Remembering the Crusades and Crusading*, edited by Megan Cassidy-Welch (London: Routledge, 2017), pp. 13–33.

Blakely, Ruth M. *The Brus Family in England and Scotland 1100–1295* (Woodbridge: Boydell, 2005).

Blumenfeld-Kosinski, Renate. 'Roles for Women in Colonial Fantasies of Fourteenth-Century France: Pierre Dubois and Philippe de Mézières'. In *The French of Outremer: Communities and Communications in the Crusading Mediterranean*, edited by Laura K. Morreale and Nicholas L. Paul (New York: Fordham University Press, 2018), pp. 247–81.

Bom, Myra Miranda. *Women in the Military Orders of the Crusades* (New York: Palgrave Macmillan, 2012).

Borchardt, Karl. 'Late Medieval Indulgences for the Hospitallers and the Teutonic Order'. In *Ablasskampagnen des Spätmittelalters: Luthers Thesen von 1517 im Kontext*, edited by Andreas Rehberg. Bibliothek des Deutschen Historischen Instituts in Rom 132 (Berlin: De Gruyter, 2017), pp. 195–218.

Bower, Canon, 'On a Brass found in Arthuret Church'. *Transactions of the Cumberland and Westmorland Antiquarian and Archaeological Society* new series 1 (1901): pp. 114–15.

Brodman, James William. *Ransoming Captives in Crusader Spain: The Order of Merced on the Christian-Islamic Frontier* (Philadelphia, PA: University of Pennsylvania Press, 1986).

Brown, Elizabeth A. R. 'The Oxford Collection of the Drawings of Roger de Gaignières and the Royal Tombs of Saint-Denis'. *Transactions of the American Philosophical Society* 78.5 (1988): pp. i–viii+1–74.

Brundage, James A. 'The Crusader's Wife: A Canonistic Quandary'. *Studia Gratiana* 12 (1967): pp. 425–41.

Brundage, James A. 'The Crusader's Wife Revisited'. *Studia Gratiana* 14 (1967): pp. 243–51.

Brundage, James A. 'The Votive Obligations of Crusaders: The Development of a Canonistic Doctrine'. *Traditio* 24 (1968): pp. 77–118.

Brundage, James, A. *Medieval Canon Law and the Crusader* (Madison, WI: University of Wisconsin Press, 1969).

Brundage, James A. 'Prostitution, Miscegenation and Sexual Purity in the First Crusade'. In *Crusade and Settlement: Papers read at the First Conference of the Society for the Study of the Crusades and the Latin East and presented to R. C. Smail*, edited by Peter W. Edbury (Cardiff: University College Cardiff Press, 1985), pp. 57–65.

Buck, Andrew D. 'Settlement, Identity, and Memory in the Latin East: An Examination of the Term "Crusader States"'. *English Historical Review* 135/573 (2020): pp. 271–302.

Buck, Andrew D. 'Women in the Principality of Antioch: Power, Status and Social Agency'. *Haskins Society Journal* 31 (2019): 95–132.

Bull, Marcus. *Knightly Piety and the Lay Response to the First Crusade: The Limousin and Gascony c. 970–c. 1130* (Oxford: Oxford University Press, 1993).

Butkens, Christophre. *Trophées tant sacrés que prophanes du Duché de Brabant*, 4 vols (The Hague: Chrétien van Lom, 1724).

Cadden, Joan. *Meanings of Sex Difference in the Middle Ages: Medicine, Science, and Culture* (Cambridge: Cambridge University Press, 1993).

Caille, Jacqueline. 'Les Seigneurs de Narbonne dans le conflit Toulouse-Barcelone au XIIe siècle'. *Annales du Midi: revue archéologique, historique et philologique de la France méridionale* 97/171 (1985): pp. 227–44.

Callahan, Leslie Abend. 'The Widow's Tears: the Pedagogy of Grief in Medieval France and the Image of the Grieving Widow'. In *Constructions of Widowhood and Virginity in the Middle Ages*, edited by Cindy L. Carlson and Angela Jane Weisl (Basingstoke: Macmillan, 1999), pp. 245–263.

Camden, William. *Remaines of a Greater Worke Concerning Britain* (London: Simon Waterson, 1605).

Carpenter, David. *Henry III: The Rise to Power and Personal Rule, 1207–1258* (New Haven, CT: Yale University Press, 2020).

Cassidy-Welch, Megan, and Anne E. Lester, 'Memory and Interpretation: New Approaches to the Study of the Crusades'. In *Crusades and Memory: Journal of Medieval History* 40.3 (2014): pp. 225–36, republished in *Crusades and Memory: Rethinking Past and Present*, edited by Megan Cassidy-Welch and Anne E. Lester (London: Routledge, 2015), pp. 1–12.

Cassidy-Welch, Megan, editor. *Remembering the Crusades and Crusading* (London: Routledge, 2017).

Cassotti, Marsilio. *D. Teresa A Primeira Rainha de Portugal*, translated by Ana Isabel Ruiz Barata (Lisbon: A Esfera dos Livros, 2008).

Casteen, Elizabeth. 'Sex and Politics in Naples: The Regnant Queenship of Johanna I'. *Journal of the Historical Society* 11.2 (2011): pp. 183–210.

Casteen, Elizabeth. *From She-Wolf to Martyr: The Reign and Disputed Reputation of Johanna I of Naples* (Ithaca, NY: Cornell University Press, 2016).

Chazan, Robert. *European Jewry and the First Crusade* (Berkeley, CA: University of California Press, 1987).

Chevedden, Paul E. 'The Islamic View and the Christian View of the Crusades: A New Synthesis'. *History* 93/310 (2008): pp. 181–200.

Cheyette, Frederic L. *Ermengard of Narbonne and the World of the Troubadours* (Ithaca, NY: Cornell University Press, 2001).

Christiansen, Eric. *The Northern Crusades*, 2nd edn (London: Penguin, 1997).

Christie, Niall. "Alī ibn Tāhir al-Sulamī'. In *Christian Muslim Relations: A Bibliographical History, volume 3 (1050–1200)*, edited by David Thomas and Alex Mallet, with Juan Pedro Monferrer Sala, Johannes Pahlitzsh, Mark Swanson, Herman Teule, and John Tolan. History of Christian-Muslim Relations 15 (Leiden: Brill, 2011), pp. 307–11.

Christie, Niall. 'Fighting Women in the Crusading Period through Muslim Eyes: Transgressing Expectations and Facing Realities?' In *Crusading and Masculinities*, edited by Natasha R. Hodgson, Katherine J. Lewis and Matthew M. Mesley, Crusades Subsidia 13 (London: Routledge, 2019), pp. 183–95.

Cohn, Norman. *The Pursuit of the Millennium: Revolutionary Millenarians and Mystical Anarchists of the Middle Ages*, revised ed. (London: Pimlico, 1993).

Cole, Penny J. '"O God, the Heathen have Come into Your Inheritance" (Ps. 78.1): The Theme of Religious Pollution in Crusade Documents, 1095–1188'. In *Crusaders and Muslims in Twelfth-Century Syria*, edited by Maya Shatzmiller (Leiden: Brill, 1993), pp. 84–111.

Constable, Giles. 'The Historiography of the Crusades'. In *The Crusades from the Perspective of Byzantium and the Muslim World*, edited by Angeliki E. Laiou and Roy Parviz Mottahedeh (Dumbarton Oaks: Dumbarton Oaks Research Library, 2001), pp. 1–22.

Corbet, Patrick. 'Entre Aliénor d'Aquitaine et Blanche de Castille. Les princesses au pouvoir dans la France de l'Est'. In *Mächtige Frauen? Königinnen und Fürstinnen im europäischen Mittelalter (11.–14. Jahrhundert)*, edited by Claudia Zey with Sophie Caflisch and Philippe Goridis. Vorträge und Forschungen 81 (Ostfildern: Jan Thorbecke, 2015), pp. 225–47.

Coss, Peter. *The Foundations of Gentry Life: The Multons of Frampton and their World, 1270–1370* (Oxford: Oxford University Press, 2010).

Cowan, Ian B. and David E. Easson, *Medieval Religious Houses: Scotland*, 2nd ed. (London: Longman, 1976).

Cowdrey, H. E. J. 'The Mahdia Campaign of 1087'. *The English Historical Review* 92/362 (1977): pp. 1–29.

Craig, Leigh Ann. ' "Stronger than Men and Braver than Knights": Women and the Pilgrimages to Jerusalem and Rome in the Later Middle Ages'. *Journal of Medieval History* 29.3 (2003): pp. 153–75.

Davis-Secord, Sarah C. *Where Three Worlds Met: Sicily in the early medieval Mediterranean* (Ithaca, NY: Cornell University Press, 2017).

Derbes, Anne and Mark Sandona. 'Amazons and Crusaders: The *Histoire Universelle* in Flanders and the Holy Land'. In *France and the Holy Land: Frankish Culture at the End of the Crusades*, edited by Daniel H. Weiss and Lisa Mahoney (Baltimore, MD: Johns Hopkins University Press, 2004), pp. 187–229.

DeVries, Kelly. *Joan of Arc: A Military Leader* (Stroud: History Press, new edition 2011).

Dickson, Gary. *The Children's Crusade: Medieval History, Modern Mythistory* (Basingstoke: Palgrave Macmillan, 2008).

Dillard, Heath. *Daughters of the Reconquest: Women in Castilian Town Society, 1100–1300* (Cambridge: Cambridge University Press, 1984).

Duff, E. Gordon. *Fifteenth century English books: a bibliography of books and documents printed in England and of books for the English market printed abroad* (Oxford: Bibliographical Society, 1917).

Dunbabin, Jean. *Charles I of Anjou: Power, Kingship and State-Making in Thirteenth-Century Europe* (London: Longman, 1998).

Dunphy, Graeme. 'Women chroniclers and chronicles for women'. In *The Encyclopedia of the Medieval Chronicle*, edited by Graeme Dunphy, 2 vols (Leiden: Brill, 2010), vol. 2, pp. 1521–4.

Eastmond, Antony. *Tamta's World: The Life and Encounters of a Medieval Noblewoman from the Middle East to Mongolia* (Cambridge: Cambridge University Press, 2017).

Edbury, Peter W., and John Gordon Rowe, *William of Tyre: Historian of the Latin East* (Cambridge: Cambridge University Press, 1988).

Edbury, Peter W. *The Kingdom of Cyprus and the Crusades, 1191–1374* (Cambridge: Cambridge University Press, 1991).

Edbury, Peter W. 'Women and the Customs of the High Court of Jerusalem according to John of Ibelin'. In *Chemins d'outre mer. Études d'histoire sur la Méditerranée médiévale offertes à Michel Balard*, edited by Damien Coulon, Catherine Otten-Froux, Paul Pagès, and Dominque Valérian (Paris: Publications de la Sorbonne, 2004), pp. 285–92.

Edbury, Peter W., 'Ernoul, *Eracles*, and the Collapse of the Kingdom of Jerusalem'. In *The French of Outremer: Communities and Communications in the Crusading Mediterranean*, edited by Laura K. Morreale and Nicholas L. Paul (New York: Fordham University Press, 2018), pp. 44–67.

Edgington, Susan B. and Sarah Lambert, editors. *Gendering the Crusades* (Cardiff: University of Wales Press, 2001).

Edgington, Susan B. 'A female physician on the Fourth Crusade?: Laurette de Saint-Valéry'. In *Knighthoods of Christ: Essays on the History of the Crusades and the Knights Templar Presented to Malcolm Barber*, edited by Norman Housley (Aldershot: Ashgate, 2007), pp. 77–85.

Edgington, Susan B. 'Crusading Chronicles'. In *Encyclopedia of the Medieval Chronicle*, edited by Graeme Dunphy, 2 vols (Leiden: Brill, 2010), vol. 1, pp. 499–500.

Edwards, David N. *The Nubian Past: An Archaeology of the Sudan* (London: Routledge, 2004).

Ehlers, Axel. *Die Ablasspraxis des Deutschen Ordens im Mittelalter*. Quellen und Studien zur Geschichte des Deutschen Ordens 64 (Marburg: N. G. Elwert, 2007).

Ellenblum, Ronnie. *The Collapse of the Eastern Mediterranean: Climate Change and the Decline of the East, 950–1072* (Cambridge: Cambridge University Press, 2012).

Evans, Michael R. '"Unfit to Bear Arms": The Gendering of Arms and Armour in Accounts of Women on Crusade'. In *Gendering the Crusades*, edited by Susan B. Edgington and Sarah Lambert (Cardiff: University of Wales Press, 2001), pp. 45–58.

Evergates, Theodore. 'Aristocratic Women in the County of Champagne'. In *Aristocratic Women in Medieval France*, edited by Theodore Evergates (Philadelphia, PA: University of Pennsylvania Press, 1999), pp. 74–110.

Evergates, Theodore. *Henry the Liberal: Count of Champagne, 1127–1181* (Philadelphia, PA: University of Pennsylvania Press, 2016).

Evergates, Theodore. *Marie of France: Countess of Champagne, 1145–1198* (Philadelphia, PA: University of Pennsylvania Press, 2019).

Fernández-Armesto, Felipe. *Before Columbus: Exploration and Colonisation from the Mediterranean to the Atlantic, 1229–1492* (Basingstoke: Macmillan, 1987).

Ferrante, Joan. 'Public Postures and Private Maneuvers: Roles Medieval Women Play'. In *Women and Power in the Middle Ages*, edited by Mary Erler and Maryanne Kowaleski (Athens GA: University of Georgia Press, 1988), pp. 213–29.

Field, Sean L. *Courting Sanctity: Holy Women and the Capetians* (Ithaca, NY: Cornell University Press, 2019).

Field, Sean L. 'Agnes of Harcourt as Intellectual: New Evidence for the Composition and Circulation of the *Vie d'Isabelle de France*'. In *Women Intellectuals and Leaders in the Middle Ages*, edited by Kathryn Kerby-Fulton, Katie Ann-Marie Bugyis, and John van Engen (Cambridge: D. S. Brewer, 2020), pp. 79–95.

Firnhaber-Baker, Justine. 'The Social Constituency of the Jacquerie Revolt of 1358'. *Speculum* 95.3 (2020): pp. 689–715.

Fleck, Cathleen A. 'The Luxury Riccardiana Psalter in the Thirteenth Century: A Nun's Prayerbook?' *Viator* 46.1 (2015): pp. 135–60.

Fleck, Cathleen A. 'The Crusader Loss of Jerusalem in the Eyes of a Thirteenth-Century Virtual Pilgrim'. In *The Crusades and Visual Culture*, edited by Elizabeth Lapina, April Jehan Morris, Susanna A. Throop, and Laura J. Whatley (Farnham: Ashgate, 2015), pp. 131–55.

Folda, Jaroslav. *Crusader Art: The Art of the Crusaders in the Holy Land, 1099–1291* (Aldershot: Lund Humphries, 2008).

Folda, Jaroslav. 'Melisende of Jerusalem: Queen and Patron of Art and Architecture in the Crusader Kingdom'. In *Reassessing the Roles of Women as 'Makers' of Medieval Art and Architecture*, edited by Therese Martin (Leiden: Brill, 2012), pp. 429–77.

Forey, Alan. 'The Military Orders and the Ransoming of Captives from Islam (Twelfth to Early Fourteenth Centuries)'. *Studia Monastica* 33 (1991): pp. 259–79.

Fort, Gavin. '"Make a Pilgrimage for Me": The Role of Place in Late Medieval Proxy Pilgrimage'. In *Travel, Time and Space in the Middle Ages and Early Modern Time: Explorations of World Perceptions and Processes of Identity Formation*, edited by Albrecht Classen (Berlin: De Gruyter, 2018), pp. 424–45.

Frankopan, Peter. *The First Crusade: The Call from the East* (London: Bodley Head, 2012).

Friedman, Yvonne. 'Captivity and Ransom: the Experience of Women'. In *Gendering the Crusades*, edited by Susan B. Edgington and Sarah Lambert (Cardiff: University of Wales Press, 2001), pp. 121–39.

Friedman, Yvonne. *Encounter between Enemies: Captivity and Ransom in the Latin Kingdom of Jerusalem* (Leiden: Brill, 2002).

Friedman, Yvonne. 'Gestures of Conciliation: Peacemaking Endeavors in the Latin East'. In *In Laudem Hierosolymitani: Studies in Crusades and Medieval Culture in Honour of Benjamin Z. Kedar*, edited by Iris Shagrir, Ronnie Ellenblum and Jonathan Riley-Smith. Crusades Subsidia 1 (Aldershot: Ashgate, 2007), pp. 31–48.

Fuller, Thomas. *The Historie of the Holy Warre*, 3rd ed. (Cambridge: John Williams, 1640).

Gaposchkin, M. Cecilia. 'The Liturgical Memory of July 15, 1099: Between History, Memory, and Eschatology'. In *Remembering the Crusades and Crusading*, edited by Megan Cassidy-Welch (London: Routledge, 2017), pp. 34–48.

Gaposchkin, M. Cecilia. *Invisible Weapons: Liturgy and the Making of Crusade Ideology* (Ithaca, NY: Cornell University Press, 2017).

Gaposchkin, M. C. 'Kingship and Crusade in the First Four Moralized Bibles'. In *The Capetian Century, 1214–1314*, edited by William Chester Jordan and Jenna Rebecca Phillips (Turnhout: Brepols, 2017), pp. 71–112.

García-Guijarro Ramos, Luis. 'The Aragonese Hospitaller Monastery of Sigena: its Early Stages, 1188–c. 1210'. In *Hospitaller Women in the Middle Ages*, edited by Anthony Luttrell and Helen J. Nicholson (Aldershot: Ashgate, 2006), pp. 113–51.

García-Guijarro Ramos, Luis. '*Reconquista* and Crusade in the Central Middle Ages. A Conceptual and Historiographical Survey'. In *Crusading on the Edge: Ideas and Practice of Crusading in Iberia and the Baltic Region, 1100–1500*, edited by Torben Kjersgaard Nielsen and Iben Fonnesberg-Schmidt. Outremer: Studies in the Crusades and the Latin East 4 (Turnhout: Brepols, 2016), pp. 55–88.

Geary, Patrick J. *Living with the Dead in the Middle Ages* (Ithaca, NY: Cornell University Press, 1994).

Gee, Loveday Lewes. *Women, Art and Patronage from Henry III to Edward III, 1216–1377* (Woodbridge: Boydell, 2002).

Geldsetzer, Sabine. *Frauen auf Kreuzzügen, 1096–1291* (Darmstadt: Wissenschaftliche Buchgesellschaft, 2003).

Gilbert, James E. 'A Medieval "Rosie the Riveter"? Women in France and Southern England during the Hundred Years War'. In *The Hundred Years*

War: A Wider Focus, edited by L. J. Andrew Villalon and Donald J. Kagay. History of Warfare 25 (Leiden, 2005), pp. 333–63.

Gillingham, John. *Richard I* (New Haven, CT: Yale University Press, 1999).

Goitein, S. D. 'Geniza Sources for the Crusader Period: A Survey'. In *Outremer: Studies in the history of the Crusading Kingdom of Jerusalem presented to Joshua Prawer*, edited by B. Z. Kedar, H. E. Mayer, and R. C. Smail (Jerusalem: Yad Izhak Ben-Zvi Institute, 1982), pp. 306–22.

Goldstone, Nancy. *The Lady Queen: The Notorious Reign of Joanna I, Queen of Naples, Jerusalem, and Sicily* (New York: Walker, 2009).

Goodman, Anthony. *John of Gaunt: The Exercise of Princely Power in Fourteenth-Century Europe* (Harlow: Longman, 1992).

Goodman, Anthony. *Margery Kempe and her World* (Harlow: Longman, 2002).

Goodman, Jennifer R. 'The Lady with the Sword: Philippa of Lancaster and the Chivalry of the Infante Dom Henrique (Prince Henry the Navigator)'. In *Queens, Regents and Potentates*, edited by Theresa M. Vann (Dallas, TX: Academia Press, 1993), pp. 149–65.

Gordo Molina, Angel G. 'Urraca I de León y Teresa de Portugal. Las Relaciones de Fronteras y el Ejercicio de la Potestad Femenina en la Primera Mitad del Siglo XII. Jurisdicción, *Imperium* y Linaje'. *Intus-Legere Historia* 2.1 (2008): pp. 9–23.

Grant, Alexander. 'The St Bees Lord and Lady, and their Lineage'. In *North-West England from the Romans to the Tudors: essays in memory of John Macnair Todd*, edited by Keith J. Stringer. *Cumberland and Westmorland Antiquarian and Archaeological Society Extra series* 41 (2014): pp. 171–200.

Grant, Lindy. 'Récit d'un ménestrel de Reims'. In *Encyclopedia of the Medieval Chronicle*, edited by Graeme Dunphy, 2 vols (Leiden: Brill, 2010), vol. 2, p. 1265.

Grant, Lindy. *Blanche of Castile, Queen of France* (New Haven, CT: Yale University Press, 2016).

Guard, Timothy. *Chivalry, Kingship and Crusade: The English Experience in the Fourteenth Century* (Woodbridge: Boydell, 2013).

Guirondet, M. 'Les Croisiés de Saint-Antonin'. *Bulletin Archéologique et Historique publié sous la direction de la Société Archéologique de Tarn-et-Garonne* 5 (1877): pp. 113–24.

Hallam, Elizabeth M., and Judith Everard. *Capetian France 987–1328*, 2nd ed. (Harlow: Longman, 2001).

Hallam, Elizabeth. 'Berengaria [Berengaria of Navarre] (c. 1165–1230)'. In *Oxford Dictionary of National Biography*, edited by H. C. G. Matthew and Brian Harrison (Oxford: Oxford University Press, 2004). https://doi-org. abc.cardiff.ac.uk/10.1093/ref:odnb/2192.

Hamilton, Bernard. 'Women in the Crusader States: the Queens of Jerusalem, 1100–1190'. In *Medieval Women*, edited by Derek Baker. Studies in Church History Subsidia 1 (Oxford: Basil Blackwell, 1978), pp. 143–74.

Hamilton, Bernard. 'Eleanor of Castile and the Crusading Movement'. *Mediterranean Historical Review* 10 (1995): pp. 92–103.

Bernard Hamilton and Andrew Jotischky, *Latin and Greek Monasticism in the Crusader States* (Cambridge: Cambridge University Press, 2020).

Hamilton, Sarah. 'The Virgin Mary in Cathar Thought'. *The Journal of Ecclesiastical History* 56.1 (2005): pp. 24–49.

Hansbery, Joseph E. 'The Children's Crusade'. *Catholic Historical Review* 24.1 (1938): pp. 30–8.

Harris, Jonathan. *Byzantium and the Crusades*, 2nd ed. (London: Bloomsbury, 2014).

Harwood, Sophie. *Medieval Women and War: Female Roles in the Old French Tradition* (London: Bloomsbury Academic, 2020).

Havice, Christine. 'The Marginal Miniatures in the Hamilton Psalter (Kupferstichkabinett 78.A.9.)'. *Jahrbuch Der Berliner Museen* 26 (1984): pp. 79–142.

Hay, David J. '"Collateral Damage?" Civilian Casualties in the Early Ideologies of Chivalry and Crusade'. In *Noble Ideals and Bloody Realities, Warfare in the Middle Ages*, edited by Niall Christie and Maya Yazigi (Leiden: Brill, 2006), pp. 3–25.

Hay, David J. *The Military Leadership of Matilda of Canossa, 1046–1115* (Manchester: Manchester University Press, 2008).

Heller, Sarah-Grace. 'Surprisingly historical women in the Old French Crusade Cycle'. In *Women and Medieval Epic: Gender, Genre, and the Limits of Epic Masculinity*, edited by Sara S. Poor and Jana K. Schulman (New York: Palgrave Macmillan, 2007), pp. 41–66.

Hemptinne, Thérèse de. 'Les épouses des croisés et pèlerins flamandes aux XIᵉ et XIIᵉ siècles: L'exemple des comtesses de Flandre Clémence et Sybille'. In *Autour de la première Croisade. Actes du colloque de la Society for the Study of the Crusades and the Latin East, Clermont-Ferrand, 22–25 juin 1995*, edited by Michel Balard (Paris: Publications de la Sorbonne, 1996), pp. 83–95.

Hendrickx, Benjamin. 'The Visit of Marie de Brienne to Cyprus in the Context of her Quest for Assistance to the Latin Empire of Constantinople'. In *Cyprus and the Crusades*, edited by Nicholas Coureas and Jonathan Riley-Smith (Nicosia: Society for the Study of the Crusades and the Latin East and the Cyprus Research Centre, 1995), pp. 59–67.

Herman, Margaux. 'Towards a History of Women in Medieval Ethiopia'. In *A Companion to Medieval Ethiopia and Eritrea*, edited by Samantha Kelly (Leiden: Brill, 2020), pp. 365–94.

Heymann, Frederick G. *John Žižka and the Hussite Revolution* (Princeton, NJ: Princeton University Press, 1955).

Hill, George. *A History of Cyprus, volume 3: The Frankish Period, 1432–1571* (Cambridge: Cambridge University Press, 1948).

Hillenbrand, Carole. *The Crusades: Islamic Perspectives* (Edinburgh: Edinburgh University Press, 1999).

Hodgson, Natasha. 'The Role of Kerbogha's Mother in the *Gesta Francorum* and Selected Chronicles of the First Crusade'. In *Gendering the Crusades*, edited by Susan B. Edgington and Sarah Lambert (Cardiff: University of Wales Press, 2001), pp. 163–76.

Hodgson, Natasha. 'Nobility, Women and Historical Narratives of the Crusades and the Latin East'. *Al-Masāq: Islam and the Medieval Mediterranean* 17.1 (2005): pp. 61–85.

Hodgson, Natasha R. *Women, Crusading and the Holy Land in Historical Narrative* (Woodbridge: Boydell, 2007).

Hodgson, Natasha R., Katherine J. Lewis, and Matthew M. Mesley, editors. *Crusading and Masculinities.* Crusades Subsidia 13 (London: Routledge, 2019).

Holloway, Julia Bolton. 'Margaret of Jerusalem/Beverley and Thomas of Beverley/Froidmont, her brother, her biographer', at http://www.umilta.net/jerusalem.html.

Holt, Andrew. 'Feminine Sexuality and the Crusades: Clerical Opposition to Women as a Strategy for Crusading Success'. In *Sexuality in the Middle Ages and Early Modern Times: New Approaches to a Fundamental Cultural-Historical and Literary-Anthropological theme*, edited by Albrecht Classen (Berlin: Walter de Gruyter, 2008), pp. 449–69.

Hotchkiss, Valerie R. *Clothes make the Man: Female Cross Dressing in Medieval Europe*, new ed. (New York: Routledge, 2012).

Housley, Norman. *The Italian Crusades: The Papal-Angevin Alliance and the Crusades against Christian Lay Powers, 1254–1343* (Oxford: Oxford University Press, 1982).

Housley, Norman. *The Avignon Papacy and the Crusades, 1305–1378* (Oxford: Oxford University Press, 1986).

Housley, Norman. *The Later Crusades: From Lyons to Alcazar, 1274–1580* (Oxford: Oxford University Press, 1992).

Hrbek, Ivan. 'Egypt, Nubia and the Eastern Deserts'. In *The Cambridge History of Africa, volume 3: from c. 1050 to c. 1600*, edited by Roland Oliver (Cambridge: Cambridge University Press, 1977), pp. 10–97.

Hurlock, Kathryn. *Wales and the Crusades, c. 1095–1291* (Cardiff: University of Wales Press, 2011).

Hurlock, Kathryn. *Britain, Ireland & the Crusades, c. 1000–1300* (Basingstoke: Palgrave Macmillan, 2013).

Husain, Adnan A., and Margaret Aziza Pappano. 'The One Kingdom Solution?: Diplomacy, Marriage, and Sovereignty in the Third Crusade'. In *Cosmopolitanism and the Middle Ages*, edited by John M. Ganim and Shayne Aaron Legassie (New York: Palgrave Macmillan, 2013), pp 121–40.

Irwin, Robert. 'The Mamlūk Conquest of the County of Tripoli'. In *Crusade and Settlement: Papers read at the First Conference of the Society for the Study of the Crusades and the Latin East and presented to R. C. Smail*, edited by Peter W. Edbury (Cardiff: University College of Cardiff Press, 1985), pp. 246–50.

Jacoby, David. 'The Latin Empire of Constantinople and the Frankish States in Greece'. In *The New Cambridge Medieval History, volume 5: c.1198–c.1300*, edited by David Abulafia (Cambridge: Cambridge University Press, 1999), pp. 523–42.

Jacoby, Zehava. 'The Tomb of Baldwin V, King of Jerusalem (1185–1186), and the Workshop of the Temple Area'. *Gesta* 18.2 (1979): pp. 3–14.

Johnson, Hannah. 'Massacre and Memory: Ethics and Method in Recent Scholarship on Jewish Martyrdom'. In *Christians and Jews in Angevin England: The York Massacre of 1190, Narratives and Contexts*, edited by Sarah Rees Jones and Sethina C. Watson (Woodbridge: Boydell, 2013), pp. 261–77.

Jordan, Erin L. 'Hostage, Sister, Abbess: The Life of Iveta of Jerusalem'. *Medieval Prosopography* 32 (2017): pp. 66–86.

Jordan, William Chester. *Louis IX and the Challenge of the Crusade: A Study in Rulership* (Princeton, NJ: Princeton University Press, 1979).

Jubb, Margaret. *The Legend of Saladin in Western Literature and Historiography* (Lewiston: Edwin Mellen, 2000).

Karl, Louis. 'Vie de sainte Elisabeth de Hongrie par Nicolas Bozon'. *Zeitschrift für romanische Philologie* 34 (1910): pp. 295–314.

Kedar, Benjamin Z. 'The Passenger List of a Crusader Ship, 1250: Towards the History of the Popular Element on the Seventh Crusade'. *Studi Medievali* 3rd series 13.1 (1972): pp. 267–79.

Kenaan-Kedar, Nurith, and Benjamin Z. Kedar, 'The Significance of a Twelfth-Century Sculptural Group: *Le Retour du Croisé*'. In *Dei gesta per Francos: Études sur les croisades dédiées à Jean Richard; Crusade Studies in Honour of Jean Richard*, edited by Michel Balard, Benjamin Z. Kedar, and Jonathan Riley-Smith (Aldershot: Ashgate, 2001), pp. 29–44.

Kenaan-Kedar, Nurith. 'The Enigmatic Sepulchral Monument of Berengaria (CA. 1170–1230), Queen of England (1191–1199)'. *Assahp. Section B, Studies in Art History* 12 (2007): pp. 49–61.

Kenaan-Kedar, Nurith. 'Pictorial and Sculptural Commemoration of Returning or Departing Crusaders'. In *The Crusades and Visual Culture*, edited by Elizabeth Lapina, April Jehan Morris, Susanna A. Throop, and Laura J. Whatley (Farnham: Ashgate, 2015), pp. 91–104.

Knowles, David, and R. Neville Hadcock, *Medieval Religious Houses, England and Wales*, 2nd edn (Harlow: Longman, 1971).

Knüsel, Christopher J., Catherine M. Batt, Gordon Cook, Janet Montgomery, Gundula Müldner, Alan R. Ogden, Carol Palmer, Ben Stern, John Todd, and Andrew S. Wilson, 'The Identity of the St Bees Lady, Cumbria: An Osteobiographical Approach'. *Medieval Archaeology* 54:1 (2010): pp. 271–311.

Kool, Robert. 'Finding French Deniers in the Latin Kingdom of Jerusalem. The Archaeological and Cultural Perspective'. In *Transferts culturels entre France et Orient latin (XIIe–XIIIe siècles)*, edited by Martin Aurell, Marisa Galvez, and Estelle Ingrand-Varenne (Paris: Classiques Garnier, 2021), pp. 101–28.

Kostick, Conor. *The Social Structure of the First Crusade* (Leiden: Brill, 2008).

Kostick, Conor. 'Women and the First Crusade: prostitutes or pilgrims?' In *Studies on Medieval and Early Modern Women 4: Victims or Viragos?* edited by Christine Meek and Catherine Lawless (Dublin: Four Courts Press, 2005), pp. 56–68.

Kosto, Adam J. *Hostages in the Middle Ages* (Oxford: Oxford University Press, 2012).

Krebs, Verena. *Medieval Ethiopian Kingship, Craft, and Diplomacy with Latin Europe* (Cham: Palgrave Macmillan, 2021).

Lambert, Sarah. 'Crusading or Spinning'. In *Gendering the Crusades*, edited by Susan B. Edgington and Sarah Lambert (Cardiff: University of Wales Press, 2001), pp. 1–15.

Landon, Lionel. *The Itinerary of Richard I*. Pipe Roll Society new series 13 (1935).

Lees, Beatrice A. 'The Letters of Queen Eleanor of Aquitaine to Pope Celestine III'. *English Historical Review* 21/81 (1906): pp. 78–93.

Leighton, Gregory. 'Written and Visual Expressions of Authority of Female Monastic Institutions in medieval Livonia: 13th to 15th centuries'. *Studia Slavica et Balcanica Petropolitana* 1 (2021): pp. 15–35.

Lejeune, Rita. 'Rôle littéraire de la famille d'Aliénor d'Aquitaine'. *Cahiers de Civilisation médiévale* 1.3 (1958): pp. 319–37.

Lejeune, Rita, and Jacques Stiennon, *The Legend of Roland in the Middle Ages*, translated by Christine Trollope, 2 vols (New York: Phaidon, 1971).

Leson, Richard A. 'Chivalry and Alterity: Saladin and the Remembrance of Crusade in a Walters *Histoire d'Outremer*'. *Journal of the Walters Art Museum* 68/69 (2011–2012): pp. 87–96.

Lespinasse, René de. *Hervé de Donzy, Comte de Nevers* (Nevers: P. Fay, 1868).

Lester, Anne E. 'Remembrance of Things Past: Memory and Material Objects in the time of the Crusades, 1095–1291'. In *Remembering the Crusades and Crusading*, edited by Megan Cassidy-Welch (London: Routledge, 2017), pp. 73–94.

Levin, Chaviva. 'Constructing Memories of Martyrdom: Contrasting Portrayals of Martyrdom in the Hebrew Narratives of the First and Second Crusade'. In *Remembering the Crusades: Myth, Image, and Identity*, edited by Nicholas Paul and Suzanne Yeager (Baltimore, MD: Johns Hopkins University Press, 2012), pp. 50–68.

Lewis, Kevin James. 'Countess Hodierna of Tripoli: From Crusader Politician to "Princess Lointaine"'. *Assuming Gender* 3.1 (2013): pp. 1–26.

Linder, Amnon. *Raising Arms: Liturgy in the Struggle to Liberate Jerusalem in the Late Middle Ages* (Turnhout: Brepols, 2003).

Lloyd, Simon. *English Society and the Crusade, 1216–1307* (Oxford: Oxford University Press, 1988).

Lloyd, Simon. 'William Longespée II: The Making of an English Crusading Hero'. *Nottingham Medieval Studies* 35 (1991): pp. 41–69 and 36 (1992): pp. 79–125.

Lock, Peter. *The Franks in the Aegean, 1204–1500* (Harlow: Longman, 1995).

Loomis, Laura Hibbard. 'Secular Dramatics in the Royal Palace, Paris, 1378, 1389, and Chaucer's "Tregetoures"'. *Speculum* 33.2 (1958): pp. 242–55.

Loomis, Roger Sherman. '*Richard Cœur de Lion* and the *Pas Saladin* in Medieval Art', *PMLA* 30.3 (1915): pp. 509–28.

LoPrete, Kimberly A. 'Adela of Blois: Familial Alliances and Female Lordship'. In *Aristocratic Women in Medieval France*, edited by Theodore Evergates (Philadelphia, PA: University of Pennsylvania Press, 1999), pp. 7–43.

Lower, Michael. *The Barons' Crusade: A Call to Arms and its Consequences* (Philadelphia, PA: University of Pennsylvania Press, 2005).

Lower, Michael. *The Tunis Crusade of 1270: A Mediterranean History* (Oxford: Oxford University Press, 2018).

Ljubarskij, Jakov. 'Why is the *Alexiad* a Masterpiece of Byzantine Literature?' In *Anna Komnene and her Times*, edited by Thalia Gouma-Peterson (New York: Garland, 2000), pp. 169–85.

Lunt, William E. *Financial Relations of the Papacy with England* [vol. 2]: *1327–1534* (Cambridge, MA: Medieval Academy of America, 1962).

Luongo, F. Thomas. *The Saintly Politics of Catherine of Siena* (Ithaca, NY: Cornell University Press, 2006).

Luttrell, Anthony T. 'The Hospitallers' Interventions in Cilician Armenia: 1291–1375'. In *The Cilician Kingdom of Armenia*, edited by T. S. R. Boase (Edinburgh: Scottish Academic Press, 1978), pp. 118–44.

Luttrell, Anthony. 'Englishwomen as Pilgrims to Jerusalem: Isolda Parewastell, 1365'. In *Equally in God's Image: Women in the Middle Ages*, edited by Julia Bolton Holloway, Constance S. Wright, and Joan Bechtold (New York: Peter Lang, 1990), pp 184–97.

Luttrell, Anthony. 'English Contributions to the Hospitaller Castle at Bodrum in Turkey: 1407–1437'. In *The Military Orders*, vol. 2: *Welfare and Warfare*, edited by Helen Nicholson (Aldershot: Ashgate, 1998), pp. 163–72.

Luttrell, Anthony and Helen J. Nicholson, eds. *Hospitaller Women in the Middle Ages* (Aldershot: Ashgate, 2006).

Luttrell, Anthony. 'Chaucer's English Knight and his Holy War'. In *Tribute to Alain Blondy* (Valetta: Fondation de Malte, 2017), pp. 211–25.

McCash, June Hall. *The Cultural Patronage of Medieval Women* (Athens, GA: University of Georgia Press, 1996).

MacKay, Angus. *Spain in the Middle Ages: From Frontier to Empire, 1000–1500* (Basingstoke: Macmillan, 1977).

MacLellan, Rory. 'Hospitaller Confraternity Scripts, Crusading and the English Reformation, c. 1440–1537'. *Historical Research* 92/256 (2019): pp. 445–57.

Maddicott, John. 'Grandson [Grandison], Sir Otto de (c. 1238–1328)'. In *Oxford Dictionary of National Biography*, edited by H. C. G. Matthew and Brian Harrison (Oxford: Oxford University Press, 2004). https://doi-org. abc.cardiff.ac.uk/10.1093/ref:odnb/37827.

Maier, Christoph T. *Preaching the Crusades: Mendicant Friars and the Cross in the Thirteenth Century* (Cambridge: Cambridge University Press, 1994).

Maier, Christoph T. 'The *bible moralisée* and the Crusades'. In *The Experience of Crusading, volume one: Western Approaches*, edited by Marcus Bull and Norman Housley (Cambridge: Cambridge University Press, 2003), pp. 209–22.

Maier, Christoph T. 'The Roles of Women in the Crusade Movement: A Survey'. *Journal of Medieval History* 30.1 (2004): pp. 61–82.

Marcombe, David. *Leper Knights: The Order of St Lazarus of Jerusalem in England, c. 1150–1544* (Woodbridge: Boydell, 2003).

Marcoux, Robert. 'Memory, Presence and the Medieval Tomb'. In *Revisiting the Monument: Fifty Years Since Panofsky's Tomb Sculpture*, edited by Ann Adams and Jessica Barker (London: Courtauld Institute of Art, 2016), pp. 49–67.

Martin, Therese. 'The Art of a Reigning Queen as Dynastic Propaganda in Twelfth-Century Spain'. *Speculum* 80.4 (2005): pp. 1134–71.

Martindale, Jane. 'Eleanor [Eleanor of Aquitaine], *suo jure* duchess of Aquitaine (*c.* 1122–1204)'. In *Oxford Dictionary of National Biography*, edited by H. C. G. Matthew and Brian Harrison (Oxford: Oxford University Press, 2004, online version 23 September 2004). https://doi-org.abc.cardiff.ac.uk/10.1093/ref:odnb/8618.

Marvin, Laurence W. *The Occitan War: A Military and Political History of the Albigensian Crusade, 1209–1218* (Cambridge: Cambridge University Press, 2008).

Mayer, Hans Eberhard. 'Studies in the History of Queen Melisende of Jerusalem'. *Dumbarton Oaks Papers* 26 (1972): pp. 93, 95–182.

Mayer, Hans Eberhard. 'Henry II of England and the Holy Land'. *The English Historical Review* 97/385 (1982): pp. 721–39.

Mayer, Hans Eberhard. 'The Wheel of Fortune: Seignorial Vicissitudes under Kings Fulk and Baldwin III of Jerusalem'. *Speculum* 65.4 (1990): pp. 860–77.

Mazeika, Rasa. ' "Nowhere was the Fragility of their Sex Apparent": Women Warriors in the Baltic Crusade Chronicles'. In *From Clermont to Jerusalem: The Crusades and Crusader Societies 1095–1500. Selected Proceedings of the International Medieval Congress, University of Leeds, 10–13 July 1995*, edited by Alan V. Murray. International Medieval Research 3 (Turnhout: Brepols, 1998), pp. 229–48.

Metcalfe, Alex. *Muslims and Christians in Norman Sicily: Arabic Speakers and the end of Islam* (London: Routledge, 2013).

Möhring, Hannes. 'Joseph Iscanus, Neffe Balduins von Canterbury, und eine anonyme englische Chronik des Dritten Kreuzzugs: Versuch einer Identifikation'. *Mittellateinisches Jahrbuch* 19 (1984): pp. 184–90.

Morris, Bridget. *St Birgitta of Sweden* (Woodbridge: Boydell, 1999).

Morris, David. 'The Servile Mother: Jerusalem as Woman in the Era of the Crusades'. In *Remembering the Crusades: Myth, Image, and Identity*, edited by Nicholas Paul and Suzanne Yeager (Baltimore, MD: Johns Hopkins University Press, 2012), pp. 174–94.

Muessig, Carolyn, George Ferzoco, and Beverly Mayne Kienzle, editors. *A Companion to Catherine of Siena* (Leiden: Brill, 2012).

Muldoon, James. 'Crusading and Canon Law'. In *Palgrave Advances in the Crusades*, edited by Helen J. Nicholson (Basingstoke: Palgrave Macmillan, 2005), pp. 37–57.

Munro, Dana. 'The Children's Crusade'. *American Historical Review* 19.3 (1914): pp. 516–24.

Murray, Alan V. 'Sex, Death and the Problem of Single Women in the Armies of the First Crusade'. In *Shipping, Trade and Crusade in the Medieval Mediterranean: Studies in Honour of John Pryor*, edited by Ruthy Gertwagen and Elizabeth Jeffreys (Farnham: Ashgate, 2012), pp. 255–70.

Murray, Alan V. 'Women in the Royal Succession of the Latin Kingdom of Jerusalem (1099–1291). In *Mächtige Frauen? Königinnen und Fürstinnen im europäischen Mittelalter (11.–14. Jahrhundert)*, edited by Claudia Zey with Sophei Caflisch and Philippe Goridis. Vorträge und Forschungen 81 (Ostfildern: Jan Thorbecke, 2015), pp. 131–62.

Murray, Alan V. 'Constance, Princess of Antioch (1130–1164): Ancestry, Marriages and Family'. In *Anglo-Norman Studies XXXVIII: Proceedings of the Battle Conference 2015*, edited by Elisabeth van Houts (Woodbridge: Boydell, 2016), pp. 81–95.

Murray, Alan V. 'Contrasting Masculinities in the Baltic Crusades: Teutonic Knights and Secular Crusaders at War and Peace in Late Medieval Prussia'. In *Crusading and Masculinities*, edited by Natasha R. Hodgson, Katherine J. Lewis, and Matthew M. Mesley. Crusades Subsidia 13 (London: Routledge, 2019), pp. 113–28.

Naum, Magdelana. 'Ambiguous Pots: Everyday Practice, Migration and Materiality. The Case of medieval Baltic Ware on the Island of Bornholm (Denmark)'. *Journal of Social Archaeology* 12.1 (2012): pp. 92–11.

Newman, Barbara. 'Possessed by the Spirit: Devout Women, Demoniacs, and the Apostolic Life in the Thirteenth Century'. *Speculum* 73.3 (1998): pp. 733–70.

Nicholas, Karen S. 'Countesses as Rulers in Flanders'. In *Aristocratic Women in Medieval France*, edited by Theodore Evergates (Philadelphia, PA: University of Pennsylvania Press, 1999), pp. 111–37.

Nicholson, Helen. *Templars, Hospitallers and Teutonic Knights: Images of the Military Orders, 1128–1291* (Leicester: Leicester University Press, 1993).

Nicholson, Helen. 'Women on the Third Crusade'. *Journal of Medieval History* 23.4 (1997): pp. 335–49.

Nicholson, Helen J. 'Margaret de Lacy and the Hospital of Saint John at Aconbury, Herefordshire'. *Journal of Ecclesiastical History* 50 (1999): pp. 629–51; reprinted in *Hospitaller Women in the Middle Ages*, edited by Anthony Luttrell and Helen J. Nicholson (Aldershot: Ashgate, 2006), pp. 153–177.

Nicholson, Helen. *Medieval Warfare: Theory and Practice of War in Europe, 300–1500* (Basingstoke: Palgrave Macmillan, 2004).

Nicholson, Helen J. ' "La roine preude femme et bonne dame": Queen Sybil of Jerusalem (1186–1190) in History and Legend, 1186–1300'. *The Haskins Society Journal* 15 (2004): pp. 110–24.

Nicholson, Helen J. 'Saints venerated in the Military Orders'. In *Selbstbild und Selbstverständnis der geistlichen Ritterorden*, edited by Roman Czaja and Jürgen Sarnowsky. Ordines Militares: Colloquia Torunensia Historica XIII (Toruń: Uniwersytetu Mikołaja Kopernika, 2005), pp. 91–113.

Nicholson, Helen J. 'Love in a Hot Climate: Gender Relations in *Florent et Octavien*'. In *Languages of Love and Hate: Conflict, Communication, and Identity in the Medieval Mediterranean*, edited by Sarah Lambert and Helen Nicholson. International Medieval Research 15 (Turnhout: Brepols, 2012), pp. 21–36.

Nicholson, Helen J. 'Remembering the Crusaders in Cyprus: the Lusignans, the Hospitallers and the 1191 Conquest of Cyprus in Jean d'Arras's *Mélusine*'. In *Literature of the Crusades*, edited by Simon Thomas Parsons and Linda M. Paterson (Cambridge: D. S. Brewer, 2018), pp. 158–72.

Nicholson, Helen J. 'The True Gentleman? Correct Behaviour towards Women according to Christian and Muslim Writers: From the Third Crusade to Sultan Baybars'. In *Crusading and Masculinities*, edited by Natasha R. Hodgson, Katherine J. Lewis, and Matthew M. Mesley. Crusades Subsidia 13 (London: Routledge, 2019), pp. 100–12.

Nicholson, Helen J. 'The Construction of a Primary Source. The Creation of *Itinerarium Peregrinorum* 1'. *Cahiers de recherches médiévales et humanistes / Journal of Medieval and Humanistic Studies* 37 (2019): pp. 143–65.

Nicholson, Helen J. 'Queen Sybil of Jerusalem as a Military Leader'. In *Von Hamburg nach Java. Studien zur mittelalterlichen, neuen und digitalen Geschichte. Festschrift zu Ehren von Jürgen Sarnowsky*, edited by Jochen Burgtorf, Christian Hoffarth, and Sebastian Kubon (Göttingen: Vandenhoeck & Ruprecht, 2020), pp. 265–76.

Noffke, Suzanne. 'Catherine of Siena'. In *Medieval Holy Women in the Christian Tradition, c. 1100–c. 1500*, edited by A. J. Minnis and Rosalynn Voaden (Turnhout: Brepols, 2010), pp. 601–22.

Nolan, Kathleen. 'Symbolic Geography in the Tomb and Seal of Berengaria of Navarre, Queen of England'. In *Moving Women Moving Objects (400–1500)*, edited by Tracy Chapman Hamilton and Mariah Proctor-Tiffany (Leiden: Brill, 2019), pp. 59–85.

O'Callaghan, Joseph F. *The Last Crusade in the West: Castile and the Conquest of Granada* (Philadelphia, PA: University of Pennsylvania Press, 2014).

Park, Danielle E. A. *Papal Protection and the Crusader: Flanders, Champagne, and the Kingdom of France, 1095–1222* (Woodbridge: Boydell, 2018).

Parker, Matthew E. '*Papa et pecunia*: Innocent III's combination of Reform and Fiscal Policy to Finance Crusades'. *Mediterranean Historical Review* 32.1 (2017): pp. 1–23.

Parsons, Simon Thomas, and Linda M. Paterson, editors. *Literature of the Crusades* (Cambridge: D. S. Brewer, 2018).

Paul, Nicholas. *To Follow in their Footsteps: The Crusades and Family Memory in the High Middle Ages* (Ithaca, NY: Cornell University Press, 2012).

Peacock, A. C. S. 'Georgia and the Anatolian Turks in the 12th and 13th Centuries'. *Anatolian Studies* 56 (2006): pp. 127–46.

Perry, Guy. *John of Brienne: King of Jerusalem, Emperor of Constantinople, c. 1175–1237* (Cambridge: Cambridge University Press, 2013).

Perry, Guy. *The Briennes: The Rise and Fall of a Champenois Dynasty in the Age of the Crusades, c. 950–1356* (Cambridge: Cambridge University Press, 2018).

Pétel, A. 'La Commanderie de Payns et ses dépendances à Savières, à Saint-Mesmin, à Messon, et au Pavillon'. *Revue Champenoise et Bourguignon* 1 (July 1904): pp. 25–54.

Phillips, Jonathan. *The Second Crusade: Extending the Frontiers of Christendom* (New Haven, CT: Yale University Press, 2007).

Phillips, Jonathan. *The Life and Legend of the Sultan Saladin* (London: Bodley Head, 2019).

Pinzino, Jane Marie. 'Just War, Joan of Arc, and the Politics of Salvation'. In *Hundred Years War: A Wider Focus*, edited by L. J. Andrew Villalon and Donald J Kagay. History of Warfare 25 (Leiden: Brill, 2005), pp. 365–98.

Pluskowski, Aleksander. *The Archaeology of the Prussian Crusade: Holy War and Colonisation* (London: Routledge 2013).

Pogossian, Zaroui. 'Women, Identity, and Power: A Review Essay of Antony Eastmond, *Tamta's World*'. *Al-ʿUṣūr al-Wusṭā: The Journal of Middle East Medievalists* 27 (2019): pp. 233–66.

Porges, Walter. 'The Clergy, the Poor, and Non-combatants on the First Crusade'. *Speculum* 21.1 (1946): pp. 1–23.

Poulet, André. 'Capetian Women and the Regency: The Genesis of a Vocation'. In *Medieval Queenship*, edited by John Carmi Parsons (Stroud: Alan Sutton, 1994), pp. 93–116.

Powell, James M. *Anatomy of a Crusade, 1213–1221* (Philadelphia, PA: University of Pennsylvania Press, 1986).

Powell, James M. 'The Role of Women in the Fifth Crusade'. In *The Horns of Ḥaṭṭīn*, edited by B. Z. Kedar (Jerusalem: Yad Izhak Ben-Zvi, 1992), pp. 294–301.

Prestwich, Michael. *Edward I* (London: Methuen, 1988).

Purcell, Maureen. 'Women Crusaders: a Temporary Canonical Aberration?' In *Principalities, Powers and Estates. Studies in Medieval and Early Modern Government and Society*, edited by L. O. Frappell (Adelaide: Adelaide University Union Press, 1979), pp. 57–64.

Queller, Donald E. *The Fourth Crusade: The Conquest of Constantinople, 1201–1204* (Leicester: Leicester University Press, 1978).

Reilly, Bernard F. *The Kingdom of León-Castilla under Queen Urraca, 1109–1126* (Princeton NJ: Princeton University Press, 1982).

Rhodes, Hilary. *The Crown and the Cross: Burgundy, France, and the Crusades, 1095–1223*. Outremer: Studies in the Crusades and the Latin East 9 (Turnhout: Brepols, 2020).

Richardson, H. G. 'The Letters and Charters of Eleanor of Aquitaine'. *English Historical Review* 74/271 (1959): pp. 193–213.

Riddy, Felicity. 'Kempe [*née* Brunham], Margery (*b. c.* 1373, *d.* in or after 1438)'. In *Oxford Dictionary of National Biography*, edited by H. C. G. Matthew and Brian Harrison (Oxford: Oxford University Press, 2004). https://doi-org. abc.cardiff.ac.uk/10.1093/ref:odnb/15337.

Riley-Smith, Jonathan. *The First Crusade and the Idea of Crusading* (London: Athlone Press, 1986).

Riley-Smith, Jonathan. 'Family Traditions and Participation in the Second Crusade'. In *The Second Crusade and the Cistercians*, edited by Michael Gervers (New York: St Martin's Press, 1992), pp. 101–8.

Riley-Smith, Jonathan. *The First Crusaders, 1095–1131* (Cambridge: Cambridge University Press, 1997).

Rodríguez, Ana. 'Remembering the Crusades while living the Reconquest: Iberia, twelfth to fourteenth centuries'. In *Remembering the Crusades and Crusading*, edited by Megan Cassidy-Welch (London: Routledge, 2017), pp. 202–15.

Röhricht, Reinhold. *Studien zur Geschichte des fünften Kreuzzuges* (Innsbruck: Wagner'schen Universitäts-Buchhandlung, 1891).

Rousseau, Constance M. 'Home Front and Battlefield: The Gendering of Papal Crusading Policy (1095–1221)'. In *Gendering the Crusades*, edited by Susan B. Edgington and Sarah Lambert (Cardiff: University of Wales Press, 2001), pp. 31–44.

Rousset, Paul. 'Sainte Catherine de Sienne et le problème de la croisade'. *Schweizerische Zeitschrift für Geschichte* 25 (1975): pp. 499–513.

Ruch, Lisa M. 'Matthew Paris'. In *Encyclopedia of the Medieval Chronicle*, edited by Graeme Dunphy, 2 vols (Leiden: Brill, 2010), vol. 2, pp. 1093–5.

Rudt de Collenberg, W. H. 'L'Empereur Isaac de Chypre et sa fille (1155–1207)', *Byzantion* 38.1 (1968): pp. 123–79.

Ruffini, Giovanni R. 'The History of Medieval Nubia'. In *The Oxford Handbook of Ancient Nubia*, edited by Geoff Emberling and Bruce Beyer Williams (Oxford: Oxford University Press, 2021), pp. 750–71.

Ruggles, D. Fairchild. *Tree of Pearls: The Extraordinary Architectural Patronage of the 13th-Century Egyptian Slave-Queen Shajar al-Durr* (Oxford: Oxford University Press, 2020).

Russell, P. E. 'Prince Henry the Navigator'. *Diamente* 11 (1960): pp. 3–30, reprinted in *Portugal, Spain and the African Atlantic, 1343–1490: Chivalry and Crusade from John of Gaunt to Henry the Navigator*, edited by P. E. Russell (London: Variorum, 1995), article XI.

Sahlin, Claire L. 'Holy Women of Scandinavia: A Survey'. In *Medieval Holy Women in the Christian Tradition, c. 1100–c. 1500*, edited by A. J. Minnis and Rosalynn Voaden (Turnhout: Brepols, 2010), pp. 689–713.

Sandys, Agnes. 'The Financial and Administrative Importance of the London Temple in the Thirteenth Century'. In *Essays in Medieval History presented to Thomas Frederick Tout*, edited by A. G. Little and F. M. Powicke (Manchester: Manchester University Press, 1925; repr. Freeport, NY: Books for Libraries, 1967), pp. 147–162.

Schein, Sylvia. *Fideles Crucis: The Papacy, the West, and the Recovery of the Holy Land 1274–1314* (Oxford: Oxford University Press, 1991).

Schein, Sylvia. 'Bridget of Sweden, Margery Kempe and Women's Jerusalem Pilgrimages in the Middle Ages'. *Mediterranean Historical Review* 14:1 (1999): pp. 44–58.

Setton, Kenneth. *The Papacy and the Levant (1204–1571)*. 4 volumes (Philadelphia, PA: American Philosophical Society, 1976–1984).

Shadis, Miriam. *Berenguela of Castile (1180–1246) and Political Women in the High Middle Ages* (New York: Palgrave Macmillan, 2009).

Shadis, Miriam. 'Unexceptional Women: Power, Authority, and Queenship in Early Portugal'. In *Medieval Elite Women and the Exercise of Power, 1100–1400: Moving beyond the Exceptionalist Debate*, edited by Heather J. Tanner (Cham: Palgrave Macmillan, 2019), pp. 247–70.

Short, Ewan. 'The Agency and Authority of Agnes of France and Margaret of Hungary in the Aftermath of the Fall of Constantinople (1204–1206)'. *Question* 3 (2019): pp. 28–37, 96–101.

Short, Ewan. 'The Socioemotional Labour Performed by Women in the Medieval Byzantine *oikos* (1000–1118)'. *Gendered Voices* 4 (2019): pp. 19–22.

Siberry, Elizabeth. 'A Crickhowell Crusader: The Case of the Missing Hands', *Brycheiniog: Cyfnodolyn Cymdeithas Brycheiniog, The Journal of the Brecknock Society* 46 (2015): pp. 101–8.

Sjursen, Katrin E. 'The War of the Two Jeannes and the Role of the Duchess in Lordship in the Fourteenth Century'. *Medieval Feminist Forum* 51.1 (2015): pp. 4–40.

Sjursen, Katrin E. 'Pirate, Traitor, Wife: Jeanne of Belleville and the Categories of Fourteenth-Century French Noblewomen'. In *Medieval Elite Women and the Exercise of Power, 1100–1400: Moving beyond the Exceptionalist Debate*, edited by Heather J. Tanner (Cham: Palgrave Macmillan, 2019), pp. 135–156.

Smith, Caroline. *Crusading in the Age of Joinville* (Aldershot: Ashgate, 2006).

Smith, Toulmin. *English Gilds*, Early English Text Society, 40 (London: Oxford University Press, 1870).

Solterer, Helen. 'Figures of Female Militancy in Medieval France'. *Signs* 16.3 (1991): pp. 522–49.

Sousa Soares, Torquato de. 'O governo de Portugal pela Infanta-Rainha D. Teresa (1112–1128)'. In *Colectânea de Estudos em Honra do Professor Doutor Damião Peres* (Lisbon: Academia Portuguesa de História, 1974), pp. 95–119.

Städtler, Katharina. 'The Sirventes by Gormonda de Monpeslier'. In *The Voice of the Trobairitz: Perspectives on the Women Troubadours*, edited by William D. Paden (Philadelphia, PA: University of Philadelphia Press, 1989), pp. 129–55.

Strayer, Joseph. 'The Crusades of Louis IX'. In *A History of the Crusades*, edited by Kenneth M. Setton, vol. 2, *The Later Crusades, 1189–1311*, edited by Robert Lee Wolff and Harry W. Hazard (Madison, WI: University of Wisconsin Press, 1969), pp. 486–518.

Strong, S. Arthur. *A Catalogue of Letters and Other Historical Documents Exhibited in the Library at Welbeck* (London: John Murray, 1903).

Stubbs, William. 'Introduction'. In *Chronicles of the Reigns of Edward I and Edward II*. Rolls Series 76, vol. 2 (London: Longman, 1883), pp. vii–cix.

Swanson, R. N. 'Crusade Administration in Fifteenth-Century England: Regulations for the Distribution of Indulgences in 1489'. *Historical Research* 84/223 (2011): pp. 183–8.

Swanson, R. N. 'Preaching Crusade in Fifteenth-Century England: Instructions for the Administration of the anti-Hussite Crusade of 1429 in the Diocese of Canterbury'. *Crusades* 12 (2013): pp. 175–96.

Talmon-Heller, Daniella. 'Arabic Sources on Muslim Villagers under Frankish Rule'. In *From Clermont to Jerusalem: The Crusades and Crusader Societies 1095–1500. Selected Proceedings of the International Medieval Congress, University of Leeds, 10–13 July 1995*, edited by Alan V. Murray. International Medieval Research 3 (Turnhout: Brepols, 1998), pp. 103–17.

Tamrat, Taddesse. 'Ethiopia, the Red Sea and the Horn'. In *The Cambridge History of Africa, volume 3: from c. 1050 to c. 1600*, edited by Roland Oliver (Cambridge: Cambridge University Press, 1977), pp. 98–182.

Tanner, Heather J., Laura L. Gathagan, and Lois L. Huneycutt. 'Introduction'. In *Medieval Elite Women and the Exercise of Power, 1100–1400: Moving beyond the Exceptionalist Debate*, edited by Heather J. Tanner (Cham: Palgrave Macmillan, 2019), pp. 1–18.

Tessera, Miriam Rita. 'Philip Count of Flanders and Hildegard of Bingen: Crusading against the Saracens or Crusading against Deadly Sin?' In *Gendering the Crusades*, edited by Susan B. Edgington and Susan Lambert (Cardiff: University of Wales Press, 2001), pp. 77–93.

Tibble, Steve. *The Crusader Armies 1099–1187* (New Haven, CT: Yale University Press, 2018).

Truax, Jean A. 'Anglo-Norman Women at War: Valiant Soldiers, Prudent Strategists or Charismatic Leaders?' In *The Circle of War in the Middle Ages: Essays on Medieval Military and Naval History*, edited by Donald J. Kagay and L. J. Andrew Villalon (Woodbridge: Boydell, 1999), pp. 111–25.

Turner, Ralph V. *Eleanor of Aquitaine: Queen of France, Queen of England* (New Haven, CT: Yale University Press, 2009).

Tyerman, Christopher. *England and the Crusades, 1095–1588* (Chicago, IL: University of Chicago Press, 1988).

Tyerman, Christopher. *The Invention of the Crusades* (Basingstoke: Macmillan, 1998).

Tyerman, Christopher. *The Debate on the Crusades* (Manchester: Manchester University Press, 2011).

Tyerman, Christopher. *How to Plan a Crusade: Reason and Religious War in the High Middle Ages* (London: Allen Lane, 2015).

Van Houts, Elisabeth, *Memory and Gender in Medieval Europe 900–1200* (Basingstoke: Macmillan, 1999).

Van Houts, Elisabeth. 'Introduction: Medieval Memories'. In *Medieval Memories: Men, Women and the Past, 700–1300*, edited by Elisabeth van Houts (Harlow: Longman, 2001), pp. 1–16.

Vann, Theresa M. '"Our father has won a great victory": the Authorship of Berenguela's Account of the Battle of Las Navas de Tolosa, 1212'. *Journal of Medieval Iberian Studies* 3.1 (2011): pp. 79–92.

Vann Theresa M., and Donald J. Kagay. *Hospitaller Piety and Crusader Propaganda: Guillaume Caoursin's Description of the Ottoman Siege of Rhodes, 1480* (Farnham: Ashgate, 2015).

Vaughan, Richard. *Philip the Good: The Apogee of Burgundy* (London: Longman, 1970).

Vertot, L'Abbé René Aubert de. *Histoire des Chevaliers Hospitaliers de S. Jean de Jerusalem, appellez depuis Chevaliers de Rhodes, et aujourd'hui Chevaliers de Malthe*, 5 vols (Paris: Rollin, Quillau and Desaint, 1726).

Vic, Claude de and Joseph Vaissete. *Histoire générale de Languedoc*, 16 vols (Toulouse: Édouard Privat, 1872–1905).

Walsh, Richard J. 'Charles the Bold and the Crusade: Politics and Propaganda'. *Journal of Medieval History* 3.1 (1977): pp. 53–86.

Weever, Jacqueline de. *Sheba's Daughters: Whitening and Demonizing the Saracen Woman in Medieval French Epic* (New York: Garland, 1998).

Whatley, Laura Julinda. 'Romance, Crusade, and the Orient in King Henry III of England's Royal Chambers'. *Viator* 44.3 (2013): pp. 175–98.

Willard, Charity Cannon. 'Isabel of Portugal and the fifteenth-century Burgundian Crusade'. In *Journeys Toward God: Pilgrimage and Crusade*, edited by Barbara N. Sargent-Baur (Kalamazoo, MI: Medieval Institute Publications, 1992), pp. 205–14.

Willard, Charity Cannon. 'The Patronage of Isabel of Portugal'. In *The Cultural Patronage of Medieval Women*, edited by June Hall McCash (Athens, GA: University of Georgia Press, 1996), pp. 306–20.

Woodacre, Elena. 'Questionable Authority: Female Sovereigns and their Consorts in Medieval and Renaissance Chronicles'. In *Authority and Gender in Medieval and Renaissance Chronicles*, edited by Juliana Dresvina and Nicholas Sparks (Newcastle Upon Tyne: Cambridge Scholars Publishing, 2012), pp. 376–83.

Zacour, Norman P. 'The Children's Crusade'. In *A History of the Crusades*, edited by Kenneth M. Setton, vol. 2, *The Later Crusades, 1189–1311*, edited by Robert Lee Wolff and Harry W. Hazard (Madison, WI: University of Wisconsin Press, 1969), pp. 325–42.

Zerner, Monique. 'L'épouse de Simon de Montfort et la croisade albigeoise'. In *Femmes, mariages, lignages: XIIe–XIVe siècles. Mélanges offerts à Georges Duby* (Brussels: De Boeck-Wesmael, 1992), pp. 449–70.

Index

Readers should note that for the benefit of digital users, indexed terms that span two pages (e.g., 52–53) may, on occasion, appear on only one of those pages.

Acre 16, 35, 37, 51–2, 56–7, 62–5, 72–5, 77, 79, 82–3, 87, 92–5, 102, 110–11, 120–3, 130, 135, 147, 158–60
Adela of Champagne, queen of France 66–7, 104, 121–2, 131–2
Adela of Normandy, countess of Blois 56–7, 105–7
al-'Adil 58–9, 66, 94
Agnes (Anna) of France, Byzantine empress 67–8
Agnes and John Groby 116
Agnes of Harcourt 40
Agnes of Middleton 74–5
Agnes of Poitou, empress 23–4
Ahmad ibn Ibrahim al-Ghazi, imam 6, 64, 79, 92
Aigeline, countess of Burgundy 138
Albert of Aachen 1–4, 10, 15–16, 65–6
Alditha, daughter of Ralph Hodeng 99
Alexander V, pope (Pisa) 116
Alexandria 8–9, 93–4, 152–3
Alexios I Komnenos, Byzantine emperor 11, 144–5
Alexios IV Angelos 42, 67–8
Alfonse of Poitiers 56–7, 78, 137
Alfonso I, 'el Batallador', king of Aragon 26–7
Alfonso II, king of Aragon 119
Alfonso VI, emperor of León and Castile 25–6
Alfonso VII, emperor or king of León and Castile 27–9
Alfonso VIII, king of Castile 28, 38, 122, 137, 143–4

Alfonso X, king of Castile 44–5
Alice, countess of Blois 62–3, 147
Alice, princess of Antioch 72
Alice, wife of Robert son of Walter 62
Alice of Goldsborough 99
Alice of Montmorency, countess of Montfort 42–4, 80, 144
Almohads 38, 143
Almoravids (Murabitun) 25–9, 79–80
Álvar García de Santa María 29–30
Amaury (Amalric), king of Jerusalem 73, 102–3
Amaury de Montfort, count of Toulouse 43–4, 144
Amazons (mythical female warriors) 13–14, 63, 147
Ambroise 1–2, 10, 16, 71, 77–8, 82–4
Anna Komnene 11, 16–17, 144–5
Anthony II de Lucy, lord of Cockermouth and Egremont 100–1, 138
Antioch vi, 12, 31, 35, 40–1, 66–9, 72–4, 80–1, 91, 107, 137, 151–2
Antoine de la Salle 22–3
Arthur, legendary king 31, 153–4
Ascalon 72–3, 86–8, 94–5

Bahā' al-Dīn ibn Shaddād 11, 80–1
Baldwin II, count of Hainaut 111
Baldwin II, king of Jerusalem 35, 102–3, 148–9
Baldwin II, Latin emperor of Constantinople 44–5, 143
Baldwin III, king of Jerusalem 35, 72

Baldwin IV, count of Hainaut 108
Baldwin IX of Flanders, first Latin
    emperor of Constantinople 95,
    110–11, 113–14
Baldwin, lord of Ardres 112–13
Baldwin of Boulogne, count of Edessa,
    first Latin king of Jerusalem 56–7,
    119–20
Barzella Merxadrus 61–2
Barziyya (Bourzey) 68–9, 80–1
battlefield roles 2–3, 26–7, 53, 80–6, 108
Beatrice, countess of Provence 14–15,
    56–7, 65
Beatrice, daughter of Charles of Anjou
    and Countess Beatrice 44–5
Beatrice of Bar, margravine of
    Tuscany 23–4
Beatrice of Vienne, countess of
    Montfort 144
Béla III, king of Hungary 62–3
Béla IV, king of Hungary 66
Benedict XIII, pope (Avignon) 29–30
Berengaria of Navarre, queen of
    England 56–7, 78–9, 87, 95, 104,
    108, 131–3, 135–6
Berenguela (Berengaria), empress
    of Castile, wife of Alfonso VII
    28–9, 79–80
Berenguela (Berengaria), queen of
    León, queen of Castile 28, 31,
    37–8, 119, 143, 159–60
Berenguela of Castile, wife of John de
    Brienne 37–8, 44, 137
Bernal Díaz de Costello 33–4, 70
Bertha of Sulzbach (Eirene), Byzantine
    empress 66–7
Bethany. See St Lazarus of
Birgitta of Sweden, saint 40, 46–9,
    123–4, 139–40, 150
Blanche of Castile, queen of
    France 37–40, 44, 56–7, 97–8, 104,
    109, 137, 143–4, 147, 161–2
Blanche of Eu 137
Blanche of Namur, queen of
    Sweden 47–8
Blanche of Navarre, countess of
    Champagne 108, 120–1, 131–3,
    143–4
Blessed Virgin Mary 6–7, 33–4, 39–40,
    79–80, 126–7, 135

Bohemond I, prince of Antioch 144–5
Boniface VIII, pope 45
Boniface IX, pope (Rome) 126
Brienne family 37–8, 44–5, 57, 130,
    137, 149–50
Brus (Bruce) family 111–12, 120–1, 152
burial of the dead 130, 138
Byzantine empire 11, 23–5, 42, 66–8,
    95, 144–5
Byzantium. See Constantinople

Caesarius of Heisterbach 46
Cairo 41, 60–1, 94–5, 133–5
Calatrava, order of 119
Calixtus II, pope 27
Canary Islands 31, 46, 70
canon law 4–5, 21–2, 111–12, 114
Canterbury, archbishop of 21–3,
    104, 114–15
captives and prisoners 2, 7, 12, 14, 22–5,
    39–40, 50–1, 59–61, 76–7, 85–9,
    91–6, 98–9, 102–3, 108–9, 120–1,
    144, 151–2
Carmen in victoriam Pisanorum 24
Castile, kingdom of 25–34, 37–8, 57, 70,
    135, 137
Catherine, lady of Oudenburg 61–2
Catherine of Brunswick-Lüneberg 74
Catherine Cornaro, queen of
    Cyprus 36–7
Catherine de Courtenay, titular Latin
    Empress of Constantinople 137
Catherine de Eyton 139
Catherine (Catalina) of Lancaster,
    queen of Castile 29–31, 37, 57
Catherine de' Medici, queen of
    France 95–6
Catherine of Siena 40–2, 49–52, 123–4
Cecilia of le Bourcq, princess of
    Antioch 73–4
Cecilia Luvel 112
Celestine III, pope 98–9, 121–2
Ceuta 30–1, 157–8
Chanson de la croisade albigeois (Song of
    the Cathar Wars) 80, 82–3, 88–9
Charlemagne 150, 153
Charles V, king of France 50, 53
Charles VI, king of France 129–30
Charles VII, king of France 51–2
Charles of Anjou 14–15, 40, 44–5, 56–7

Charles the Bold, duke of Burgundy 37
Charlotte de Lusignan, queen of
    Cyprus 36–7, 149
chastity 1–2, 12, 55, 133–5
Châteaudun, viscount of 56–7
childbirth 3–4, 56–7, 60, 65, 77, 108, 124
children 3–4, 27, 38–9, 43, 54–6, 71–2,
    74–7, 80–3, 86, 88–96, 98–9, 104–8,
    119–21, 157–8
chivalric ideals 12, 29–31, 79–80,
    126, 129–30
Chrétien de Troyes 153–4
Christiana de Brus, countess of Dunbar
    120–1
Christiana, widow of Roger Mubray
    120–1
Christina, widow of Walter le
    Tayllur 101
Christina of Ireby 111–12
Christine, daughter of Roger of Haifa
    120–1
Christine, lady of Ardres 112–13
Christine de Pizan (Pisan) 51–2, 103–4
Christopher Columbus 33–4
Chronica Adefonsi Imperatoris 28–9,
    79–80
'Chronicle of Ernoul' 69, 95
chronicles 9–12, 142, 158
Cilician Armenia, kingdom of 41,
    122–3, 149
Cistercian order 46, 133, 135–7, 139–40
Clarice, daughter of Elena 74–5
Clemence of Burgundy, countess of
    Flanders 56–7, 105–7
Clement III, pope 121–2
Clement V, pope 122–3, 141–2
Clement VI, pope 40, 144
Clement VII, pope (Avignon) 30–1
Coimbra 27–8
command roles, women in 3, 26–7,
    29–33, 35–6, 38–9, 51–2, 59–61, 63,
    70–4, 79–80, 85, 103–4, 108,
    114, 155
commutation of vows 8, 17–20
confraternities and guilds 119–21, 123
Conrad III, king of Germany 66–7
Conrad of Marburg 109–10
Conrad of Montferrat 73
Constance of Burgundy, queen of
    Castile 26

Constantinople 13–15, 41–2, 44–5,
    66–8, 92–3, 110–11, 127,
    138–9, 153–5
    Latin Empire of 41, 44–5, 48–9, 137
Constanza of Castile, wife of John of
    Gaunt 30–1, 57, 160
conversion 6–7, 31–4, 46–50, 55–6,
    58–9, 65–6, 70, 89, 95–6,
    126, 139–40
Cornwall 114–15
Coucy, baroness of 110
Cristóvão da Gama 6, 34
Cross, of Christ 6–7, 10–11, 33–4, 46,
    50, 79, 121–3, 126–7, 131–2, 135–6,
    138–42, 152–3, 161
    taking the vi–vii, 1–2, 7, 21–2, 37, 39,
    46–7, 53, 57, 62–3, 65–6, 76–7,
    114–15, 118, 131–2, 146, 151–5,
    160–2 (see also vows)
crossdressing 17
crucesignatae 1–2, 37, 62–3. See also Cross,
    taking the; vows
Crusades
    First (1096–1099) vi, 1–2, 11–13,
    15–17, 23–5, 56–7, 65–6, 80–1,
    87–91, 105–7, 129–30, 144,
    148–50, 152–3
    1101 expedition 15–16, 62–3, 107
    Second (1147–1148) 7–8, 13–14, 35,
    56–7, 66–7, 87, 90–1, 98, 105–6,
    112–13, 138
    Third (1188–1192) 1–2, 11, 16, 21–3,
    36, 38, 51–2, 56–7, 62–3, 68–9,
    71–3, 77–84, 87, 91, 95, 98, 104–5,
    107, 129–30, 133, 155
    Fourth (1202–1204) 10, 13–14, 67–8,
    95, 108, 110–11, 127, 131–2, 138–9
    Albigensian (1209–1226) 38–9, 42–4,
    46–7, 80, 82–3, 88–9, 146–7, 160
    Children's (1212) 5–6, 75–6
    Fifth (1218–1221) 37, 61–2, 74–5, 78,
    82, 99, 101–2, 118, 122, 138–9, 146
    Richard earl of Cornwall's
    (1240–1241) 115
    Louis IX's first (1248–1254) 10,
    18–19, 39–40, 44–5, 56–7, 59–61,
    64–5, 76–9, 126–7, 130, 137, 140,
    144, 151–2
    pastoureaux (Shepherds') (1251, 1320)
    39–40, 76–7, 97–8

Crusades (*cont.*)
  Louis IX's second, to Tunis (1270)
    56–7, 78–9, 137, 150
  Lord Edward's (1271–1272) 63–5,
    100, 105, 111–12, 135, 140, 147
  French against Aragon (1285) 85–6
  Henry Despenser's (1383) 115–16
  Hussite (1420–1431) 74, 82–4, 88,
    115–16, 160
  Alonso de Luga's (1492) 46
  in Baltic (*see* Lithuania; Livonia;
    Prussia)
  definition of vi, 5–8, 122–3
  ideals and images of 6–7, 25–6,
    28–34, 37, 41–2, 47–8, 50–1, 71, 79,
    123, 126–7, 131–2
  plans 53–6, 150
  preaching the 21–2, 37, 46–7,
    92–3, 146
  songs of 21
  in Spain and Portugal (*see* Iberian
    Peninsula)
Cyprus v, 36–7, 41, 44, 48–9, 87, 93–5,
    149, 152–3

Damietta 3–4, 18–19, 59–62, 64–5,
    78–9, 82–3, 159–60
death of women on crusade 2–4, 9,
    15–16, 41, 56–7, 72–5, 80–4,
    86–93, 107, 110–11, 147. *See also*
    murder; suicide
debts 101–2, 117–18
diplomacy 3, 13–14, 28–30, 55–6, 65–70
Domatilla, would-be crusader 50–1
Doña Marina 33–4, 70
Dorothea of Montau 124–6
dower 100–2, 106, 112
Dulce of Aragon 119

Edith of Navenby 117–18
Edmund Crouchback 63–4, 105
education 55–6, 147, 150–2
Edward I, king of England 55–6, 63–4,
    105, 114–15, 135, 147. *See also*
    Crusade: Lord Edward's
Edward II, king of England 160
Egypt 5–6, 10, 39–40, 54–5, 59–61,
    76–7, 94–5. *See also* Mamluks.
Ela, countess of Salisbury 142–3

Eleanor, duchess of Aquitaine, queen of
    France, queen of England 2,
    13–14, 38, 56–7, 66–7, 87, 98–9, 104,
    106, 131–2, 135–6, 153, 155
Eleanor, widow of John de Verdun 100
Eleanor of Aragon, queen of
    Cyprus 41, 48–9
Eleanor de Bohun, duchess of
    Gloucester 152–3
Eleanor of Castile, queen of England 2,
    63–5, 135, 147
Eleanor (Leonor) of England, queen of
    León-Castile 38
Eleanor of Provence, queen of
    England 105, 144, 151–2
Eleni, queen (empress) of
    Ethiopia 34, 58–9
Elizabeth of Asheton 9
Elizabeth of Combe Keynes 9
Elizabeth the Cuman 66
Elizabeth Daneys 102
Elizabeth of Hungary (Thuringia),
    landgravine of Thuringia 67–8,
    100, 109–10, 123–4, 151, 161–2
Elvira of Castile, countess of
    Toulouse 56–7, 65
Emerias of Alteias 53
Emma and Simon Mountfort 116–17
Enrique III, king of Castile 29–30, 57
Enrique IV, king of Castile 32, 79–80
Erard of Ramerupt 108
Ermengarde, vicecountess of
    Narbonne 70–1
Erneburg, wife of William of
    Hokesoure 62–3
Eschiva of Bures, lady of Tiberias and
    Galilee 73–4
Estoire de la Guerre Sainte. See Ambroise
Estonia 77, 139–40
Ethiopia, kingdom of 6, 34, 58–9,
    64, 79, 92
Eu, countess of 103–4, 110
Eugenius III, pope 101–2, 108
Eva, widow of Robert Tiptoft 114

family connections, interests, and
    influence 19–20, 37–42, 49, 66–8,
    76–7, 88–9, 94–8, 106, 130–3, 136–7,
    147, 152–3, 157–8

Fati (baptised Catherine), Muslim captive 95–6
Felix Fabri 9
Ferdinand II, king of Aragon 25–6, 32–4
Fernando III, king of Castile and León 28–31, 37–8
Fernando of Antequera, regent of Castile (King Ferdinand I of Aragon) 29–31
Fernando de Pulgar 32–3
Ferrand, count of Flanders 120–1
Finland 47–8
Florina of Burgundy, fictional crusader 15
Fontevrault abbey 135–6, 141
foundations. See patronage
Francesco Balbi di Correggio 14, 82–3
Francisca de Gazmira 46, 70
Fulcher of Chartres 1–2, 10, 91
Fulk V, count of Anjou 38, 105–6, 147–9

Garnier de Traînel, bishop of Troyes 127
Gaza, battle of (1239) 144
gender stereotypes v, 12–17, 46–7, 53, 71, 77, 79–81, 83–4, 97, 133–5, 158–60. See also queenship
Genoa, Genoese 24–5, 37, 41, 45, 60–2, 118
Geoffrey of Villehardouin 10, 68
Georgians 88
Gerald of Wales 21–2
Gesta Francorum 12–13
Gilles Berthout, lord of Oudenburg 61–2
Giovanni dale Celle of Vallombrosa 50–1
Girauda of Lavaur 88–9
Godfrey de Bouillon 65–6, 119–20, 129–30, 152–3
Godvere of Tosni 56–7
Gormonda de Monpeslier 146
Granada 25–6, 29–30, 32–3, 69–70, 79–80
Great Schism (Western Schism, 1378–1417) 40, 51
Greek Orthodox Church 55–6, 95, 139–40, 146
Gregory I, pope 6, 23–4
Gregory VIII, pope 121–2
Gregory IX, pope 127–8

Gregory XI, pope 41–2, 49–50
grief 39, 97, 109–10, 127–8, 142
Guibert, abbot of Nogent 80–1
guilds. See confraternities
Guiletta of Bologna 61–2
Guillaume Caoursin 82–3
Guy de Lusignan, king of Jerusalem, lord of Cyprus 14, 36, 72–4

Hainaut 108, 111, 113–14, 120–1, 129–30
Hattin, battle of (1187) 36, 69, 72–4, 121–2
Hawis of Trevisac 114–15
Hawisa, wife of Peter of Duffield 99
Hawise, sister of Hamo LeStrange 100
health 1–2, 19, 55, 77–8. See also medical practitioners
Heilwig of Lippe, countess of Holstein 56–7
Helewyse Palmer 8, 17–18, 117
Henry I, 'the Liberal', count of Champagne 102, 106, 131–2, 141–2, 153–4
Henry II, count of Champagne, ruler of Jerusalem 73, 107–9, 131–2, 137
Henry, 'the Lion', duke of Saxony and Bavaria 153
Henry II, king of England 38, 136, 148–9, 153–5
Henry III, king of England 105, 113–14, 144, 151–2
Henry IV, king of England 30–1, 152–3
Henry V, king of England 153
Henry Bolingbroke. See Henry IV, king of England
Henry Borwin III of Mecklenburg 95–6
Henry Knighton 115–16
Henry the Navigator, infante of Portugal 31
Henry of Rodez 74–5, 102, 158–9
Henry of Trastamara 30–1
heretics 5–6, 38–9, 46–7, 51–2, 85, 88–9, 124–7, 133–5, 146–7. See also Crusade: Albigensian; Crusade: Hussite
Hernán Cortés 6–7, 33–4, 70
Hersenda phisica 64–5
Hervé de Donzy, count of Nevers 61–2, 138–9

Hildegard of Bingen, abbess 52, 123–4
Hildegund von Schönau 17–18
Histoire Universelle 63, 147
'History of Eracles' 10–11, 58, 69, 151–2
Hodierna, countess of Tripoli 155
Holy Sepulchre, church of 5–6, 71, 75–6, 141, 148–50. *See also* Jerusalem
Honoré Bonet (Bouvet) 87
Honorius III, pope 122
Hospitallers (Hospital of St John of Jerusalem, Knights Hospitaller) 6, 9, 14, 26–7, 36, 41–2, 55–6, 82–3, 86, 95–6, 102, 113–14, 116, 119–24, 126–7, 130
hospitals and hospices 19, 53, 109–10, 123–4
Hostiensis (Henry de Susa) 63
Humbert II of Viennois 56–7, 144

Iberian Peninsula 24–34, 37, 44–5, 153. *See also* Castile; Granada; Portugal; Spain
Ibn al-Athīr 11, 22–3, 68–9, 88, 94
Ibn Hawqal 58
Ibn al-Kardabus 26–7
Ibn Khaldūn 58–9
Ida of Cham, margravine of Austria 15–16, 62–3
Ida of Louvain, countess of Hainaut 111
Idonea de Camville 142
'Imād al-Dīn al-Iṣfahānī 11, 71, 73–4, 77, 80–1, 91
imposters 112–14
indulgences vi–vii, 4–5, 36, 50–1, 114–17, 161
Innocent III, pope 4–5, 121–2
Innocent VIII, pope 33, 149
intelligence and spying 3, 68–9
Ireland 74–5, 119
Irene Angela (Eirene Angelina) 42
Isaac II Angelos, Byzantine emperor 67–8
Isaac Doukas Komnenos 87, 95
  daughter of 95–6
Isabel I, 'the Catholic', queen of Castile 25–6, 32–4, 37
Isabel I, queen of Jerusalem 73, 137
Isabel II, queen of Jerusalem 149–50
Isabel Bruce, queen of Norway 152
Isabel de Ibelin, lady of Beirut 73–4

Isabel Palmer 8, 17–18, 117
Isabel of Portugal, duchess of Burgundy 37, 159
Isabelle of Aragon, queen of France 56–7, 65, 78, 137, 158–9
Isabelle of Bavaria, queen of France 129–30
Isabelle of France, countess of Champagne and queen of Navarre 56–7, 150
Isabelle of France, daughter of Blanche of Castile 40
Isabelle of France, queen of England 160
Isolda Parewastell 8–9, 93–4, 139
Itinerarium peregrinorum et gesta regis Ricardi. See Richard de Templo
Iveta (Yveta) of Jerusalem, abbess of Bethany 102–3, 139–40

James II, king of Cyprus 36
James of Vitry 37, 46–7, 118
Jaufré Rudel 155
Jean de Joinville. *See* John, lord of Joinville
Jeanne (Joanna), countess of Flanders 113–14, 120–1
Jeanne (Joanna), countess of Toulouse 56–7
Jeanne of Mayenne 133
Jerusalem, city and kingdom of vi, 5–11, 13–14, 21–3, 26–7, 33–8, 40–1, 45, 48–52, 56–9, 62–3, 68–9, 72–5, 84–8, 93–4, 99, 102–3, 105–6, 108, 112, 117–23, 127–8, 131–2, 139–43, 147–50, 153–6. *See also* Holy Sepulchre
Jews and Jewish communities 76–7, 82–3, 87–91, 94–5
Joan, wife of Anthony de Lucy 138
Joan of Arc 51–2, 123–4
Joan Beaufort, countess of Westmorland 153
Joanna of England, queen of Sicily, countess of Toulouse 56–9, 66, 78–9, 87, 95, 136, 155
João I, king of Portugal 30–1, 57, 69–70
Johanna, queen of Naples 40–2, 48–51, 157–8
Johannina 74–5, 158–9

John I, king of Portugal. *See* João I
John, lord of Joinville 10, 39, 44, 59–60,
    78, 126–7, 130, 140
John XXIII, pope (Pisa) 116
John of Acre, count of
    Montfort 44, 137
John de Brienne, king of Jerusalem 37–8,
    44, 57, 137, 143, 149–50
John of Gaunt, duke of
    Lancaster 30–1, 57
John Hawkwood 41–2, 49–50
John de Moulton 100–1
John Stillingflete 119–20
John de Verdun (Verdon) 100
Jordan Valette 15–16
Juan I, king of Castile-León 57
Juan II, king of Castile-León 29–30
Juana of Portugal, queen of
    Castile 79–80
Judith, biblical heroine 122–3
Juliana, wife of John Guer 62

al-Kāmil, sultan of Egypt 134–5
Katherine, wife of John Danthorpe 117
Katherine and John Frisden 116–17
Katherine and Henry Langley 116–17
Katherine of Vadstena 40
Kerbogha's mother 12–13
killing by women 83–6, 88–91, 93
Knights Hospitaller. *See* Hospitallers
Knights Templar. *See* Templars
Konrad the Priest 153

labouring and other support work 3–4,
    16, 82–5, 160
Lambert de Waterlos 108
Las Navas de Tolosa, battle of (1212) 38,
    122, 143–4
Latin Chronicle of the Kings of Castile 28
laundresses 71, 77–8, 90–1
Lavaur 43, 88–9
Lebnä Dengel, emperor of Ethiopia 34,
    58–9
Lecia of Walton 74–5
Leon VI, king of Cilician Armenia 41
Leopold V, duke of Austria 95, 104
Leopold II, margrave of Austria 15–16,
    62–3
letter writing 17–18, 38, 41–2, 49–50,
    66–7, 98–9, 143–4

libraries 150–2
Lithuania, Lithuanians 22–3, 30–1,
    65–6, 71–2, 92–3, 125–6
liturgy in support of crusades 5, 98,
    121–3, 141–2, 161
Livonia 56–7, 126–7, 139–40
Livonian Rhymed Chronicle 65–6, 77
Louis VII, king of France 13–14, 56–7,
    66–8, 106, 138
Louis VIII, king of France 38–40, 43–4,
    97, 109, 113–14, 137, 147
Louis IX, king of France 38–40, 44–5,
    56–7, 59–61, 64–5, 76–9, 97–8, 104,
    109, 130, 135–6, 140, 144, 147,
    150, 161–2
Louis of Savoy, king of Cyprus 36
Lucy, countess of Tripoli 73–4
Lucy, sister of the Trinitarian Order 83
Ludolf von Sudheim 84
Ludwig IV, landgrave of Thuringia 100,
    109–10, 123–4, 151, 161–2, 223n.1
Lusignan family 14, 36–7, 41, 72–4,
    149, 155

Magnus Eriksson, king of Sweden 47–8
al-Mahdiya (Mahdia) 24
Malta 6, 14, 82–3
Mamluk sultans of Egypt 5–6, 8–9,
    36–7, 41, 45, 53, 92, 94–5, 122–3
Mansura, battle of (1250) 60–1,
    134–5, 142
Manuel I, king of Portugal 34, 58–9
Manuel Komnenos, Byzantine
    emperor 66–8
Mara of Serbia 66
Margaret, baptised Muslim
    captive 95–6
Margaret, countess of Warwick
    119–20
Margaret, niece of John de Brienne 57
Margaret, princess of Antioch and
    countess of Tripoli 137
Margaret Beaufort, countess of
    Richmond 77–8
Margaret of Beverley 84–5, 93–4
Margaret of France, queen of
    Hungary 62–3, 107, 109
Margaret (Maria) of Hungary,
    Byzantine empress 68
Margaret de Lacy (née Braose) 119

Margaret of Provence (of Savoy), queen
of France 14–15, 56–7, 59–61, 65,
78–9, 135–6, 140, 144, 147, 159–60
Margaret de Reynel, lady of Sidon 130
Margaret of Soissons, queen of Cilician
Armenia 41
Margaret of Valois, duchess of
Savoy 95–6
Margery (Margaret), countess of
Winchester 101–2
Margery, wife of William fitzHugh 116
Margery Kempe 8–9
Margery de Lacy, wife of John de
Verdun 100
Maria (Mary), mother of Walter of
Beirut 102–3
Maria of Antioch, Byzantine
empress 67–8
Maria of Antioch, heiress to kingdom
of Jerusalem 40
Maria of Montferrat, queen of
Jerusalem 149–50
Marie des Baux 56–7, 144, 160
Marie de Brienne, Latin empress of
Constantinople 37–8, 44–5,
137, 143
Marie of Champagne, countess of
Flanders 110–11, 113–14
Marie of France, countess of
Champagne 101–2, 106–7, 109,
131, 153–4
Marie de France, poet 154–5
Marie of Oignies 46–7
Marino Sanudo Torsello 54–5, 162
Mariotta, daughter of William 74–5
Marjorie, countess of Carrick 111–12
Marriage and marriage alliances 57–9,
65–8, 95–6, 99, 111–12
Martha (Morta), queen of
Lithuania 65–6
martyrdom 6, 12, 46–7, 49–50, 86,
89–91, 93, 134–5, 142
Mary, wife of John de Moulton 100–1
Mary of St Pol, countess of
Pembroke 140
Mathilde de Garlande 88–9
Matilda of Boulogne, queen of
England 119–20
Matilda of Brabant, countess of
Artois 56–7, 65

Matilda of Canossa (of Tuscany) 23–4
Matilda de Courtenay, countess of
Nevers 61–2, 138–9, 161
Matilda of England, duchess of Saxony
and Bavaria 153
Matthew Paris 10–11, 39–40, 97,
115, 142–3
Mecca 14, 95–6
medical practitioners 53, 55–6, 63–5
Melisende, queen of Jerusalem 35, 38,
72, 102–3, 105–6, 139–40,
147–9, 155
Melisende psalter 147–9
Mélusine 155
menstruation 3–4
merchants 20, 60, 78, 82–3, 152
Mexico 6–7, 33–4, 70
midwives 65
Miguel de Castanhoso 6, 64
military orders. See Calatrava,
Hospitallers, St Lazarus, Templars,
Teutonic Order
military service 73–4, 87
Mindaugas, king of Lithuania 65–6
Minstrel of Reims 10–11, 13–14, 39, 97,
113–14, 155
miracles 6, 33–4, 93–4, 126–7
Montgey, battle of (1211) 46–7
Montlhéry, family of 37
monuments and tombs 4, 130–8
motivation 19–20, 47–8, 57, 62–3, 77,
91, 120–1
Murad II, Ottoman sultan 66
murder 42, 48–9, 61, 67–8, 74–5, 89–93,
98–9, 133–5
Muriel, widow of Adam of Croxby 112

navies. See shipping
Nevers, counts of 37, 61–2, 110,
138–9, 161
Nicolas de Bozon 151
Nicolaus von Jeroschin 71–2, 93
Nicopolis, battle of (1396) 103–4,
110, 141–2
Niketas Choniates 13–14, 42
Novgorod 47–8, 126–7
Nubia 58–9
nuns and nunneries 95–6, 102–4,
115–16, 119, 135–7, 139–43,
149–51

Odo I, duke of Burgundy 15
Odo of Deuil 13–14, 66–7
Orderic Vitalis 107
Otto de Grandison 135
Ottomans 6–9, 14, 34, 41–2, 66, 77–8,
    82–3, 86, 91–3, 103–4, 116–17,
    122–3, 126–7, 155–6

Le Pas Saladin 129–30
Pascal II, pope 27–8
patronage and donations 4, 114–21,
    123–4, 130–1, 133, 135–40, 147–50,
    153–4, 158–9
Pere (Pedro) II, king of Aragon 28,
    119, 143–4
Peter I, king of Cyprus 41, 48–9,
    93–4, 152–3
Peter von Dusburg 69, 71–2, 83,
    85–6, 92–3
Peter of les Vaux-de-Cernay 43,
    80, 88–9
Petronilla de Lacy 101
Philip II Augustus, king of France 38,
    62–3, 67–9, 104–5, 121–2,
    131–2, 155
Philip III, king of France 56–7, 78, 150
Philip IV, king of France 76–7, 160
Philip of Alsace, count of Flanders 52,
    153–4
Philip the Good, duke of
    Burgundy 37, 159
Philippa of Champagne 108, 137
Philippa of Lancaster, queen of
    Portugal 30–1, 37, 57, 69–70, 159–60
Philippe de Mézières 54–5, 77,
    160, 162
Philippe Mouskes 109–10
Pierre Dubois 55–6, 63–6
pilgrimage and pilgrims 7–9, 18–19,
    37–8, 48–51, 53, 62–3, 70–1, 74–5,
    84–6, 93–6, 109–10, 123, 131–2,
    139–40, 149–50, 152, 160
Pisa, Pisans 24–5, 40, 60
Pleshey 129–30, 152–3
pollution, spiritual 1–2, 12, 77, 89–91
Portugal, kingdom of 26–8, 30–1,
    33–4, 69–70
Portuguese 6, 64, 79, 92, 157–60
prayer 23–4, 50–1, 53, 82–3, 130–1,
    135–6. See also liturgy

pregnancy 3–4, 59–60, 75–7, 88, 92–3,
    108, 110–11, 116–17
prisoners. See captives
protection for crusaders 7–8, 98–9,
    101–2, 108, 161
Prussia 22–3, 71–2, 79–80, 83, 85–6, 92,
    100–1, 138, 152–3

queenship 28–33, 133–7, 152

Rachel, biblical heroine 127–8
Rachel, daughter of Rabbi Isaac ben
    Rabbi Asher 89–90
Rachel suum videns 127–8
Ralph of Coggeshall 68–9
Ramon Muntaner 14–15, 85–6
ransom 39, 41, 60–1, 93–5, 98, 102–3,
    108–9, 120–1, 138
rape 87–8, 91–5, 99
Raymond VI, count of Toulouse 95
Raymond VII, count of Toulouse 80, 146
Raymond of Poitiers, prince of
    Antioch 13–14, 35, 66–7
Raymond of Saint-Gilles, count of
    Toulouse 56–7
Récits d'un ménestrel de Reims.
    See Minstrel of Reims
Reconquista (Reconquest) 25–34
recruitment 4, 37, 42–52, 80
regency 29–30, 38–9, 56–7, 74,
    97–8, 102–11
Rhodes, island of 6, 9, 36, 56–7, 82–4,
    86, 91, 116–17, 126–7
Riccardiana psalter 149–50
Richard, earl of Cornwall 115, 144
Richard I, king of England 38,
    56–8, 68–9, 71, 73, 95, 98, 104,
    131–2, 136
Richard de Templo 1–2, 10, 16, 71,
    78, 82–4
Robert I, count of Artois 56–7, 97
Robert II, count of Artois 137
Robert II, count of Flanders 56–7,
    105–7
Robert of Clari 67–8
Robert of Sablonnières 101
Roger of Howden 62–3
Rome 36, 40, 47–51, 123
Rosceline of La Ferté 120–1
Russia 47–8, 126–7

Säblä Wängel (Seble Wongel), queen of Ethiopia 6, 64, 79
Saher de Quenci (Saher de Quincy), earl of Winchester 101–2
St Birgitta. *See* Birgitta
St Catherine's monastery in Sinai 147
St Euphemia 127
St Helen of Athyra 127
St James of Santiago (de Compostella) 6–8, 33–4, 37–8, 117
St John of Jerusalem. *See* Hospitallers
St Lazarus, order of 119–20, 154–5
St Lazarus of Bethany, abbey of 102–3, 139–40
St Mary. *See* Blessed Virgin Mary
'St Victor', ship 18–19, 62, 71
saints 46–8, 123–7, 131, 140, 149–50, 161
Saladin, sultan of Egypt and Damascus vi, 11, 13–14, 36, 58, 68–9, 72–4, 80–1, 84–5, 91, 93–4, 121–2, 129–30, 141–2, 149–50, 155–6
al-Ṣalih Ayyūb, sultan of Egypt 60–1, 133–5
Sancha, queen of Aragon 28, 119
Sancho VII, king of Navarre 131–2, 143–4
Santiago de Compostella. *See* St James of Santiago
Saura de St Jean 117–18
Scotland 111–12, 120–1, 152
Seble Wongel. *See* Säblä Wängel
servants 2–4, 18–20, 54–5, 65, 71, 74–5, 77–8, 82–3, 158–9
sexual activity 1–4, 12–14, 54–5, 77, 116–17. *See also* chastity; health; pollution; rape
Shajar al-Durr, sultana of Egypt 60–1, 133–5, 161
shipping 9, 18–19, 36, 40–2, 54–5, 59, 62, 79, 84, 87, 140
Sicily, kingdom of 14–15, 18–19, 56–8, 104, 144–5, 149–50
sick, care for. *See* hospitals; medical practitioners
sieges 3–4, 16, 27–9, 32–3, 79–86, 160
Sigena, Hospitaller house 119
Sigismund of Luxembourg, king of Hungary 74, 83

Simon de Montfort the Elder, count of Toulouse 42–4, 80, 83, 144
single women 18–19, 62–3, 70–7, 82–3
Sixtus IV, pope 32, 116–17
slavery, slaves 2, 31, 50–1, 69, 87, 91–2, 94, 158
social status 4, 16–20, 46–7, 49, 54–6, 61–2, 87–9, 95–6, 103–4, 114, 124, 149–50, 157–9
'Song of the Cathar Wars'. See *Chanson de la croisade albigeois*
'Song of Roland' 153
sorcery 69
Spain 25–6, 32–4. *See also* Iberian Peninsula
Stephanie de Milly, lady of Transjordan 73–4
Stephen, count of Blois 56–7, 105–7
suicide 71–2, 87, 89–91, 109
Sulieman the Magnificent, Ottoman sultan 82–3, 95–6
Swantopolk (Swietopelk II), duke of Pomerania 83, 92
Sybil, princess of Antioch 68–9
Sybil, queen of Jerusalem 36, 72–3, 155
Sybil of Anjou, countess of Flanders 56–7, 105–6, 108

T'amt'a, ruler of Akhlat 58, 66
Tangier 37
Templars (Knights Templar) 27, 55–6, 68–9, 101–2, 119–20, 126–7, 140, 151–2, 154–5
Teresa, queen of Portugal 26–8, 35, 119
Teresa Gil 118
Teutonic Order 53, 61–2, 65–6, 69, 71–2, 77, 79–80, 83, 92–3, 123–7
Thibaut (Theobald) III, count of Champagne 107–8, 131–2
Thibaut IV, count of Champagne and king of Navarre 108, 120–1, 132–3
Thibaut V, count of Champagne and king of Navarre 56–7
Thierry of Alsace, count of Flanders 35, 56–7, 105–6, 108

Toledo 25–9, 32, 79–80
tombs. *See* monuments
Toulouse 39, 43–4, 80, 82–3
   counts of. *See* Amaury de Montfort;
      Elvira of Castile; Jeanne (Joanna),
      Raymond VI; Raymond VII;
      Raymond of Saint-Gilles;
      Simon de Montfort
Trinitarian order 120–1
Tripoli (Syria) 73–4, 92, 137, 155

Urban II, pope 53
Urban V, pope 93–4, 139
Urban VI, pope (Rome) 30–1, 40, 51
Urraca, queen of Castile 26–8, 35, 119
Usama ibn Munqidh 11, 85–7, 91, 94

Valette. *See* Jordan Valette
Vegetius, *De re militari* 147
Venice, Venetians 24–5, 36–7, 41, 54–5,
   67–8, 93
Via ad Terram Sanctam 54–5
victims 12, 14, 87–96, 139, 158
visions 46–9, 142–3
vows of crusade vi–vii, 1–2, 4–5, 7–8,
   17–22, 39, 53, 62–3, 114–15, 117,
   151–2, 160. *See also* Cross, of
   Christ, taking the

Wales 21–2, 119–20, 138
widows 15–16, 27, 34, 38–9, 41, 43–4,
   48–9, 54–7, 62–3, 73–4, 100–2,
   108–12, 114, 118, 120–1, 131–5,
   137–9, 144, 161–2
wills 61–2, 65, 74–5, 78, 100–2, 114–15,
   118, 140, 152–3, 158–9
William, archbishop of Reims 105,
   121–2
William II, archbishop of Tyre 10–11,
   35, 72, 151–2
William II, king of Sicily 56–7
William Longespee II 142–3
William Trussel 99
William of Tripoli, *De statu
   Saracenorum* 150
William of Tudela 88–9
wives 3–4, 12, 16, 18–23, 37–8, 42–4,
   54–63, 65–6, 79, 82–3, 88–90, 92,
   98–102, 105–6, 109–14, 124, 131–8,
   158–60, 162

Yusuf III of Granada 30, 69–70, 159–60
Yveta. *See* Iveta

Zaragoza (Saragossa) 26–7
Zengi of Mosul 35, 72, 153–4
Zurara, Gomes Eanes de 31, 69–70